Elements of Culture

An Applied Perspective

Susan Andreatta
THE UNIVERSITY OF NORTH
CAROLINA AT GREENSBORO

Gary Ferraro
THE UNIVERSITY OF NORTH
CAROLINA AT CHARLOTTE

WADSWORTH
CENGAGE Learning

Australia • Brazil • Japan • Korea • Mexico • Singapore • Spain • United Kingdom • United States

WADSWORTH
CENGAGE Learning·

Elements of Culture: An Applied Perspective

Susan Andreatta and Gary Ferraro

Acquiring Editor: Erin Mitchell

Developmental Editor: Lin Gaylord

Assistant Editor: Linda Stewart

Editorial Assistant: Mallory Ortberg

Media Editor: Mary Noel

Marketing Manager: Andrew Keay

Marketing Assistant: Jack Ward

Marketing Communications Manager: Laura Localio

Content Project Manager: Cheri Palmer

Design Director: Rob Hugel

Art Director: Caryl Gorska

Manufacturing Planner: Judy Inouye

Rights Acquisitions Specialist: Dean Dauphinais

Production Service: Joan Keyes, Dovetail Publishing Services

Text Designer: Tom Ingalls

Photo Researcher: Wendy Granger, Bill Smith Group

Text Researcher: Ashley Liening

Copy Editor: Carol Reitz

Illustrator: Graphic World

Cover Designer: Ingalls Design

Cover Image: David Bathgate/ Corbis

Compositor: PreMediaGlobal

For product information and technology assistance, contact us at **Cengage Learning Customer & Sales Support, 1-800-354-9706.**

For permission to use material from this text or product, submit all requests online at **www.cengage.com/permissions.** Further permissions questions can be e-mailed to **permissionrequest@cengage.com.**

Library of Congress Control Number: 2011938554

ISBN-13: 978-1-111-83000-7

ISBN-10: 1-111-83000-2

Wadsworth
20 Davis Drive
Belmont, CA 94002-3098
USA

Cengage Learning is a leading provider of customized learning solutions with office locations around the globe, including Singapore, the United Kingdom, Australia, Mexico, Brazil, and Japan. Locate your local office at **www.cengage.com/global.**

Cengage Learning products are represented in Canada by Nelson Education, Ltd.

To learn more about Wadsworth, visit **www.cengage.com/wadsworth**

Purchase any of our products at your local college store or at our preferred online store **www.cengagebrain.com.**

Printed in the United States of America
2 3 4 5 6 7 15 14 13

Brief Contents

Detailed Contents

Preface

Our purpose in this first edition of *Elements of Culture: An Applied Perspective* is to provide students with a grounding in the basic principles and practices of cultural anthropology using ethnographic anthropology and its application to contemporary issues and problem solving. We believe that teaching students the foundations of cultural anthropology from an applied perspective will better engage students and may encourage some of them to consider career opportunities in applied anthropology; it will also give them a clearer sense of the relevance of the discipline in their first anthropology course. Students who are seeking careers that will make differences in their communities or who want to join multicultural or interdisciplinary teams elsewhere in the world will especially benefit from our applied ethnographic perspective.

We recognize that many faculty and their students enjoy learning about contemporary cultures from a variety of perspectives. We developed this 12-chapter textbook with the idea that faculty might wish to incorporate additional readings, video streams, and other activities during the course of their semester. We believe that fewer chapters will allow faculty to engage the students in other ways of learning without feeling the pressure to rush through textbook chapters or to skip chapters due to a lack of time. So, there are only 12 chapters and we have kept them brief, but without compromising content.

The need for our students to become culturally competent, irrespective of what occupation(s) they pursue, speaks to the importance of taking courses in cultural anthropology, and preferably more than just the introductory course. Cultural anthropology is the academic discipline best positioned to enhance students' cultural awareness and educate them about cultural differences. Making an introductory course as relevant and applied as possible serves multiple purposes. Not only do we want to have students actually read the material and to attract anthropology majors; we also want to provide useful tools and concepts for those pursuing other careers and professions that require critical thinking, cross-cultural knowledge, or research skills.

To be certain, training the next generation of students with the skill sets needed to operate in a more globalized and socially networked world cries out for new ways in which we can engage students and apply anthropological concepts to real-world issues. Showing our students how others have used their anthropological expertise to help solve contemporary problems might inspire them to do the same. Increasingly, applied anthropology has become more mainstream among anthropologists, including those who work in the academy as well as those in both the private and nonprofit sectors. The range of contexts in which one may apply anthropological concepts as well as collaborate on interdisciplinary teams requires that we think from the outset about the diversity of settings in which one may find employment, contribute to problem solving, and engage in community-based research.

Co-authors Susan Andreatta and Gary Ferraro previously collaborated on the Eighth and Ninth Editions of *Cultural Anthropology: An Applied Perspective.* They bring to the table complementary styles of pedagogy as well as a shared commitment to applied research and scholarship. Andreatta's research has focused on environmental and medical anthropology, while Ferraro has concentrated on business, education, and organizational structures. With our Senior Developmental Editor, Lin Gaylord, we have co-conducted five workshops at the annual meetings of the Society for Applied Anthropology and for the National Association for the Practice of Anthropology at the American Anthropological Association, where we focused on how we can make our anthropology courses more applied and more hands-on for students.

We recognize that to be a successful applied anthropologist one needs to be grounded in ethnographic methods, theory, and terminology, and so these basic building blocks of descriptive anthropology make up the core of our textbook. However, we have presented applied examples throughout the text to illustrate various terms and concepts and to work through longer analyses.

In order to engage students quickly and with the ever-increasing interest in applied anthropology, we put practical cases up front and make them accessible in each chapter. Our intent directly and indirectly is to have instructors and their students think about concepts, issues, and world and local problems at the very beginning and end of each chapter. Two special features in this textbook guide both the student and instructor through the applied focus of each chapter. First, each chapter begins with an **applied chapter-opening vignette**, a case study, which is followed by two or three discussion questions for further thought to facilitate conversations both in class and out of class. For example, in Chapter 4 the opening vignette focuses on a medical anthropologist, Patricia Omidian, and her work among Afghani families. Her training in ethnography and medical anthropology and her knowledge of the local language (Dari) allowed her to train and mentor local staff so that they could conduct their own surveys, evaluations, and training in strategic planning after she was evacuated.

Second, we conclude each chapter with a section called **Out in the Real World,** which encourages the reader to think about contemporary issues as they relate to the material they have just read. This feature is our way of reinforcing the pedagogical emphasis on applied anthropology. It also provides a context for what students can *do* with anthropology and the anthropological concepts they have been exposed to in this book. Each Out in the Real World case also has two or three discussion questions to facilitate conversations both in class and out of class. For example, in Chapter 5, Language and Communication, the Out in the Real World example draws students' attention to American Sign Language (ASL). In addition, the example goes on to illustrate the ways in which language and communication differ among other hearing-challenged (deaf) people around the world and describes the alternative hand-signing systems some have developed as a means of communication.

Living and working in the twenty-first century requires us to understand a wide variety of cultures and subcultures and thus to develop a number of skills and capacities that can be mastered through studying applied cultural anthropology. With this in mind we designed the textbook in such a way as to provide a foundation in ethnographic theory, methods, and examples while also highlighting applied research projects in each of the chapters.

Chapter 1 opens with a letter to the student in which we describe the purpose of the textbook, why we have taken the applied perspective, what the book is designed to accomplish, and how to get the most from the book. We thought it would be helpful for students to understand from the beginning why an applied perspective is important to anthropology and how they may be able to use or pursue it even after their introductory course in cultural anthropology. The Out in the Real World vignette discusses an apologist's role in developing a new breakfast cereal. We use Chapter 1 to define anthropology using a four-field approach, and we provide applied examples for each of the four fields. Each of the remaining chapters draws from cultural anthropology with an applied perspective.

In **Chapter 2** we address the concept of culture. Studying culture is at the core of what anthropology is and what anthropologists do. By opening with a case on the need for considering culture in designing houses, we get students thinking about how culture is taken for granted. We then present culture as a combination of things, ideas, and behavior patterns transmitted from generation to generation through the process of learning. We also recognize that culture is not static; that it changes with time, with contact with other ethnic groups, and sometimes for no obvious reason. The chapter concludes with an applied case from business anthropology on cross-cultural coaching.

Chapter 3 is where we illustrate the difference between descriptive anthropology (ethnography) and applied anthropology. We note that applied anthropology relies on the ethnographic methods used by descriptive anthropologists, but applies them in solving contemporary problems or issues. As an example, the chapter opens with a case about working on HIV/AIDS in Zimbabwe. We also list various employment opportunities in which applied anthropologists have been able to establish rewarding careers, and we highlight several of them with case studies. The Out in the Real World feature describes how a study-abroad experience may lead to a career in anthropology or possibly in applied anthropology.

Chapter 4 covers theory and methods in anthropology and begins with an inspiring case about how training in medical anthropology successfully equipped a researcher for fieldwork in Afghanistan. The first half of the chapter concentrates on major anthropological theorists and their contributions. The second half emphasizes ethnographic field methods—in particular, participant observation and interviewing—and concludes with methods used in applied anthropology. The Out in the Real World example on climate change and scarce resources illustrates the applied approach.

In **Chapter 5** we discuss language and communication and consider such topics as the differences between human and nonhuman communications, how languages change, the relationships between language and culture, and nonverbal forms of communication, including American Sign Language. We also address how technology in the twenty-first century has influenced and changed how we communicate culturally and globally, especially with the introduction of Facebook and the iPad, as illustrated in the chapter-opening case.

As we move through our understanding of anthropology and culture, we examine environments, subsistence patterns, and economics in **Chapter 6.** We open with a case discussing the influence of secondary education on East African pastoralist survival strategies to illustrate the connection between environments and subsistence strategies. Anthropologists generally agree that the environment does not determine food-getting patterns but rather sets broad limits on the possibilities, especially when we consider that culture defines what is considered a food item. The specific mode of food getting is influenced by the environment itself and its interface with a people—both their culture and their technology. Drawing on Stewardian cultural ecology to examine cultural adaptations to the environment, this chapter examines subsistence strategies (hunting, gathering, fishing; pastoralism, horticulture, and agriculture) among various groups around the world. In recent times industrial agriculture has been changing the foods one has access to eat, and in response some groups have formed to emphasize eating local foods, such as the Slow Food Movement and niche marketing for organic farmers and fishermen (as described in the Out in the Real World case).

We discuss kinship, marriage, and family in **Chapter 7.** The chapter-opening case looks at the ways in which kinship and family relationships affect the spread of infectious diseases such as Ebola hemorrhagic fever.

This example draws our attention to the fact that a medical anthropologist can use kinship patterns, the concept of family, and the role of marriage to understand the spread of epidemics and to create a treatment program for a community. The chapter teaches that the way relatives are defined is not the same everywhere, nor is the concept of marriage or what may constitute a family. In modern times, the task of understanding kinship systems has been made even more complex by such phenomena as transnational adoptions, gay and lesbian families, and new reproductive technologies, such as sperm banks, in vitro fertilization (IVF), and surrogate motherhood. The Out in the Real World feature looks at low birth rates and family planning in Italy.

Chapter 8 continues the preceding chapter's discussion of kinship, marriage, and family by examining sex, gender, and sexuality. It opens with a case on sex-selective abortion in India. After defining who can marry whom, we turn our attention to cultural influences on gender roles and sexual preferences and practices, while recognizing that biology (genetics) governs the sex (male or female) of the individual and family members. We conclude the chapter with a discussion of differential access to power and decision making, specifically sexual asymmetry, gender stratification, and gender ideology. The Out in the Real World case looks at assisting Afghan women in health care and education.

In Chapter 9 we discuss political organization and social control, beginning with a case on monolingualism and the Department of Homeland Security. All societies have political systems to manage public affairs, maintain social order, and resolve conflict. The study of political organization involves topics such as the allocation of political roles, levels of political integration, concentrations of power and authority, mechanisms of social control, and means for resolving conflict. Drawing on traditional anthropology, we introduce the concepts of bands, tribes, chiefdoms, and state societies. Political structures vary from very informal structures such as bands at one extreme to highly complex state systems of government at the other extreme. Whatever form of political organization a society has, however, it must inevitably address the issue of social control, including the formal and informal means by which a society maintains harmony and avoids chaos. We also raise the question in this chapter of what role anthropology and anthropologists play in the military. Can our cross-cultural understandings help to reduce conflict? The Out in the Real World feature tackles this question by asking whether anthropologists should work for the military.

Anthropologists have long observed that all societies have a recognizable set of beliefs and behaviors that can be called religious or supernatural. In Chapter 10 we focus our attention on supernatural belief systems. The chapter opens by looking at Islamic religious freedom in Florida.

Contemporary anthropological studies of religion focus on how religious systems function for both the individual and the society as a whole as mechanisms for social control, conflict resolution, and reinforcing group solidarity as well as on the psychological functions of religion. We address the cognitive and emotional appeal of organized belief systems, which takes us to a more symbolic aspect of our understanding of culture and again leads nicely into the following chapter, one of our favorites. The Out in the Real World case combines anthropology, medicine, and religion to illustrate the importance medical anthropology has had in sensitizing medical caregivers who may tend to culturally different patients. Research has confirmed that culture is a critical variable in the diagnosis and treatment of illnesses. Understanding and accommodating the supernatural beliefs of culturally different patients are absolutely essential for providing them with the best possible health care. The case describes how medical anthropologists are developing systems of medical knowledge and patient care in a clinic for Chinese immigrants in Brooklyn, New York.

In **Chapter 11** we focus on various forms of artistic expression, opening with a case on music and urban revitalization in Brazil. In all societies people apply imagination, creativity, and technical skills to transform matter, sound, and movement into works of art. The various types of artistic expression include the graphic or plastic arts—such as painting, carving, weaving, basket making, and sculpting out of clay, metal, or glass; the creative manipulation of sounds and words in such artistic forms as music, poetry, and folklore; and the application of skill and creativity to body movement that gives rise to dance. The very fact that artistic expression is found in every known society suggests that it functions in some important ways in human societies, as illustrated by the concluding ethnographic case, which looks at how a cultural anthropologist helped track down stolen statues critical to the Mijikenda people for appeasing the ancestor-spirits and honoring and protecting the deceased.

Our final chapter, **Chapter 12**, addresses global challenges and the role of applied anthropology. We have written a concluding letter to students. The letter is our way of reminding them of the importance of the applied aspect of the book and of applied anthropology and how anthropological understandings are essential for addressing the human challenges of the twenty-first century—namely, climate change, population growth, environmental degradation including water shortages and lack of clean drinking water, the spread of world health pandemics, and increased poverty throughout the world. The chapter itself examines the basic trends of the post–World War II era that concern anthropologists, such as immigration patterns; the rise of religious fundamentalism; rapid urbanization in Africa, Asia, and Latin America; the spread of world health pandemics such as AIDS; environmental degradation; and the widening gap between the rich and the poor throughout the world. The Out in the Real World case tells how a cultural anthropologist is revitalizing the small town of Star, North Carolina. There are many take-away messages in this chapter for faculty and students that will provide opportunities both inside and outside of the classroom for meaningful conversations on culture.

We close by reminding instructors and their students how the applied examples used in this text highlight the interdisciplinary nature of applied anthropology. There is a diverse and wide range of professional areas in which students may pursue further studies or employment; the list below, while by no means exhaustive, illustrates some of these possibilities:

Public school educators	International businesspeople
Human resource managers	Architects
Energy officials or consultants	University professors
International development workers	Family planners
	Social workers
Public health educators	Market researchers
Antipoverty program officials	Product designers
Criminal justice workers	Medical caregivers
Advertising employees	Postwar national builders

Supplements for Instructors

CourseReader: Cultural Anthropology

CourseReader: Cultural Anthropology allows you to create a fully customized online reader in minutes. Access a rich collection of thousands of primary and secondary sources, readings, and audio and video selections from multiple disciplines, including the *Editor's Choice* readings edited by co-author Gary Ferraro, for readings that complement the contemporary applied perspective. Each selection includes a descriptive introduction that puts it into context, and every selection is further supported by both critical-thinking and multiple-choice questions designed to reinforce key points. This easy-to-use solution allows you to select exactly the content you need for your courses, and is loaded with convenient pedagogical features like highlighting, printing, note taking, and downloadable MP3 audio files for each reading. You have the freedom to assign and customize individualized content at an affordable price. (1-111-76955-9; 978-1-111-76955-0)

Online Instructor's Manual with Test Bank

Prepare for class more quickly and effectively with such resources as detailed chapter outlines, learning objectives, key terms, suggested films, and teaching and learning activities as well as additional print and online resources. For assessment support, the Test Bank includes true/false, multiple-choice, short-answer, and essay questions for each chapter. (1-111-83178-5; 978-1-111-83178-3)

Online PowerPoint™ Lecture Slides

Create dynamic lectures with these new, highly visual PowerPoint slides. Available for download on the instructor companion website, the slides include photos and figures from the book, chapter overviews, key terms, and helpful notes for instructors. There are presentations for each chapter, plus at least one slide on each reading in the CourseReader: Cultural Anthropology Editor's Choice for a fully integrated experience. The slides will help you emphasize key points in the readings and contextualize the readings in the scope of applied cultural anthropology.

ExamView® for Elements of Culture: An Applied Perspective

Available for download from the instructor website, ExamView® testing software includes all the test items from the Test Bank in electronic format, enabling you to create customized tests in print or online. (1-111-94236-6; 978-1-111-94236-6)

Anthropology CourseMate

Anthropology CourseMate brings course concepts to life with interactive learning, study, and exam preparation tools that support the printed textbook. A textbook-specific website, Anthropology CourseMate includes an interactive eBook and other interactive learning tools, including quizzes, flashcards, videos, and more. Go to www.cengagebrain.com.

WebTutor™ on WebCT® and Blackboard® for Elements of Culture: An Applied Perspective

Jumpstart your course with customizable, rich, text-specific content within your Course Management System. Students gain access to a full array of study tools, including glossaries, chapter-specific quizzing material, flashcards, and videos. With WebTutor™, instructors can provide virtual office hours, post syllabi, track student progress with the quizzing material, and even customize the content to suit their needs. Go to webtutor.cengage.com for more information.

Wadsworth Anthropology Video Library

Enhance your lectures with new video clips from the BBC Motion Gallery and CBS News. Addressing topics from the four fields, these videos are divided into short segments, perfect for introducing key concepts with footage sourced from some of the most remarkable collections in the world. (1-111-30615-X)

AIDS in Africa DVD

Expand your students' global perspective of HIV/AIDS with this award-winning documentary series focused on controlling HIV/AIDS in southern Africa. Films focus on caregivers in the faith community; how young people share messages of hope through song and dance; the relationship of HIV/AIDS to gender, poverty, stigma, education, and justice; and the story of two HIV-positive women helping others. (0-495-17183-2)

Readings and Case Studies

Classic Readings in Cultural Anthropology, Third Edition

Practical and insightful, this concise and accessible reader by Gary Ferraro presents a core selection of historical and contemporary works that have been instrumental in shaping anthropological thought and research over the past decades. Readings are organized around eight topics that closely mirror most introductory textbooks and are selected from scholarly works on the basis of their enduring themes and contributions to the discipline. (ISBN 1-111-29792-4)

Case Studies in Cultural Anthropology, edited by Janice E. Stockard and George Spindler

Select from more than seventy contemporary and classic ethnographies representing geographic and topical diversity, and emphasizing culture change and the factors influencing change, in the peoples depicted. Look for new revisions of these popular classic case studies: Napoleon Chagnon's *The Yąnomamö*, Sixth Edition (publishing in January 2012, ISBN: 978-1-111-82874-5); and *The Dobe Ju/'hoansi*, Fourth Edition, by Richard Lee (publishing in February 2012, ISBN: 978-1-111-82877-6).

Case Studies on Contemporary Social Issues, edited by John A. Young

Framed around social issues, these contemporary case studies are globally comparative and represent the cutting-edge work of anthropologists today. This series offers a variety of case studies that explore how anthropology is used today in understanding and addressing problems faced by human societies around the world. New topics include *Seeking Food Rights: Nation, Inequality and Repression in Uzbekistan* by Nancy R. Rosenberger (ISBN: 978-1-111-30149-1); new editions of *Slaughterhouse Blues: The Meat and Poultry Industry in North America*, Second Edition, by Donald D. Stull and Michael J. Broadway (publishing in January 2012, ISBN: 978-1-111-82878-3); and *Bravo for the Marshallese: Regaining Control in a Post-Nuclear, Post-Colonial World*, Second Edition, by Holly M. Barker (publishing in February 2012, ISBN: 978-1-111-83384-8).

Supplements for Students

Anthropology CourseMate

The more you study, the better the results. Make the most of your study time by accessing everything you need to succeed in one place. Read your textbook, take notes, review flashcards, watch videos, and take practice quizzes—online with CourseMate. Go to webtutor.cengage.com for more information.

Acknowledgments

To one degree or another, many people have contributed to this textbook. Others have contributed less directly, yet their fingerprints are found throughout the text. We are particularly grateful to the many professors with whom we have studied at Michigan State University (Andreatta) and Syracuse University (Ferraro). We owe a similar debt to the many colleagues over the years who have shared with us their thinking on anthropological research and teaching. While there are far too many names to fit into a small preface, they have had an important impact on our thinking and our careers as anthropologists and, thus, on the content of this book. They have always responded graciously to our requests for information in their various areas of expertise and have taught us a great deal about teaching introductory anthropology. We are confident that they know who they are and will accept our most sincere gratitude.

This textbook has benefited enormously from excellent editorial guidance and the comments of many reviewers. We want to thank our Senior Developmental Editor, Lin Marshall Gaylord, and our Acquiring Editor, Erin Mitchell, for their vision, counsel, and many excellent suggestions for developing this introductory textbook. Thanks are also extended to the entire Wadsworth editorial, marketing, and production team including Linda Stewart, Assistant Editor; Mallory Ortberg, Editorial Assistant; Melanie Cregger, Associate Media Editor; Andrew Keay, Marketing Manager; Cheri Palmer, Senior Project Manager, Content & Media Production; Joan Keyes, Dovetail Production Services; Carol Reitz, Copy Editor; and Wendy Granger, Photo Researcher.

As with many good textbooks, they are made better because of the conscientious comments made by reviewers. We are grateful to our reviewers, who made valuable and insightful suggestions for strengthening the text, including: Nancy Anson, Darton Community College; Laura Gonzalez, San Diego City College; Vanessa Martinez, Holyoke Community College; and Melinda Thoele, Allegany College of Maryland. For this First Edition we would also like to express our gratitude to the many colleagues who wish to remain anonymous. We trust that these reviewers will see that many of their helpful suggestions have been incorporated into this edition. We encourage any readers, professors, or students to send us comments, corrections, and suggestions for future improvements via e-mail at the following addresses:

gpferrar@uncc.edu

s_andrea@uncg.edu

After nearly a half century (cumulative) of full-time university teaching, we want to express our deepest gratitude to our many students who have helped us define and refine our anthropological perspectives and, consequently, the concepts and interpretations in this book.

About the Authors

Photo by Penelope Pynes

Susan Andreatta, Associate Professor of Anthropology at the University of North Carolina at Greensboro, received her BA in anthropology and Spanish at the University of Delaware, her MA in anthropology from Iowa State University, and her PhD, also in anthropology, from Michigan State University. Andreatta also did a two-year post-doc in England at the University of Hull. During the past twenty-five years she has conducted fieldwork in Costa Rica, Jamaica, St. Vincent, Barbados, Antigua, Dominica, Mexico, Uganda, China, and North Carolina. Her theoretical orientation lies in political economy and political ecology as they are applied to the environment and health. Since 1985 she has participated in a wide range of applied projects, including those that focused on tourism, migration and resettlement, health and nutrition, agriculture, agroforestry, and direct marketing of fresh local produce and seafood. Her interests in small-scale family farms, rural communities, and their transformation or resistance to the expansion of agribusiness and the globalization of agriculture have enabled her to work both overseas and domestically. In addition, she has been examining traditional and Western approaches to health care in changing economic and political systems. Her work has been published in *Human Organization, Culture & Agriculture, Southern Rural Sociology, Urban Anthropology*, and *Home Health Care Management & Practice*. Andreatta is the Director of Project Greenleaf at UNCG, a project she started in 2001 that provides undergraduate students with hands-on applied research experiences. She is a past board member and former secretary for the Society for Applied Anthropology (SfAA) as well as a past president of the Society for Applied Anthropology (2007–2009).

Gary Ferraro, Professor Emeritus of Anthropology at the University of North Carolina at Charlotte, received his BA in history from Hamilton College and his MA and PhD from Syracuse University. He has been a Fulbright Scholar at the University of Swaziland in Southern Africa (1979–80) and again at Masaryk University in the Czech Republic (2003) and has served twice as a visiting professor of anthropology in the University of Pittsburgh's Semester at Sea Program, a floating university that travels around the world. He has conducted research for extended periods of time in Kenya and Swaziland and has traveled widely throughout many other parts of the world. He has served as a consultant/trainer for such organizations as USAID, the Peace Corps, the World Bank, IBM, G.E. Plastics, and Georgia Pacific, among others. From 1996 to 2000 he served as the Director of the Intercultural Training Institute at UNC–Charlotte, a consortium of cross-cultural trainers/educators from academia, government, and business, designed to help regional organizations cope with cultural differences at home and abroad. He is the author of:

Photo by Lorne Lassiter

The Two Worlds of Kamau (1978)

Cultural Anthropology: An Applied Perspective (1992, 1995, 1998, 2001, 2004, 2006, 2008, 2010, 2012)

The Cultural Dimension of International Business (1990, 1994, 1998, 2002, 2006, 2010, 2013)

Anthropology: An Applied Perspective (1994)

Applying Cultural Anthropology: Readings (1998)

Global Brains: Knowledge and Competencies for the Twenty-First Century (2002)

Classic Readings in Cultural Anthropology (2004, 2009, 2012)

These people are celebrating the Songkran festival in Chiang Mai, Thailand, by gleefully engaging in "water fights."

Alain Evrard/PhotoLibrary

CHAPTER 1

What Is Anthropology?

A LETTER TO STUDENTS

Greetings! We would like to welcome you to the First Edition of *Elements of Culture: An Applied Perspective.*

We are very proud of this textbook and the difference we bet it will make in your lives after you read and learn from the text. All introductory textbooks in cultural anthropology are designed to introduce the reader to the content of cultural anthropology. But this textbook, with its "applied perspective," goes beyond the content of the discipline by showing you how the research findings, theories, methods, and insights of cultural anthropology can be useful *in your everyday personal and professional lives.*

The study of cultural anthropology, in other words, is far more than the study of the similarities and differences among the thousands of distinct and discrete cultures of the world and, in today's interconnected world, it is far more relevant. The "applied" orientation of this book illustrates (through specific examples and scenarios) how understanding the ideas and behavior patterns of culturally different people, both at home and abroad, enables us to better meet our own personal and professional objectives. Conversely, when we fail to take our cultural environments seriously, we are likely to commit some serious cultural *faux pas,* which can have negative social, political, and economic ramifications.

The book's applied orientation is woven throughout the text. Each chapter (except this one) begins with a scenario that illustrates how knowledge of different cultures can affect our everyday lives. Moreover, all chapters conclude with an applied feature entitled "Out in the Real World" that presents examples of how anthropological data, theories, insights, and methods are being applied to a wide range of social issues and professions. In between these beginning and ending features, you will find other examples in the body of each chapter of how cultural anthropology can make a difference in our everyday personal and professional lives.

We are writing to you at the beginning of Chapter 1 so that you know from the outset that this book has a twofold purpose: (1) it introduces you to the basic field of cultural anthropology, and (2) it demonstrates how cross-cultural awareness is highly relevant in the interconnected world of the twenty-first century. We also want to alert you to pay close attention to the cases at the beginning and ending of each chapter because they are reminders of the importance of cultural knowledge to our everyday lives. Since we all play out our lives in a cultural context—and, to an increasing degree, in a multicultural or cross-cultural context—an understanding of cultural anthropology is crucial for maximizing our personal and professional success in the twenty-first century, irrespective of what line of work you might pursue.

When most North Americans hear the word *anthropologist,* a number of images come to mind. They picture, for example:

- Dian Fossey devoting years of her life to making systematic observations of mountain gorillas in their natural environment in Rwanda
- A field anthropologist interviewing an exotic tribesman about his kinship system
- The excavation of a jawbone that will be used to demonstrate the evolutionary link between early and modern humans
- A linguist meticulously recording the words and sounds of a native informant speaking a language that has never been written down
- A cultural anthropologist studying the culture of the hard-core unemployed in Washington, DC
- A team of archaeologists in pith helmets unearthing an ancient temple from a rain forest in Guatemala

Each of these impressions—to one degree or another—accurately represents the concerns of scientists who call themselves anthropologists. Anthropologists do in fact travel to different parts of the world to study little-known cultures (cultural anthropologists) and languages (anthropological linguists), but they also study culturally distinct groups within their own cultures. Anthropologists also unearth fossil remains (physical anthropologists) and various artifacts (archaeologists) of people who lived thousands and, in some cases, millions of years ago. Even though anthropologists in these subspecialties engage in substantially different types of activities and generate different types of data, they are all directed toward a single purpose: the scientific study of humans, both biologically and culturally, in whatever form, time period, or region of the world they might be found.

Anthropology—derived from the Greek words *anthropos* for "human" and logos for "study"—is, if we take it literally, the study of humans. In one sense this is an accurate description to the extent that anthropology raises a wide variety of questions about the human condition. And yet this literal definition is not particularly illuminating because a number of other academic disciplines—including sociology, biology, psychology, political science, economics, and history—also study human beings. What is it that distinguishes anthropology from all of these other disciplines?

Anthropology is the study of people—their origins, their development, and their contemporary variations, wherever and whenever they have been found. What distinguishes anthropology from all the disciplines that study humans is that it is by far the broadest in scope. The subject matter of anthropology includes fossilized skeletal remains of early humans, artifacts and other material remains from prehistoric and historic archaeological sites, as well as all of the contemporary and historical cultures of the world. The task that anthropology has set for itself is enormous. Anthropologists strive for an understanding of the biological and cultural origins and evolutionary development of the species. They are concerned with all humans, both past and present, as well as their behavior patterns, thought systems, and material possessions. In short, anthropology aims to describe, in the broadest sense, what it means to be human.

In their search to understand the human condition, anthropologists draw on a wide variety of data and methods, some unique to this field. They also work with specialists in other fields, such as geologists and geneticists, to create a diverse field of study that is often directly relevant to other fields. Anthropologist Eric Wolf (1964) suggested that anthropology spans the gap between the humanities, the social sciences, and the natural sciences. To illustrate, anthropological investigations of native art, folklore, values, and supernatural belief systems are primarily humanistic in nature; studies of social stratification, comparative political systems, and means of distribution are common in sociology, political science, and economics, respectively; and studies of comparative anatomy and radiocarbon dating are central to the natural sciences of biology and chemistry.

The global scope of anthropological studies has actually increased over the past century. In the early 1900s, anthropologists concentrated on the non-Western, preliterate, and technologically simple societies of the world and were content to leave the study of industrial societies to other disciplines such as sociology. In recent decades, however, anthropologists have devoted increasing attention to cultural and subcultural groups in industrial societies while continuing their studies of more exotic peoples of the world. It is not uncommon today for anthropologists to apply their field methods, for example, to the study of Hutterite colonies in North Dakota, rural communes in California, and urban street gangs in Chicago. Only when the whole range of human cultural variation is examined will anthropologists be in a position to test the accuracy of theories about human behavior.

Traditionally, the discipline of anthropology is divided into four distinct branches or subfields: *physical anthropology,* which deals with humans as biological organisms; *archaeology,* which attempts to reconstruct the cultures of the past, most of which have left no written records; *anthropological linguistics,* which focuses on the study of language in historical, structural, and social contexts; and *cultural anthropology,* which examines similarities and differences among contemporary cultures of the world. Within each of these broad subfields, anthropologists specialize in many specific topic areas (see Table 1.1). In recent years each subfield has developed an applied (or more practical) component, which is directed more toward solving societal problems and less toward collecting knowledge purely for the sake of developing theory.

TABLE 1.1 Branches of Anthropology

PHYSICAL ANTHROPOLOGY	ARCHAEOLOGY	ANTHROPOLOGICAL LINGUISTICS	CULTURAL ANTHROPOLOGY
Paleoanthropology	Historical archaeology	Historical linguistics	Development anthropology
Primatology	Prehistoric archaeology	Descriptive linguistics	Psychological anthropology
Human variation	Contract archaeology	Ethnolinguistics	Environmental anthropology
Forensic anthropology	Applied archaeology	Sociolinguistics	Medical anthropology
Applied physical anthropology	Cultural resource management	Applied linguistics	Urban anthropology
			Political anthropology
			Applied anthropology

© Cengage Learning 2013

Despite this four-field division, the discipline of anthropology has a long-standing tradition of emphasizing the interrelations among these four subfields. One of the major sections of the American Anthropological Association is the General Anthropology Division (GAD), founded in 1984 to foster scholarly exchange on unifying the four major subfields of the discipline. Moreover, in recent years there has been considerable blurring of the boundaries among the four branches. For example, the specialized area known as medical anthropology draws heavily from both physical and cultural anthropology, educational anthropology addresses issues that bridge the gap between cultural anthropology and linguistics, and sociobiology looks at the interaction between culture and biology.

Although cultural anthropology is the central focus of this textbook, a brief discussion of the other three branches will provide an adequate description of the discipline as a whole.

Physical Anthropology

The scientific study of humans from a biological perspective is called **physical anthropology**. Physical, or biological, anthropology looks at the biological and behavioral characteristics of humans and nonhuman primates (apes, monkeys, lemurs, lorises, and tarsiers), including their ancestors. The research of physical anthropologists, which helps to explain what it means to be human, is concerned with three broad areas of investigation. First, they are interested in reconstructing the anatomical and behavioral evolutionary record of the human species from fossil remains; they ask questions about the emergence of humans and how humans have evolved up to the present time. This area of physical anthropology is known as

paleoanthropology. The second area of concern to physical anthropologists is **primatology**—the study of the evolutionary fossil record of our nearest living relatives (apes, monkeys, and prosimians) and the behavior of living populations in their natural habitats. And the third area of investigation, called **human variation**, deals with how and why the physical traits (skin color, body proportions, head shape, and facial features) of contemporary human populations vary throughout the world. Today it is important to study human variation because of what it tells us about human adaptation. Unlike comparative biologists, physical anthropologists study how both culture and the environment have influenced biological evolution and contemporary variations.

Paleoanthropology

In their attempts to reconstruct human evolution, paleoanthropologists draw heavily on fossil remains (hardened organic matter such as bones and teeth) of humans, protohumans, and other primates. Once these fossil remains have been unearthed, the difficult job of comparison, analysis, and interpretation begins. To which species do the remains belong? Are the remains human or those of our prehuman ancestors? If not human, what do the remains tell us about our own species? When did these primates live? How did they adapt to their environment? To answer these questions, paleoanthropologists use the techniques of comparative anatomy. They compare such physical features as cranial capacity, teeth, hands, position of the pelvis, and shape of the head of the fossil remains with those of humans or other nonhuman primates. In addition to comparing physical features, paleoanthropologists look for signs of culture (such as tools) to help determine the humanity of the fossil remains. For example, if fossil remains are found in association with tools, and if it can be determined that the tools were made by these creatures, then it is likely that the remains will be considered human.

In addition to reconstructing the human evolutionary record, paleoanthropology has led to various applications of physical anthropology, most notably in the areas of medical anthropology, forensic anthropology, and the study of the effects of infectious diseases on humans. For example, for years forensic anthropologists have used traditional methods and theories from physical anthropology to help identify the remains of crime and disaster victims for legal purposes. Forensic anthropologists can determine from skeletal remains the age, sex, and stature of the deceased as well as other traits such as physical abnormalities, traumas (such as broken bones), and nutritional history. In recent years, forensic anthropologists have been called on to testify in murder trials and to study the physical remains of victims of mass human rights abuses, such as those that occurred in Bosnia and Kosovo in the 1990s. Forensic anthropologists played a significant role in helping to identify victims of the 9/11 attacks on New York City and Washington, DC. The life and work of one forensic anthropologist, Kathy Reichs (who worked to identify victims from the World Trade Center), have inspired the prime-time TV series *Bones*.

Primatology

Since the 1950s, physical anthropologists have developed their own area of specialization that helps shed light on human evolution and adaptation over time and space. This field of study is known as primatology—the study of our nearest living relatives (apes, monkeys, and prosimians) in their natural habitats. Primatologists study the anatomy and social behavior of such nonhuman primate species as gorillas, baboons, and chimpanzees in an effort to gain clues about our own evolution as a species. Because physical anthropologists do not have the luxury of observing the behavior of human ancestors several million years ago, they learn how early humans could have responded to certain environmental conditions and changes in their developmental past by studying contemporary nonhuman primates (such as baboons and chimps) in similar environments.

The Dian Fossey Gorilla Fund International

Primatologist Dian Fossey (1932–1985) spent decades in Central Africa studying mountain gorillas in their natural environment. Although she was killed in 1985, the work she devoted her life to—studying and protecting the mountain gorillas of Rwanda—has resulted in the stabilization and growth of the population of this most endangered of the great apes. In 1988 Sigourney Weaver starred as Dian Fossey in **Gorillas in the Mist**, a feature film about Fossey's life and work as a primatologist.

For example, the simple yet very real division of labor among baboon troops can shed light on role specialization and social stratification in early human societies, and the rudimentary tool-making skills found among chimpanzees in Tanzania may help explain early human strategies for adapting to the environment.

Physical Variations Among Humans

Although all humans are members of the same species and therefore are capable of interbreeding, considerable physical variation exists among human populations. Some of these differences are based on visible physical traits, such as the shape of the nose, body stature, and color of the skin. Other variations are based on less visible biochemical factors, such as blood type or susceptibility to diseases.

During the first half of the twentieth century, physical anthropologists attempted to document human physical variations throughout the world by dividing the world's population into various racial categories. A **race** was defined as a group of people who share a greater statistical frequency of genes and physical traits with one another than they do with people outside the group. Today, however, no anthropologists subscribe to the notion that races are fixed biological entities whose members all share the same physical features. Despite the efforts of earlier anthropologists to classify people into discrete racial categories, most anthropologists today do not consider these categories to be particularly useful. Thus most anthropologists view these early-twentieth-century racial typologies as largely an oversimplification of our present state of genetic knowledge.

Although contemporary anthropologists continue to be interested in human physical variation, they are concerned with how physical variations help people adapt to their environments. Physical anthropologists have found that populations with the greatest amount of melanin in their skin are found in tropical regions, whereas lighter-skinned populations generally reside in more northern latitudes. This suggests that natural selection has favored dark skin in tropical areas because it protects people from dangerous ultraviolet light. In colder climates, people tend to have considerable body mass (less body surface), which is a natural protection from the deadly cold. And sickle cells, found widely in the blood of people living in sub-Saharan Africa, protect people against the ravages of malaria.

Archaeology

Experts in the field of **archaeology** study the lifeways of people from the past by excavating and analyzing the material culture they have left behind. The purpose of archaeology is not to fill up museums by collecting exotic relics from prehistoric societies. Rather, it is to understand the cultural adaptations of ancient peoples (prehistoric and historic) by at least partially reconstructing their cultures. Because archaeologists concentrate on societies of the past, they are limited to working with material culture including, in some cases, written records. From these material remains, however, archaeologists are able to make inferences about many nonmaterial cultural characteristics (ideas and behavior patterns) of people who lived thousands, and in some cases millions, of years ago.

Archaeologists work with three types of material remains: artifacts, features, and ecofacts. **Artifacts** are objects that have been made or modified by humans and that can be removed from the site and taken to the laboratory for further analysis. Tools, arrowheads, and fragments of pottery are examples of artifacts. **Features**, like artifacts, are made or modified by people, but they cannot be readily carried away from the dig site. Archaeological features include such things as house foundations, fireplaces, and postholes. **Ecofacts** are objects found in the natural environment (such as bones, seeds, and wood) that were not made or altered by humans but were used by them. Ecofacts provide archaeologists with important data concerning the environment and how people used natural resources.

The data that archaeologists have at their disposal are very restricted. Not only are archaeologists limited to material remains, but also the overwhelming majority of material possessions that may have been part of a culture do not survive thousands of years under the ground. As a result, archaeologists search for fragments of material evidence (such items as projectile points, hearths, beads, and postholes) that will enable them to piece together a culture. A prehistoric garbage dump is particularly revealing because the archaeologist can learn a great deal about how people lived from what they threw away. These material remains are then used to make inferences about the nonmaterial aspects of the culture (i.e., values, ideas, and behaviors) being studied. For example, the finding that all women and children are buried with their heads pointing in one direction, whereas the heads of adult males point in a different direction, could lead to the possible explanation that the society practiced matrilineal kinship (that is, children followed their mother's line of descent rather than their father's).

Once the archaeologist has collected the physical evidence, the difficult work of analysis and interpretation begins. By studying the bits and pieces of material culture left behind (both environmental data and anatomical remains), the archaeologist seeks to determine how the people supported themselves, whether they had a notion of an afterlife, how roles were allocated between men and women, whether some people were more powerful than others, whether the people engaged in trade with neighboring peoples, and how lifestyles have changed over time.

Archaeologist Darius Arya works at the excavation of Caligula's house at Fori Imperiali in Rome.

Present-day archaeologists work with both historic and prehistoric cultures. Historic archaeologists help to reconstruct the cultures of people who used writing and about whom historical documents have been written. For example, historical archaeologists have contributed significantly to our understanding of colonial American cultures by analyzing material remains that can supplement such historical documents as books, letters, graffiti, and government reports. Prehistoric archaeology, on the other hand, deals with the vast segment of the human record (several million years) that predates the advent of writing about 5,500 years ago. Because archaeology remains the one scientific enterprise that systematically focuses on prehistoric cultures, it has provided us with a much longer time frame than written history for understanding the record of human development.

The relevance of archaeology often goes beyond helping us better understand our prehistoric past. During the 1960s and 1970s, a number of preservation and environmental protection laws were passed to identify and protect cultural and historic resources (such as landmarks, buildings, and archaeological sites) from being bulldozed. The laws require environmental impact studies to be conducted prior to the start of federally funded projects such as dams, highways, airports, and office buildings.

If the building project would destroy the cultural resource, then the law requires that archaeological research be conducted to preserve the information from the site. In response to these laws, archaeologists developed the specialty area of **cultural resource management**. The goal of this form of applied archaeology is to ensure that the laws are properly followed, that high-quality research is conducted, and that the data from archaeological sites are not destroyed by federally funded building projects.

Anthropological Linguistics

The branch of anthropology that studies human speech and language is called **anthropological linguistics**. Although humans are not the only species that has systems of symbolic communication, ours is by far the most complex form. In fact, some would argue that language is the most distinctive feature of being human because without language we could not acquire and transmit our culture from one generation to the next or think abstractly about a concept or the future.

Linguistic anthropology, which studies contemporary human languages as well as those of the past, looks not only at the structure and patterning of language but also at the origins of language, how it is learned, how it changes, and the social context in which it is used. Linguistic anthropologists also examine whether the language we speak causes us to view the world differently from others and how the use of the words we use may change our experiences. Linguistic anthropology is divided into four distinct branches: historical linguistics, descriptive linguistics, ethnolinguistics, and sociolinguistics.

Historical linguistics deals with the emergence of language in general and how specific languages have diverged over time. Some of the earliest anthropological interest in language focused on the historical connections between languages. For example, nineteenth-century linguists working with European languages demonstrated similarities in the sound systems between a particular language and an earlier parent language from which the language was derived. By comparing contemporary languages, linguists have been able to identify certain language families. Through techniques such as *glottochronology*, linguists can approximate when two related languages began to diverge from each other. Today this historical linguistic technique (which is based on some controversial assumptions) is used in conjunction with archaeological and biological evidence (e.g., DNA). For example, it can help archaeologists to more accurately trace population movements and to identify the inhabitants of a site.

Descriptive linguistics is the study of sound systems, grammatical systems, and the meanings attached to words in specific languages. Every culture has a distinctive language with its own logical structure and set of rules for putting words and sounds together for the purpose of communicating. In its simplest form, the task of the descriptive linguist is to compile dictionaries and grammar books for previously unwritten languages.

Cultural linguistics (also known as **ethnolinguistics**) is the branch of anthropological linguistics that examines the relationship between language and culture. In any language, certain cultural aspects that are emphasized (such as types of snow among the Inuit, cows among the pastoral Maasai, or automobiles in U.S. culture) are reflected in the vocabulary. Moreover, cultural linguists explore how different linguistic categories can affect how people organize their experiences, how they think, and how they perceive the world around them.

The fourth branch of anthropological linguistics, known as **sociolinguistics**, examines the relationship between language and social relations. For example, sociolinguists are interested in investigating how social class influences the particular dialect a person speaks. They also study the situational use of language—that is, how people use different forms of a language depending on the social situation they find themselves in at any given time. To illustrate, the words and grammatical structures a U.S. college student chooses when conversing with a roommate are significantly different from the linguistic style used when talking to a grandparent, a rabbi, or a potential employer during a job interview.

Anthropological linguists also engage in applied activities. For example, after describing the structure of a language, descriptive linguists frequently take the next logical step and work with educators to plan effective strategies for teaching English as a second language. Some anthropological linguists serve as consultants to government and educational leaders responsible for setting language policy in a state or country. Anthropological linguists sometimes work with local (small-scale) minority groups whose languages are spoken by so few people that they are in danger of becoming extinct. Still other applied linguists help design foreign language and culture programs for people who are preparing to live and work abroad. Moreover, linguists like Deborah Tannen (1990) apply their knowledge of gender differences in language to help men and women better understand one another.

Cultural Anthropology

The branch of anthropology that deals with the study of specific contemporary cultures (**ethnography**) and the more general underlying patterns of human culture derived through cultural comparisons (**ethnology**) is called **cultural anthropology** (see Table 1.2). Before cultural anthropologists can examine cultural differences and similarities throughout the

TABLE 1.2 Two Facets of Cultural Anthropology

ETHNOGRAPHY	ETHNOLOGY
Descriptive	Comparative
Based on direct fieldwork	Based on data collected by other ethnographers
Focuses on a single culture or subculture	Generalizes across cultures or subcultures

© Cengage Learning 2013

world, they must first describe the features of specific cultures in as much detail as possible. These detailed descriptions (ethnographies) are the result of extensive field studies (usually a year or two in duration) in which the anthropologist observes, talks to, and lives with the people he or she is studying. The large number of ethnographies written over the course of the twentieth century have provided an empirical basis for the comparative study of cultures. In the process of developing these descriptive accounts, cultural anthropologists provide insights into questions such as: How are the marriage customs of a group of people related to the group's economy? What effect does urban migration have on the kinship system? In what ways have supernatural beliefs helped a group of people adapt more effectively to their environment? Thus, while describing the essential features of a culture, the cultural anthropologist may also explain why certain cultural patterns exist and how they may be related to one another.

Ethnology is the comparative study of contemporary cultures, wherever they may be found. Ethnologists seek to understand both why people today and in the recent past differ in their ideas and behavior patterns and what all cultures in the world have in common with one another. The primary objective of ethnology is to uncover general cultural principles, the "rules" that govern human behavior. Because all humans have culture and live in groups called societies, there are no populations in the world today that are not viable subjects for the ethnologist. The lifeways of Inuit in the Arctic tundra, Greek peasants, Maasai herdsmen in Tanzania, and the residents of a retirement home in southern California have all been studied by cultural anthropologists.

Ethnographers and ethnologists face a daunting task as they describe and compare the many peoples of the world today. Cultural anthropologists must deal with enormous cultural diversity (thousands of distinct cultures in which people speak mutually unintelligible languages), numerous features of culture that can be compared, and a wide range of theoretical frameworks for comparing them. To describe even the least complex cultures requires many months of interviewing people and observing their behavior. Even with this large expenditure of time, rarely do contemporary ethnographers describe total cultures. Instead, they usually describe only the more outstanding features of a culture and then investigate a particular aspect or problem in greater depth.

Areas of Specialization

Because the description of a total culture is usually beyond the scope of a single ethnographer, in recent decades cultural anthropologists have tended to specialize, often identifying themselves with one or more of these five areas of specialization:

1. *Urban anthropology:* Cultural anthropologists during the first half of the twentieth century tended to concentrate their research on rural societies in non-Western areas. In the immediate post–World War II era, however, anthropologists in greater numbers turned their attention to the study of more complex urban social systems. With increases in rural-to-urban migration in many parts of the world, it was becoming more difficult to think of rural populations as isolated, insulated entities. During the 1950s and 1960s, which saw even more rural–urban interaction, cultural anthropologists began to assess the impacts that cities were having on traditional rural societies. It was then a natural development to follow rural people into the cities to see how the two systems interacted. Thus was born the subdiscipline of urban anthropology.

   By focusing on how factors such as size, density, and heterogeneity affect customary ways of behaving, urban anthropologists have examined such important topics as ethnic neighborhoods, rural–urban linkages, labor migration, urban kinship patterns, social networks, urban stratification, squatter settlements, and informal economies. Urban anthropology has also focused on social problems such as homelessness, troubled race relations, poverty, social injustice, unemployment, crime, and poor public health.

2. *Medical anthropology:* Another recent area of specialization is medical anthropology, which studies the relationship of biological and sociocultural factors to health, disease, and illness—both now and in the past. Medical anthropology includes a variety of perspectives and concerns, ranging from a biological pole at one end of the spectrum to a sociocultural pole at the other. Medical anthropologists with a more biological focus tend to concentrate on interests such as the role of disease in human evolution, nutrition, growth and development, and **paleopathology** (the analysis of disease in ancient populations). Medical anthropologists with more social or cultural interests focus on ethnomedicine (belief systems that affect sickness and health), medical practitioners, and the relationship between traditional and Western medical systems.

Dr. Paul Farmer, an applied medical anthropologist as well as a medical doctor, is the founder of Partners in Health, an international medical organization. For more than 20 years Dr. Farmer has been working with the people of Haiti on a successful treatment program for infectious diseases such as tuberculosis and AIDS.

3. *Development anthropology:* Dating back to the nineteenth century, colonial powers were interested in the economic development of their colonies, which in the early days meant building infrastructure such as power plants, roads, railroads, and communication systems to support new, viable industries. Later, other development projects were initiated in such areas as agriculture, education, medicine, and job training. Although anthropologists were sometimes consulted on these multimillion-dollar projects, it was not until the 1960s (when development anthropology became a recognized subdiscipline) that anthropologists played a more active and comprehensive role in the development process. In the early 1960s, development anthropologists focused their efforts on pointing out why and how development programs were unsuccessful because they failed to account for local cultural factors. By the 1970s and 1980s, development anthropologists were becoming more involved in the entire development cycle, including project identification, design, budgetary considerations, implementation, and evaluation.

The development anthropology that has emerged in the twenty-first century focuses more on people (rather than on the economy) and on assessing value. Many development anthropologists no longer start by asking: How can I make this large development project successful? Rather, they are asking: Will this project benefit the target population? If the answer is yes, then the new breed of twenty-first-century development anthropologists will likely become involved in the project by providing the vital local cultural information needed to make it successful. The focus is no longer on the international development agencies, governments, or multinational corporations financing the development project. Rather, the criteria for success are the benefits for the local populations, such as reduced poverty, equitable economic growth, environmental protection, and respect for human rights.

4. *Environmental anthropology:* Tracing its roots to early ecological anthropologists, environmental anthropology—which examines how human populations interact with their environments—is concerned with two fundamental questions: What role does the physical environment play in the formation and evolution of specific cultures, and how do specific sociocultural groups perceive, manage, and modify their environments? Most of the leading environmental anthropologists have demonstrated repeatedly that culture and environment cannot be treated in isolation because they are so intimately interconnected. Although twenty-first-century anthropologists are still interested in the relationships between culture and the natural environment *per se,* they have expanded their research interests to include theories and approaches that are useful for addressing contemporary problems of environmental degradation and scarce resources like water. These concerns include (but are not limited to) conflicts over land use, biodiversity conservation, air and water pollution, deforestation, soil erosion, human rights, sustainable development, mineral extraction, and the effects of biochemicals on the health of local populations. Often working collaboratively with scholars from many other disciplines, environmental anthropologists assist policy makers and planners by providing valuable insights into the local cultures of the people who are negatively affected by environmental changes.

5. *Psychological anthropology:* Psychological anthropology, one of the oldest subspecialties of cultural anthropology, looks at the relationship between culture and the psychological makeup of individuals and groups. Concerned with the relationships between psychological processes and cultural factors, psychological anthropologists examine how culture may affect personality, cognition, attitudes, and emotions.

Between the 1920s and 1950s, early practitioners of psychological anthropology—namely, Ruth Benedict, Franz Boas, and Edward Sapir—were interested in the relationship between culture and personality. Many of these early theorists studied the effects of cultural features (such as feeding, weaning, and toilet training) on personality; others, led by Abraham Kardiner, were interested in how *group* personality traits were reflected in entire cultures. Stimulated by the need to know more about America's allies and enemies during and after World War II, some psychological anthropologists turned their attention to "national character studies." For example, Geoffrey Gorer and John Rickman (1949) studied Russia, and Ruth Benedict wrote her classic study of the Japanese national character in 1946. Today these studies are not taken very seriously because of the methodological difficulties involved in generalizing about large and diverse societies. Since the 1960s, psychological anthropology has moved away from these broad national character studies and has focused on a more narrowly drawn set of problems, such as symbolism, cognition, and consciousness in specific societies. Now methodologies are more varied, statistics are more widely used, and psychological anthropologists collaborate with people working in other disciplines, such as psychology and linguistics.

These five areas are only a partial list of the specializations within cultural anthropology. Other specialties include agricultural anthropology, legal anthropology, educational anthropology, the anthropology of religion, business anthropology, economic anthropology, political anthropology, the anthropology of tourism, the anthropology of work, and nutritional anthropology.

Guiding Principles

For the past century, cultural anthropology has distinguished itself from other disciplines in the humanities and social sciences by following several guiding principles. Although other disciplines have adopted some of these major themes over the decades, they remain central to the discipline of cultural anthropology.

Holism

A distinguishing feature of anthropology is its holistic approach to the study of human groups. Anthropological **holism** is evidenced in a number of important ways. First, the anthropological approach is comprehensive and involves looking at both biological and sociocultural aspects of humanity—that is, people's genetic endowment as well as what they acquire from their environment after birth. Second, anthropology has the longest possible time frame, from the earliest beginnings of humans several million years ago right up to the present. Third, anthropology is holistic to the extent that it studies all varieties of people wherever they may be found, from East African pastoralists to Korean factory workers. And, finally, anthropologists study many different aspects of human experience, including family structure, marital regulations, house construction, methods of conflict resolution, means of livelihood, religious beliefs, language, space usage, and art.

In the past, cultural anthropologists have made every effort to be holistic by covering as many aspects of a culture as possible in the total cultural context. More recently, however, the accumulated information from all over the world has become so vast that most anthropologists have needed to become more specialized or focused. To illustrate, one anthropologist may concentrate on marital patterns, whereas another may focus on farming and land-use patterns. Despite this trend toward specialization, though, anthropologists continue to analyze their findings within a wider cultural context.

Ethnocentrism

While waiting to cross the street in Mumbai, India, an American tourist stood next to a local resident, who proceeded to blow his nose, without handkerchief or tissue, into the street. The tourist's reaction was instantaneous and unequivocal: *How disgusting!* He responded to this cross-cultural incident by evaluating the Indian's behavior on the basis of standards of etiquette established by his own culture. According to those standards, it is considered proper to use a handkerchief in such a situation. But if the man from Mumbai were to see the American tourist blowing his nose into a handkerchief, he would be equally repulsed, thinking it strange indeed for the man to blow his nose into a handkerchief and then put the handkerchief back into his pocket and carry it around for the rest of the day.

Both the American and the Indian are evaluating each other's behavior based on the standards of their own cultural assumptions and practices. This way of responding to culturally different behavior is known as ethnocentrism: the belief that one's own culture is superior to all others. In other words, it means viewing the rest of the world through the narrow lens of one's own cultural perspectives.

Incidents of ethnocentrism are extensive. During the recent war in Iraq, both American troops and civilian contractors expressed disdain for what they saw as blatant Iraqi dishonesty in their everyday dealings. Brought up to value honesty and straight talk, most Americans fail to appreciate that some other cultures, such as in Iraq, place a higher value on personal and family honor than on transparency. From an Iraqi perspective, if one's honor is threatened, it is far more important to preserve honor than to tell the unvarnished truth. Often Iraqis tell Americans that they understand something when they do not. Americans see this as a lie, while Iraqis see it as a face-saving mechanism designed to preserve their personal honor and dignity. Both Americans and Iraqis failed to recognize the inherent logic of the others' value system and, as a result, were being ethnocentric (Tierney 2003).

It should be quite obvious why ethnocentrism is so pervasive throughout the world. Because most people are raised in a single culture and never learn about other cultures, it is only logical that their own way of life—their values, attitudes, ideas, and ways of behaving—seems to be the most natural and correct. Our ethnocentrism should not be a source of embarrassment because it is a natural by-product of growing up in any society. In fact, from a functionalist perspective, ethnocentrism may serve the positive societal function of enhancing group solidarity. Even though ethnocentrism is present in all cultures, however, it is a major obstacle to the understanding of other cultures and to peaceful coexistence, which are, after all, the primary objectives of cultural anthropology. Although we cannot eliminate ethnocentrism totally, we can reduce it. By becoming aware of our own ethnocentrism, we can temporarily set aside our own value judgments long enough to learn how other cultures operate and what they consider to be natural.

Cultural Relativism

Since the beginning of the twentieth century, the discipline of anthropology has led a vigorous campaign against the perils of ethnocentrism. As cultural anthropologists began to conduct empirical fieldwork among the different cultures of the world, they recognized a need for dispassionate and objective descriptions of the people they were studying. Following the lead of Franz Boas in the United States and Bronislaw Malinowski in Britain, twentieth-century anthropologists participated in a tradition that called on the researcher to strive to prevent his or her own cultural values from coloring the descriptive accounts of the people under study.

According to Boas, the father of modern anthropology in the United States, anthropologists could achieve that level of detachment through **cultural relativism**.

This is the notion that any part of a culture (such as an idea, a thing, or a behavior pattern) must be viewed in its proper cultural context rather than from the viewpoint of the observer's culture. Rather than asking, how does this fit into *my* cultural perspective, the cultural relativist asks, how does a cultural item fit into the rest of the cultural system of which it is a part? First formulated by Boas and later developed by one of his students, Melville Herskovits (1972), cultural relativism rejects the notion that any culture, including our own, possesses a set of absolute standards by which all other cultures can be judged. Cultural relativity is a cognitive tool that helps us understand why people think and act the way they do.

Perhaps a specific example of cultural relativity will help to clarify the concept. Anthropologists over the years have described a number of cultural practices from around the world that appear to be morally reprehensible to most Westerners. For example, the Dani of western New Guinea customarily cut off a finger from the hand of any close female relative of a man who dies, the Kikuyu of Kenya routinely remove part of the genitalia of teenage girls in order to suppress their maleness, and the Dodoth of Uganda extract the lower front teeth of young girls in an attempt to make them more attractive. Some Inuit groups practice a custom that would strike the typical Westerner as inhumane at best: When aging parents become too old to carry their share of the workload, they are left out in the cold to die. If we view such a practice by the standards of our Western culture (that is, ethnocentrically), we would have to conclude that it is cruel and heartless, hardly a way to treat those who brought you into the world. But the cultural relativist would look at this form of homicide in the context of the total culture of which it is a part. John Friedl and John Pfeiffer provide a culturally relativistic explanation of this custom:

> It is important to know . . . that this . . . [custom is not practiced] against the will of the old person. It is also necessary to recognize that this is an accepted practice for which people are adequately prepared throughout their lives, and not some kind of treachery sprung upon an individual as a result of a criminal conspiracy. Finally, it should be considered in light of the ecological situation in which the Eskimos [sic] live. Making a living in the Arctic is difficult at best, and the necessity of feeding an extra mouth, especially when there is little hope that the individual will again become productive in the food-procurement process, would mean that the whole group would suffer. It is not a question of Eskimos not liking old people, but rather a question of what is best for the entire group. We would not expect—and indeed we do not find—this practice to exist where there was adequate food to support those who were not able to contribute to the hunting effort. (1977: 331)

There is a problem with taking the notion of cultural relativism too literally. If cultural relativism is taken to its logical extreme, we would have to conclude that absolutely no behavior found in the world is immoral provided that the people who practice it concur that it is morally acceptable or that it performs a function in the interest of the society. Practicing cultural relativism, however, does not require that we view all cultural practices as morally equivalent; that is, not all cultural practices are equally worthy of tolerance and respect. To be certain, some cultural practices (such as genocide) are morally indefensible in any cultural context. Also, keep in mind that to practice cultural relativism does not require that you give up your own culture and practice another. In fact, it doesn't even require that you like, or approve of, the other culture.

Yet, if our goal is to *understand* human behavior in its myriad forms, then cultural relativism can help us identify the inherent logic behind certain ideas and customs.

Contributions of Anthropology

One of the major contributions of anthropology to the understanding of the human condition stems from the very broad task it has set for itself. Whereas disciplines such as economics, political science, and psychology are considerably narrower in scope, anthropology has carved out the task of examining all aspects of humanity for all periods of time and all parts of the globe. Because of the magnitude of this task, anthropologists must draw on theories and data from other disciplines in the humanities, the social sciences, and the physical sciences. As a result, anthropology is in a good position to integrate the various disciplines dealing with human physiology and culture.

Enhancing Understanding

In comparison with people in other countries, people from the United States generally have less knowledge about other countries and other cultures. Americans' knowledge about other parts of the world has been dismal for decades and is not improving to any significant degree. Knowledge about the rest of the world is particularly important today because the world has become increasingly interconnected. Forty years ago it made relatively little difference whether North Americans spoke a second language, knew the name of the British prime minister, or held a passport. But now, in the twenty-first century, we live in a world in which decisions made in Geneva or Tokyo send ripples throughout the rest of the world.

For the past several decades, the world has experienced globalization, which involves rapidly growing free-market economies, the lowering of tariff barriers, and the worldwide use of high-speed information technology. This recent intensification of the flow of money, goods, services, and information to all parts of the globe has greatly accelerated culture change and has made the study of different cultures more complex. Increasing numbers of people today are moving, both geographically and through cyberspace, outside their own familiar cultural borders, causing dramatic increases in cross-cultural contact and the potential for culture change. Through its distinctive methodology of long-term, intensive, participant-observation research, cultural anthropology offers an in-depth look at how local cultural groups are reacting to the process of globalization. Although many pundits study the consequences of globalization by talking only to government and business leaders, cultural anthropologists are more likely to see what is actually occurring on the ground and how the local people

themselves talk about their life experiences in a time of rapid globalization.

Still another contribution of anthropology is that it helps us better understand ourselves. The early Greeks claimed that the educated person was the person with self-knowledge ("Know thyself"). One of the best ways to gain self-knowledge is to know as much as possible about one's own culture—that is, to understand the forces that shape our thinking, values, and behaviors. And the best way of learning about our culture is to examine the similarities and differences between ourselves and others. The anthropological perspective, with its emphasis on the comparative study of cultures, should lead us to the conclusion that our culture is just one way of life among many found in the world and that it represents one way (among many possible ways) to adapt to a particular set of environmental conditions. Through the process of contrasting and comparing, we gain a fuller understanding of other cultures as well as our

Dr. Ann Dunham Soetoro, a cultural anthropologist who spent many years studying local craftsmen and economically depressed peoples in rural Indonesia, was a shining example of the type of understanding derived from anthropological fieldwork. Oh, incidentally, did we mention that Soetoro was the mother of President Barack Obama? Do you think her anthropological perspective and cross-cultural sensitivities have had an influence on the thinking of her son?

National Anthropological Archives, Smithsonian Institution

own, which then allows us to operate more effectively (both personally and professionally) in our increasingly interconnected world.

Building Skills for the Twenty-First Century

As discussed in the "Letter to Students" at the beginning of this chapter, the study of cultural anthropology has relevance for our everyday lives. The data, concepts, and insights derived from the study of other cultures can help us better meet our professional goals and lead more satisfying lives in a multicultural society. But the very *process* of studying cultural anthropology is also valuable because of the skills and competencies that it helps develop. Activities such as taking courses about different cultures, working in local internships with international organizations, living in the university's international dormitory, and participating in study-abroad programs all combine to provide students with valuable carryover skills that go beyond the mere mastery of subject content.

Educators, business leaders, and policy makers have written volumes about the behavioral traits, skills, and competencies needed for success in the twenty-first century (Cash 2010; Larson, Brown, and Mortimer 2003; Trilling and Fadel 2009). Although many of these writers have put a unique spin on their own list of competencies, there remains a basic core on which most can agree. These skills involve developing a broad perspective, appreciating other points of view, operating comfortably in ambiguous situations, working effectively as part of cross-cultural teams, and becoming emotionally resilient, open-minded, and perceptually aware. These traits have been identified as essential for coping with a rapidly changing world that has become increasingly interdependent. And, because the study of cultural anthropology involves immersing oneself in other cultures, it is perhaps the best single training ground for developing those competencies needed for a wide range of professional areas. Table 1.3 provides a partial list of careers that benefit from the study of cultural anthropology.

DEVELOP A BROAD PERSPECTIVE This skill involves seeing the big picture and the interrelatedness of the parts. A basic anthropological strategy for understanding other cultures is to look at a cultural feature from within its original cultural context rather than from the perspective of one's own culture. In other words, the student of anthropology is continually being asked to analyze a part of a culture in relationship to the whole. What better way to develop this type of systems thinking?

APPRECIATE OTHER PERSPECTIVES Being inquisitive, nonjudgmental, and open to new ways of thinking is vital if we are to adapt to ever-changing environments. This involves, essentially, a willingness to learn and postpone making evaluations until more facts are known. Such a capacity also requires suppressing one's ego and letting go of old paradigms. It does not mean giving up one's cultural values in favor of others. But it does entail (at least temporarily) letting go of cultural certainty, learning how other cultures view us, and being willing to see the internal logic of another culture. This is exactly what students of cultural anthropology are encouraged to do in order to learn about other cultures and their diverse perspectives.

BALANCE CONTRADICTIONS A major requirement for working and living effectively in a global society is to be able to balance contradictory needs and demands rather than trying to eliminate them. Contradictions and conflicts should be seen as opportunities, not as liabilities. Conflicting

TABLE 1.3 Non-Academic Career Opportunities in Anthropology

SUBFIELD	EXAMPLES
Physical anthropology	Forensic specialist with law enforcement
	Museum curator
	Genetic counselor
	Human rights investigator
	Zoologist/primatologist
	Public health official
Archaeology	Cultural resource manager
	Museum curator
	Environmental impact specialist
	Historical archaeologist
	Contract (salvage) archaeologist
Anthropological linguistics	ESL teacher
	International business trainer
	Foreign-language teacher
	Cross-cultural advertising/marketing specialist
	Translator/interpreter
Cultural anthropology	International business consultant
	Cross-cultural consultant in hospitals
	Museum curator
	International economic development worker
	Cross-cultural trainer
	International human resources manager
	School educator
	Immigration/refugee counselor

values, behaviors, and ideas are a fact of life in today's world. The study of cultural anthropology provides insights into the nature of the world's diversity and how each culture is a logical and coherent entity. When anthropology students are exposed to logical alternatives to their own ways of thinking and behaving, they learn to cope with differences and contradictions and actually use these differences to achieve synergy.

EMPHASIZE GLOBAL TEAMWORK Success in the twenty-first century requires an emphasis on cultural awareness and cross-cultural teamwork, not just personal awareness and individual mastery. Both private and public institutions are becoming increasingly global in focus. For example,

The study of cultural anthropology prepares people for working in the global economy of the twenty-first century.

foreign subsidiaries, joint ventures with foreign firms, and overseas facilities are commonplace in the world of business. If young adults are to be successful at working within and leading these culturally complex organizations, they will need to know the underlying cultural assumptions of the diverse people on those multicultural teams. There is no academic discipline in higher education today that addresses this competency better than cultural anthropology.

DEVELOP COGNITIVE COMPLEXITY Citizens of the new millennium need what is referred to as *cognitive complexity,* which is made up of the twin abilities of differentiating and integrating. Differentiation involves being able to see how a single entity is composed of a number of different parts; integration, on the other hand, involves the capacity to identify how the various parts are interconnected. The cognitively complex person is able to engage in both types of thinking and can move comfortably between the two. One must be able to focus on the unique needs of the local situation while at the same time understanding how it fits into the operations of the total organization. The study of cultural anthropology encourages one to examine another culture as well as one's own, compare the two, and understand the relationship of both cultures to the generalized concept of culture. Thus the student of anthropology gets practice at becoming cognitively complex by moving from the specific parts to the whole and back again.

DEVELOP PERCEPTUAL ACUITY Living and working in the twenty-first century require people to be perceptually acute. We need to accurately derive meaning from interactions with others from a wide variety of cultures and subcultures. This involves being attentive to both verbal and nonverbal communication by being an active listener, deriving meaning from social context, and being sensitive to the feelings of others and to one's effect on others. Studying other cultures—and particularly living in other cultures—forces the anthropology student to derive meaning not only from the words exchanged in cross-cultural encounters but also from the nonverbal cues, the social context, and the assumptions embedded in the other culture.

Thus, a number of skills and capacities that are considered essential for effective living and working in the twenty-first century can be mastered while studying cultural anthropology. Although a mere exposure to cultural anthropology does not guarantee that these skills will be developed, the comparative study of the world's cultural diversity and shared heritage is the single best classroom for acquiring these competencies. Even if you don't major in anthropology, you can develop skills for the twenty-first century by doing what anthropologists do—that is, throwing themselves into other cultures by traveling and living abroad, either before, during, or after college. For example, an increasing number of recent high school graduates are opting to take a "gap year," a time to travel and intern with organizations abroad before attending college (Mohn 2006: 6). In addition, it has become increasingly important for university students to have some type of experiential international learning opportunity during their undergraduate years. An appreciable number of college graduates (both anthropology majors and others) are beginning to recognize the value of immersing oneself in a different culture. It has been estimated (Chura 2006) that approximately thirty-five thousand recent U.S. college graduates have taken a year or two off to travel and work in a culture different from their own. In most cases this is not frivolous "bumming around," but rather a way of developing vital global skills for the twenty-first century. For many it has been a way to leverage their position in the job market when they return home.

The Bottom Line: Understanding Other Cultures

This book, and indeed cultural anthropology as a discipline, focuses on understanding other cultures, wherever they may be found. Although gaining this understanding involves acquiring accurate information about the world's cultures, it also involves learning about one's own culture. However, what we know, or think we know, about our own culture is not necessarily perceived in the same way by people from different cultures. In other words, we may hold a particular value or cultural trait and then describe that trait in only the most positive ways. Those looking at us from the outside, however, are more likely to see some of the negative implications as well. Thus, if cultural anthropology is to help us function more effectively in an increasingly interconnected world, we will have to focus on accomplishing three tasks: understanding culture-specific information about other cultures, understanding our own culture, and understanding how culturally different people view us and our cultural patterns.

Out in the Real World: Anthropologist Develops a New Breakfast Food

While most anthropologists work in academic institutions (e.g., colleges, universities, and museums), a growing number of applied anthropologists are working in non-academic settings such as hospitals, government agencies, international development agencies, public health organizations, and for-profit businesses, among others. One of the many practical (non-academic) careers opening up to cultural anthropologists today is *new product developer*. Research and design firms, which develop new products, are actively recruiting anthropologists to help them gain deeper insights into their customers through ethnographic research. One such cultural anthropologist, Susan Squires, who has worked in product development for more than a decade, conducted participant-observation research on U.S. families during breakfast time [National Association of Practicing Anthropologists (NAPA) website 2010]. Her research has not only shed light on new ways of thinking about food consumption in the mornings but also led to the development of a successful new breakfast food product. By actually sitting at the breakfast table with parents and their children, Squires learned a number of interesting features about the morning meal for the modern U.S. family:

- With both parents working, children have to be dropped off at school or day care relatively early, and consequently breakfast time is hectic. Children often eat "on the run" rather than sitting down to a large traditional breakfast.
- Since children are not very hungry when they wake up at 6:30 in the morning, they often leave the house at 7:00 a.m. without eating much of anything.
- Both children and adults eat bananas because they are nutritious, portable, disposable, and fun to eat.

- Parents, children, and even grandparents, while agreeing that breakfast is an important meal, have different ideas about what constitutes a good breakfast. Mothers believe that breakfast food should be nutritious and free of preservatives; fathers prefer less nutritional "comfort food"; grandparents think that the best breakfast is warm and high in cholesterol (bacon, eggs, and buttered toast); and children prefer sweet foods such as sweetened cereal, donuts, or pancakes with plenty of maple syrup.

If a new breakfast food product were developed, it would have to meet the family's needs. For example, it should be nutritious, portable, disposable, versatile, and fun to eat. Based on her ethnographic research—which determined *actual* eating patterns rather than asking people what they had for breakfast—Susan Squires developed a new breakfast food product designed for the two-parent, working family on the go called "Go-gurts." The first yogurt served in a tube, "Go-gurts" is a healthy, high-protein food; it is smooth and creamy and comes in a number of fun and tasty flavors such as Strawberry Splash and Cool Cotton Candy. This alternative breakfast supplement, developed by an anthropologist and based on ethnographic research, had sales of more than $37 million during its first year on the market.

Is cultural anthropology practical in our everyday lives? Stay tuned for many other examples of how anthropological data, insights, research, methods, and theories inform a wide range of professions, some of which *you* might be practicing in the not-too-distant future.

QUESTIONS FOR FURTHER THOUGHT

1. What problems of data collection do you think Squires may have encountered when conducting her field research?

2. Can you think of other healthy, portable, and disposable breakfast foods that would be appropriate for the busy American family?

SUMMARY

1. This textbook takes an *applied* perspective. This means that, in addition to surveying the content material of cultural anthropology, this book takes a number of opportunities to emphasize how the theories, methods, and insights of cultural anthropology can be used to help solve societal problems, both at home and abroad.

2. The academic discipline of anthropology involves the study of the biological and cultural origins of humans. The subject matter of anthropology is wide-ranging, including fossil remains, nonhuman primate anatomy and behavior, artifacts from past cultures, past and present

languages, and all of the prehistoric, historic, and contemporary cultures of the world.

3. As practiced in the United States, the discipline of anthropology follows an integrated four-field approach comprising physical anthropology, archaeology, anthropological linguistics, and cultural anthropology. All four subdisciplines have both theoretical and applied components.

4. The subdiscipline of physical anthropology focuses on three primary concerns: paleoanthropology (the study of fossil remains in order to decipher the biological record of human evolution), primatology (the study of nonhuman primate anatomy and behavior for the purpose of gaining insights into human adaptation to the environment), and studies of human physical variations (skin color, stature, facial structure, genetics) and how biological variations contribute to adaptation to one's environment.

5. The subfield of archaeology has as its primary objective the reconstruction of past cultures, both historic and prehistoric, from the material objects the cultures leave behind.

6. Anthropological linguistics, which studies both present and past languages, is divided into four major subdivisions: historical linguistics (studying the emergence and divergence of languages over time), descriptive linguistics (analyzing the structure of phonetic and grammar systems in contemporary languages), ethnolinguistics (exploring the relationship between language and culture), and sociolinguistics (understanding how social relations affect language).

7. Cultural anthropology focuses on the study of contemporary cultures wherever they are found in the world. One part of the task of cultural anthropology involves describing particular cultures (ethnography), and the other part involves comparing two or more cultures (ethnology).

8. A long-standing tradition in anthropology is the holistic approach. The discipline is holistic (or comprehensive) in four important respects: It looks at both the biological and cultural aspects of human behavior; it encompasses the longest possible time frame by looking at contemporary, historic, and prehistoric societies; it examines human cultures in every part of the world; and it studies many different aspects of human cultures.

9. There are essentially two ways to respond to unfamiliar cultures. One way is ethnocentrically—that is, through the lens of one's own cultural perspective. The other way is from the perspective of a cultural relativist—that is, within the context of the other culture. Cultural anthropologists strongly recommend the second mode, although they are aware of certain limitations.

10. The discipline of cultural anthropology helps students develop the skills and competencies needed to live in the twenty-first century, including developing a broad perspective, appreciating other perspectives, balancing contradictions, emphasizing global teamwork, developing cognitive complexity, and developing perceptual acuity.

KEY TERMS

anthropological
  linguistics 11
archaeology 8
artifacts 9
cultural anthropology 12
cultural relativism 19
cultural resource
  management 11
descriptive linguistics 11

ecofacts 9
ethnocentrism 18
ethnography 12
ethnolinguistics 12
ethnology 12
features 9
historical linguistics 11
holism 17
human variation 6

paleoanthropology 6
paleopathology 14
physical
  anthropology 5
primatology 6
race 8
sociolinguistics 12

These monks use laptops in their temple.

© Corbis Flirt/Alamy

CHAPTER 2

The Concept of Culture

THE NEED TO UNDERSTAND CULTURE
WHEN DESIGNING HOUSING

Jason, an associate in an internationally known architectural firm in Philadelphia, was assigned to head up a project designing public housing units in Nairobi, Kenya. With a small team of colleagues, Jason spent about three months designing and preparing the schematics for a large, nine-building project consisting of more than two hundred separate units. The units were laid out in much the same way that public housing units are designed in Philadelphia, Atlanta, or Chicago—that is, with two bedrooms, a large bathroom, a living room, and a dining area with an adjoining open kitchen. The plans were accepted by the Nairobi City Council, and the buildings were constructed over a period of several years.

Once completed, the units were rented (with substantial government subsidies) to needy families. Unfortunately, many of the new residents, while grateful to live in new housing with modern conveniences, were not at all satisfied with one particular design feature. Jason and his team of Western architects had designed every unit with a dining room that opened up into the kitchen. This design reflects the typical American practice of using the kitchen for both food preparation and socializing. For example, it is not at all unusual for dinner guests in the United States to socialize in the kitchen while the host puts the final touches on the dinner.

For Kenyans (most of whom retain strong ties to their traditional rural cultures), however, the place where food is cleaned, prepared, and cooked is considered unclean and is totally unsuitable for entertaining one's guests or, for that matter, even being seen by guests. To serve dinner to guests in the dining room while they can look into the "unclean" place where food is prepared is as unthinkable as having a bathroom without a door next to the dining room. After residents complained to the public housing officials, the units were modified by the addition of a door between the dining room and kitchen.

Jason and his design team were guilty of failing to remove their cultural blinders. They assumed that people the world over deal with their personal domestic space in similar ways. Perhaps the municipal government of Nairobi could have been spared the needless expense of altering the kitchens if Jason had taken a cultural anthropology course while he was studying architecture.

QUESTIONS FOR FURTHER THOUGHT

1. How can you explain the fact that the original plans for this public housing project were approved by the Nairobi City Council, which should have known better?

2. Can you think of any other examples of how architects must understand the cultural values of the people who use the buildings they design?

Although the term *culture* is used in most of the social sciences today, over the years it has received its most precise and comprehensive definition from the discipline of anthropology. Whereas sociology has concentrated on the notion of society and social relations; economics on the concepts of production, distribution, and consumption; and political science on the concept of power; anthropology has focused on the culture concept. From anthropology's nineteenth-century beginnings, culture has been central to both ethnology (comparing cultures) and archaeology and has been an important, if not major, concern of physical anthropology. Anthropology, through its examination of different lifeways throughout space and time, has done more than any other scientific discipline to refine our understanding of the concept of culture.

Culture Defined

In nonscientific Western usage, the term *culture* refers to personal refinements such as classical music, the fine arts, world philosophy, and gourmet cuisine. For example, according to this popular use of the term, the cultured person listens to Bach rather than Lady Gaga, orders prime rib rather than barbecued ribs when dining out, can distinguish between the artistic styles of Monet and Toulouse-Lautrec, prefers Cabernet to Kool-Aid, and attends the ballet instead of staying home and watching TV. The anthropologist, however, uses the term in a broader sense to include far more than just "the finer things in life." The anthropologist does not distinguish between cultured people (those who have the finer things) and uncultured people. All people have culture, according to the anthropological definition. An Australian aboriginal, living with a bare minimum of technology, has as much culture as Yo-Yo Ma or Placido Domingo. Thus, for the anthropologist, projectile points, creation myths, and mud huts are items of culture and contribute to rich discussions about understanding humans and their ways of life across time and space.

Over the past century, anthropologists have formulated a number of definitions of the concept of culture. In fact, in the often-cited work by Alfred Kroeber and

© Charles and Josette Lenars/Corbis

According to the anthropological definition, this Australian aboriginal man has as much culture as world-class cellist Yo-Yo-Ma or Broadway lyricist Stephen Sondheim.

Clyde Kluckhohn (1952), more than 160 different definitions of culture were identified. Nineteenth-century British anthropologist Edward Tylor (1871: 1) suggested one definition: Culture is "that complex whole which includes knowledge, belief, art, morals, law, custom, and any other capabilities and habits acquired by man as a member of society."

Adding to the already sizable number of definitions, we will define culture as "everything that people have, think, and do as members of a society." This definition can be instructive because the three verbs (*have*, *think*, and *do*) correspond to the three major components of culture. That is, everything that people *have* refers to material possessions; everything that people *think* refers to the things they carry around in their heads, such as ideas, values, and attitudes; and everything that people *do* refers to behavior patterns. Thus all cultures are composed of material objects; ideas, values, and attitudes; and patterned ways of behaving (see Figure 2.1).

Although we compartmentalize these components of culture, we should not conclude that they are unrelated. In fact, the components are so intimately connected that it is frequently hard to separate them in real life. To illustrate, a non-American anthropologist studying the mainstream culture of the United States would observe people engaged in writing in a wide variety of contexts. Middle-class North Americans fill out job applications, post information on Facebook, scribble messages on Post-it notes, write books, and compose e-mail and text messages, to mention only a few examples. When we write, we use tangible *things* (or artifacts), such as pens, pencils, computers, word processing software,

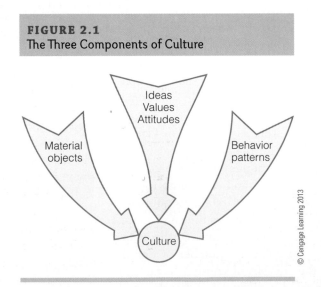

FIGURE 2.1
The Three Components of Culture

Ideas
Values
Attitudes

Material objects

Behavior patterns

Culture

© Cengage Learning 2013

smart phones, and paper. Although these artifacts are both obvious and visible, they represent only one part of writing. To understand the full significance of writing in U.S. culture, it is imperative that we look below the surface to other components of culture such as ideas, knowledge, attitudes, and behavior patterns. For example, in order for a New Yorker to use English in its written form, she must know the alphabet, how to spell, basic English grammar and syntax, and the rule that words are written from left to right and from top to bottom. She must know how to manipulate a writing implement (pen or pencil) or have basic computer skills. She needs to know a wealth of cultural information in order to communicate written messages coherently. In addition, she must follow certain behavioral conventions, like not writing while sitting in her bathing suit in a public library. Thus the cultural process of writing involves an intimate knowledge of the three fundamental components of culture: things or artifacts, ideas and knowledge, and patterns of behavior that are passed on from one generation to the next.

Perhaps the most fundamental aspect of culture, and what makes humans unique in the animal world, is the capacity to symbolize. A **symbol** is something that stands for (represents) something else. When North Americans see a Nazi swastika, a multitude of images come to mind: the Holocaust, Adolf Hitler, concentration camps, and goose-stepping storm troopers. Most citizens of the United States have a positive feeling when they see the red, white, and blue stars and stripes. That particular arrangement of colors and shapes symbolizes, among other things, freedom, democracy, the Bill of Rights, and due process. Yet, as we have seen in recent years, the American flag represents a host of very different meanings for angry young men who delight in burning it in the streets of Tehran, Djakarta, and Karachi. Whether the U.S. flag symbolizes positive or negative ideas, it is true that all human behavior begins with the use of symbols.

As Leslie White (1959) stated so eloquently, the ability to symbolize is the single most important hallmark of humanity. It is this capacity to create and give meaning to symbols that helps people identify, sort, and classify things, ideas, and behaviors. When people symbolize by using language, they are able to express experiences that took place at an earlier time or suggest events that may happen in the future. Without symbols we would not be able to store the collective wisdom of past generations, and consequently we would be prone to repeat the mistakes of the past. Symbols tie together people who otherwise might not be part of a unified group. The power of our shared symbols becomes clear when we meet others from our own culture in a far-off country. We generally are drawn to them because we share a common set of symbols, such as language, nonverbal forms of communication, and material culture like clothing.

It is the shared meaning of our symbols that enables us to interact with one another with the least amount of ambiguity and misunderstanding.

An inescapable conclusion from studying cultural anthropology is that there are an enormous number of discrete societies with their own unique cultures. Just how many distinct cultures there are depends largely on how one defines the term *culture,* an issue on which there is no absolute consensus among anthropologists. Many scholars equate the number of discrete cultures with the number of mutually unintelligible languages. That is, they assume that if two groups speak mutually unintelligible languages, then other parts of their cultures are sufficiently different to consider them distinct (unique) cultures. By making this assumption, we estimate that there are approximately 850 separate cultures on the continent of Africa alone and more than 5,000 throughout the world. And, in addition to linguistic differences, there are literally hundreds of cultural features that vary from one society to another, including ideas, values, ideologies, religions, material objects, and behavior patterns.

Culture Is Shared

The last phrase in our working definition—*as members of a society*—reminds us that culture is a shared phenomenon. For a thing, idea, or behavior pattern to qualify as being cultural, it must have a meaning shared by most people in a society. It is this shared nature of culture that makes our lives less complicated. Because people share a common culture, they are able to predict, within limits, how others will think and behave. For example, when two people meet for the first time in Toronto, it is customary for them to shake hands. If both people grew up in Toronto, neither party will have to wonder what is meant by an outstretched hand. They will know, with nearly absolute certainty, that the extended hand is a nonverbal gesture signifying friendship rather than a sexual advance, a hostile attack, or an attempt to steal one's wallet. It is when we step outside our familiar cultural setting— where meanings are not shared with other people—that misunderstandings occur. In fact, the uncertainty one experiences when trying to operate in an unfamiliar culture often leads to **culture shock,** a form of psychological distress that can result in depression, overeating, or irritability.

The degree to which people in any given society share their culture varies from culture to culture. Even in small-scale, homogeneous societies, one can expect to find a certain amount of differentiation based on gender, class, age, religion, or ethnicity. The daughter of a wealthy physician in Athens, for example, is likely to have a somewhat different set of values and behavioral expectations than the daughter of a rural Greek farmer. Moreover societal rules are never adhered to strictly. Although culture exerts a powerful influence, people exercise free will by reinterpreting rules, downplaying their consequences, or disregarding them altogether (such as the Catholic who practices birth control or the conscientious objector who flees the country rather than serve in a war).

In larger, highly complex societies, such as the United States and Canada, one is likely to find a number of subcultural groups in addition to the mainstream culture. The use of the terms **subculture** and *mainstream culture* should in no way imply that subcultures are inferior or any less worthy of study. Rather, subcultures are subsets of the wider culture. They share a number of cultural features with the mainstream, but they retain a certain level of cultural uniqueness that sets them apart. Examples of subcultural groups are hyphenated American communities, such as Japanese-Americans in Seattle, Cuban-Americans in Miami, and Islamic-Americans in Detroit, as well as the Amish communities in Pennsylvania, Indiana, and Wisconsin. Subcultures can also include students at universities and colleges.

© H. Mark Weidman Photography/Alamy

The culturally distinct Amish people, in Pennsylvania's Lancaster County, still use horse-drawn buggies for transportation.

Culture Is Learned

Culture is not transmitted genetically. Rather, it is acquired through learning and interacting with one's cultural environment. This process of acquiring culture after we are born is called **enculturation.** We acquire our culture (ideas, values, and behavior patterns) by growing up in it. When an infant is born, he or she enters a cultural environment in which many solutions already exist to the universal problems facing all human populations. The child merely needs to learn or internalize those solutions in order to make a reasonable adjustment to his or her surroundings. A male child who is born in Kansas will probably watch a good deal of TV; attend schools with books, desks, and professionally trained teachers; learn to drive a car; and marry one wife at a time. In contrast, a male child who is born among the Jie of Uganda is likely to grow up playing with cows, learn most of what he knows from peers and elders rather than teachers, undergo an initiation ceremony into adulthood that involves being anointed with the undigested stomach contents of an ox slaughtered for the occasion, and have at least three or four wives at one time. Even though these children are born into radically different cultures, they have something important in common: Both children are born into an already existing culture, and they have only to learn the ways of thinking and acting set down by their culture.

If we stop to think about it, a great deal of what we do during our waking hours is learned. Brushing our teeth, eating three meals a day, sweeping the floor, attending school, wearing a wristwatch, knowing to stop at a red light, sleeping on a mattress, and waving good-bye are all learned responses to our cultural environment. To be certain, some aspects of our behavior are not learned but are genetically based or instinctive. For example, a newborn infant does not need to attend a workshop on the "art of sucking." Or, if someone throws a brick at your head, you do not have to be taught to duck or throw your hands up in front of your face. Nevertheless, the overwhelming majority of our behavioral responses are the result of complex learning processes.

Learning Versus Instincts

During the first half of the twentieth century, psychologists and other social scientists tended to explain human behavior in terms of various instincts or genetically based propensities. Gypsies traveled about because they were thought to have "wanderlust" in their blood; Black people were musical because they were believed to have natural rhythm; and some people, owing to their genetic makeup, were supposedly born criminals. Today the discipline of anthropology has dismissed this type of biological determinism.

In a statement adopted in 1998 by its executive board, the American Anthropological Association weighed in on this topic:

> At the end of the twentieth century, we now understand that human cultural behavior is learned, conditioned into infants beginning at birth, and always subject to modification. No human is born with a built-in culture or language. Our temperaments, dispositions, and personalities, regardless of genetic propensities, are developed within a set of meanings and values that we call "culture." Studies of infant and early childhood learning and behavior attest to the reality of our cultures in forming who we are.

Learning Different Cultural Content

Even though there is an enormous range of variation in cultural behavior throughout the world, all people acquire their culture by the same process. People often assume erroneously that if a Hadza adult of Tanzania does not know how to solve an algebraic equation, then she or he must be less intelligent than we are. Yet there is no evidence to suggest that people from some cultures are fast learners and people from others are slow learners. The study of comparative cultures has taught us that people in different cultures learn *different* cultural content (attitudes, values, ideas, and behavioral patterns) and that they accomplish this with similar efficiency. The traditional Hadza hunter has not learned algebra because such knowledge would not particularly facilitate his adaptation to life in the East African grasslands. However, he does know how to track a wounded bushbuck that he has not seen for three days, how to locate groundwater, and how to build a house out of locally available materials. In short, people learn (with relatively equal efficiency) what they need to know to best adapt to their environment.

Culture Is Taken for Granted

Culture is so embedded in our psyche that we frequently take it for granted. We live out our lives without thinking too much about how our culture influences our thinking and behavior. How we act and what we think are often so automatic and habitual that we rarely give them any thought at all. Unfortunately, this leads to the uncritical conclusion that how we live out our lives is really no different from how people from other cultures live out theirs. The job of cultural anthropology is to heighten our awareness of other cultures, as well as our own, in hopes that we will be less likely to take our own culture for granted. Learning *not* to take our own culture for granted is the best way to combat *ethnocentrism* (the belief that one's own culture is superior and "right" compared to other cultures).

Perhaps an example of taking one's culture for granted will be helpful. Anthropologist Edward T. Hall, who devoted much of his career to the study of time across cultures, identified two fundamentally different ways of dealing with time: monochronically and polychronically. People from **monochronic cultures**—such as the United States, Germany, and Switzerland—view time in a linear fashion, prefer to do one thing at a time, place a high value on punctuality, and keep precise schedules. Most middle-class North Americans would never think of leaving the house without that little gadget strapped to their wrist or their cell phones that tell them, no matter where they may be, exactly what time it is.

© LWA-Dan Tardif/Corbis

North Americans, who tend to be monochronic, place a high value on punctuality, schedules, and deadlines.

Other cultures tend to be **polychronic**, preferring to do many things at the same time and seeing no particular value in punctuality for its own sake. Rather than reacting to the hands of a clock, polychronic people strive to create and maintain social relationships. Their de-emphasis on schedules and punctuality should not be interpreted as laziness, however. Rather, they *choose* to place a greater value on social relationships than on completing a particular task on time. Polychronic people often view the typical North American's obsession with time as being rude and dehumanizing because time and punctuality take precedence over meaningful social relationships.

How we deal with time varies greatly from culture to culture. Middle-class North Americans pay close attention to time, take deadlines very seriously, move rapidly, start their meetings on time, and eat because it is time to eat. People in polychronic cultures, on the other hand, are much less attentive to the hour of the day, view deadlines much less rigidly, build in a lot of socializing time before starting the business portion of their meetings, and eat because there are others with whom to share food. When we uncritically expect everyone to operate according to our sense of time, we are taking our own culture for granted.

Culture Influences Biological Processes

Human existence, by its very nature, is biocultural—that is, the product of both biological and cultural factors. All animals, including humans, have certain biologically determined needs that must be met if they are to stay alive and well. We all need to ingest a minimum number of calories each day, protect ourselves from the elements, sleep, and eliminate wastes from our body, to mention a few. It is vital for us to distinguish between these needs and the ways in which we satisfy them. To illustrate, even though all people need to eliminate wastes from the body through defecation, how often, where, in what physical position, and under what social circumstances we defecate are all questions that are answered by our individual culture. Thus, to say that life is biocultural means that our bodies and their biological processes are heavily influenced by our cultures.

A dramatic example of how culture can influence or channel our biological processes was provided by anthropologist Clyde Kluckhohn (1949), who spent much of his career in the American Southwest studying the Navajo culture. Kluckhohn tells of a non-Navajo woman he knew in Arizona who took a somewhat perverse pleasure in causing a cultural response to food. At luncheon parties she often served sandwiches filled with a light meat that resembled tuna or chicken but had a distinctive taste. Only after everyone had finished lunch would the hostess inform her guests that what they had just eaten was neither tuna salad nor chicken salad but rather rattlesnake salad. Invariably, someone would vomit upon learning what he or she had eaten. This is an excellent example of how the biological process of digestion can be influenced by a cultural idea. Not only was the process influenced; it was reversed! That is, the culturally based *idea* that rattlesnake meat should not be eaten triggered a violent reversal of the normal digestive process.

The nonmaterial aspects of our culture, such as ideas, values, and attitudes, can have an appreciable effect on the human body. Culturally defined attitudes concerning male and female attractiveness, for example, have resulted in some dramatic effects on the body. Burmese women elongate their necks by depressing their clavicles and scapulas with heavy brass rings, traditional Chinese bound the feet of young girls, men in New Guinea put bones through their noses, and scarification and tattooing are practiced in various parts of the world for the same reasons that women and men in the United States pierce their ear lobes (that is, because their cultures tell them that it looks good). People who are intolerant of different cultural practices often fail to realize that if they had been raised in one of those other cultures, they would also be practicing those allegedly disgusting or irrational customs.

© Reuters,/Fred Prouser/Landov

People in all cultures alter their bodies because they believe it makes them look more attractive.

Cultural Universals

Since the early twentieth century, hundreds of cultural anthropologists have described the wide variety of cultures found in the contemporary world. As a result, the discipline of anthropology has been far more effective at documenting cultural differences than at showing similarities among cultures. This preoccupation with different forms of behavior and different ways of meeting human needs was the result, at least in part, of wanting to move away from the premature generalizing about human nature that was so prevalent a century earlier.

This vast documentation of culturally different ways of behaving has been essential to our understanding of the human condition. The significant number of cultural differences illustrates how flexible and adaptable humans are in comparison with other animals, because each culture has developed its own set of solutions to the universal human problems facing all societies. For example, every society, if it is to survive as an entity, needs a system of communication that enables its members to send and receive messages efficiently. That there are thousands of mutually unintelligible languages in the world today certainly attests to human flexibility. Yet, when viewed at a somewhat higher level of abstraction, all of these different linguistic communities have an important common denominator; that is, they all have developed some form of language. Thus it is important to bear in mind that despite their many differences, all cultures of the world share a number of common features (**cultural universals**) because they have all worked out solutions to a whole series of problems that face all human societies. We can perhaps gain a clearer picture of cultural universals by looking in greater detail at the universal societal problems or needs that give rise to them.

One of the most fundamental requirements of any society is to see that the basic physiological needs of its people are met. Clearly, people cannot live unless they receive a minimum amount of food, water, and protection from the elements. Because a society will not last without living people, every society needs to work out systematic ways of producing (or procuring from the environment) absolutely essential commodities and then distributing them to its members. In the United States, goods and services are distributed according to the capitalistic principle of "to each according to his or her capacity to pay." In classic socialist countries of the mid-twentieth century, distribution took place according to the principle of "to each according to his or her need." The Hadza of Tanzania distribute meat according to how an individual is related to the person who killed the animal. The Mbuti of Central Africa engage in a system of distribution called silent barter, in which they avoid face-to-face interaction with their trading partners. Many societies distribute valuable commodities as part of the marriage system, with the family of the groom sending livestock to the family of the bride. Even though the details of each of these systems of distribution vary greatly, every society has worked out systems of production and distribution to ensure that people get what they need for survival. As a result, we can say that every society has an *economic system*.

All societies face other universal needs besides the need to produce and distribute vital commodities to their members. For example, all societies need to make provisions for orderly mating and child-rearing that give rise to patterned *systems of marriage and family*. If a society is to endure, it needs to develop a systematic way of passing on its culture from one generation to the next. This universal societal need for cultural transmission leads to some form of *educational system* in all societies. A prerequisite for the longevity of any society is the maintenance of social order; that is, most of the people must obey most of the rules most of the time. This universal need to avoid chaos and anarchy leads to a set of mechanisms that coerce people to obey the social norms, which we call a *social control system*. Because people in all societies are faced with life occurrences that defy explanation or prediction, all societies have developed systems for explaining the unexplainable, most of which rely on some form of supernatural beliefs such as religion, witchcraft, magic, or sorcery. Thus all societies have developed a *system of supernatural beliefs* that serves to explain otherwise inexplicable phenomena. And because all societies, if they are to function, need their members to be able to send and receive messages efficiently, they have developed *systems of communication,* both verbal and nonverbal.

Despite what may appear to be an overwhelming amount of cultural variety found in the world today, all cultures, because they must meet certain universal needs, have a number of traits in common.

Culture Is Adaptive and Maladaptive

Culture represents the major way by which human populations adapt or relate to their environments so that they can continue to reproduce and survive. Most living organisms other than humans adapt to their environments by developing physiological features that equip them to maximize their chances for survival. For example, certain species of predators such as wolves, lions, and leopards have developed powerful jaws and canine teeth to be used for killing animals and ripping the flesh of the animal. Humans, on the other hand, have relied more on cultural than on biological features for adapting to their environments. Through the invention and use of tools such as spears, arrows, guns, and knives, humans are able to kill and butcher animals even more efficiently than an animal could with its massive jaws and teeth. The discovery of chemical substances such as penicillin, quinine, and the polio vaccine has provided the human species a measure of protection against disease and death. The proliferation of agricultural technology over the past century has dramatically increased humans' capacity to feed themselves. Because humans rely much more heavily on cultural adaptation than on biological adaptation, we are enormously flexible in our ability to survive and thrive in a wide variety of natural environments. Because of the **adaptive nature of culture**, people are now able to live in many previously uninhabitable places, such as deserts, the polar region, the ocean, and even outer space.

Culture provides humans with an enormous adaptive advantage over all other forms of life. Biological adaptation depends on the Darwinian theory of natural selection. According to this theory, nature selects those members of a species that happen to already possess certain biologically based features that make them better adapted to a particular environment. But what if those adaptive characteristics do not exist in the gene pool? Then evolutionary change in the traits of the species will not happen over time, and as a result, the species may become extinct. Moreover, even when natural selection works, it works very slowly. But because culture is learned, humans can find technological solutions to better and more quickly adapt to the environment. For example, when one's environment becomes increasingly colder over a number of years, nonhumans (relying on Darwinian natural selection) must wait generations to develop more protective body hair. Humans with culture, however, need only to develop methods for making clothing and shelters to protect themselves from the elements. Thus culture is a much quicker and more efficient means of adaptation than is a purely biological approach.

The notion that culture is adaptive should not lead us to conclude that every aspect of a culture is adaptive. It is possible for some features to be adaptively neutral—neither enhancing nor diminishing the capacity of a people to survive. Moreover it is even possible for some features of a culture to be maladaptive or dysfunctional. To illustrate, the large-scale use of automobiles, coupled with environmental pollution from oil spills and burning carbon fuels, is currently destroying the quality of the air in our environment. If this set of cultural behaviors continues unchecked, it will degrade our environment to such an extent that it will be unfit for human habitation. Thus it is not likely that such a maladaptive practice will persist indefinitely. Either the practice will disappear when the people become extinct, or the culture will change so that the people will survive. Whichever outcome occurs, the maladaptive cultural feature will eventually disappear.

Cultures Are Generally Integrated

To suggest that all cultures share some universal characteristics is not to imply that cultures comprise a laundry list of norms, values, and material objects. Instead, cultures should be thought of as integrated wholes, the parts of which, to some degree, are interconnected. When we view cultures as integrated systems, we can begin to see how particular cultural traits fit into the whole system and, consequently, how they tend to make sense *within that context*. Equipped with such a perspective, we can begin to better understand the "strange" customs found throughout the world.

One way of describing this integrated nature of cultures is by using the **organic analogy** made popular by some of the early functionalist anthropologists, most notably Herbert Spencer and Bronislaw Malinowski. This approach makes the analogy between a culture and a living organism such as the human body. The physical human body comprises a number of systems, all functioning to maintain the overall health of the organism; these include the respiratory, digestive, skeletal, excretory, reproductive, muscular, circulatory, endocrine, and lymphatic systems. Any anatomist or surgeon knows where these systems are located in the body, what function each plays, and how the parts of the body are interconnected.

In the same way that human organisms comprise various parts that are both functional and interrelated, so too do cultures. When conducting empirical field research, the cultural anthropologist must describe the various parts of the culture, show how they function, and explain how they are interconnected. When describing cultures, anthropologists often identify such parts as the economic, kinship, social control, marriage, military, religious, aesthetic, technological, and linguistic systems—among others. These parts of a culture are more than a random assortment of customs. Even though anthropologists often fail to spell out clearly the nature and dimensions of these relationships, it is believed that the many parts of a culture are to some degree interconnected (see Figure 2.2). Thus we can speak of cultures as being logical and coherent systems.

The integrated nature of culture enables anthropologists to explain certain sociocultural facts on the basis of other sociocultural facts. When we say that cultures are integrated, we are suggesting that many parts

FIGURE 2.2
Interconnectedness of the Parts of Culture

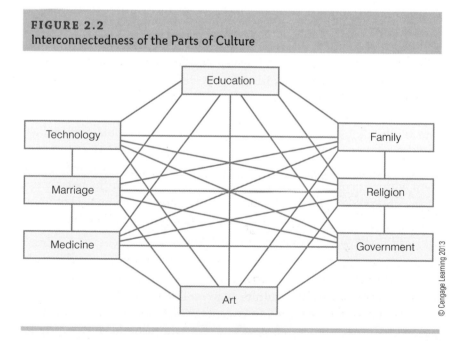

© Cengage Learning 2013

not only are connected to one another but in fact influence one another. To illustrate this point, consider the fact that Japan has the third largest economy in the world, yet Japanese scholars have received only 14 Nobel Prizes since 1901 as compared to 116 for the United Kingdom, 126 for Germany, and 320 for the United States (Coutsoukis 2010). If we want to explain or understand this phenomenon, it is important to seek answers in other parts of the culture. For example, Japanese culture is steeped in Confucianism, which emphasizes piety toward elders, age-graded promotions, and a general penchant for incremental advances rather than bold experimentation. Moreover, in a society that has always valued cooperation and harmony, Japanese scholars avoid the intense peer review that has stimulated creativity and experimentation in other industrialized nations. Professional advancement for Japanese scholars has been based more on seniority than on actual contributions, and relationships among scientists are cordial, friendly, and nonconfrontational. Thus, if we are to understand why the Japanese have received so few Nobel Prizes in science, we need to look at other parts of the Japanese culture that have influenced the behavior (and the creativity) of Japanese scientists.

Although the organic analogy is a useful model for looking at culture, it should not lead us to believe that *all* parts of a culture are intimately interconnected. If this were the case, every culture would be a smooth-running operation, like a well-oiled machine, with all of the parts working in harmony. But cultures, like machines, often have parts that are out of sync and detract from the well-being of the whole. And yet the culture, or the machine, does not come to a grinding halt. There are, in other words, parts of culture that may not be mutually supportive or may even be in conflict with one another. For example, the goals of a family are not always compatible with those of the workplace. Moreover, within the workplace itself, there are built-in conflicts between labor (interested in maximizing wages) and management (interested in maximizing profits). To be certain, cultures can be viewed as systems, but they also have certain parts that grind against one another. Thus cultures are characterized by both harmony and conflict.

The concept of integrated cultures is directly related to the concept of cultural relativism (discussed in Chapter 1), which involves viewing any item within its proper cultural context rather than from the perspective of the observer's culture. The fact that all cultures are composed of interrelated parts prompts us to explore how a feature from a new and different culture fits into its original cultural context.

Cultures Change

Thus far we have presented culture as a combination of things, ideas, and behavior patterns transmitted from generation to generation through the process of learning. This view of culture, focusing as it does on continuity among the generations, tends to emphasize its static rather than dynamic aspects. And yet a fundamental principle underlying all cultures is that there is nothing as constant as change. Some cultures—those that remain relatively insulated from the global economy—change quite slowly, whereas for others change occurs more rapidly. Despite the wide variation in the speed with which cultures change, one thing is certain: No culture remains completely static year after year.

One need not be a scholar of cultural change to notice that cultures have been changing more rapidly with each passing decade. Cultural change occurs at such an accelerated pace today that it is difficult to keep up with the latest developments. The recent revolutions in transportation and electronic communications have made the world seem smaller. Today it is possible to travel to the other side of the earth in a commercial airliner in about the same time it took our great-grandparents to travel fifty miles in a horse and carriage. Via satellite we can view instant transmissions of live newscasts from anywhere in the world. Indeed the global exchange of commodities and information is bringing the world's population closer to the notion of living in a global village. Because of this rapid and dramatic increase in our capacity to interact with people in other parts of the world, the likelihood of cultures diffusing (or spreading) has increased dramatically in recent decades.

Processes of Culture Change

Cultural change is brought about by both internal and external factors. Internal factors include inventions and innovations, and external factors include cultural diffusion (spreading) between cultures. Although diffusion is responsible for the greatest amount of cultural change, it is important to examine both processes of change in greater detail.

INVENTIONS AND INNOVATIONS Any new thing, idea, or behavior pattern that emerges from within a society is an **invention** (a new combination of existing cultural features) or an **innovation** (a recombination of existing cultural items). Some inventions are deliberate and purposeful, while others are unconscious and unintentional. Ralph Linton, one of the most prominent scholars of cultural change in the twentieth century, suggested that over the long run, the unconscious inventor has had a greater impact on cultural change than has the conscious inventor. The unconscious or accidental inventor contributes to cultural change without being driven by an unmet societal need or even realizing that she or he is making a contribution. As Linton (1936: 31) put it, "Their inventions are, as a rule, of little individual importance, but they loom large in the aggregate."

These numerous unintentional inventors sometimes go unrecognized, even though they may make a significant cumulative contribution to their culture. (An example of an unintentional invention—which actually had

Inventor Ron Popeil has made millions of dollars marketing such products as his Showtime Rotisserie on TV infomercials ("Just set it, and forget it!").

an important impact—was the scientist at 3M who, while trying to invent a very strong adhesive, failed and produced instead a very weak adhesive that was ideal for Post-it notes.) Most often it is the deliberate, intentional inventor who is recognized, rewarded, and remembered. From our own history, Eli Whitney was sufficiently motivated by the need to produce more cotton to invent the cotton gin, Jonas Salk discovered the polio vaccine to eradicate a crippling disease, and hundreds of other inventors have come up with new discoveries, gadgets, and ideas because they wanted to do something better or more efficiently.

CULTURAL DIFFUSION In addition to changing as a result of inventions and discoveries, cultures change through the process of **cultural diffusion**: the spreading of a thing, an idea, or a behavior pattern from one culture to another. As important as inventions and discoveries are to cultural change, the total number of inventions in any given society is generally quite small. If every culture had to rely solely on its own inventions, human progress over the centuries would indeed be slow. Cultures have been able to develop rapidly because the process of diffusion has enabled humans to pool their creative and inventive resources.

Comparing the importance of independent invention and diffusion has been an ongoing debate in anthropological circles for more than a century. Ralph Linton (1936) suggested that no more than 10 percent of all cultural items found in any culture, including our own, originated in that culture. Most cultural anthropologists today, however, have abandoned their quest to determine which cultural features were original to a culture and which entered through the process of diffusion. Instead, they have recognized that all cultures exhibit a mixture of the two in some proportion.

Before we leave the topic of cultural diffusion, it is important to distinguish between it and the related anthropological concept of acculturation. The concepts of diffusion and acculturation have some things in common. In fact, **acculturation** is a special type of diffusion that takes place as a result of sustained contact between two societies, one of which is subordinate to the other. Thus both diffusion and acculturation involve cultural change as a result of contact with another group. But whereas diffusion involves a single trait or a complex set of traits, acculturation involves the widespread reorganization of one or both cultures over a short period of time. Both the dominant and subordinate cultures may experience changes, but the subordinate culture always changes more dramatically. Acculturation can have a variety of consequences. The subordinate culture could become extinct, it could be incorporated as a distinct subculture of the dominant group, or it could be assimilated (blended) into the dominant group. But whatever form it takes, acculturation is *forced* borrowing under conditions of external pressure.

Linked Cultural Changes

We have introduced the idea that cultures are more than the sum of their parts. Rather, cultures are systematic wholes, the parts of which are, to some degree, interconnected. If cultures truly are integrated wholes, it would follow that a change in one part of the culture would be likely to bring about changes in other parts. In other words, most changes that occur in cultures tend to be **linked changes**. The introduction of a single technological innovation may well set off a series of changes in other parts of the culture.

An example of linked cultural changes is the boom in cell-phone usage throughout the world. A mere fifteen years ago, a person who used a cell phone on the streets of Chicago would, in all likelihood, have been a wealthy investor who was calling his stockbroker on a mobile phone the size of a gallon container of milk. Today it seems as though there are more people than not walking the streets of our cities either speaking or, more frequently, texting on their cell phones. One change linked to the cell phone has been the increase in car accidents caused by multitasking Americans making business calls or chatting with friends while driving to work. Moreover, in some of our major cities, the number of traffic accidents has further increased because of inattentive pedestrians talking or texting on their cell phones. In fact, the New York City Department

TABLE 2.1 Features of the Concept of Culture

Culture defined	Culture is everything that people have, think, and do as members of a society.
Culture is shared	The shared meanings connected to things, ideas, and behavior patterns make life less ambiguous and more predictable for members of the same cultural group.
Culture is learned	Culture is transmitted not genetically but through interactions with one's cultural environment.
Culture is taken for granted	Our own culture is so ingrained in us that we are often unaware that it even exists.
Culture influences biological processes	Our bodies and biological processes are influenced by culture.
Cultural universals	Despite variations in specific details, all cultures have certain common features, such as systems of governing, patterns of producing and distributing food, forms of enculturation, and family patterns.
Culture is adaptive	Culture enables people to adapt to their environments and thus increase their chances of survival.
Cultures are generally integrated	The various parts of a culture (things, ideas, and behavior patterns) are interconnected to some degree. Thus a change in one part of the culture is likely to bring about changes in other parts of the culture.
Cultures change	The things, ideas, and behavior patterns of some cultures change more rapidly than others, but all cultures experience change, both internally and externally.

© Cengage Learning 2013

of Transportation has sponsored campaigns warning cell phone–toting pedestrians of the dangers of not paying attention when crossing the street (Belson 2004).

Table 2.1 is a summary of the features we have presented in our discussion of the concept of culture.

Culture, Race, and Ethnicity

The discipline of anthropology has as its primary goal to study the extraordinary physical and cultural diversity found among the world's populations. This vast physical and cultural diversity is also of great interest to the people themselves, because human relationships are often shaped by the differences, either real or imagined, between groups of people. To one degree or another, all societies differentiate among their members, and these differences can become the basis for social inequalities. People are often characterized on the basis of their distinctive physical characteristics or their learned cultural traits. Those who share similar physical traits are often defined as belonging to the same **race**. Shared physical traits may include blood types, eye color and shape, skin color, hair texture, ability to digest certain foods, and resistance or susceptibility to particular diseases—to mention just a few. By way of contrast, *culture* refers to *nonbiological* and *nongenetic* traits, which characterize an **ethnic group** in which the members share beliefs, values, customs, and often a common language, religion, dietary practices, humor, clothing, history, national origin, and kinship. People who share ethnicity, therefore, claim a certain cultural group identity for themselves and are defined by others as having that identity. Ethnic feelings and associated behaviors may vary in intensity within ethnic groups and countries over time, as illustrated by recent events in Egypt, Syria, Libya, Iran, and Iraq.

In everyday usage the term *race* often is used as a synonym for *culture* or *ethnic group*. But anthropologists consider these to be *very* different concepts. And, even though many groups share both a common culture and a similar set of physical traits, these characteristics vary quite independently of each other. The concept of race has generally been used to justify behaviors, actions, and beliefs against others who look and act differently.

Throughout history, and in many parts of the world, racial and eth nic differences have led to inequality, discrimination, antagonism, and in some cases violence. Each day we read about racial or ethnic conflict in the world: terrorist attacks on Palestinians and Jews in Israel and internal conflicts in Sudan, the Ivory Coast, the Middle East, and northern Africa. Closer to home, there are ethnic gang wars in U.S. cities, immigration disputes along the U.S.–Mexican border, and racial and ethnic profiling in the aftermath of September 11. So, even in the United States—a country constitutionally and legally committed to social justice—racial and ethnic differences still greatly affect relationships among groups and their relative positions in the social hierarchy.

When people who share a large number of biological traits intermarry, it is likely (but by no means certain) that they will have offspring who also share those traits. Based on our knowledge of genetics, we know that there are no pure races because recessive traits are not lost but can reappear in future generations. Because different populations have been interbreeding for thousands of years, a continuum of human physical types has resulted.

The widespread use of DNA evidence has been a major reason for the success of such TV shows as *CSI, CSI: Miami, CSI: NY, Bones,* and *Body of Proof.* DNA testing is also a very effective mechanism for teaching university students a central concept about race: that is, racial groups or categories, as we normally define them, are not pure, mutually exclusive biological entities, but rather are arbitrary and socially constructed. In a sociology class on "race and ethnic relations" at Penn State University, students learn that they are not quite who they thought they were (Daly 2005). As part of this course, students are able to have their DNA analyzed. Most students want to have their DNA tested for a variety of reasons. Some want to prove to themselves that they are 100 percent racially pure;

others think it might be cool to find traces of some other racial or biological groups; still others hope to find some unexpected racial footprints so they will be able to shock their parents. One black student from Philadelphia learned that 52 percent of his DNA was associated with Africans and 48 percent with Europeans. Even though this Black student is genetically 48 percent white, he was brought up in a Black family and neighborhood, has always identified himself as Black, and has no intention of altering that identity. This example is significant because it reminded him (and his classmates) that race is not a neat and tidy way of compartmentalizing people into one biological category or another.

As a scientific concept, then, race does not provide insight into human behavior. Nevertheless, because of the way people interpret physical differences, race is important *socially* and is a *social construct* in that societies give race meaning. The "races" we hear about are cultural or social rather than biological categories. In fact, race relations and stratification based on race are affected by people's beliefs, not necessarily by scientific facts. In some states in the United States, a person is defined as Black, for legal purposes, if one of his or her great-grandparents is Black. Brazil, on the other hand, has at least seven categories of race, all based on gradations of skin color, hair texture, and facial features (Fish 1995). Because a husband and wife may have children who differ considerably on all of these traits, Brazilians acknowledge that two children who have the same biological parents can be classified as racially different. Using the Brazilian criteria for determining race, many U.S. Blacks would not be considered Black in Brazil. Nevertheless, no matter how racial categories are defined, the accompanying beliefs about race are socially constructed and can have very real social consequences. All too often in human history, groups have separated themselves according to physical differences. They soon decide that physically different people are inferior and then use that belief to exclude, exploit, or brutalize them.

Culture and the Individual

Throughout this chapter we have used the term *culture* to refer to everything that people have, think, and do as members of a society. All cultures, both large and small, have shared sets of meanings that serve as a collective guide to behavior. Because people from the same culture learn essentially the same values, rules, and expected behaviors, their lives are made somewhat less complicated because they know, within broad limits, what to expect from one another. To illustrate, when people walk down a crowded hallway in the United States, there is a general understanding that they will keep to the right. Because most people share that understanding, the traffic flows without serious interruption. If, however, someone walks down the left side of the hallway, traffic slows down because people are unsure how to cope with the oncoming person. Such an incident is disruptive and produces anxiety for the simple reason that normal, expected, and predictable behavior has not occurred.

Our cultures exert a powerful influence on our conduct, often without our even being aware of it. However, to assert that culture influences our behavior is hardly the same as asserting that it determines our behavior. Deviance from cultural norms is found in all societies. Because individual members of any society maintain, to varying degrees, a free will, they have the freedom to say no to cultural expectations. Unlike the honeybee, which behaves according to its genetic programming, humans can make a range of behavioral choices. Of course, choosing an alternative may result in unpleasant consequences, but all people have the option of doing things differently from what is culturally expected.

People may choose to go against cultural conventions for a number of reasons. In cases where adherence to a social norm involves a hardship, people may justify their noncompliance by stretching the meaning of the norm. Or sometimes people flout a social norm or custom in order to make a social statement. Whatever the reason, the fact remains that social norms rarely, if ever, receive total compliance. For this reason, cultural anthropologists distinguish between ideal behavior (what people are expected to do) and real behavior (what people actually do).

Out in the Real World: Cross-Cultural Coaching

An increasing number of organizations are beginning to employ cultural anthropologists to help valued foreign employees adjust to the organization's culture. In 2000 one of your authors (Ferraro) was hired by a U.S.-based multinational company to "coach" one of its foreign research scientists who was having difficulty becoming part of a research team located in rural Georgia. The researcher, whom we will call "Kwanda," grew up in French-speaking Zaire (today the Democratic Republic of the Congo), completed his undergraduate degree in France, and earned a PhD from a Canadian university. Kwanda's supervisor described him as someone who, though highly competent, (1) was not a good "team player" (i.e., collaborative researcher), (2) did not take criticism well, and (3) was seen as aloof and arrogant by his colleagues. Your author, in his role as cross-cultural coach, met with Kwanda on five different occasions over a three-month period (with each session lasting three to four hours).

A major issue addressed in the coaching sessions was the "prima donna" factor. Arriving at his first job with a brand new PhD, Kwanda, no doubt, held his academic credentials (i.e., the highest level of training in his field) in very high esteem. He was not prepared, like most new PhDs, for the fact that American society in general does not share his high opinion of a doctoral degree. Moreover he was raised in Zaire, which when it gained its independence from Belgium in 1960 had a total of eight college graduates employed in its government. For youngsters growing up in Zaire at that time, education of any type was limited and competition to get into school was fierce. Thus anyone who managed to receive even a high school education in Zaire was truly a very rare, fortunate, and highly competent student. To then go on to college and graduate school must have been a very heady experience. Clearly, Kwanda had overcome enormous odds to achieve his high level of education. It is little wonder that he held his academic credentials in higher esteem than most people in corporate America.

Thus part of the cross-cultural coaching challenge was to help Kwanda become more comfortable with the fact that his degrees did not automatically give him instant celebrity. Within the corporate culture of Kwanda's employer, people earned respect and credibility by accomplishing things, rather than solely on the basis of their academic degrees. Kwanda's view of education and the view of his colleagues are simply two different ways of approaching the world, and neither is better than the other.

Another issue addressed in the coaching sessions was communication—that is, the sending and receiving of messages. Part of Kwanda's difficulty involved linguistic style. Growing up in French-speaking Zaire, Kwanda had learned not only the French language but also the attitudes that go along with speaking French. French speakers, perhaps to a greater degree than any other linguistic group in the world, believe that their language is far more than just a mechanism for sending and receiving messages; rather, they perceive it as an art form like prose or poetry. Coming from such a linguistic tradition, Kwanda had difficulty with typically terse, functional American English. The function of everyday discourse in the United States is to communicate as quickly and effectively as possible. The words need not be beautifully constructed; they simply need to do the job efficiently. So, when Kwanda received a cryptic two-word e-mail message in the form of a question, he immediately interpreted this as a linguistic "slap in the face." Kwanda viewed this type of communication as offensive because he interpreted it as being sent by someone who did not care enough about the intended receiver to use the proper level of eloquence. Again Kwanda needed to see that the American sender was not purposefully being rude. Kwanda simply came from a very different linguistic tradition, one in which linguistic style communicates respect for the recipient of the message. Neither party, in other words, is right or wrong. Although Kwanda may never stop cringing at overly terse ways of communicating in the United States, he came to understand (through this anthropological intervention) the nature of this linguistic difference and learned that he should not take it as a personal affront.

During the early coaching sessions, Kwanda came to understand the nature of the cross-cultural differences that were preventing him from making a smooth adjustment to his new work environment. After identifying behavioral changes that he could make to facilitate his adjustment, Kwanda was asked to keep a journal of his new behaviors in the workplace, as well as his thoughts and feelings about them. And because communicating across cultures is a two-way process, it was also recommended that Kwanda's supervisor and colleagues learn more about the cultural differences that were operating in their laboratory setting.

QUESTIONS FOR FURTHER THOUGHT

1. Can you think of any other cultural issues that may have impeded Kwanda from making a smooth adjustment to the corporate culture?

2. Should Kwanda be solely responsible for modifying his attitudes and behavior so as to adjust to the corporate culture, or does the corporation have a responsibility to make certain accommodations?

3. In what other situations could you envision a cross-cultural coach working?

SUMMARY

1. For the purposes of this book, we define the term *culture* as everything that people have, think, and do as members of a society.

2. Culture is something that is shared by members of the same society. This shared nature of culture enables people to predict—within broad limits—the behavior of others in the society. Conversely, people become disoriented when attempting to interact in a culturally different society because they do not share the same behavioral expectations as members of that society.

3. Rather than being inborn, culture is acquired through a learning process that anthropologists call enculturation. People in different cultures learn different things, but there is no evidence to suggest that people in some cultures learn more efficiently than do people in other cultures.

4. Culture is so embedded in our psyche that we frequently take it for granted. The job of cultural anthropologists is to heighten our awareness of other cultures, as well as our own, in hopes that we will be less likely to take our own culture for granted.

5. Certain aspects of culture—such as ideas, beliefs, and values—can affect our physical bodies and our biological processes. More specifically, certain culturally produced ideas concerning physical beauty can influence the ways in which people alter their bodies.

6. Although cultures throughout the world vary considerably, certain common features (cultural universals) are found in all cultures. Cultural anthropology—the scientific study of cultures—looks at both similarities and differences in human cultures wherever they are found.

7. Cultures function to help people adapt to their environments and consequently increase their chances for survival. It is also possible for cultures to negatively alter or even destroy their environments.

8. A culture is more than the sum of its parts. Rather, a culture should be seen as an integrated system with its parts interrelated to some degree. This cultural integration has important implications for the process of culture change because a change in one part of the system is likely to bring about changes in other parts.

9. Cultures—and their three basic components of things, ideas, and behavior patterns—are constantly experiencing change. Although the pace of culture change varies from society to society, no culture is totally static. Cultures change internally (innovation) and by borrowing from other cultures (diffusion).

10. Acculturation is a specialized form of cultural diffusion that involves forced borrowing under conditions of external pressure.

11. People are characterized on the basis of their distinctive physical traits (e.g., skin color, hair texture, and blood type) or their learned cultural traits (e.g., language, religion, and dietary practices). Those who share similar physical traits are said to belong to the same race, whereas those who share learned cultural traits are said to belong to the same ethnic group. Even though the terms *race* and *ethnic group* are often used interchangeably, anthropologists consider them to be very different concepts.

12. Although culture exerts considerable influence on a person's thoughts and behaviors, it does not determine them.

KEY TERMS

Women are making clay bricks
beneath wind turbines in
Tamil Nadu, India.

CHAPTER 3
Applied Anthropology

WORKING ON HIV/AIDS IN ZIMBABWE:
AN APPLIED ANTHROPOLOGIST'S CONTRIBUTION

Applied anthropologists work in many settings, including disaster relief. Some disasters take a while to unfold, as in the case of slow water contamination altering a population's access to safe drinking water, while other disasters develop rapidly from a naturally occurring event such as earthquakes, hurricanes, and tornadoes. Unfortunately, the myriad of disasters and crises occurring with some regularity provides ample employment opportunities for applied social scientists.

Pauline Gwatirisa and Lenore Manderson (2009) reported on a different kind of disaster in urban Zimbabwe, where economic, political, social, and environmental factors are converging on a population with high levels of illness and early mortality as a result of HIV infection. The combination of these factors has produced a food crisis for the country. Gwatirisa and Manderson recognized the important need to identify vulnerable groups and target where immediate food aid was needed if food relief programs were to be successful.

Like much of Africa, Zimbabwe has a long history of extreme climate variation, which has led to an unpredictable food supply—feast or famine. Colonialism and structural adjustment also contributed to Zimbabwe's food problems. Historically, Zimbabwe produced enough grain (maize and wheat) domestically to meet its own needs. Yet, in recent times, the country's grain reserves decreased due to drought and land degradation, economic changes, mono-cropping, and concentrated land-ownership, making agricultural communities vulnerable.

Gwatirisa conducted fieldwork in three high-density townships in Mutare, the capital of the eastern province of Manicaland. These townships were characterized by high rates of poverty, HIV infection, unemployment, and inflation. Her research project documented the experiences of twenty-five primary caregivers of people living with HIV/AIDS in poor salaried households, identified their coping mechanisms, and examined the impact that food insecurity had on the care recipients and their fellow householders. Gwatirisa found that all of the urban households that participated in her study were living below the poverty line in rental accommodations. After the most basic needs had been paid for, including monthly rent, utility bills, school fees, and health care costs, there was not much left over for the household to use for additional expenses like food. In fact, food was found not to be a priority! Food items were purchased with whatever funds remained in the household budget.

Identifying food aid recipients at the time of a disaster is always contentious. In the case of Zimbabwe, it was determined that anyone who lived in a household in which an income earner generated a regular monthly salary was excluded from food aid. Gwatirisa and Manderson reported that this meant that even when more than one family shared a living space, if any one adult earned a monthly salary, then all household members were disqualified from food assistance.

Gwatirisa and Manderson's research is compelling for a number of reasons. It helps us to see how applied anthropology can identify social issues and positively influence social policy. By conducting basic ethnographic research on some extremely sensitive issues, these anthropologists were able to provide insights into the macro-level forces that have a significant impact on household food security. They noted that regularity of income was not a reliable indicator of household food security because of inflation and expanding household sizes, and was therefore an inappropriate exclusion criterion in food aid programs. HIV further complicated people's ability to provide food and to work for wages. As the authors suggest, poverty, health issues (HIV/AIDS), and food insecurity were either a cause or consequence of one another and were key factors in the experiences of participants. They stress that future food aid and relief programs designed to mitigate the impact of food insecurity need to take into account the complex relationships and interactions of these forces and the ways in which they shape people's lives.

QUESTIONS FOR FURTHER THOUGHT

1. Is long-term food aid the only approach that might be considered when providing assistance to a nation facing economic, political, environmental, and health-related disasters?

2. What other assistance might be offered during a crisis to help single-income households in which many family members depend on one wage earner?

The very nature of cultural anthropology research—which involves living with people, sharing in their lives, and often befriending them—makes it difficult for anthropologists to ignore the enormity of the problems societies face everyday. Anthropologists may learn first-hand about poor health and living conditions, inadequate food production, lack of drinking water, high infant mortality, political repression, and any number of factors that impinge on the quality of life for a society. It should therefore come as no surprise that many cultural anthropologists feel a sense of responsibility for helping to solve—or at least identify—some of these pressing social problems.

Although, to some extent, anthropologists have always applied their findings to the solution of human problems, an increasing number of anthropologists since the mid-twentieth century have conducted research aimed explicitly at practical applications. These practitioners conduct research known as **applied anthropology**, which is characterized by **problem-oriented research** among the world's contemporary populations. These pragmatic anthropologists attempt to apply anthropological data, concepts, and strategies to the solution of social, economic, environmental, and technological problems, both at home and abroad. Specific examples of such applied projects include lowering the incidence of obesity in certain segments of populations, ameliorating conflicts between police and immigrant populations in urban areas, and developing economic opportunities in third world communities. In recent decades a number of terms have been given to these attempts to use anthropological research to improve human conditions: *action anthropology, advocacy anthropology, development anthropology,* and *practicing anthropology.* For the purposes of this chapter, however, we will use the more widely accepted and generic term *applied anthropology.*

Our use of this term requires some delineation because applied anthropology cuts across all of the traditional four fields. Most anthropologists who identify with an applied perspective are cultural anthropologists, but the other three traditional subdisciplines are certainly involved in their share of applied activities, as discussed in Chapter 1.

Much of the applied anthropology carried out in recent decades has been supported by large public and private organizations seeking to better understand the cultural dimensions of their sponsored programs. These organizations include international agencies such as the U.S. Agency for International Development (USAID), the World Bank, the World Health Organization (WHO), the Ford Foundation, and the Population Council; certain national organizations such as the National Institutes of Health (NIH), the Bureau of Indian Affairs (BIA), the Centers for Disease Control and Prevention (CDC), and the U.S. Department of Agriculture (USDA); and on a more local level, various hospitals, private corporations, school systems, urban planning departments, substance abuse programs, facilities for the aged, and family planning clinics.

Applied Versus Non-Applied Anthropology

For much of the past century, many anthropologists have distinguished applied anthropology from descriptive or academic anthropology. Descriptive or academic anthropology was seen as being concerned only with the advancement of the discipline in terms of refining its methods and theories and adding more valid and reliable data. Applied anthropology, on the other hand, was characterized as being primarily aimed at changing human behavior in order to ameliorate contemporary problems. The two types of anthropology are not mutually exclusive enterprises, however.

Applied anthropology is considerably more difficult to define than are the four traditional subfields, precisely because it has always been a part of the discipline; in fact, applied and theoretical anthropology have developed alongside each other. Anthropologists with applied interests were involved in shaping the professional organizations from the beginning. To illustrate, from its founding in 1902, the American Anthropological Association (today's largest professional organization of anthropologists) was linked to the Anthropological Society of Washington (founded in 1879), an organization that helped organize applied research on inequities in low-income housing in Washington, DC, during the nineteenth century. Also, some of the major subfields of cultural anthropology evolved out of early applied research, including political, urban, medical, agricultural, educational, and environmental anthropology. Moreover, the first code of ethics for the profession of anthropology was established by the Society for Applied Anthropology (SfAA) in 1949, while the American Anthropological Association (AAA) did not follow with its own code until 1971. Thus, as we can see, applied anthropology has played a key role in shaping the entire discipline of anthropology (Rylko-Bauer, Singer, and Van Willigen 2006: 179).

Throughout the history of anthropology, its practitioners have been concerned with the utility of their findings for solving social problems. For example, in the early 1930s, the Applied Anthropology Unit of Indian Affairs was created by President Franklin Roosevelt's Commissioner of Indian Affairs, John Collier (an anthropologist himself). The aim of this unit was to study the progress of self-governing organizations among some Native American groups as called for in the 1934 Indian Reorganization Act. As part of the Interdisciplinary Committee on Human Relations at the University of Chicago, anthropologists W. Lloyd Warner, Burleigh Gardner, and others conducted applied research in the areas of industrial management, productivity, and working conditions. Moreover World War II provided vast opportunities for anthropologists to apply their skills and insights to the war effort. In the decades following World War II, cultural anthropologists conducted applied research in a wide variety of areas, including agriculture, medicine, criminal justice, alcohol and drug use, housing, tourism, geriatric services, education, and business, among others. Thus many cultural anthropologists have very purposefully engaged in applied research throughout the twentieth and into the twenty-first century, others have applied secondary anthropological data to help solve certain social problems, and still others— engaging in the investigation of a theoretical problem—have taken the additional step of explaining the practical implications of their findings for policy makers.

If we take the descriptive/applied distinction too literally, we might conclude that applied anthropologists have no theoretical concerns and

© Jesper Jensen/Alamy

Applied anthropologists are often consulted by international development agencies on projects such as this well-digging project in rural Ghana.

academic purists have no concern for the practical implications of their work. In actual practice, neither of these is true. Applied anthropology takes into account and contributes to the theories, methods, and data that have been developed by the discipline as a whole. And, similarly, the more theoretically oriented anthropologists are indebted to applied anthropologists for stimulating their interest in new areas of research and, in some cases, for contributing to the development of new theory. The beneficial consequences that can accrue from the interaction of theoretical and applied anthropologists have been well described by Walter Goldschmidt (1979: 5): "The more a field is engaged in practical affairs, the greater the intellectual ferment; for programmatic activities raise issues and often new approaches which would otherwise escape the attention of the discipline." For a more well-developed discussion of how applied and theoretical anthropology can inform each other, see the article by Barbara Rylko-Bauer, Merrill Singer, and John Van Willigen (2006: 184–85).

It is not surprising that the line between descriptive and applied anthropology is so murky because both groups receive the same form of training and draw on the same methods—notably, **participant-observation** and ethnographic interviewing (which we will discuss in the next chapter). The line is blurred still further by the fact that the two have experienced parallel development, have been mutually supportive, and often have claimed the same personnel. Nevertheless a major distinction is drawn between descriptive and applied anthropology. Applied anthropologists are action driven in that their problem-oriented approach to solving contemporary problems enables them to go beyond theorizing to facilitating change, whereas descriptive or academic anthropologists are driven to contribute to anthropology's field of knowledge, especially to its theoretical framework.

It might be useful to think of the different approaches to cultural anthropology in terms of a continuum, with five different types of cultural anthropology ranging from most theoretical to most applied. Alexander Ervin (2005: 2–5) suggests such a model containing five types of cultural anthropology as shown in Table 3.1 and described in the subsequent list.

TABLE 3.1 A Continuum of Theoretical and Applied Cultural Anthropology

DESCRIPTIVE/ THEORETICAL POLARITY				APPLIED POLARITY
Descriptive ethnography/ ethnology	Studies of social issues	Policy studies	Applied anthropology	Practicing anthropology

© Cengage Learning 2013

1. *Descriptive ethnography/ethnology:* For the past century, traditional ethnography (describing) and ethnology (comparing and theorizing) have accounted for most of the anthropological studies conducted on cultures and subcultures throughout the world. These wide-ranging studies have examined everything from nomadic pastoralists in Kenya to schoolchildren in New York City, and from subsistence farmers in Honduras to an urban street gang in Chicago. The meticulousness with which these many and varied cultural groups have been described, analyzed, and compared has led to the development of the accumulated knowledge (cultural practices, behaviors, values, ideologies, and institutions) of cultural anthropology.

2. *Studies of social issues:* The ethnographic study of contemporary social issues often generates findings that have relevance for policy makers. For example, in his ethnographic account *Living with Bad Surroundings: War, History and Everyday Moments in Northern Uganda,* Sverker Finnström (2008) writes about the Acholi people in Uganda. Using narrative, he focuses on members of the younger generation as they cope with a civil war and the prevalence of AIDS while trying to provide viable futures for themselves and their families.

3. *Policy studies:* Moving further toward the applied pole of the continuum, anthropological studies of social policy focus on analyzing the values, social structure, and decision-making processes of those institutions that work to solve social problems. Although ethnographic studies of powerful institutions in our own society can lead to beneficial changes, they are relatively rare for the simple reason that influential policy setters are often unwilling to be studied (up close and personal) as a small-scale tribal society might be studied.

4. *Applied anthropology:* Applied cultural anthropology is most often commissioned by organizations (businesses, governments, and nonprofits) that are interested in receiving concrete recommendations for solving specific problems. For example, a foreign development program may be interested in knowing how a proposed dam-building project might negatively affect a local group of people displaced by the dam project, or health professionals might want to design and implement a community-based program to reduce the incidence of tuberculosis or other communicable diseases.

5. *Practicing anthropology:* The term *practicing anthropology* has become popular since the 1970s to refer to that group of professionally trained anthropologists (at the MA or PhD level) who work full time outside of academia by applying their cultural expertise to advance the goals of their employing organizations. Unlike their academically based counterparts, practicing anthropologists not only conduct needs assessments, program evaluations, and social impact studies, but frequently implement and administer the programs as well.

Unlike theoretical (academic) anthropology, the work of applied anthropology involves generating (to varying degrees) three major products: information, policy, and action. The first of these products is the collection of solid sociocultural *information* on the people under study (the project participants). This information, obtained by conducting research, includes raw data and data that have been analyzed as well as general anthropological theories. Using these research findings as a foundation, the applied anthropologist next develops *policy*, which can be used to help alleviate a problem or condition identified during the information-gathering phase. Although anthropologists may, in fact, be involved in the policy-making process, it is more likely that they will include the policy implications in their findings or even make policy recommendations. The final product of the applied anthropologist is a plan of *action*, or intervention, designed to correct the problem or undesirable condition. Thus, as John Van Willigen (2002: 11) reminds us, "information is obtained through research, information is used to formulate policy, and policy guides action."

Recent History of Applied Anthropology

Even though anthropologists have been applying their insights since the beginning of the twentieth century, the real stimulus came in the 1940s, when many of the leading cultural anthropologists were asked to participate in efforts related to World War II. The National Research Council recruited anthropologists to examine national morale during wartime, to learn about food preferences and wartime rationing, and to perform national character studies on our adversaries—the Germans, Italians, and Japanese. After the war most anthropologists left government service and returned to academia and more theoretical concerns. This trend continued throughout the 1950s and 1960s. Starting in the mid-1960s and going into the 1970s, anthropologists conducted fieldwork in another wartime period, with some carrying out research in Vietnam and Thailand. Ethical issues and concerns were raised about anthropologists being involved with the military and clandestine research, and this prompted both the AAA and SfAA to revise their code of ethical responsibilities.

From the 1970s to the present, a new brand of applied anthropology has emerged. These applied anthropologists are not university professors but full-time employees of the hiring agencies. The Center for Innovation and Research in Graduate Education at the University of Washington in Seattle recently completed a survey of relatively new social science PhDs in six fields, including anthropology. The survey included students who were beginning graduate school up to those who had completed their doctorates six to ten years ago (Baba 2009). The findings reveal that 47 percent of anthropology PhDs work outside of academic settings for government organizations or nonprofit or private sector firms. This trend is largely the result of two factors that are essentially external to the discipline of anthropology. First, over the past four decades, the market for most academic jobs has decreased dramatically. The abundance of jobs that marked the 1950s and 1960s turned into a shortage of jobs in the 1970s and afterward. Second, federal legislation has mandated policy research that can be accomplished effectively by cultural anthropologists. For example, the National Historic Preservation Act of 1966 (aiming to preserve the historical and cultural foundations of the nation), the National Environmental Policy Act of 1969 (requiring assessments of the impact of federally funded construction projects on the cultural environment), and the Foreign Assistance Act of 1961 (establishing USAID, the foreign aid arm of the federal government) all provide for policy research of a cultural nature. As a result of fewer academic jobs and more applied research opportunities, more anthropology PhDs are finding permanent employment outside academia. This trend has been accompanied by increases in the number of MA programs in applied anthropology (see Appendix A) and growing membership in applied anthropology organizations, such as the Society for Applied Anthropology (SfAA) and the National Association of Practicing Anthropologists (NAPA).

Special Features of Anthropology

What does the discipline of anthropology have to offer as an applied social science? What unique contributions can anthropology make to social programs and agencies? The answers to these questions rest largely on the unique approach to the study of humans that anthropology has taken from its earliest beginnings. Among some of the basic features of anthropology that applied cultural anthropologists draw from are the following: participant-observation, the holistic perspective, the development of regional expertise, the emic view, the value orientation of cultural relativism, and topical expertise.

- *Participant-observation:* Direct field observation, a hallmark of twentieth-century anthropology, can lead to a fuller understanding

The understandings that emerge from applied anthropological studies of peasant farmers (such as these in Madagascar) can be helpful in agricultural development programs.

of sociocultural realities than might be possible by relying on secondary sources alone. Also, the rapport developed while conducting participant-observation research can be drawn upon in the implementation stage of the applied project.

- *The emic view:* Whatever the setting of a particular project—be it an agricultural development scheme in Zimbabwe, an inner-city hospital in Detroit, or a classroom in rural Peru—the applied anthropologist brings to the project the perspective of the local people, what anthropologists call the emic view. By using the emic view (the mental categories and assumptions of the local people) rather than their own technical/professional view (the etic view), anthropologists can provide program planners and administrators with strategic information that can seriously affect the outcome of programs of planned change.

- *The holistic perspective:* This distinctive feature of anthropology forces us to look at multiple variables and see human problems in their historical, economic, and cultural contexts. This conceptual orientation reminds us that the various parts of a sociocultural system are interconnected, and therefore a change in one part of the system is likely to cause changes in other parts. The holistic perspective also encourages us to look at problems in terms of both the short run and the long run.

- *Regional expertise:* Many anthropologists, despite recent trends toward specialization, continue to function as culture area specialists (such as Africanists and Latin Americanists). The cultural anthropologist who has conducted doctoral research in Zambia, for example, often returns to that country for subsequent field studies. Thus long-term association with a region provides a depth of geographic knowledge that most policy makers lack.

- *Cultural relativism:* The basic principle of cultural relativism—a vital part of every cultural anthropologist's training—tends to foster tolerance, which can be particularly relevant for applied anthropologists working in complex organizations. For example, tolerance stemming from the perspective of cultural relativism can help anthropologists cross class lines and relate to a wide range of people within a complex organization (such as a hospital or school system) in which they are working.

- *Topical expertise:* It is generally recognized that the topical knowledge gleaned from fairly specific anthropological studies in one part of the world is likely to have policy relevance in other parts of the world. For example, cultural anthropologists who have studied pastoralism in East Africa have topical experience with and knowledge about pastoralism that can be applied not just elsewhere in Africa but also in the Middle East or Central Asia (Scudder 1999: 359).

© Tina Manley/Alamy

Applied anthropologists help medical personnel provide more efficient and culturally relevant services to people throughout the world. Here a Western doctor provides medical assistance in rural Honduras.

These six features of anthropology enhance the discipline's effectiveness in developing programs, projects, and policies that contribute to ameliorating contemporary social problems.

Specialized Roles of Applied Anthropologists

Applied anthropologists also play a number of specialized roles, which are more thoroughly described by John Van Willigen (2002: 3–6):

Policy researcher: This role, perhaps a common role for applied anthropologists, involves providing cultural data to policy makers so that they can make the most informed policy decisions.

Evaluator: In another role that is also quite common, evaluators use their research skills to determine how well a program or policy has succeeded in fulfilling its objectives.

Impact assessor: This role entails measuring the effects of a particular project, program, or policy on local peoples. For example, impact assessors may determine the consequences, both intended and unintended, that a federal highway construction project might have for the community through which the highway runs.

Planner: In this fairly common role, applied anthropologists actively participate in the design of various programs and policies.

Needs assessor: This role involves conducting research to determine ahead of time the need for a proposed program or project.

Trainer: Adopting what is essentially a teaching role, the applied anthropologist imparts cultural knowledge about certain populations to different professional groups working in cross-cultural situations (such as Peace Corps volunteers or international businesspeople).

Advocate: This rare role involves becoming an active supporter of a particular group of people. Usually involving political action, this role is most often combined with other roles.

Expert witness: This role involves the presentation of culturally relevant research findings as part of judicial proceedings through legal briefs, depositions, or direct testimony.

Administrator/manager: An applied anthropologist who assumes direct administrative responsibility for a particular project is working in this specialized role.

Cultural broker: This role may involve serving as a liaison between the program planner and administrators on one hand and local ethnic communities on the other, or between mainstream hospital personnel and their ethnically distinct patients.

These specialized roles are not mutually exclusive. In many cases, applied anthropologists play two or more of these roles as part of the same job. For example, an applied anthropologist who is working as a policy researcher may also conduct research as a needs assessor before a program is initiated and then conduct an impact assessment and evaluation after the program has concluded.

Examples of Applied Anthropology

An Ethnographic Study of Adolescent Drug Dealers (Urban Anthropology)

Because of cocaine's high cost, cocaine addiction historically has been viewed as a rich person's problem. In the last several decades, however, the introduction of a cheaper variety of cocaine—crack—has made this drug accessible to all segments of the population. By and large, the appearance of crack cocaine has been a destructive force for both individuals and society as a whole. Increased trafficking in crack cocaine has been responsible, at least in part, for increases in crime, in the incidence of HIV/AIDS (sex-for-crack exchanges), and in the number of children born with drug addictions. One of the more disturbing aspects of the crack cocaine epidemic is the high incidence of cocaine dealing among adolescents. In 2008, "5.3 million Americans age 12 and older had abused cocaine in any form and 1.1 million had abused crack at least once in the year prior to being surveyed" (Substance Abuse and Mental Health Administration 2010). This is not a new problem, but it is clearly an increasing problem.

In an attempt to learn more about adolescent drug dealing, Richard Dembo and his colleagues (1993) conducted an ethnographic study of adolescent drug dealers in west central Florida. Dembo interviewed thirty-four drug-dealing youths and sixteen non-drug-dealing youths on topics such as the extent to which they used income from selling drugs to help meet family expenses, their reasons for selling crack cocaine, the perceived risks of dealing in cocaine, and the negative effects of drug trafficking on the neighborhood. The adolescents who were dealing needed to work on average twenty-one weeks out of the year. Most of the dealers said that they were not currently using cocaine. Two out of three adolescent dealers said they had killed or hurt someone through their association with cocaine. The great majority of the dealers reported that they spent most of their income on personal luxury items (such as clothes and jewelry) or on business expenses such as guns or protection. It is estimated that they contributed less than 10 percent of their income to their families. Most adolescent dealers said that they sold cocaine to earn a lot of money (because legitimate jobs pay too little), which gives them higher status among their peers.

This ethnographic study of the culture of adolescent cocaine dealers has important policy implications because the findings suggest certain strategies for dealing with this problem. For example, because wanting to make money is the major reason for selling cocaine, intervention strategies must include ways of improving the vocational and educational skills of adolescents so they will have more access to legitimate work. Because most of the adolescent dealers were not using cocaine, there is little reason to treat the problem as drug dependency. This study suggests that adolescent dealing is motivated by economics, not drug addiction. Knowing this fact about the culture of adolescent dealers suggests a rational strategy for addressing the problem: Former teenage dealers who have been successful in legitimate careers could serve as positive role models for adolescent dealers by encouraging and supporting those who are willing to pursue legitimate career alternatives.

The Nestlé Baby Formula Controversy (Medical Anthropology)

As we have mentioned, one of the roles applied anthropologists play is advocate, whereby one's own research is used to support a public cause or protest movement. Penny Van Esterik (1989), an applied anthropologist from York University in Toronto, played such a role during the late 1970s and early 1980s in the controversy surrounding Nestlé's active marketing of baby formula in impoverished third world countries.

Because increasing numbers of new mothers in the United States and Europe were choosing breast feeding rather than bottle feeding during this time, Nestlé, a major manufacturer of baby formula, aggressively marketed its products to third world mothers in an effort to increase the company's worldwide market share.

Opponents of Nestlé argued that the company's aggressive marketing in third world countries was highly irresponsible because of the health risks the formula posed to infants and the risks associated with not breast feeding. The major problem was that the formula needed to be mixed with clean, potable water, which in many third world countries is in short supply. Moreover the fuel needed to boil the local water to remove contaminants was often unavailable or unaffordable. Thus, more often than not, children in Africa, Asia, and South America were being fed overly diluted formula made with contaminated water. The result was a marked increase in infant illness and mortality due to diarrhea, dehydration, and intestinal infections.

The scientific evidence supported the superiority of breast feeding over infant formula because breast milk is safe, renewable, and free. Nevertheless, Nestlé, as well as some American and European companies, persisted in promoting its products to third world mothers for more than a decade. Spurred on by widespread international protests, the World Health Organization and UNICEF developed the Code of Marketing of Breast-milk Substitutes in 1981 to ensure the ethical marketing of all baby foods. Interestingly, the United States was the only country that refused to endorse the guidelines owing to its insistence on unregulated worldwide trade. The protests, debates, and boycotts lasted until 1984, when Nestlé finally agreed to comply with the internationally agreed-upon guidelines. Because of poor compliance, the boycott continues in many countries.

Throughout this period when Nestlé seemed to be thumbing its nose at the rest of the world, applied anthropologist Van Esterik played an important advocacy role in the debate. Having conducted fieldwork in Thailand, she brought her research on the deleterious health effects of baby formula to the public debate on this issue. She participated in a large-scale research project on the topic in Colombia, Kenya, Indonesia, and Thailand. And on many occasions since the late 1970s, she has participated in public debates on the topic, some of which involved official Nestlé spokespersons. Thus Van Esterik provides an excellent example of the role of advocacy, in which the applied anthropologist not only conducts research on a controversial topic but also takes the next step of directly advocating a particular position in the public debate.

Socioeconomic Barriers to Biogas in China (Development Anthropology)

In 1997 the Chinese government declared biogas to be part of its clean-energy initiative and thus provided subsidies (about one-third of the initial investment) for rural households that were willing to adopt biogas as their source of fuel. Household-based biogas systems, as they are developing in China, are small-scale systems that convert ordinary farm waste into methane gas used for cooking, lighting, and heating. Each system is made up of a 25' × 35' concrete digester in which human and animal wastes (along with straw) are naturally fermented to produce the inexpensive and environmentally friendly alternative fuel. Recent research (Abraham, Ramachandran, and Ramalingam 2007; Balsam and Ryan 2006; Gan and Yu 2008) has suggested that biogas offers a number of health, environmental, and economic benefits for rural Chinese households. Unfortunately, during the first twelve years after the start of government subsidies, biogas contributed only about 1 percent of the energy consumption in rural China. Development anthropologist Li Jian (2009) of the University of Northern Iowa has conducted extensive research on the sociocultural barriers to biogas technology in southwestern China and offers suggestions to policy makers on how these barriers might be removed.

Li Jian found five basic barriers to the adoption of biogas technology in rural China. The most prominently cited barrier was *financial*. Nearly two of every three households interviewed stated that, even with a government subsidy, they could not buy a biogas system without taking out a substantial loan equivalent to roughly 16 percent of a household's total annual income. When one considers that most rural households have easy access to firewood and that electricity generated by coal and other fossil fuels is relatively inexpensive, there is little economic incentive for rural households to convert to biogas energy systems. A second barrier is a *shortage of labor* because biogas systems are labor intensive. The digester needs constant surveillance to ensure that it remains airtight and watertight, farm residues need to be shredded and composted before use, old sludge must be removed periodically and spread on crops as a fertilizer, the contents of the digester must be stirred once a day with a long stick, and steel parts need to be painted and repaired periodically. All of these maintenance tasks must be performed, even though most rural Chinese households have lost many adult members to urban migration. A third challenge for the widespread use of biogas systems is that the average household does not have a *sufficient number of pigs* (a minimum of four) to produce the amount of manure needed to run the system efficiently. A fourth barrier to adopting biogas systems is a *lack of general education* and specific technical knowledge of how to acquire and maintain the biogas system. This finding confirms a general tenet of development anthropology (worldwide)—that is, that level of education is the major factor in the adoption of new technologies. And, finally, biogas use in rural China has been inhibited by the *high cost of repairing* biogas systems as well as a lack of qualified repairpersons.

While all of these barriers are significant, they should not prevent rural economies from successfully converting to biogas use. Experts and policy planners are convinced that biogas systems have the potential to alleviate environmental, medical, agricultural, and economic development challenges in rural China. Chinese government officials claim that by subsidizing one-third of the cost of each biogas system, they are contributing as much as possible. But, as Jian suggests, they should take a more comprehensive view of the *real* cost to rural residents of getting behind the conversion to biogas technology. The more people who convert to biogas to meet their domestic energy needs, the fewer local trees will be cut down to make charcoal, the fewer respiratory and eye diseases will be caused by air pollution, the more money individual farmers will have to invest in their farming operations, and the more fertile their land will become through the use of the organic fertilizers produced by the biogas systems. With all of these cost savings associated with using biogas, the government can surely afford to provide larger subsidies and better support services for rural Chinese biogas users.

Agrochemical Effects on the Human and Natural Environments (Ecological Anthropology)

As the world became increasingly industrialized and globalized during the twentieth century, environmental anthropologists became more and more interested in the effects of technology on both the natural and human environments. In the 1990s, one of your authors (Susan Andreatta) studied the impact of the use of agrochemicals (i.e., insecticides, fungicides, and herbicides) on the health of both local farmers and their physical environments in the Caribbean islands of Antigua, Barbados, and

St. Vincent. Andreatta collected her data in 1994–1995 from a network of players in the agricultural sector of these three island nations, including farm owners, farm laborers, government officials, and international corporations.

Andreatta (1998) found that the increased use of chemical biocides was driven by a number of factors: a world marketplace demanding blemish-free fruits and vegetables, international chemical companies wishing to expand their markets into developing countries, growers interested in producing the most marketable produce possible, and a lack of government control of the importation and use of potentially dangerous chemical biocides. Andreatta's findings confirmed that the continued use of agrochemicals over the decades in Antigua, Barbados, and St. Vincent has had harmful consequences for the health of local producers as well as the quality of their physical environments. Farm workers were at risk of overexposure to toxic chemical biocides due to both use and misuse. Because most of the chemical products did not come with mixing instructions, farm workers often used more powerful concentrations of the chemicals than were necessary. Moreover, workers often mixed and applied the chemicals without wearing adequate protective clothing. Direct exposure to the biocides used on banana trees caused eye damage, skin rashes, and fingernail loss. The literature on other banana-producing nations, such

© Jan Sochor/Alamy

A farmworker on a banana plantation uses a pump spayer to apply chemicals.

as Costa Rica, indicates that overexposure or continued exposure to such biochemicals could lead to lower sperm counts and sterility for men, while women reported increased reproductive problems, including producing infants with serious birth defects.

The widespread use and misuse of biocides also had major negative effects on the natural environments of these three Caribbean islands. First, the use of biocides on some fruits and vegetables often contaminated other food crops as well, such as peppers, tomatoes, broccoli, and strawberries. Second, biocides often leached into natural drinking water supplies. And, finally, chemical run-off into streams and rivers killed off fish populations, thereby endangering a source of protein in the diets of local populations.

After documenting the risks of agrochemicals to both both human and environmental health, Andreatta offered some useful suggestions to help ameliorate some of the more negative consequences of using agrochemicals. To illustrate, there was a pressing need for the departments of agriculture on these three islands to take a more proactive role in regulating both the importation and use of these biocides. Some products could be banned from entering the country because they are simply too toxic. The governments could require by law that biocide products contain explicit instructions on their packaging for mixing and application. The governments need to ensure that local producers receive adequate training (and perhaps even certification) on the safe use of agrochemicals, including wearing protective clothing, marking recently sprayed fields with appropriate signs or flags, and adhering to a safe re-entry schedule.

Similar concerns about the health and safety of farm workers in the United States have been a topic for some time. Industrialized agriculture has increased its use of synthetic chemicals in its production of more fruits and vegetables. By the early 1980s, Cesar Chavez had raised the issue of farm workers' health and exposure to chemicals in raising grapes and strawberries in California. Similar exposure was found among farm workers who worked in vegetable and fruit production elsewhere in the United States as well (Barlett 1989; Chavez 1999; Lyson 2004).

Career Opportunities in Applied Anthropology

With the cost of a college education continuing to skyrocket, more and more parents are asking their college-aged children why they are majoring in anthropology. Behind such a question, of course, is the more pragmatic question: What kind of job can you get with a BA in anthropology? It is important to bear in mind that a BA in cultural anthropology is a liberal arts degree, not a type of professional certification. An undergraduate degree in anthropology does not prepare a person to become a professional research anthropologist any more than an undergraduate degree in economics equips a person to be the head of the Federal Reserve. However, the BA in anthropology does provide an excellent background for graduate study in anthropology as well as other related fields such as sociology, history, public health, and social work; it also provides students with the skills needed for any entry-level job, particularly those that require analytical, research, and writing skills. For those interested in becoming a professional anthropologist, graduate school is a must in order to obtain the advanced training in methods, research and writing skills, fieldwork experiences, and the appropriate credentials necessary to apply for academic and non-academic positions.

For those not interested in pursuing a traditional career as an academic anthropologist, the BA in anthropology provides valuable skills and insights that can be relevant for a wide variety of other professions. The terms *applied anthropologist* and *cross-cultural expert* are not standard job categories used in Internet searches for employment. In recent decades, however, the governmental, industrial, and nonprofit sectors have created jobs that require sensitivity to cross-cultural issues and involve working with people from different cultural backgrounds. To illustrate, anthropological skills and insights are being used with increasing frequency to (1) help architects design culturally appropriate housing, (2) enable agronomists to implement successful reforestation programs, (3) educate health care providers about the public health aspects of the AIDS epidemic, and (4) provide criminal justice officials with culturally relevant information for the resolution of legal cases, to mention but a few applications. This textbook contains many case studies that illustrate the wide variety of occupational domains in which anthropological data and insights are being utilized. Many other areas draw on the insights and skills of applied anthropologists, as shown in Table 3.2.

As more and more PhD-level anthropologists are working in non-academic jobs, employment opportunities for those with less than PhD training in anthropology are also increasing. Today people with training in cultural anthropology are putting their observational and analytic skills to work in the public (government), private (business), and nonprofit sectors of the economy. In fact, as we have noted, more professionally trained anthropologists are employed in non-academic positions today than in colleges and universities. As you consider your own career

TABLE 3.2 Recent Growth Areas for Careers
in Applied/Practicing Anthropology

Agriculture	Forestry	Peace and conflict resolution
Alcohol and drug use	Geriatric services	Policy making
Architectural design	Health and medicine	Population and demography
Community action	Housing	Public administration
Criminal justice and law enforcement	Human rights	Recreation and tourism
Disaster research	Industry and business	Resettlement
Economic development	Land use	Urban affairs
Education and training	Language policy	Water resource management
Employment and labor	Media and broadcasting	Wildlife management
Environment	Nutrition	
Fisheries research	Missions	

© Cengage Learning 2013

options, you need to ask several important questions. Are you more interested in an academically based job that permits some part-time applied research or in a full-time job with a government agency, a nonprofit, or a business that involves using anthropological skills on an everyday basis? If you are interested in a non-academic career, how much additional education (beyond the BA) will you need? Do you want to work in the private, public, or nonprofit sector of the economy? Do you want to work for a local, regional, national, or international organization? Do you see yourself working as a full-time, permanent employee of an organization or as an independent, contracting consultant to larger organizations? Since jobs in public or nonprofit organizations generally have lower salaries than jobs in the private (business) sector, what are your realistic income expectations? And, since academic anthropologists tend to work alone and control the pace of their own research, how comfortable would you be with working on collaborative research projects with a number of colleagues and having many aspects of that research controlled by your employing organization? Once you have answered these questions (and perhaps others as well), you will be in the best position to embark on a career path based on applied anthropology. This involves both applying for posted jobs that seek the skills of an applied cultural anthropologist and presenting yourself (with your valuable anthropological perspective and competencies) as the best candidate for a wide variety of traditional jobs within an organization, such as a grant writer for a nongovernmental organization located in the third world.

The study of cultural anthropology prepares people for working in the global economy of the twenty-first century.

Out in the Real World: How a Study-Abroad Experince Can Lead to a Career in Applied Anthropology

Getting involved is the next step for students in applied anthropology programs. Many students look for hands-on experiences before they start graduate school—be it an MA or a PhD program. For those students there are a number of opportunities; however, the competition is stiff. Prior to graduating from an undergraduate program, you may want to engage in activities that set yourself apart from other students who also have a BA in anthropology. We offer a few ways for you to distinguish yourself from a traditional anthropologist as well as from the run-of-the-mill social scientist interested in describing what is out there in the world.

Consider seeking a study-abroad experience for a semester or even a year if your academic program permits it. At most universities there is no additional cost to go abroad—only the extracurricular activities, which might include sightseeing and buying postcards and souvenirs. The best time to go abroad is in your junior year, when you have several anthropology courses under your belt as well as a methods course and advanced courses in some of the specialized areas of anthropology involving the environment, health, economics, education, or any other topic that takes you to the next step of collecting original data in your field of interest (along with your academic advisor's). These experiences, especially if you learn another language, are invaluable and transforming.

Consider working with one of your professors on a local project. There may be opportunities to take part in independent study, internships, or service learning that will provide you with skills that take you to the next level. There may be local opportunities to conduct research with immigrant populations, farmers, fishermen, health care providers, educators, and others. Critical experiences include writing surveys and grants and interviewing and transcribing your results (see later chapters for more ideas). Your professors may suggest other ways for you to use your talents and interests. Just make sure you are in a position to write a final paper about your experience when you are finished, not just a reflection piece. Perhaps your experience will lend itself to a conference presentation at an SfAA annual meeting. What will set you apart from others is not just a high GPA but a range of experiences as well as a demonstration of your perseverance and accomplishments.

Last, students who work in their own communities or participate in national or international causes can and do make a difference. For example, they may collect data that lead to fund-raising efforts to assist people in need. Students may be involved in projects that gather information about the resources needed to make drinking water safe in countries where potable water is scarce. Other projects raise awareness about rape victims or victims of collateral damage in civil wars in the Sudan, the Congo, Somalia, Uganda, and Rwanda. This list is by no means exhaustive in terms of place or issue. Developing the skills for organizing and following through with activities like these will help you develop the skills for further projects that rely on grant writing and ethnographic skills.

There are many projects that you as an undergraduate may want to consider for an independent experience or a final project as an anthropology major. In applied anthropology, the field is wide open. Applied anthropology is everywhere and deals with problem solving for contemporary issues in cultural and physical anthropology, archaeology, and linguistics. Most universities encourage collaborative research among faculty members, and we assume this creates opportunities for students, too. You might consider building your own collaborative team around a local issue to get started on your journey of applied work. Imagine what students with skills in interviewing, geographic information systems (GIS), statistics, methods for data collection and entry, and grant writing could do together.

We leave you with these possibilities of how to *use* anthropology. The following chapters will give you more ideas that you may use to plan future study-abroad experiences or your own independent research.

QUESTIONS FOR FURTHER THOUGHT

1. How can a study-abroad experience or first-hand research on a local project be a transformative learning experience for an anthropologist?

2. What research skills would it be helpful to have before engaging in applied research?

SUMMARY

1. Traditionally, many anthropologists have distinguished between descriptive anthropology (aimed at refining the discipline's theory, methods, and data) and applied anthropology (focused on using anthropological insights to solve practical social problems).

2. World War II provided many opportunities for anthropologists to turn their efforts to applied projects related to the war. Then the postwar boom in higher education lured many anthropologists back into academic positions during the 1950s and 1960s. The decline in the number of academic positions for anthropologists since the 1970s has coincided with more applied types of employment outside of academia.

3. Cultural anthropology can make unique contributions as a policy science. For example, anthropologists bring to a research setting their skills as participant-observers, the ability to view sociocultural phenomena from a holistic perspective, their regional and topical expertise, a willingness to see the world from the perspective of the local people (emic view), and the value orientation of cultural relativism.

4. Applied anthropologists work in a wide range of settings, both at home and abroad. Moreover they play a number of specialized roles, including policy researcher, impact assessor, expert witness, trainer, planner, and cultural broker.

5. Examples of applied anthropology include Richard Dembo's ethnographic research on teenage cocaine dealing in Florida, Penny Van Esterik's advocacy involvement in the Nestlé baby formula controversy, Li Jian's analysis of barriers to the development of biogas technology in China, and Susan Andreatta's research on the effects of agrochemicals on the human and natural environments in three Caribbean island nations.

6. Today there is a growing need for applied anthropologists to develop strategies that will increase the likelihood of policy makers using their research findings.

7. In the last several decades, there has been significant growth in areas that attract applied and practicing anthropologists. These include architecture, environmental studies, fisheries research, geriatric services, the military, tourism, and water resource management.

KEY TERMS

applied anthropology 60	participant-observation 62	problem-oriented research 60

Using a flip chart, a female trainer conducts a course for community health workers in Parwan Province, Afghanistan.

CHAPTER 4

Anthropological Theory and Methods

TRAINING IN MEDICAL ANTHROPOLOGY EQUIPS RESEARCHER FOR FIELDWORK IN AFGHANISTAN

What would you need to do to prepare for fieldwork? Would you know what to do if your assignment took you to Afghanistan? After you read this chapter, we hope you will have a number of ideas for responding to these questions. Many anthropologists are interested in doing ethnographic fieldwork to learn about and describe people from another culture. As we have seen, many of these ethnographic anthropologists use a theoretical orientation to guide their questioning and frame the scope of their research. Other anthropologists use a more applied approach; they are interested in a wide range of contemporary issues, problem solving at the grassroots level, and ways in which their work may influence policies that benefit the local people.

One such anthropologist, Patricia Omidian, wrote a book entitled *When Bamboo Bloom* (2010) about her experiences working in Taliban-controlled Afghanistan in Kabul, Hazarajat, and Herat prior to 9/11. Omidian recounts the choices she made in her fieldwork based on her anthropological training and her particular interests in psychosocial wellness and the anthropology of emotions.

As an applied medical anthropologist, Omidian relied heavily on her methods training, which is critical to both ethnographic and applied research, as well as on her experience in training people. Most of the work she did in Afghanistan involved training and mentoring local staff so that they could conduct their own surveys, evaluations, and training in strategic planning (Omidian 2010:2).

She went into the field fluent in the local language, Dari (the Persian dialect spoken in Afghanistan), and she showed respect for the cultural norms that prescribe a specific dress code and limited mobility for women. In this way, Omidian was able not only to fulfill her employment obligations but also to provide anthropological insights about the rural areas of Afghanistan, where she pointed out project needs in a culturally sensitive manner. By using anthropological tools and techniques, she became an expert in training local people to design surveys, collect and enter data, and analyze these data in a region that had no electricity, sophisticated technology, or freedom of movement.

Concerned with psychosocial wellness, Omidian lived under the conditions imposed by the Taliban and saw firsthand the impact their edicts had on the education, health, and everyday lives of men and women. She found, for example, that the life expectancy at birth is forty-three years and more than half of the population is under the age of eighteen. Though improving, the country's maternal and infant mortality conditions are the worst in the world today.

She heard about the horrors of war from men and women alike. Men could be beaten or whipped if their beards were too short, and women (or their fathers, husbands, and brothers) could be punished if their pants were the wrong color or they visited a market to get food for the family unescorted by a male family member. Each time Omidian visited or interviewed Afghani families, she was putting them and herself at risk, since no one knew from one day to the next what the Taliban would decree.

Clearly Omidian was able to gain a wealth of cultural understanding that enabled her to navigate in Afghanistan while the Taliban were in control as well as contribute to local efforts to improve conditions. The hospitality of those who hosted and protected her while she was "doing her job" is also clear. In the end, however, she was evacuated in the aftermath of 9/11, and today she continues her work in the region but from the country of Pakistan.

QUESTIONS FOR FURTHER THOUGHT

1. What is the difference between an ethnographic anthropologist and an applied anthropologist?

2. If asked what kind of anthropologist you are studying to be, how would you respond?

3. What are some key personal qualities one should possess to do good fieldwork?

Anthropologists have always been interested in explaining the cultural differences and similarities they find among people. This desire to account for vast cultural variations has given rise to anthropological theories that attempt to shed light on why cultures operate in certain ways. A **theory** is a statement that suggests a relationship among phenomena and explains that relationship. A good theory is one that both explains and predicts. In other words, theories are models of reality that enable us to understand cultural phenomena and predict their occurrence.

Even when theories remain unproven, they are useful for research because they can generate hypotheses (unproven propositions that provide a basis for further investigation) to be tested in an empirical research investigation. In tests of a hypothesis, it is possible to determine how close the actual findings are to the expected findings. If what is found is consistent with what was expected, the theory is strengthened; if not, the theory will probably be revised or abandoned. But, either way, the original theory serves the important function of guiding empirical research, and it changes as new data become available.

Anthropological theories attempt to answer such questions as Why do people behave as they do? and How do we account for human cultural diversity? These questions guided early attempts to theorize, and they continue to be relevant today. In this chapter we will explore the major theoretical schools of cultural anthropology that have developed since the mid-nineteenth century, and we will look at how they have changed as new research either supported or weakened their perspectives. We will also explore some of the basic methods that cultural and applied anthropologists use in data collection and analysis. A number of the methods we discuss, founded by early anthropologists, are still used today.

Evolutionism

Trying to account for the vast diversity in human cultures, the first group of early anthropologists, writing during the last half of the nineteenth century, suggested the theory of cultural **evolutionism**. Their basic premise was that all societies pass through a series of distinct evolutionary stages, and we find differences in cultures because they are at different evolutionary stages of development. This theory, developed by Edward Tylor in England and Lewis Henry Morgan in the United States, placed Euro-American cultures at the top of the evolutionary ladder and "less-developed" cultures on the lower rungs. The evolutionary process was thought to progress from simpler (lower) forms of culture to increasingly more complex (higher) forms of culture. Thus the "simpler" societies at the bottom of the evolutionary ladder had only to wait an indeterminable length of time before eventually (and inevitably) rising to the top. It was assumed that all cultures would pass through the same set of preordained evolutionary stages.

While Tylor (1832–1917) was writing in England, Morgan (1818–1881) was founding the evolutionary school in the United States. Morgan, a lawyer in Rochester, New York, was hired to represent the neighboring Iroquois Indians in a land grant dispute. After the lawsuit was resolved, Morgan conducted an ethnographic study of the Seneca Indians (an Iroquois group). Fascinated by the Senecas' matrilineal kinship system, Morgan circulated questionnaires and traveled around the United States and elsewhere in the world gathering information about kinship systems among native North Americans and other native cultures. This kinship research—which may be Morgan's most enduring contribution to the comparative study of culture—was published in his *Systems of Consanguinity and Affinity of the Human Family* in 1871.

Six years later Morgan wrote his famous book *Ancient Society* (1877). In keeping with the general tenor of the times, he developed a system of classifying cultures to determine their evolutionary niche. Morgan, like Tylor, used the categories *savagery, barbarism,* and *civilization* but was more specific in defining them according to the presence or absence of certain *technological* features. Subdividing the stages of savagery and barbarism into three distinct subcategories (lower, middle, and upper), Morgan (1877: 12) defined seven evolutionary stages—through which all societies allegedly passed.

The theories of Tylor and Morgan have been criticized by succeeding generations of anthropologists for being ethnocentric because they concluded that Western societies represented the highest levels of human achievement. Also, Tylor and Morgan have been criticized for being armchair speculators, putting forth grand schemes to explain cultural diversity based on fragmentary data at best. As David Kaplan and Robert Manners (1986: 39–43) remind us, Tylor and Morgan may have overstated their case somewhat because they were trying to establish what Tylor called "the science of culture," whereby human behavior was explained in terms of secular evolutionary processes rather than supernatural causes.

In defense of Tylor and Morgan, we should acknowledge that they firmly established the notion that differences in human lifestyles are the result of certain identifiable cultural processes rather than biological processes or divine intervention. Moreover Morgan's use of techno-economic factors to distinguish among fundamentally different types of cultures remains a viable concept. Although this evolutionary scheme is ethnocentric by today's standards because it assumes the superiority of one culture, we must remember that it replaced the prevailing theory that small-scale, preliterate societies were composed of people whose ancestors had fallen from God's grace. Hunters and gatherers, it had been argued, possessed such simple levels of technology because their degeneration had made them intellectually inferior to peoples with greater technological complexity.

Diffusionism

During the late nineteenth and early twentieth centuries, diffusionists, like evolutionists, addressed the question of cultural differences in the world but came up with a radically different answer. Evolutionism may have overestimated human inventiveness by claiming that cultural features arose in different parts of the world independently of one another, due in large measure to the **psychic unity** of human kind. According to **diffusionism**, however, certain cultural features were invented originally in one or several parts of the world and then spread, through the process of diffusion, to other cultures.

By the early part of the twentieth century, diffusionism had run its course. Early diffusionists suggested that everything found in the world could ultimately be traced back to the early Egyptians. However, despite collecting considerable historical data, diffusionists were not able to prove primary centers of invention. They could not explain when cultures come into contact with one another and what accounted for the diffusion of some cultural items but not others. They were not able to clarify what conditions were required to bring about diffusion of a cultural item or what determines the rate at which a cultural item spreads throughout a geographic region. Despite these limitations, diffusionists were the first to point out the need to develop theories dealing with contact and inter-action among cultures.

As we have seen, both evolutionists and diffusionists tried to explain why the world was inhabited by highly diverse cultures. Although they offered different explanations for the diversity, both schools took a deductive approach to the discipline (reasoning from the general to the specific). Each started with a general principle and then used that principle to explain a universal history; they were less interested in discovering how different people of the world actually lived their lives.

American Historicism

American historicism, which was a reaction to the deductive approach, began under the leadership of Franz Boas (1858–1942). Coming from an academic background in physics and geography, Boas was appalled by what he saw as speculative theorizing masquerading as science. Rather than dreaming up all-encompassing theories to explain why particular societies are the way they are, Boas wanted to put the discipline on a sound inductive footing by collecting specific data and then developing general theories. Thus Boas and his students insisted on collecting detailed ethnographic (descriptive cultural information) data through fieldwork and at the same time called for a moratorium on theorizing.

Franz Boas, the teacher of the first generation of cultural anthropologists in the United States, put the discipline on a firm empirical basis.

Some of Boas's more severe critics claimed that this antitheoretical stance was responsible for retarding the discipline of anthropology as a science. In retrospect, most commentators would agree that his experience in the area of physics enabled Boas to bring to the young discipline of anthropology both methodological rigor and a sense of how to define problems in scientific terms. And, equally important, he left the discipline on a sound empirical footing so that those who followed could develop cultural theories.

Functionalism

While Franz Boas was putting anthropology on a more empirical footing in the United States, Bronislaw Malinowski (1884–1942) was also proceeding inductively by establishing a tradition of firsthand data collection in the United Kingdom. Malinowski, like Boas, was a strong advocate of fieldwork. Both men insisted on learning the local language and trying to understand a culture from an insider's (emic) perspective. They differed, however, in that Malinowski had no interest in asking how a cultural item got to be the way it is. Malinowski concentrated instead on exploring how contemporary cultures operated or functioned. This theoretical orientation, known as **functionalism**, assumed that cultures provided various means for satisfying both societal and individual needs. The job of the fieldworker was to become sufficiently immersed in the culture and language to be able to identify these functions.

Not only do all aspects of a culture have a function, but, according to Malinowski, they are also related to one another. This functionalist tenet is well illustrated in Malinowski's description of the *kula ring*, a system of trade found among the Trobriand Islanders. The kula not only performs the function of distributing goods within the society but also is related to many other areas of Trobriand culture—including political structure, magic, technology, kinship, social status, myth, and social control.

Another form of functionalism was developed by the British anthropologist Alfred Reginald Radcliffe-Brown (1881–1955). Like Malinowski, Radcliffe-Brown held that the various aspects of a society should be studied in terms of the functions they perform. Whereas Malinowski viewed functions mostly as meeting the needs of the *individual,* Radcliffe-Brown saw them in terms of contributing to the well-being of the *society.* Because of this emphasis on social rather than individual functions, Radcliffe-Brown's theory has the name **structural functionalism**.

Psychological Anthropology

As early as the 1920s, American anthropologists became interested in the relationship between culture and the individual. Radcliffe-Brown, warning against what he called psychological reductionism, looked almost exclusively to social structure for his explanations of human behavior. The early practitioners of **psychological anthropology** looked at child-rearing practices and personality from a cross-cultural perspective. They held that child-rearing practices help shape the personality of the individual, which in turn influences the culture.

Margaret Mead (1901–1978), a student of Boas, was one of the earliest and most prolific writers in the field of culture and personality. Mead became fascinated with the general topic of the emotional disruption that seemed to accompany adolescence in the United States. Psychologists at the time maintained that the stress and emotional problems found among American adolescents were a biological fact of life and occurred during

Margaret Mead devoted much of her long and distinguished career in anthropology to the study of how culture affects the process of growing up. Here she is conducting fieldwork in the Admiralty Islands in 1953.

puberty in all societies. But Mead wanted to know whether this emotional turbulence was the result of being an adolescent or of being an adolescent in the United States. In 1925 she left for Samoa to try to determine whether the strains of adolescence were universal (that is, biologically based) or varied from one culture to another. In her first book, *Coming of Age in Samoa* (1928), Mead reported that the family structure and relaxed sexual patterns among Samoans were responsible for a calm adolescence. Thus she concluded that the emotional turbulence found among U.S. adolescents was culturally rather than biologically based. Mead was criticized, however, because, while conducting fieldwork, she did not interview the Samoan "elite" and therefore her research results were thought to be overreaching. In other words, one should not overgeneralize one's research conclusions—for example, doing a study in only one community and then speaking about all the people of a country in one's conclusions.

From the turbulence of adolescence, Mead turned to the question of gender roles. Based on her research among the Arapesh, Tchambuli, and Mundugumor of New Guinea, she attempted to demonstrate that there were no universal temperaments that were exclusively masculine or feminine. Based on her findings, Mead concluded in her *Sex and Temperament in Three Primitive Societies* (1935) that our own Western conception of masculine and feminine is not genetically based but rather is culturally determined and remains the prevailing view today.

Neoevolutionism

As we have seen, Franz Boas and others were critical of the nineteenth-century evolutionists, in part because they made sweeping generalizations based on inadequate data. Despite these criticisms, however, no one, including Boas himself, was able to demonstrate that cultures do *not* develop or evolve in certain ways over time.

In the 1930s another American anthropologist trained in the Boasian tradition, Leslie White (1900–1975), resurrected the theories of the nineteenth-century evolutionists. Like Tylor and Morgan, White believed that cultures evolve from simple to increasingly more complex forms and that cultural evolution is as real as biological evolution. White's contribution was to suggest the cause of evolution, which he called his "basic law of evolution."

According to White's **neoevolutionism**, culture evolves when people are able to increase the amount of energy under their control. For most of human prehistory, while people were hunters and gatherers, the major source of energy available to them was human power. But with the invention of agriculture, animal domestication, the steam engine, the internal combustion engine, and nuclear power, humans have been able to dramatically increase the levels of energy at their disposal. For White, the significant equation is $C = ET$, where C is culture, E is energy, and T is technology. Cultural evolution is caused by advancing levels of technology and a culture's increasing capacity to "capture energy."

Another anthropologist who rejected the *particularist* orientation (gathering a wide range of data from a particular culture) of Boas in the mid-twentieth century was Julian Steward (1902–1972). Like White, Steward was interested in the relationship between cultural evolution and adaptation to the environment. But White's approach—which focused on the whole of human culture—was far too general for Steward. Steward's main problem with White's theory was that it cannot explain why some cultures evolve by "capturing energy" whereas others do not. One way of characterizing the difference between them is that White was interested in the broad concept of culture and Steward was more interested in developing propositions about specific cultures or groups of cultures.

Steward called his own form of neoevolutionism **multilinear evolution**, which focused on the evolution of specific cultures without assuming that all cultures follow the same evolutionary process. Steward held that by examining sequences of change in different parts of the world, one could identify paths of development and some limited causal principles that hold true for a number of societies. To test his formulation, Steward selected areas of the world that had produced complex societies (civilizations), such as Egypt and the Middle East in the Old World and Mexico and Peru in the New World. Steward tried to show certain recurring developmental sequences from earliest agriculture up through large, complex urbanized societies. In these areas, people were faced with dry environments that required them to develop methods of irrigation to obtain water for farming.

Steward's approach was based on an analysis of the interaction between culture and environment. He argued that people who face similar environmental challenges (such as arid or semiarid conditions) are likely to develop similar technological solutions, which, in turn, lead to the parallel development of social and political institutions. Even though environment is a key variable in Steward's theory, he was not an environmental determinist because he recognized the variety of human responses to similar environmental conditions. By focusing on the relationships among people, environment, and culture, Steward was the first and leading proponent of the study of **cultural ecology**.

Steward's approach is still used today as a useful way to describe how a society (culture group) interacts with its environment, obtains food and other natural resources, and makes a living. There are those, however, who criticize this approach as being static and descriptive. Critics contend there is no mechanism in his approach that facilitates change or adaptation—be it cultural or environmental.

French Structuralism

White's and Steward's approach to understanding cultural adaptation is from a behavioral perspective: That is what people do to survive and sustain their culture. There are more symbolic anthropological perspectives, however, in which the anthropologist focuses on the unconscious processes of the human mind shared by members of a particular culture. Anthropologist Claude Lévi-Strauss (1908–2009) concentrated on identifying the mental structures that undergird social behavior. This theoretical orientation, very closely aligned with Lévi-Strauss, is known as **French structuralism**.

For Lévi-Strauss ethnology tends to be more psychological or cognitive. He relied heavily on the science of linguistics to understand patterns found in culture. Many linguists in recent years have hypothesized that basic grammatical structures are preprogrammed in the human mind. Likewise Lévi-Strauss argued that certain codes programmed in the human mind are responsible for shaping cultures. Cultural differences occur, according to Lévi-Strauss, because history and the environment alter these innate mental codes. Although he recognized surface differences, Lévi-Strauss suggested that in the final analysis the mental structure of all humans is essentially the same. The content of a cultural element may vary from one society to another, but the structure of these elements is limited by the very nature of the human mind. In essence, Lévi-Strauss reintroduced his own version of the psychic unity of humankind.

One of the basic characteristics of the human mind from the perspective of Lévi-Strauss is that it is programmed to think in **binary oppositions**, or opposites. All people have a tendency to think in terms of pairs of opposites, such as male–female, hot–cold, old–young, night–day, and right–left. To Lévi-Strauss binary opposites were universals, yet the actual paired opposites were a cultural construct. Lévi-Strauss's theories have been criticized for being overly abstract and not susceptible to empirical testing. Nevertheless, Lévi-Strauss has made a major contribution by directing our attention to the relationship between culture and cognition.

Ethnoscience

The theoretical approach of Lévi-Strauss is similar in several significant respects to that of the ethnoscientists, a small but vocal group of American cultural anthropologists who gained recognition during the 1950s and 1960s. **Ethnoscientists** such as Ward Goodenough (1956) and William Sturtevant (1964) attempted to understand a culture from the point of view of the people themselves.

In an effort to make ethnographic description more accurate than in the past, ethnoscientists try to describe a culture in terms of how it is perceived, ordered, and categorized by the members of that culture (an emic approach) rather than by imposing the categories of the ethnographer (an etic approach). To illustrate, traditionally Western ethnographers used categories from their own cultures to describe another culture. Whereas English speakers have different words for turquoise, aqua, and green, other cultures might include them all within a single color term, and still others might have thirty or more different words for various shades of blues and greens. Whereas some cultures have different linguistic categories for mother's brother's daughter and mother's sister's daughter, in the United States these two family members are lumped together under the single kinship category *cousin*. Thus the primary aim of ethnoscience is to identify the implicit rules, principles, and codes that people use to classify the things and events in their world.

Ethnoscientists have been criticized on several fronts. First, though admitting that it may be desirable to get the natives' viewpoint, some anthropologists feel that one's own conditioning and preconceptions make it impossible to get into the minds of culturally different people. Second, even if it is possible to understand another culture from the natives' point of view, how does one communicate one's findings to others in one's own linguistic/cultural group? Third, if every ethnographer described specific cultures using native categories, every society would be unique; there would be few areas of common ground and little or no basis for comparison.

Feminist Anthropology

Feminist anthropology developed alongside the wider women's movement in the 1960s and 1970s and focused on the fact that anthropological fieldwork was male-centered. Critics argued that, although some anthropologists were women, the women in those societies studied by anthropologists were often neglected as objects of study. Even when women were put under the anthropological lens, they were often portrayed as passive objects (as in bridewealth transactions) rather than as prime players in the mainstream of social life.

As a long-overdue corrective to this neglect, marginalization, and misrepresentation of women in anthropology, **feminist anthropology** called for a systematic reanalysis of the role women play in the social structure. Feminist anthropologists such as Louise Lamphere (1974), Sherry Ortner (1974), and Michelle Zimbalist Rosaldo (1974), among others, tried to rectify this male bias by focusing on women's positions within society. More recent studies have looked at the social construction of gender, work and production, reproduction and sexuality, variations among different groups of women, and how gender influences economic, political, and social power, resulting in multiple interpretations of feminist anthropology (see Lewin 2006).

Although feminist anthropology is diverse in terms of areas of investigation and theoretical indebtedness, a number of basic features are generally agreed upon. First, feminist anthropology takes as a given that gender is an important variable when studying any aspect of cultural life. Just as economics, politics, and religion vary according to status, class, power, and age, they also vary according to gender. Second, the feminist critique rejects **positivism** (a philosophical system based on observable scientific facts and their relationship to one another) because the language of science is seen as repressive and serving the interests of the dominant class or group of a society. Instead, feminist ethnographies are more subjective and collaborative in working with subjects. Third, this anti-positivist approach led to a preference for qualitative methods over quantitative methods. And finally, feminist anthropology does not assume a value-neutral position; it is aimed at consciousness raising and empowerment of women.

The new attention given to gender issues by the feminist anthropologists of the 1970s led some anthropologists to return to sites where earlier studies had been conducted from a largely male-centric perspective. Annette Weiner, a feminist anthropologist, returned to look at Malinowski's classic study of the Trobriand Islanders. According to Malinowski's (1922) original ethnography, Trobriand men gave gifts of yams at harvest time to their sisters' husbands. Malinowski viewed these gifts as a type of tribute from the girl's family to her husband's family, and thus as a way of consolidating male power, but Weiner (1976) had a very different interpretation. She found that, because the yams were given *in the wife's name,* the gift was as much a symbol of the high value placed on women as it was a symbol of power and status for men. Thus, in her restudy of Trobriand culture, Weiner was able to show that men were much more dependent on women for their status and power than Malinowski's earlier description would have us believe.

Cultural Materialism

As the discipline of anthropology expanded with more research and increased knowledge about culture, adaptation, and variation, the theoretical orientations continued to get more complex. Gradually this complexity led to theoretical orientations that furthered our cultural understanding from both a behavioral and a symbolic perspective. We see this clearly in cultural materialism, which is most closely associated with Marvin Harris (1927–2001). **Cultural materialism** is the theoretical position based on the concept that material conditions or modes of production determine human thoughts and behavior. According to this approach, the primary task of anthropology is to provide causal explanations for the similarities and differences in thought and behavior found among human groups (Harris 1968, 1979b, 1999). Cultural materialists accomplish this task by studying material constraints that arise from the universal needs of producing food, technology, tools, and shelter. Harris and other cultural materialists see material constraints as the primary factors that cause cultural variations.

Cultural materialists rely heavily on an etic (the outsider's perspective) research methodology—that is, one that assumes the viewpoint of the anthropologist rather than the native informant. This research strategy utilizes the scientific method, logical analysis, the testing of hypotheses, measurement, and quantification. This approach differs from an emic (the insider's perspective) approach, whereby the anthropologist relies on ethnographic methods that provide insights from members of a culture group and give voice to their indigenous knowledge.

As Harris (1979b) argued, a culture group's code of conduct and rules for behavior and language are not very helpful in explaining phenomena such as poverty, underdevelopment, imperialism, population explosions, ethnic and class conflict, exploitation, taxation, private property, pollution, the military-industrial complex, political repression, crime, urban blight, unemployment, and war. Critics of cultural materialism criticize its heavy scientific emphasis from an outsider's perspective. They argue that it limits the analysis to a discussion of the costs and benefits of activities in a particular society.

Postmodernism

Like the other social science disciplines trying to compete for recognition and distinguish themselves from the humanities, anthropology saw itself as essentially a scientific enterprise for the better part of the twentieth century. Although many of the schools of anthropology discussed so far varied between hard and soft scientific approaches, they never abandoned such scientific canons as gathering empirical data, testing hypotheses, looking for cause-and-effect relationships, and adhering to the scientific method. However, in the 1970s and 1980s, a number of anthropologists, collectively referred to as postmodernists, questioned the scientific methods of anthropology.

Although **postmodernism** means different things to different people, it grew out of the traditions of structuralism, interpretative anthropology, and feminist anthropology. A basic tenet of postmodernism is that the "modernists" (scientific anthropologists) are arrogant to think that they can describe, interpret, and give meaning to the lives of people in other cultures. The modernists' enterprise for much of the twentieth century, they claim, was based on the privileged status of science and reflected the basic power imbalances between the wealthy colonial countries and those developing countries where much anthropological research was conducted. It is impossible, they contend, for predominantly male, Euro-American anthropologists to step outside of their own culture to produce an objective view of another culture.

Postmodernists hold that all ethnographic accounts are subjective because they are conditioned by the experiences and personal histories of the ethnographer. Therefore postmodernists believe the written ethnography should represent a dialogue between the anthropologist and the people being studied, giving voice to the research subjects themselves. Postmodernists contend that only through this dialogical process can meaning and interpretation emerge.

Another tenet of the postmodernist philosophy is the rejection of generalizing (deductive reasoning) and developing predictable theories. By emphasizing the uniqueness of every culture, postmodernists view culture as a changing set of individual meanings that require continual reinterpretation. Postmodernists therefore see cultural anthropology as more of a humanistic enterprise than a scientific one that allows for cross-cultural comparisons, having more in common with descriptive literature than with human geography, biology, or psychology.

Interpretive anthropology, advocated by Clifford Geertz (1926–2006), is a major force in postmodernism. Rather than searching for general propositions about human behavior, interpretive anthropologists such as Geertz (1973, 1983) take a more descriptive approach by examining how the people themselves interpret their own values and behaviors. Interpretive anthropologists are strongly wedded to the emic, rather than the etic, approach to the discipline. According to Geertz, the job of the anthropologist is not to generate laws or models that will predict human behavior, for these predictive devices tend to ignore the complexity and living qualities of human cultures. Rather, Geertz would have anthropology concentrate on cultural description, literature, folklore, myths, and symbols.

The interpretive orientation is admittedly relativistic (understanding another culture with reference to one's own values) and is designed to sensitize anthropologists to their own views and values as well as those of the informant. Geertz advocates combining self-knowledge with knowledge of the people under study so that anthropologists learn something about themselves as they are learning about the culture of the informant. In fact, a postmodernist ethnography usually reveals as much about the anthropologist as it does about the people being studied.

The writings of Cuban American anthropologist Ruth Behar of the University of Michigan are an excellent example of what Geertz had in mind for interpretive anthropology. In her book *Translated Woman: Crossing the Border with Esperanza's Story* (1993), Behar tells how she started her research by listening to the life story of Esperanza, a Mexican woman she had befriended. Before long Behar found that learning about Esperanza's life history was causing her to reflect on her own life. Behar began to question aspects of her own life and work, including the role of the ethnographer, the validity of comparing her life with Esperanza's, and her achievements as an affluent and successful academic. The book, written from an interpretive perspective, turned out to be two life stories rather than one.

Concluding Thoughts on Anthropological Theory

We have covered a wide range of anthropological theories and their proponents, beginning with some of the earliest anthropologists, Tylor and Morgan, from the nineteenth century. Table 4.1 summarizes the primary theories and their proponents. Each theoretical orientation has been presented in a way that introduces general terms and places it chronologically in the history of anthropological theory. And, although many of these earlier theoretical perspectives have been criticized, they all have strengths that cause them to remain prominent within the discipline. In fact, they are the building blocks for the development of new theories, resulting in a complex array of schools of anthropological thought. Few anthropologists today would tie themselves to a single school or theoretical orientation such as postmodernism or cultural materialism. Contemporary anthropologists tend to be more eclectic and problem oriented, focusing on explaining cultural phenomena while drawing on a wide variety of theories, research methods, and sources of data. Anthropologists recognize that you do not throw the baby out with the bath water; it has been worth retaining elements of earlier theories. Those applied anthropologists who focus more on solving problems than on contributing new theories to the discipline rely on existing theories to frame their research and conduct their fieldwork. Next we will look at some methods cultural and applied anthropologists use to obtain and analyze data and interpret their findings.

TABLE 4.1 Anthropological Theories and Their Proponents

SCHOOL	MAJOR ASSUMPTION	ADVOCATES
Evolutionism	All societies pass through a series of stages.	Tylor, Morgan
Diffusionism	All societies change as a result of cultural borrowing from one another.	Graebner, Smith
American historicism	Fieldwork must precede cultural theories.	Boas, Kroeber
Functionalism	The task of anthropology is to understand how parts of contemporary cultures contribute to the well-being of individuals.	Malinowski
Structural functionalism	Anthropology's task is to determine how cultural elements function for the well-being of the society.	Radcliffe-Brown
Psychological anthropology	Anthropology's task is to show relationships among psychological and cultural variables.	Benedict, Mead
Neoevolutionism	Cultures evolve in direct proportion to their capacity to harness energy.	White, Steward
French structuralism	Human cultures are shaped by certain preprogrammed codes in the human mind.	Lévi-Strauss
Ethnoscience	Cultures must be described in terms of native categories.	Sturtevant, Goodenough
Feminist anthropology	Social relationships should be viewed as being gendered.	Lamphere, Ortner, and Rosaldo
Cultural materialism	Material conditions determine human consciousness and behavior.	Harris
Postmodernism	Human behavior stems from the way people perceive and classify the world around them.	Geertz

Ethnographic Methods—Doing Cultural Anthropology

A distinctive feature of present-day cultural anthropology is the reliance on **fieldwork** as the primary way to conduct research. Cultural anthropologists may carry out their research in other contexts, including libraries and museums, but most rely on experiential fieldwork, where they describe and explain cultural features by collecting data on site and engaging in *participant-observation* (observing and learning in the field while participating in an activity) as part of their **ethnographic fieldwork**.

Cultural anthropologists collect their primary data by living with the people they study. They learn the language of the people, ask questions, survey the environment, inventory material possessions, and spend long periods of time observing and participating in everyday life.

Before the 1960s, it was usual for an anthropologist to produce a book on "his" or "her" people several years after returning from a fieldwork

Anthropologist Marjorie Shostak conducts anthropological fieldwork among the indigenous peoples of the Kalahari Desert in Botswana, southern Africa. She and her husband worked among the Ju/'hoansi.

experience. Such a work is called an **ethnography,** an in-depth account of a people's culture studied by the anthropologist who conducted the on-site fieldwork. Frequently these books did not contain a detailed description or explanation of field methods or the fieldwork experience itself. A reader had no way of knowing how long the anthropologist stayed in the field, how many people were interviewed and observed, or what data-gathering techniques were used. Because the credibility of any ethnographic study depends on its methodology, cultural anthropologists since the 1960s have been producing excellent accounts of their fieldwork experiences and data-collection methods.

By the late 1970s, applied anthropologists began to involve members of the cultural group they were studying with the project design, data collection, and data analyses. Involving local people in the applied research process is known as **participatory action research**. This participation facilitates local training and monitoring of the projects. In addition, such training may help the community conduct its own projects to better their futures, as we saw with Omidian's (2010, p. 82–83) work in Afghanistan.

To get a better handle on a particular culture, an anthropologist begins by listening to stories, narratives, and other kinds of talk that provide insight into the community. Anthropologists refer to this form of data as qualitative data. **Qualitative data** are gathered from personal interviews, oral histories, observations, and interactions with community members.

These data are important to the research process and may be logged in anthropologists' **fieldnotes** or tape recorded and transcribed for later analyses. The patterns in the shared worldviews within a culture provide perspective on the numerical data obtained from gathering quantitative data. **Quantitative data** are numerical data such as population trends, numbers of births and marriages, morbidity and mortality rates, household and community size, landholding size, income and education levels, and any other data that can be counted. Anthropologists use these data to conduct statistical analyses. For example, if the anthropologist has been collecting data on household size and the sex and age of its members, he or she can determine from these data what percentages of the adult members of the community are female or male. Of course, more complex quantitative data analyses may also be conducted. For example, if the anthropologist has asked the appropriate questions, she or he might be able to find out from the data how many women of childbearing age have children under five who are malnourished. Ideally, ethnographic methods should blend qualitative and quantitative approaches to identify patterns and trends.

Like ethnographic anthropologists, applied anthropologists use similar methods to conduct their research, which is grounded in ethnography—in the methods of gathering and analyzing data. Applied anthropologists, however, focus on contemporary problems and social issues, rather than aiming to examine the whole culture. Given the nature of their work, applied anthropologists often collaborate on projects with other scientists as well as community members. They may work as facilitators, where they assist in project design, implementation, or evaluation, or they may be interested in specific issues such as the incidence of malnutrition in a village, the rate at which deforestation is taking place in a region, or how a community has been able to slow the spread of tuberculosis. Each of these topics requires that the applied anthropologist be specialized in something beyond the knowledge of a particular people's culture. Such specializations may include (but are not limited to) nutritional anthropology, medical anthropology, and environmental anthropology, and with these specializations comes additional training in related methods of data collection. Most important, though, the applied anthropologist's role is to provide a cultural understanding of how a problem came to be and how it may be lessened or solved.

Preparing for Fieldwork

Whether one is an academic or an applied anthropologist, many essential preparations must be made in order to ensure the success of the fieldwork project. First, because doing fieldwork is expensive, it is necessary to obtain funding from a source that supports anthropological research.

Financial support (covering living expenses, transportation, and other research-related costs) is awarded on a highly competitive basis to the proposals that have the greatest merit. Even though a proposal may require months of preparation, there is no guarantee that it will be funded. Most anthropologists spend time writing and submitting more than one grant proposal with the hope that at least one will take them to the field.

Second, preparation for fieldwork involves taking the proper health precautions. Before leaving home, a fieldworker should obtain all relevant immunizations. It is also prudent to get information about available health facilities ahead of time in case the anthropologist or a family member becomes ill while in the field.

Third, if the field research is to be conducted in a foreign country (as is often the case), permission or clearance must be obtained from the host government. The host government officials often want to make sure that the research will not be embarrassing or politically sensitive, that the findings will be useful, and that the researcher's presence in the host country will not jeopardize any local citizens.

A fourth concern that must be addressed before leaving for the field is proficiency in the local language. An important part of the tradition of anthropological fieldwork is that it is conducted in the native language. If the fieldworker is not fluent in the language of the culture to be studied prior to going into the field, language instruction should be built into the fieldwork timeline, which may lengthen one's stay in the field.

Finally, the soon-to-be fieldworker must take care of a host of personal details before leaving home, such as arranging for the payment of bills and house sitting. Recognizing these pre-departure details should put an end to the illusion that fieldwork is a romantic holiday.

Stages of Field Research

Although no two fieldwork experiences are the same, every study should progress through the same five basic stages.

Stage 1: Selecting a Research Problem

In the early twentieth century, the major aim of fieldwork was to describe a culture in as much ethnographic detail as possible. In recent decades fieldworkers have moved away from general ethnographies of particular cultures. Rather than studying all the parts of a culture with equal attention, contemporary cultural anthropologists are more likely to examine specific issues or phenomena. The shift to a problem-oriented approach lends itself to research that builds on a series of descriptive questions that are progressively more complex to better understand not only *how* and *why* particular problems have come to be, but also *what* may be done about them. This can take the research project into the realm of applied anthropology.

Stage 2: Formulating a Research Design

The **research design** is the overall strategy for conducting the research. In the research design stage, the would-be fieldworker must decide on sampling approaches that will identify who might be willing to participate in the project. For example, how many or what percentage of the people in a village or community should the anthropologist attempt to interview?

Stage 3: Collecting the Data

Once a series of big-picture questions, driven by a theoretical perspective(s), have been developed, the next step—**collecting data**—involves selecting the appropriate data-gathering techniques.

Through participant-observation and interviewing—the two primary field techniques used by cultural anthropologists—data can be collected on a variety of topics related to the research questions or problem at hand. For example, from interviews with farmers, data can be gathered on the following topics: *land* (tenure, size, and use), *labor* (wage labor, family labor, and tasks), *gender* (who is doing what work, when, and why), *crops* (number, acreage, and type), *livestock* (number and type), *trees* (species of fruit and fodder trees, location, and use), *markets* (frequency of marketing, where products are sold, and the means of getting goods to market), *technology* used in farming (inputs and tools used), and the *natural environmental* (climate, seasonal variation, soils, erosion, and access to water), *political,* and *economic factors* that influence farming practices over time.

Stage 4: Analyzing the Data

Once the data have been collected from a fieldwork experience, the process of data analysis begins. The anthropologist starts by transcribing recordings of interviews with codes (marks or labels) that help the anthropologist identify patterns and trends. For qualitative data, software such as ATLAS.ti helps facilitate the coding of the narrative to identify forms with shared meaning. For example, if an anthropologist interviewed a number of young women going about their daily routines, he or she could mark (code) the text for all the different activities the women describe as part of their morning, afternoon, and evening duties (qualitative data). For quantitative data, most anthropologists (and social scientists for that matter) use the statistical package SPSS. Using the same example, an anthropologist could count how many women engage in the same activities (quantitative data) as part of their daily routines.

Stage 5: Interpreting the Data

Like any science, anthropology does more than simply describe specific cultures. **Interpreting data**—perhaps the most difficult step—involves explaining the findings. Have the research questions been answered? What patterns and trends emerged from the analyses, and what do they mean? What factors can be identified that will help explain the findings? How do these findings compare with the findings of other similar studies? How generalizable are the findings to wider populations? Have these findings raised methodological or theoretical issues that have a bearing on the discipline? In applied cultural anthropology, the questions may revolve around how the findings contribute to a project's design, implementation, impact, or evaluation. These are the types of questions anthropologists must answer in a project report, journal article, or book chapter, generally written after returning home from the fieldwork experience.

Data-Gathering Techniques

A central problem facing any anthropological fieldworker is determining the most appropriate methods for collecting data. Some data-collection methods, such as interviewing with a tape recorder, that might work in one culture may be totally inappropriate for a neighboring culture. Given the wide variety of cultures in the world, it is important that anthropologists have a number of options so that they can match the appropriate set of data-gathering techniques to each fieldwork situation. There is a need to be flexible because the techniques originally planned in a research proposal may prove to be inappropriate when actually used in the field.

Participant-Observation

It seems only fitting to start a discussion of data-gathering techniques with participant-observation because anthropologists use this method more than any other single technique and more extensively than any other social science discipline. Participant-observation means becoming involved in the culture under study while making systematic observations of what people actually do.

From the very first day of fieldwork, gaining entry into the community presents some challenges for the participant-observer. In order to learn the appropriate behavior for participating in a local community in a nonobstructive way, the anthropologist begins by observing the community before participating in the social life. Often the beginning fieldworker must overcome a wide variety of fears, suspicions, and hostilities from the local people.

A general piece of advice for most fieldworkers is to proceed slowly. Coming from a society that places a high value on time, most U.S. anthropologists do not take kindly to the suggestion to slow down. After all, because they will be in the field for a limited amount of time, most Western anthropologists think they must make the best use of that time by collecting as much data as they can, as quickly as possible.

There are compelling reasons for not rushing into asking specific questions from day one. Since most fieldworkers have an imperfect understanding of the culture during the initial weeks and months they live in a community, they often do not know enough to even ask the right specific questions. The quality of one's data will vary directly with the amount of groundwork the fieldworker has been able to lay. Ethnographers must invest a considerable amount of time and energy while allowing the local people to get to know them.

ADVANTAGES OF PARTICIPANT-OBSERVATION Using participant-observation has certain methodological advantages for obtaining the best possible data. For example, people in most cultures appreciate any attempt on the part of the anthropologist to live according to the rules of their culture. Another major advantage of participant-observation is that it enables the fieldworker to distinguish between normative and real behavior—that is, between what people *say they do* and what people *actually do*. When a fieldworker conducts an interview, there is no way to know for certain whether people behave as they say they do. The participant-observer, however, has the advantage of seeing actual behavior rather than relying on hearsay.

DISADVANTAGES OF PARTICIPANT-OBSERVATION Participant-observation has certain methodological problems that can jeopardize the quality of the data. First, the very nature of participant-observation precludes a large sample size because these studies are time-consuming. A second problem is that the data are often hard to code or categorize, which makes comparing data challenging. And, third, a major methodological shortcoming of participant-observation is that it has an obtrusive effect on the very thing that is being studied. Inhibited by the anthropologist's presence, many people are likely to behave in a way they would not behave if the anthropologist were not there.

Interviewing

In addition to using participant-observation, cultural anthropologists in the field rely heavily on ethnographic interviewing. Interviewing is used for obtaining information on what people think or feel (**attitudinal data**) as well as on what they do (**behavioral data**). Even though interviewing is used widely by many disciplines (including sociology and psychology), the ethnographic interview is unique in a number of respects. First, in the ethnographic interview, the interviewer and the participant almost always speak different first languages. Second, the ethnographic interview cannot be used alone but must be used in conjunction with other data-gathering techniques.

STRUCTURED AND UNSTRUCTURED INTERVIEWS Ethnographic interviews may be unstructured or structured, depending on the level of control retained by the interviewer. In **unstructured interviews**, the interviewer asks open-ended questions on a general topic and allows participants to respond at their own pace using their own words. At the other extreme are **structured interviews**, in which the interviewer asks all participants exactly the same set of questions, in the same sequence, and preferably under the same set of conditions.

Structured and unstructured interviews have advantages that tend to complement each other. Unstructured interviews, which are most often used early in the data-gathering process, have the advantage of allowing participants to decide what is important to include in their responses to anthropologist's questions. In an unstructured interview, a participant might be asked to describe all of the steps involved in getting married in her or his culture. Structured interviews, on the other hand, have the advantage of producing large quantities of data that lend themselves well to more rapid statistical analyses.

Mapping

Another data-gathering tool used in the early stages of fieldwork is **ethnographic mapping**, which attempts to locate people, material culture, and environmental features in space. To illustrate, anthropologists are interested in mapping where people live, where their livestock graze, where various public and private buildings are located, where playing fields and sacred places are located, how people divide up their land, and how the people position themselves in relation to environmental features such as rivers, mountains, and oceans. Aerial and panoramic photographs are particularly useful for mapping a community's ecology. Advanced training in GIS (geographic information system), remote sensing, and collaborating with a geographer trained in these mapping techniques offer additional understanding of the people and how they interact with their environment and with one another.

Document Analysis

Cultural anthropologists engage in **document analysis** to supplement the information they collect through interviews and observation. For example, some anthropologists study personal diaries, colonial administrative records, newspapers, marriage registration data, deeds and property titles, government census information, and various aspects of popular culture, such as song lyrics and television programs.

Photography

A particularly important aid to the fieldworker's collection of data is **photography**, both still photography and ethnographic documentaries. Although ethnographic documentaries are valuable for introducing

Photographs taken in the field can serve as probes during an interview as well as useful sources of information. Answers to questions about activities or actions can provide insight into gender roles and other appropriate or inappropriate behaviors.

anthropology students to different cultures, they also have more specific uses in anthropological research. To illustrate, ethnographic documentaries can be extremely helpful in **proxemic analysis** (that is, the study of how people in different cultures distance themselves from one another in normal interactions) and **event analysis** (that is, documentation of who participates in events such as circumcision ceremonies, marriages, and funerals).

Applied Field Methods

As pointed out in Chapter 3, there are fundamental differences in the research conducted by descriptive (academic or theoretical) and applied cultural anthropologists. When compared to more traditional anthropological research, applied research is (1) more collaborative and interdisciplinary, (2) more inclusive of local people in all stages of the research, and (3) faced with real-time limitations (weeks or months rather than years). Although the same research techniques are used by both academic and applied anthropologists, the latter have developed additional fieldwork techniques that are particularly well suited for applied research projects:

- *Participatory action research (PAR):* This process begins when members of a community recognize a problem they want to solve and they contact a professional researcher to help bring about positive change. The overall approach stresses the nondominating orientation of the practitioner as well as community involvement in the process (Van Willigen 2002: 78–82).
- *Participatory rural appraisal (PRA):* This is one of the most effective methods used by applied anthropologists because of its strong commitment to community participation. "It enables rural people to share, enhance and analyze their knowledge of life and conditions, and to plan and to act" (R. Chambers 1994: 953). Through PRA and with the cooperation of community members, development professionals (including applied anthropologists) can discover and document local conditions that are relevant to planning programs and projects that are culturally appropriate.

The Pains and Gains of Fieldwork

It should be clear by now that the process of ethnographic fieldwork is central to cultural anthropology. Anthropological fieldwork tends to have a powerful impact not only on the community studied but also on the life of the practitioner. Spending a period of time living and working in an unfamiliar culture is bound to have life-altering consequences; the anthropologist is never quite the same after completing a fieldwork project (see DeVita 1992, 2000).

Sometimes cultural anthropologists can be in life-threatening situations while in the field. By conducting fieldwork in remote parts of the world, anthropologists may encounter potentially fatal dangers from the physical environment; others may be exposed to contagious diseases that can result in serious illnesses and even death. And, in certain situations, anthropologists may be exposed to various forms of social violence, including civil wars, intergroup warfare, muggings, and other crimes.

Culture Shock

Not all introductions to fieldwork are unsettling. But even anthropologists whose fieldwork experience is less traumatic encounter some level of stress from **culture shock**, the psychological disorientation caused by trying to adjust to major differences in lifestyles and living conditions. *Culture shock*, a term introduced by anthropologist Kalervo Oberg (1960), ranges from mild irritation to out-and-out panic. The fieldworker, struggling to learn what is meaningful in the new culture, never really knows when she or he may be committing a serious social indiscretion that might severely jeopardize the entire fieldwork project, such as using the wrong hand when giving a gift, speaking out of turn, or failing to show proper respect for an elder. Table 4.2 lists twenty-two symptoms of culture shock.

When culture shock sets in, everything seems to be wrong. One may become irritated over minor inconveniences and view things critically and negatively. For example, one might think the food is strange, people do not keep their appointments, everything seems unhygienic, and on and on. Generally the negative effects of culture shock subside as time passes, but culture shock is unlikely to go away completely. Success or failure depends largely on how well the ethnographer can adjust to the new culture and overcome the effects of culture shock.

Biculturalism

The total immersion experience of fieldwork provides opportunities for personal growth and increased understanding of the intricacies of a culture. Spending weeks and months living in a different culture can

TABLE 4.2 Symptoms of Culture Shock

Homesickness	Chauvinistic excesses
Boredom	Stereotyping of host nationals
Withdrawal (for example, spending excessive amounts of time reading, seeing only other Americans, and avoiding contact with host nationals)	Hostility toward host nationals
	Loss of ability to work effectively
	Unexplainable fits of weeping
Need for excessive amounts of sleep	Physical ailments (psychosomatic illnesses)
Compulsive eating	Feelings of isolation
Compulsive drinking	Weight loss
Irritability	Feelings of helplessness
Exaggerated cleanliness	Tenseness, moodiness, and irritability
Marital stress	Loss of confidence
Family tension and conflict	Fear of the worst happening

Sources: L. Robert Kohls, Survival Kit for Overseas Living *(Yarmouth, ME: Intercultural Press, 1984), p. 65; Elizabeth Marx,* Breaking Through Culture Shock: What You Need to Succeed in International Business *(London: Nicholas Brealey Publishing, 1999), p. 32.*

provide new insights into how the local people think, act, and feel. In the process of learning about another culture, we unavoidably learn a good deal about our own culture as well (Gmelch 1994a). When learning about another culture in depth, we become bicultural and develop a much broader view of human behavior.

The Ethics of Cultural Anthropology

All field anthropologists—both those who do applied work and those who do theoretical work—find themselves in social situations that are varied and complex because they work with and have different role relationships with a range of people. Under such socially complex conditions, the anthropologist will likely face a number of ethical dilemmas. For example, how do you make your findings public without jeopardizing the anonymity of your informants? Can you ever be certain that the data your informants gave you will not eventually be used to harm them? How can you be certain that the project you are working on will benefit the people with whom you worked? To what extent should you become personally involved in the lives of the people you are studying? Should you intervene to stop illegal activity? Though recognizing that anthropologists continually face such ethical dilemmas, the profession has made it clear that each anthropologist is ultimately responsible for anticipating these ethical problems and for resolving them in a way that avoids causing harm to subjects or to other scholars.

Today U.S. federal law and policies at most research oriented universities require that any faculty research must comply with accepted ethical and professional standards. Anthropologists are required to submit a description of their research to their university's committee on human subjects and obtain approval for conducting the research.

Although anthropologists have long been aware of ethical considerations, it was the Society for Applied Anthropology (SfAA) that first developed an ethics statement in 1949 and then revised its "Statement on Professional and Ethical Responsibilities" in 1975. In 1971 the American Anthropological Association (AAA) adopted its "Principles of Professional Responsibility" and established a Committee on Ethics. See the websites of the AAA (www.aaanet.org) and the SfAA (www.sfaa.net) for the most recent versions of these statements.

The growth in applied anthropology in recent decades raises some important ethical dilemmas because today's applied anthropologists may not have control over the uses of their own research. For example, they may not be able to ensure that their research findings will not be used to harm the informants or to legitimize illegal or immoral activities. All anthropologists agree that they have a responsibility to their subjects and their profession to be aware of the motives, objectives, and assumptions of the organizations that sponsor their research. All anthropologists have an ethical responsibility to avoid being hired by or receiving funds from any organization that might use their research findings in morally questionable ways.

© Images of Africa Photobank/Alamy

Applied anthropologists are getting involved in a number of water projects because potable water is in short supply in many parts of the world. Here children use their donkeys to transport the water they collect at Lake Langano in Ethiopia.

Out in the Real World: Climate Change and Scarce Resources

The challenge of finding food and water creates insecurity for human health and well-being in many parts of the world. Food and water insecurity occurs when there is insufficient and uncertain access to nutritious food and potable (drinkable) water to maintain a healthy and active lifestyle (FAO 2005). Climatic change combined with uncertain economic, political, and social conditions have made inequitable access to food and water a global crisis. Some societies face these uncertain conditions with some regularity. We ask: How do they cope with food and water insecurity? As social scientists, how do we measure the degree of food and water insecurity? Should there be a standard measure we can use to determine who is at risk?

Drawing on their years of community-based research, applied anthropologists are poised to develop appropriate tools to measure and monitor local access to food and water. Medical and nutritional anthropologists rely on anthropometric indicators, such as weight for age, height for age, and body mass index, in their fieldwork. Other studies focus on caloric consumption and measures of daily water use. These data can provide insights into the households and individuals that are experiencing food insecurity, but they are incomplete.

Researchers Craig Hadley, Amber Wutich, and Christopher McCarty (2009) have developed new ways to measure food insecurity based on their fieldwork in Tanzania and Bolivia. For evaluating access to food, they look at: the distance to food markets, the availability of land or livestock to produce food locally, household income, socioeconomic status, and food prices. For looking at access to water, they examine: the distance to water sources, seasonality in water availability, water expenditures, time spent acquiring water, and storage capacity. They stress the link between inequities in access and the health of the community. Research that only focuses on the physiological demands for food and water and does not take into account culture, experience, and perceptions may present an incomplete picture of insecurity and its health consequences.

In Tanzania among the Pimbwe, who are horticulturalists, and the Sukuma, who are agropastoralists, the data reveal there is a *hunger season,* a period of time when a substantial portion of the population experiences food insecurity. Community members report that children often go to bed hungry. Insecure access to food and the presence of hunger are key dimensions of poverty, but the question remains: How do we measure food security systematically? The authors first thought that they could measure it when stores ran out of food and thus households had limited access to food items. They came to realize that this measure was useless, especially for people who ran small shops or those who were employed in jobs other than farming. It also didn't work for larger families that depleted their stocks more quickly than those with smaller families or smaller social networks. In the end, the authors recognized that if they reworded their questions to ask respondents how they acquired food, they could assess food insecurity in both the wet and dry seasons. More important, they learned that the uncertainty that goes with providing food for one's family was a burden carried by all of the mothers and it affected their mental health.

In Bolivia the researchers developed an ethnographically grounded measure for assessing water insecurity. They worked in a semiarid region of the Bolivian Andes, in a squatters' settlement on the south side of the city of Cochabamba. Nearly 38 percent of the population there has no municipal water service, which forces these households to collect rainwater, dig wells, or seek out private water sources for cooking, bathing, and cleaning. Using their ethnographic knowledge, the authors asked a variety of questions to develop a scale for assessing water insecurity during the wet and dry seasons among different types of households. After spending five months living in the community, the researchers learned how water insecurity affects people's lives.

Their research reminds us of the increasing importance of learning more about water and food uncertainty globally. There is no one measure that will work for all conditions. Rural or urban settings, highlands or lowlands, levels of poverty, education, access to employment, gender, age, and household size are only a few of the variables that influence the strategies people use to cope with food and water insecurity. Biological demands for food and water should not be separated from biocultural needs, which are deeply embedded in all cultural systems. It is from these varied approaches that we can develop an understanding of how adaptations and coping strategies affect the incidence and experience of food and water insecurity across cultures, including one's own.

QUESTIONS FOR FURTHER THOUGHT

1. Why is it important to develop a community-based tool to measure food and water insecurity?

2. How does an ethnographic approach contribute to applied research? Does this mean there is only one way to collect empirical data?

SUMMARY

1. Nineteenth-century evolutionists, such as Tylor and Morgan, suggested that all societies passed through a series of distinct evolutionary stages. These early evolutionists established that human behavior was the result of cultural processes rather than biological or supernatural processes.

2. In contrast to the evolutionists and diffusionists, Boas took a more inductive approach to anthropology, insisting on the collection of firsthand empirical data on a wide range of cultures before developing anthropological theories.

3. The British functionalists Malinowski and Radcliffe-Brown concentrated on how contemporary cultures functioned to meet the needs of the individual and perpetuate the society.

4. The early psychological anthropologists, most notably Margaret Mead, were interested in exploring the relationships between culture and the individual.

5. White and Steward brought the theory of evolution back into fashion during the twentieth century. White held that cultures evolved from simple to complex forms. Steward's major contribution was the concept of multilinear evolution; he did not assume that all cultures passed through the same stages.

6. Feminist anthropology called for a systematic analysis of the role women play in the social structure. The feminist critique, by and large, does not embrace positivism, quantitative methods, or a value-neutral orientation.

7. Led by Harris, cultural materialists believe that tools, technology, and material well-being are the most critical aspects of cultural systems.

8. Postmodernists advocate cultural description and interpretation rather than a search for generalizations and explanatory theories.

9. Anthropologists must make preparations before they embark on a fieldwork experience, including securing research funds, obtaining government clearance, and gaining proficiency in the local language.

10. Although every fieldwork project in cultural anthropology has its own character, all projects go through five stages: selecting a research problem, formulating a research design, collecting data, analyzing the data, and interpreting the data.

11. Cultural anthropologists must determine the appropriate data-gathering technique for their own fieldwork situations. Among the tools at the fieldworker's disposal are participant-observation, interviewing, ethnographic mapping, document analysis, and photography.

KEY TERMS

American historicism 86
attitudinal data 102
behavioral data 102
binary oppositions 90
collecting data 100
cultural ecology 90
cultural materialism 93
culture shock 105
diffusionism 85
document analysis 103
ethnographic
  fieldwork 96
ethnographic
  mapping 103
ethnography 97
ethnoscience 91

event analysis 104
evolutionism 84
feminist anthropology
  92
fieldnotes 98
fieldwork 96
French structuralism 90
functionalism 87
interpreting data 100
interpretive
  anthropology 94
multilinear evolution 89
neoevolutionism 89
participatory action
  research 97
photography 103

positivism 92
postmodernism 94
proxemic analysis 104
psychic unity 85
psychological
  anthropology 87
qualitative data 97
quantitative data 98
research design 100
structural
  functionalism 87
structured interview 103
theory 83
unstructured interview
  103

Using the latest technology, an American couple enjoys free time with each other while connecting to their social network.

CHAPTER 5

Language and Communication

SOCIAL NETWORKING INFLUENCES LANGUAGE AND CULTURE ON A GLOBAL SCALE

Do you tweet on Twitter, or have you set up a blog? Do you use the Internet to connect to Google or some other search engine? Are you on a listserv, or do you enjoy watching YouTube videos? If you have done any of these activities, you are aware that your own language and culture are changing, especially the way you communicate with others. Mark Zuckerberg, *Time* magazine's Person of the Year 2010, was recognized for creating a website that has transformed the world in a very short time. What started out in 2004 as a project to help college students connect to one another expanded into Facebook, Inc., a global social network with more than 600 million participants. This achievement is a historic transformation in human culture, especially in communication and the use of technology.

Facebook has transformed the way friends, family members, and strangers communicate with one another. Conversations that family and friends may once have held in private, details of the unmentionable or the routine of everyday life, sad events, and joyous moments are now out there for anyone to view and comment on, if one is "linked" as a friend. Facebook has enabled the communication of what was once private to become public and interactive, even among total strangers.

The global, social, and cultural phenomenon of being on Facebook has given new meaning to the concepts of *friend* and *community*. Not everyone to whom one is connected on a network is a real person. The concept of friend has morphed to include not only people but also entities: One can be a "friend" to CNN or to Target. So how does it work?

To be included in this social network, *users* create a personal profile where they can add other users as friends and exchange messages. They can share photographs, video clips, stories—anything digital and all uncensored. Users can join or create interest groups organized by workplace, college, or anything else held in common. To be in the loop and kept up to date with the latest news and information means being connected to the social network.

Facebook has fundamentally changed the way people interact with one another. It allows you to stay in touch with people who might otherwise drift away because of either distance or time commitments. It allows you to talk to people when they are not present. You can use a computer, an enhanced cell phone, a Droid, an iPod, or any of the other latest technologies that provide Internet access. Updates are made available to your "friends" so that they can keep up with your activities.

In just a few short years, Facebook has become extremely popular and powerful, serving as a new way to interact and voice opinions. For example, it has been used to launch political campaigns and raise funds, and it is widely used in commerce and advertising. In 2008 a Facebook group organized an event at which users saw hundreds of thousands of Colombians march in protest against the Revolutionary Armed Forces of Colombia; in 2010 one of North Korea's official government websites, Uriminzokkiri, joined Facebook.

Yet Facebook is not universally accepted as a good thing or as a desirable global social network. In some countries governments censor the Internet when they deem it is too politically sensitive or incendiary. Countries such as the People's Republic of China, Vietnam, Iran, Pakistan, and Syria have blocked public access to Facebook for political or religious reasons. It has also been banned in some work places in the United States so that employees don't waste company time.

QUESTIONS FOR FURTHER THOUGHT

1. Why has Facebook been able to transform how people communicate with one another? What is it about this online service that seems to draw people in?

2. In what ways do you see language and culture changing in the future? Have some cultures lost the art of speaking face to face and telling stories?

Perhaps the most distinctive feature of being human is the capacity to create and use language and other symbolic forms of communication. In this chapter on language and communication, we will consider such topics as the differences between human and nonhuman communications, how languages change, the relationships between language and culture, and nonverbal forms of communication.

It is hard to imagine how a culture could even exist without language. Fundamental aspects of any culture, such as religion, family relationships, and technology, would be virtually impossible without a symbolic form of communication. Our ability to adapt to the physical environment—which involves identifying usable resources, developing ways of acquiring them, and then forming groups to exploit them—is made possible by language. It is generally held that language is the major vehicle for human thought because our linguistic categories provide the basis for perception and concept formation. Moreover it is largely through language that we pass on our cultural heritage from one generation to the next. By translating our experiences into linguistic symbols, we are able to store them, manipulate them, and pass them on to future generations. Without the capacity to symbolize, we would not be able to practice religion, create and maintain systems of law, engage in science, or compose a symphony. Language, then, is such an integral part of the human condition that it permeates everything we do. In other words, humans are humans because, among other things, we can symbolize through the use of language.

The Nature of Language

Like so many other words we think we understand, the term *language* is far more complex than we might imagine. Language, which is found in all cultures of the world, is a symbolic system of sounds that, when put together according to a certain set of rules, conveys meanings to its speakers. The meanings attached to any given word in all languages are totally **arbitrary**; that is, the word *cow* has no particular connection to the large bovine animal that the English language refers to as a cow. The word *cow* is no more or less reasonable as a word for that animal than would be *kazunk*. The word *cow* does not look like a cow, sound like a cow, or have any particular physical connection to a cow. The only explanation for the use of the word is that somewhere during the evolution of the English language the word *cow* came to be used to refer to a large, milk-giving, domesticated animal. Other languages use different, and equally arbitrary, words to describe the same animal.

Nowhere is the arbitrariness of languages more evident than in how people in different language communities select names for their children. In some East African societies, a boy is given the name of his grandfather. For centuries certain segments of the U.S. population have named male children after their fathers, and in fact this may extend for multiple generations, as in the name Harold Bennett IV. People in the United States also have been known to name their children after celebrities (Kathryn, for Kathryn Hepburn), presidents (Jefferson), jewelry stores (Tiffany), and even scientists (Booker T.). In Thailand children are given playful nicknames, such as Pig, Chubby, and Money, which usually stay with them through adulthood (T. Fuller 2007: 4). And in Zimbabwe we can find people with the first names God Knows, chosen by the parents when the child was gravely ill and the parents did not know whether he would survive; Smile, whose parents wanted to raise a happy child; and Enough, the youngest of thirteen children (Wines 2007: 4).

Diversity of Language

Given the arbitrary nature of languages, it should come as no surprise that there is enormous linguistic diversity among human populations. Even though linguists do not agree on precisely how many discrete languages exist, a reasonable estimate is six thousand (Diamond 2001). The criterion used to establish such estimates is called mutual intelligibility; that is, linguists assume that if people can understand one another, they speak the same language, and if they are unable to understand one another, they speak different languages. The application of this criterion is not as straightforward as it might seem, because there are differing degrees of intelligibility. Despite our inability to establish the precise number of discrete languages found in the world today, the amount of linguistic diversity is vast.

Not only is there considerable variation in the number of languages of the world, but the sizes of the different language communities vary widely as well. It has been estimated (Katzner 1975) that 95 percent of the world's people speak fewer than one hundred of the approximately six thousand different languages. Mandarin alone accounts for about one in every five people on earth. When we add English, Hindi, Spanish, and Russian, the figure jumps to about 45 percent. Thus the remaining 5 percent of the world's people speak thousands of discrete languages that have relatively few speakers.

Linguists today are particularly concerned about this last group of the world's languages, which are in danger of disappearing along with their cultures. Some linguists, such as Michael Krauss of the University of Alaska, estimate that as many as 90 percent of all languages will be extinct within a hundred years. If they do not die out altogether, they will become moribund—spoken by only a few older people and unknown to children (Dreifus 2001). Some linguistic anthropologists have taken action to help native populations hold on to their language traditions. For example, Pam Innes at the University of Wyoming has been active in retention and revitalization work with members of the Muskogee and Seminole nations of Oklahoma as well as the Apache and Comanche tribes of Oklahoma. In Innes's work language and culture are closely intertwined, so preserving the language goes hand in hand with retaining the culture for future generations.

Traditional North American languages are tragic examples of how languages become moribund and eventually extinct. Of the many hundreds of languages that existed in North America when Europeans arrived, only about two hundred have survived into the twenty-first century, and most of these face a dubious future. Historically, the Bureau of Indian Affairs took Native American children from their families, put them into boarding schools, and forced them to speak only English in an effort to assimilate them into the dominant culture. Native American children were punished or expelled from publicly funded schools if they were caught speaking their traditional languages. Yet today anthropological linguists such as Innes are working to retain and revitalize tribal languages while preserving the cultural heritage and tribal identity of Native Americans for both today and tomorrow.

Although efforts to revive dying languages can be a great benefit to society, daunting challenges face those who try to reverse the extinction process. Not all of the extinctions are the direct result of hostility and repression from a dominant government, as was the case with Native Americans throughout most of U.S. history. The recent revolution in communications technology has provided powerful tools (through the airwaves and cyberspace) for the spread of mainstream Western culture and language. Either directly or indirectly, indigenous populations have been inundated with the constant message that they should abandon their own traditional languages and cultures.

Communication: Human Versus Nonhuman

Communication is certainly not unique to humans because most animals have ways of sending and receiving messages. Some bird species use specific calls to communicate a desire to mate, honeybees communicate the distance and direction of sources of food very accurately through a series of body movements, certain antelope species give off a cry that warns of impending danger, and even amoebae seem to send and receive crude messages chemically by discharging small amounts of carbon dioxide.

Human communication differs from other animal communication systems in at least two important respects. One feature of human language is its capacity to convey information about a thing or an event that is not present. This characteristic, known as **displacement**, enables humans to speak of purely hypothetical things—events that have happened in the past and events that might happen in the future. In contrast to other animals, which communicate only about particular things that are in the present and in the immediate environment, language enables humans to think abstractly. A second feature of human communication that distinguishes it from nonhuman communication is that it is transmitted largely through tradition rather than through experience alone. Although our propensity (and our physical equipment) for communicating is biologically based, the specific language that any given person speaks is passed from one generation to another through the process of learning. Adults in a linguistic community who already know the language teach the language to the children.

Communication among primates is considerably more complex. Some nonhuman primate species, such as gorillas and chimpanzees, draw on a large number of modes of communication, including various calls as well as nonverbal forms of communication such as facial expressions, body movements, and gestures. Yet despite the relative complexity of communication patterns among nonhuman primates, these patterns differ from human patterns of communication in significant ways. For example, because animal call systems are to a large extent genetically based, they are rigidly inflexible to the extent that each call always has the same form and conveys the same meaning.

Open and Closed Communication Systems

Chimpanzees make one sound when they have found a plentiful source of food, another when threatened, and a third when announcing their

Joyce Butler of Columbia University shows famous chimpanzee Nim Chimpsky the sign configuration for "drink," and Nim imitates her. Even though Nim has been trained to use sign language, the differences between his form of communication and human language are vast.

presence. Each of these three sounds is unique in both form and message. And each sound (call) is mutually exclusive; that is, the chimpanzee cannot combine elements of two or more calls to develop a new call. For this reason, we speak of nonhuman forms of communication as being **closed systems of communication**. Humans, on the other hand, operate with languages that are **open systems of communication** because they are capable of sending messages that have never been sent before.

Unlike nonhuman primates, humans use language to send an infinite array of messages, including abstract ideas, highly technical information, and subtle shades of meaning. Starting with a limited number of sounds, humans are capable of producing an infinite number of meanings by combining sounds and words into meanings that may have never been sent before. To illustrate, by combining a series of words in a certain order, we can convey a unique message that has, in all likelihood, never been previously uttered: "I think that the woman named Kelee with the bright orange hair left her leather handbag in the 1951 Studebaker that was involved in a hit-and-run accident later in the day." This productive capacity of human language illustrates how efficient and flexible human communication is.

To suggest that the communication system of nonhuman primates such as chimps and gorillas is closed in contrast to the open system used by humans is an oversimplification. Some linguistic scholars, such as Noam Chomsky (1972), posited that because human language is so radically different from other forms of animal communication, humans must be endowed with certain genetically based mental capacities found in no other species. As we have learned more about the communication systems of nonhuman primates, however, a growing number of scholars have questioned this theory by claiming that certain species, such as chimpanzees and gorillas, have a latent capacity to learn language.

A major limitation to the development of language among gorillas and chimps is physical: They do not possess the vocal equipment for speech. In an effort to circumvent this physical limitation, researchers have taught some signs of American Sign Language to chimpanzees and gorillas with surprising results. In four years Allen and Beatrice Gardner (1969) taught a chimp named Washoe (1965–2007) to use 130 different signs. Of even greater significance is the fact that Washoe was able to manipulate the signs in ways that previously had been thought possible only by humans. For example, Washoe was able to combine several signs to create a new word (having no sign for the word *duck,* she called it *waterbird),* thereby "opening up" her system of communication. In another research effort in nonhuman communication, a gorilla named Koko by age four was able to use more than 250 different signs and, like Washoe, was able to name new objects by combining several different signs.

These developments suggest that chimps and gorillas have more complex powers of reasoning than had been believed earlier. Some have used this evidence to support the notion that chimpanzee and gorilla linguistic abilities differ from those of humans only in degree, not in kind. We must keep in mind, however, that nonhuman primates, despite their capacity to master signs of American Sign Language, do not have a language in the human sense of the term. There are still many features of human language that nonhuman primates, left to their own devices, do not possess and never will, such as speaking in the third person, lying to another person, or speaking of a subject without seeing it first. Nonhuman primate systems of communication are complex and functional. They deserve to be studied on their own terms, rather than with the false impression that chimps and gorillas are really incipient humans (linguistically speaking) who simply need a little more time and assistance before they are able to debate the sociopolitical complexities of globalization.

The Structure of Language

Every language has a logical structure. When people encounter an unfamiliar language for the first time, they are confused and disoriented, but after becoming familiar with the language, they eventually discover its rules and how the various parts are interrelated. All languages have rules and principles governing what sounds are to be used and how those sounds are to be combined to convey meanings. Human languages have two aspects of structure: a sound (or phonological) structure and a grammatical structure. The **descriptive linguist**, whose job is to make explicit the structure of any given language, studies both the sound system and the grammatical system of as many different human languages as possible. This work is vital in efforts to retain and revitalize a language because it documents the sounds and grammar used by native speakers.

Phonology

The initial step in describing any language is to determine the sounds that it uses; this is the study of **phonology**. Humans have the vocal apparatus to make an extraordinarily large number of sounds, but no single language uses all possible sounds. Instead, each language uses a finite number of sounds, called **phonemes**, which are the smallest units of sound that signal a difference in meaning. The number of phonemes in a language varies from a low of about fifteen to a high of about one hundred. The twenty-six letters of the English alphabet do not correspond to the total number of phonemes in the English language, which is forty-six. This is largely because English has a number of inconsistent features. For example, sometimes we pronounce the same word differently (as in the present and past tenses of the verb *read*), and we have different spellings for some words that sound identical (such as *meet* and *meat*). To address this difficulty, linguists have developed the International Phonetic Alphabet, which takes into account all of the possible sound units (phonemes) found in all languages of the world.

The manner in which sounds are grouped into phonemes varies from one language to another. In English, for example, the sounds represented by *b* and *v* are two separate phonemes. This distinction is absolutely necessary if an English speaker is to differentiate between such words as *ban* and *van* or *bent* and *vent*. The Spanish language, however, does not distinguish between these two sounds; they belong to the same sound class (or phoneme). When a Spanish speaker says the word *ver* ("to see"), it is impossible for the English speaker to determine with absolute precision whether the word begins with a *v* or a *b*.

Morphemes

Sounds and phonemes, though linguistically significant, usually do not convey meaning in themselves. The phonemes *r, a,* and *t* taken by themselves convey no meaning whatsoever. But when combined, they can form the words *rat, tar,* and *art,* each of which conveys meaning. Thus two or more phonemes can be combined to form a **morpheme**.

Even though some words are made up of a single morpheme, we should not equate morphemes with words. In our example, the words *rat, tar,* and *art,* each a single morpheme, cannot be subdivided into smaller units of meaning. In these cases each word is a single morpheme. However, the majority of words in any language are made up of two or more morphemes. The word *rats,* for example, contains two morphemes: the root word *rat* and the plural suffix *-s,* which conveys the meaning of more than one. Some of these morphemes, like *art, tar,* and *rat,* can occur in a language unattached. Because they can stand alone, they are called **free morphemes**. Other morphemes, such as the suffix *-ist,* cannot stand alone because they have no meaning except when attached to other morphemes. These are called **bound morphemes**.

Grammar

When people send linguistic messages by combining sounds into phonemes, phonemes into morphemes, and morphemes into words, they do so according to a highly complex set of rules. These rules, which are unique for each language, make up the **grammar** of the language and are well understood and followed by the speakers of that language. These grammatical systems, which constitute the formal structure of the language, consist of two parts: the rules governing how morphemes are combined to make words (**morphology**) and the principles guiding how words are arranged into phrases and sentences (**syntax**). In some languages meanings are determined primarily by the way morphemes are combined to form words (morphological features), whereas in other languages meanings are determined primarily by the order of words in a sentence (syntactical features).

We can illustrate the distinction between morphology and syntax by looking at an example from the English language. From a grammatical point of view, the statement "Mary fix Tom phone" does not make much sense. The order of the words in the statement (the syntax) is correct, but clearly some revision in the way that the words themselves are formed (morphology) is required for the statement to make grammatical sense. Because the English language requires information about verb tense, we must specify whether Mary fixed, is fixing, or will fix the phone. The English grammar system also requires information about the number of phones and the nature of the relationship between the phone and Tom. To make this statement grammatical, we can add an *-ed* to *fix,* an *-s* to *phone,* and an *-'s* to *Tom.* The revised statement ("Mary fixed Tom's phones"), which is now grammatically correct, tells us that Mary has already fixed two or more phones that belong to Tom.

Syntax is the aspect of grammar that governs the arrangement of words and phrases into sentences. In our original example ("Mary fix Tom phone"), the syntax is correct because the words are in the proper sequence. The statement would be meaningless if the words were ordered "fix Tom phone Mary" because the parts of speech are not in the proper relationship to one another. Moreover, in English, adjectives generally precede the nouns they describe (such as "white horse"), whereas in Spanish adjectives generally follow the nouns they describe (such as "caballo blanco"). The order of the words determines—at least in part—the meaning conveyed in any given language.

Language Change

When linguists look at the sound system or the structure of a language, they are engaging in **synchronic analysis** (that is, analysis at a single point in time). Like all other aspects of culture, however, language is not static but rather is constantly changing. When linguists study how languages change over time, they are engaged in **diachronic analysis** (that is, analysis over a period of time). Languages can be studied diachronically or historically in various ways. For example, historical linguists may study changes in a single language, such as changes from Old English to modern English. Or linguists can look at changes that have occurred in related languages (comparative linguistics). Thus historical linguists are interested in studying both the changes that have occurred in a single language over time and the historical relationship of languages to one another.

Just as languages change for internal reasons, they also are changed by external forces, or linguistic borrowing. It is generally thought that languages borrow from one another for two primary reasons: need and prestige. When a language community acquires a new cultural item such as a concept or a material object, it needs a word to describe it. This explains why different cultures have similar words to refer to the same item, such as automobiles, computers, and coffee. The other reason that words are borrowed from other languages is that they convey prestige to the speakers of the recipient language. To illustrate, the French word *cuisine* (from *kitchen*) was adopted into English because French food was considered more prestigious than English food during the period of French dominance (700 to 950 years ago).

Language and Culture

For the cultural anthropologist, the study of language is important not only for the practical purpose of communicating while doing fieldwork but also because of the close relationship between language and culture.

More specifically, **ethnolinguistics (cultural linguistics)** is the field of linguistic anthropology that studies the relationship between language and culture. It would be difficult, if not impossible, to understand a culture without first understanding its language, and it would be equally impossible to understand a language outside of its cultural context. For this reason, any effective language teacher will go beyond vocabulary and grammar by teaching students something about such topics as the eating habits, values, and behavior patterns of native speakers. Beginning with Franz Boas (the father of American anthropology) in the early twentieth century, the relationship between language and culture was recognized as critical and raised interesting questions. Did language influence culture, or did culture influence language? How did each influence people's perceptions (worldviews) and customs?

How Culture Influences Language

Although little research has been conducted to explore how culture influences the grammatical system of a language, there is considerable evidence to demonstrate how culture affects vocabulary. As a general rule, the vocabulary in any language tends to emphasize the words that are considered to be adaptively important in that culture. This concept, known as *cultural emphasis,* is reflected in the size and specialization of vocabulary.

In standard American English, a large number of words refer to technological gadgetry (such as *microchip* and *intake valve*) and occupational specialties (such as *teacher* and *pediatrician*) for the simple reason that technology and occupation are emphasized in our culture. Thus the English language helps North Americans adapt effectively to their culture by providing a vocabulary well suited for that culture. Other cultures have other areas of emphasis.

THE NUER A particularly good example of how culture influences language through the elaboration of vocabularies is provided by the Nuer, a pastoral people of the Sudan, whose daily preoccupation with cattle is reflected in their language (Evans-Pritchard 1940). The Nuer have a large vocabulary to describe and identify their cattle according to physical features such as color, markings, and horn configuration. The Nuer have ten major color terms for describing cattle: *white (bor), black (car), brown (lual), chestnut (dol), tawny (yan), mouse-gray (lou), bay (thiang), sandy gray (lith), blue and strawberry roan (yil),* and *chocolate (gwir).* When these color possibilities are merged with the many possible marking patterns, there are several hundred combinations. And when these several hundred possibilities are combined with terminology based on horn configuration, there are potentially thousands of ways of describing cattle with considerable precision in the Nuer language.

How Language Influences Culture

A major concern of linguistic anthropology since the 1930s has been whether language influences or perhaps even determines culture. There is no consensus on this topic among ethnolinguists, but some have suggested that language is more than a symbolic inventory of experience and the physical world, and that it actually shapes our thoughts and perceptions—the very way in which we see the world. Edward Sapir stated this notion in its most explicit form:

> The real world is to a large extent unconsciously built up on the language habits of the group. No two languages are ever sufficiently similar to be considered as representing the same social reality. The worlds in which different societies live are distinct worlds, not merely the same world with different labels attached. (1929: 214)

THE SAPIR-WHORF HYPOTHESIS Drawing on Sapir's original formulation, Benjamin Lee Whorf, a student of Sapir, conducted ethnolinguistic research among the Hopi Indians to determine whether different linguistic structures produced different ways of viewing the world. Whorf's observations convinced him that linguistic structure was in fact the causal variable for different views of the world. This notion has come to be known as the **Sapir-Whorf hypothesis**.

Both Sapir and Whorf were suggesting that language is more than a vehicle for communication; it actually establishes mental categories that predispose people to see things in a certain way. For example, if my language has a single word—*aunt*—that refers to my mother's sister, my father's sister, my mother's brother's wife, and my father's brother's wife, it is likely that I will perceive all of these family members as genealogically equivalent and consequently will behave toward them in essentially the same way. Sapir and Whorf were primarily concerned with the effects

© Joel Gordon

Although the Navajo and English languages have very different structures, these Navajo speakers can express abstract ideas every bit as effectively as native English speakers can.

of language on perception, and they suggested that both perception and the resulting behavior are determined (or at least influenced) by the linguistic categories we use to group some things under one heading and other things under another heading.

Although Sapir and Whorf did not conduct systematic scientific research with empirical evidence on the relationship among language, thought, and culture, subsequent linguistic scholars did. These later scholars focused on two main ideas: (1) a theory of linguistic determinism that states that the language you speak *determines* the way you perceive the world around you, and (2) a weaker theory of linguistic relativism that states that your language merely *influences* your thoughts about the real world.

Lera Boroditsky (2009) of Stanford University has demonstrated how even frivolous aspects of language, like grammatical gender, can have significant effects on perception. In many languages, such as the Romance languages, nouns are classified as either masculine or feminine; masculine and feminine nouns are then treated differently grammatically. In these languages, speakers must use pronouns, adjectives, and verb endings that correspond to the gender of the noun. For example, in a language that designates the word *sofa* as masculine, to say "my sofa is old" requires that the words *my, is,* and *old* be used in their masculine forms in order to agree with the masculine noun. And, the same grammatical forms are used when speaking of a person, such as an uncle, since *uncle* is also a masculine noun. Likewise, when referring to a *table* or an *aunt* (which are both feminine nouns), one must use the feminine forms of pronouns, verb endings, and adjectives.

Boroditsky asked: Does treating words as either masculine or feminine make speakers think of sofas and uncles as masculine (having the traits of males) and tables and aunts as feminine (having the traits of females)? In one of many studies, Boroditsky asked German and Spanish speakers to describe the characteristics of objects that have opposite gender assignments. To illustrate, she asked them to describe a key; the word for key is masculine in German and feminine in Spanish. In describing a key, German speakers used such words as *heavy, hard, jagged, metal,* and *serrated,* whereas Spanish speakers used such words as *lovely, intricate, golden, little, shiny,* and *tiny.* The word for expansion bridge is feminine in German and masculine in Spanish. When asked to describe an expansion bridge, German speakers used such descriptors as *beautiful, elegant, fragile, pretty,* and *slender,* whereas Spanish speakers used such words as *big, strong, dangerous, sturdy,* and *towering.* Boroditsky (2009) concluded that "apparently even small flukes of grammar, like the seemingly arbitrary assignment of gender to a noun, can have an effect on people's ideas of concrete objects in the world."

Linguistic Style

When we state that there are approximately six thousand mutually unintelligible languages spoken in the world today, we are implying that they all have unique vocabularies, grammar systems, and syntax. But each language group also varies in linguistic style. For example, some linguistic groups send explicit messages directly, while other groups communicate indirectly by sending more implicit messages. In Canada and the United States, where words and eloquence are highly valued, people strive to communicate in a way that is precise, straightforward, and unambiguous. We are expected to "tell it like it is" and avoid "beating around the bush." Communication in some Asian cultures, by way of contrast, is noticeably more ambiguous, implicit, and inexact. Placing much less emphasis on words, many Asian cultures rely heavily on nonverbal cues and social context to derive meaning.

These differing linguistic styles can lead to cross-cultural misunderstandings. The indirect style of the Japanese has been known to test the patience of Westerners, who mistakenly interpret it as sneaky and devious. In fact Japanese indirectness stems from a predominating concern to allow others to "save face" and avoid shame. Direct communicators, such as Americans, Canadians, and Germans, choose their words carefully because they want to be as clear and unambiguous as possible. Japanese also choose their words carefully, but for different reasons. Their meticulous choice of words stems from their desire to avoid blunt, offensive language, which might cause others to "lose face."

Another aspect of indirect versus direct linguistic style is the role of silence in communication. People from indirect societies see silence as useful; they tolerate intermittent periods of silence so as to gain a better understanding of their communication partners. Direct communicators, such as the majority of North Americans, avoid silence at all costs. Many Native American groups use silence as an integral part of their normal mode of discourse. Keith Basso (1970) described the role of silence among the Apache of Arizona, who define silence as the proper way of dealing with certain categories of people. For example, Basso found that the Apache used silence with strangers, during the initial stages of courtship, with children coming home after a long absence, with people who "cuss them out," with people who are sad, and with those involved in curing ceremonies. Interestingly, what was common to these six categories of people was that all involved relationships that were ambiguous and unpredictable. Thus, in some cultures, silence is determined by the nature of the social relationship between people and their social context.

In addition, there are stylistic variations in the extent to which some linguistic groups assign greater importance to *words* (that is, the content

Japanese and Americans have very different communication styles, which can influence the outcomes of negotiations.

of the message) than to *nonverbal cues,* such as tone or body language. Keiko Ishii, Jose Alberto Reyes, and Shinobu Kitayama (2003), for example, found that Americans have greater difficulty ignoring the content of a message than ignoring how the message is intoned. Their findings showed just the opposite for Japanese; that is, Japanese have greater difficulty ignoring vocal tone than ignoring verbal content. This stylistic difference between these two linguistic groups at least partially explains why both sides have a propensity to misunderstand each other. Americans are often perplexed because they think their Japanese counterparts do not seem to mean the same thing that they mean by the word *yes.* Many Japanese, conversely, feel perplexed that Americans just don't seem to get it because they fail to read the available nonverbal cues such as intonation.

Sociolinguistics

Anthropological linguistics has devoted much of its time and energy to the study of languages as logical systems of knowledge and communication. Recently, however, linguists have taken a keen interest in how people actually speak to one another in any given situation in a society. Whereas earlier linguists tended to focus on unified structures (morphology, phonology, and syntax), sociolinguists concentrate on variations in language use depending on the social situation or context in which the speaker is operating.

In much the same way that entire speech communities adapt their language to changing situations, so do the individuals in those speech communities. Bilingualism and multilingualism are obvious examples of the situational use of language. A Hispanic middle school student in Miami, for example, may speak English in the classroom and Spanish at home. But often people who are monolingual speak different forms of the same language depending on the social situation. To illustrate, the language that a college sophomore uses with a roommate is appreciably different from the language used when talking to grandparents; the expressions heard in a football locker room would hardly be appropriate to use in a job interview. In short, what is said and how it is said are influenced by variables such as the age, sex, and relative social status of the people involved.

Whether we are talking about selectively using an entirely different language or variations on the same language, the process is known as **code switching**. Code switching between two distinct languages involves *blending* the two languages simultaneously. So-called Spanglish (the blending of Spanish and English) has become a popular vernacular in places like Los Angeles and Miami. Words from both languages are combined into a single sentence, such as "Vamos a la store para comprar milk." (Translation: "Let's go to the store to buy milk.") Though once disparaged by language purists, Spanglish is gaining considerable respectability among academics such as Amherst College Professor Ilan Stavans, who published a Spanglish dictionary with 4,500 entries (Stavans 2003). Today Spanglish has become more mainstream, showing up in television and film scripts, in McDonald's advertisements, and even on a line of Hallmark greeting cards. Interestingly, a similar composite language called Denglish (a combination of Deutsch and English) is becoming commonplace in Germany and is finding its way into advertisements for such German companies as Lufthansa and Douglas Perfumes.

Specialized Vocabularies

Code switching is seen quite dramatically in complex societies made up of a number of special interest groups, each with its own specialized vocabulary. Jean Lave and Etienne Wenger (1991) introduced the concept of "community of practice," a group of people within a large society who interact regularly around specialized activities. They may be snowboarders or stockbrokers, prostitutes or politicians, truck drivers or computer geeks. They may spend much time together or have only limited contact. Members of a community of practice may meet with one another for decades, or their membership may be short lived. From a linguistic perspective, however, these communities develop unique ways of communicating, each complete with its own signature expressions.

Language, Nationalism, and Ethnic Identity

It should be recognized that language plays an important symbolic role in the development of national and ethnic identities. In some situations powerful political leaders or factions attempt to suppress local languages for the sake of standardization across a nation-state. The country of Tanzania is a case in point. When Tanzania became independent in the 1960s, its leaders were faced with the task of running a country that contained 120 mutually unintelligible languages. In order to administer a country with such linguistic diversity, the government adopted Swahili as the official national language. This meant that Swahili became the language used in schools, government bureaucracies, and parliament. Although Swahili (an Arabicized Bantu language) is no one's first language, it has served as a unifying *lingua franca* (common language) for the many linguistic communities that reside in Tanzania. To be certain, each linguistic group would have preferred to have had its own language declared the official language, but the adoption of Swahili early in Tanzania's history as a sovereign nation enabled the country to standardize its language and get on with the business of nation building.

In many other situations, the establishment of official languages has not gone so smoothly. In an attempt to strengthen Spain's power, the Franco government made a number of unsuccessful attempts to suppress the minority Basque and Catalan languages by forbidding people from speaking them in public or using them on signs or billboards. Language is an essential component of individual and group identity. When a strong national government tries to suppress a minority language or establish the majority language as the official one, it is likely that minority populations will strongly resist. The government of India, for example, has had to abort its several attempts to establish Hindi as the official language of India because riots erupted in non-Hindi-speaking areas of the country. And closer to home, the French-speaking province of Quebec, which for decades has had laws restricting the use of the English language in schools and on signs, nearly won its independence from Canada in 1995 largely over the issue of language policy.

In 2004 official languages were a hot topic in the news when the European Union expanded from fifteen nations to twenty-five. The inclusion of ten new member nations increased the number of official languages from eleven to twenty and the number of translations needed from 110 to 380. Unlike the United Nations with its 192 members, which conducts its business in six official languages, the European Union decided to adopt the democratic principle of allowing business to be conducted in *all* of the twenty official languages. So, unlike many nations that have excluded certain languages from the conduct of business, the European Union has affirmed the democratic ideal of cooperation and linguistic parity (Riding 2004: 3).

In some parts of the world, the influence of culture on language is a deliberate and indeed political process. In France the Académie Française, an official branch of the French government created by Cardinal Richelieu in 1635, has served as a form of "language police," protecting the French people from having to accept foreign words into their language. The Internet revolution of the 1990s has spawned a number of "e-words" from English that have been incorporated directly into many world languages. For example, many language communities have adopted nouns such as *web, spam,* and *virus* and verbs such as *surf, chat,* and *boot* in their original English forms. But not so with the French. The recommended term for the World Wide Web is not *le web,* but rather *la toile* (the spider's web); moreover the French "language police" prefer to use the term *les fouineurs* (nosy people) rather than the English word *hacker* for someone who breaks into computer systems illegally.

Nonverbal Communication

To comprehend fully how people in any particular culture communicate, we must become familiar with their nonverbal forms of communication in addition to their language—specifically body language and the somatic use of physical space. **Nonverbal communication** is important because it helps us to interpret linguistic messages and often carries messages of its own.

Like language, nonverbal forms of communication are learned and therefore vary from one culture to another. Even though some nonverbal cues have the same meaning in different cultures, an enormous range of variation in nonverbal communication exists among cultures. In some cases a certain message can be sent in a number of different ways by different cultures. For example, whereas in the United States we signify affirmation by nodding, the very same message is sent by throwing the head back in Ethiopia, by sharply thrusting the head forward among the Semang of Malaya, and by raising the eyebrows among the Dyaks of Borneo.

Humans communicate without words in a number of important ways, including hand gestures, facial expressions, eye contact, touching, space usage, scents, gait, and stance. A thorough discussion of these and other aspects of nonverbal communication, based on the recent literature, is beyond the scope of this textbook. A brief examination of three salient types of nonverbal communication—hand gestures, posture (kinesics), and touching (haptics)—will demonstrate the importance of this form of human communication.

Hand Gestures

Consider how many hand gestures we use every day. We cup our hand behind the ear as a nonverbal way of communicating that we cannot hear.

In June 2007 these two American women were eating their box lunches while waiting for a train in a Tokyo metro station. Even though the women spoke no Japanese and the two Japanese businessmen spoke no English, they were able to communicate by using such nonverbal forms of communication as facial expressions and hand gestures.

We thumb our noses at those we don't like. We can thumb a ride on the side of the highway. We can wave hello or good-bye. We tell people to be quiet by holding our forefinger vertically against our lips. We give the peace sign by holding up our forefinger and middle finger, but we send a very different message when we flash half of the peace sign. Or, by making a circle with our thumb and forefinger, we can communicate that everything is A-OK. Problems arise with these gestures when we cross national boundaries, however. Although the A-OK sign carries a positive, upbeat message in North America, it refers to money in Japan, zero (worthless) in France, male homosexuality in Malta, and an obscenity in parts of South America. Thus a single hand gesture carries with it many different meanings throughout the world. There are also many examples of the opposite phenomenon—namely, the use of different gestures to send the same message. For example, the nonverbal ways of communicating admiration for an attractive woman vary widely throughout the world. The Frenchman kisses his fingertips, the Italian twists an imaginary moustache, and the Brazilian curls one hand in front of another as if he is looking through an imaginary telescope.

Posture (Body Stance)

The way that people hold their bodies can communicate information about their social status, religious practices, feelings of submissiveness, desires to maintain social distance, and sexual intentions—to mention several areas. When communicating, people tend to orient their bodies toward others by assuming a certain stance or posture. A person can stand over another person, kneel, or "turn a cold shoulder," and in each case the body posture communicates something different. The meanings attached to different body postures vary from one culture to another and are learned in the same way that other aspects of a culture are internalized.

Perhaps one of the most visible and dramatic nonverbal messages sent by posture is submissiveness. Generally submissiveness is conveyed by making oneself appear smaller by lowering the body (crouching, cowering, or groveling). As part of their religious practices, some Christians kneel, Catholics genuflect, and Muslims kowtow, an extreme form of body lowering in which the forehead is brought to the ground. Nowhere is bowing more important to the process of communication today than in Japanese society. Bowing initiates interaction between two Japanese, it enhances and embellishes many parts of the ensuing conversation, and it is used to signal the end of a conversation. As an indication of how pervasive bowing is in contemporary Japan, some Japanese department stores employ people whose sole function is to bow to customers as they enter the store.

Touching

Touching is perhaps the most personal and intimate form of nonverbal communication. Humans communicate through touch in a variety of ways and for a variety of purposes, including patting a person on the head or back, slapping, kissing, punching, stroking, embracing, tickling, shaking hands, and laying-on of hands. Every culture has a well-defined set of meanings connected with touching; that is, each culture defines who can touch whom, on what parts of the body, and under what circumstances. Some cultures have been described as high-touch cultures and others as low-touch. Some studies (Mehrabian 1981; Montagu 1972; Sheflen 1972) have suggested that eastern European, Jewish, and Arab cultures tend to be high-touch cultures, whereas northern European cultures such as German and Scandinavian cultures tend to be low-touch. The difference between high- and low-touch cultures can be observed in public places, such as subways or elevators. For example, Londoners (from a low-touch culture) traveling in a crowded subway are likely to assume a rigid posture, studiously avoid eye contact, and refuse to even acknowledge the presence of other passengers. The French (from a high-touch culture), on the other hand, have no difficulty leaning and pressing against one another in a crowded Parisian subway.

Communication and Technology in the Twenty-First Century

The revolution in information technology (IT)—which started a mere three decades ago—has had profound consequences on the way humans communicate in the twenty-first century as well as on human societies in general. Most "twenty-somethings" today fail to realize how their parents communicated just a generation ago. In the 1980s people could communicate (that is, send and receive messages) by writing letters, speaking face to face, or by speaking or writing via such technology as the telephone, telegraph, radio, television, or carrier pigeon. It was not until the 2000s that the Internet and cell phones emerged as the communication technologies of choice. When viewed from this short time frame, the changes in the number of ways of communicating at our disposal today are truly revolutionary.

Innovations in Internet technology have revolutionized how information is delivered and how we produce and consume information. At the same time, they have transformed our social lives and behaviors as citizens. Many IT commentators argue that the new technology of e-mail, online discussions, Twitter, networking websites such as Myspace and Facebook, and high-speed, web-powered information diffusion creates a more informed, engaged, and influential population. Others contend that the communications revolution spawns a population of impressionable, impersonal, and easily manipulated people. While the impact of the Internet and cell phone technology on society is still widely debated, one thing is certain: The new twenty-first-century technologies are powerful vehicles for change in the way humans communicate and share information.

New technologies—instant messaging, cell phones, Blackberries, Droids, tweets, websites, chat rooms, and blogs—have altered the way people are communicating and accessing information. Because it is less expensive to text-message than to actually speak on one's cell phone, there has been an explosion of text messaging in recent years. According to the International Association for the Wireless Telecommunications Industry (www.ctia.org), approximately 4.1 billion text messages were sent over U.S. carrier networks every day in 2009, nearly twice as many as in the preceding year. Although an enormous number of text messages are being sent, however, the messages themselves lack both intimacy and detail.

Because texting is now second nature to young people in the United States, it serves as a communication divide between generations. Since most people over age forty do not engage in social texting, their children use it as a way to communicate with their friends out of earshot of their elders. Young people, having developed their own texting abbreviations, are now able to send and receive messages in school, at the dinner table, and even during church services without sacrificing their privacy. Teens in the United States use text messaging as a way to exclude their parents from their youth culture.

Text messaging frees us from having to communicate intimately about what we are feeling and allows us to be brief. One can flirt, make a date, or even break up with a "significant other" without divulging any emotions. In fact, this may be the major attraction of this new twenty-first century mode of communication: It preserves the immediacy and efficiency of face-to-face communication without the burden of emotional self disclosure.

Text messaging is widely used by young people in rural India as a way to circumvent the long-standing traditional barriers against premarital mingling. Unlike their counterparts in the United States, or even in Mumbai or Delhi, singles in rural India can't flirt or "cruise for dates" at crowded bars or clubs. Unmarried women are expected to show no interest in men's flirtatious advances, marry young, and marry a man chosen for them by their families. And, since most singles in India live with their families and share rooms with siblings, they have few opportunities to speak privately with a member of the opposite sex. Text messaging offers young Indian singles an opportunity to communicate in private without having to worry about either violating traditional customs or revealing intimate feelings.

Out in the Real World: Learning a Foreign Language or American Sign Language

Mastering a second or even a third language is an asset in today's global world. The migration of peoples because of war, famine, environmental events, or political and economic hardships creates culturally diverse communities. If you are proficient in more than one language, it opens up a wide range of employment opportunities—both domestically and internationally. The top spoken languages taught in U.S. colleges and universities in 2009, as noted by how many students were studying a particular language, were Spanish (51 percent), French (12 percent), German (5.7 percent), and Italian (4.8 percent). Although Arabic is rapidly becoming more popular, it is still studied by only 2 percent of students enrolled in language courses. Even if you have already mastered one or possibly two spoken languages, have you ever considered learning American Sign Language (ASL)? A recent article in *USA Today* (2010) reports that ASL is now the fourth most studied foreign language in the United States, with 5.4 percent of students enrolled in college ASL courses.

Although some members of the deaf and hearing-impaired communities take issue with using the term *foreign language* when referring to ASL (because the language does not come from a foreign country), it is certainly a language in its own right. ASL is not a gestural translation of English. ASL has its own specific syntax, with regional variations, slang, humor, and jokes. Like other languages, ASL evolves over time, especially from contact with signers from different countries and the introduction of new technologies (the iPod, the electric car, the Tweet, etc.) into the sign vocabulary.

An estimated 20 million Americans have measurable hearing loss, and ASL is the primary language of 250,000 to 500,000 people (Weise 2010). Students of ASL have become interpreters for the deaf and hearing-impaired communities. And a growing number of professions incorporate sign language in their work, such as special education teachers and speech and language pathologists. In fact, sign language has been shown to be a helpful method of communication for children with special needs who have trouble speaking, including those with autism, cerebral palsy, and Down's syndrome. Believe it or not, it has become popular to teach hearing babies to sign, as they are able to use gestures to communicate before they can form words.

Not surprisingly, sign language is used in many countries around the world. Each country has its own sign language dictionary depending on the size of the deaf population in that country. There are also regional dialects and slang even if the sign language is indigenous to the country, as it is in Honduras, or if the sign language is modeled after ASL. In fact, ASL is modeled on the French sign system, which dates back to the 1750s and has influenced many other European sign languages as well.

An interesting area of further research would be to examine the deaf and hearing-challenged communities from a cross-cultural perspective. Do the challenges that deaf and hearing-impaired people face differ from one country to another? How are their health, educational, and legal needs met in other countries compared to the United States? Are they overlooked because of barriers to language and culture? Being an interpreter for the deaf and hearing-impaired community is an important job in today's global world, much like being an interpreter for non-native speakers in health settings and classrooms.

QUESTIONS FOR FURTHER THOUGHT

1. Why is ASL considered a foreign language at many universities and colleges?

2. What kinds of applied research projects could one become involved in if fluent in ASL?

SUMMARY

1. Language—and the capacity to use symbols to convey abstract thoughts about the past or future—is perhaps the most distinctive hallmark of our humanity.

2. There are approximately six thousand discrete languages in the world today, but languages spoken in small-scale societies are becoming extinct at an alarming rate.

3. Although nonhumans also engage in communication, human communication systems are unique in important respects. Human communication systems are open; that is, they are capable of sending an infinite number of messages. Humans are also the only animals that can communicate about events that happened in the past or might happen in the future.

4. All human languages are structured in two ways. First, each language has a phonological structure made up of rules that govern how sounds (phonemes) are combined to convey meanings. Second, each language has its own grammatical structure comprising the rules that govern how morphemes are formed into words (morphology) and how words are arranged into phrases and sentences (syntax).

5. Like other aspects of culture, languages change over time in response to internal and external factors. Historical linguists want to know not only how languages change but also why they change.

6. There is a close relationship between language and culture. Culture influences language to the extent that the vocabulary in any language tends to emphasize words that are adaptively important in that culture.

7. Language influences culture. According to the Sapir-Whorf hypothesis, language influences perception. Language establishes mental categories that affect the ways in which people conceptualize the real world.

8. Sociolinguists are interested in studying how people's use of language depends on the social situation or context in which they are operating.

9. Language plays an important symbolic role in the development of national and ethnic identities, as exemplified in Canada, Tanzania, and the European Union.

10. Examples of human nonverbal communication—which, like language, is learned and culturally variable—include kinesics (facial expressions, hand gestures, eye contact, and posture) and haptics (touching).

11. The revolution in information technology (cell phones, instant messaging, social networking, blogs, etc.) has had a profound impact on how humans communicate. These technological innovations have led to a proliferation of messages sent and received quickly and efficiently, but many messages lack both details and personal intimacy.

KEY TERMS

Young pastoral children are learning their lessons. Studies show that adults who have had some formal education make creative business decisions that help their families and livestock survive during drought periods.

CHAPTER **6**

Subsistence Patterns, Environment, and Economics

SECONDARY EDUCATION INFLUENCES SURVIVAL STRATEGIES FOR EAST AFRICAN PASTORALISTS

When we think of East African pastoralists, we may imagine nomadic people and their animals—cattle, goats, sheep, and camels—inhabiting semiarid environments. Many East African pastoralists, such as the Ariaal, Gabra, Maasai, Pokot, Sumburu, and Turkana, live in drought-prone environments. Droughts adversely affect the survival and economic well-being of these pastoral groups as well as the environment itself. Past studies indicate that formal education was not widespread among herding communities in the rangelands of northern Kenya and that the educational levels there were much lower than in other parts of the country.

In 2009 Peter Little, Abdillahi Aboud, and Clement Lenachuru conducted a study in northern Kenya to examine whether formal education reduced the risk of food shortages for pastoralists living in drought-prone areas. They worked particularly with the Maa-speaking (Maasai-related) Il Chamus of Baringo District, where the levels of formal education had risen throughout the 1980s and 1990s (Little 1992). Using archival and ethnographic data, Little and Lenachuru conducted a longitudinal study to examine drought conditions and recovery after droughts for the pastoralists of northern Kenya.

In addition to raising livestock, the Il Chamus have always engaged in other economic activities such as dryland farming and wage employment. During times of drought, the Il Chamus have experienced serious livestock losses. These losses kindled their interest in formal education as a way to expand their economic diversification. The Il Chamus also contended with a decreased amount of grazing land due to the growing human population, agricultural expansion, violence from the neighboring Pokot, and loss of pastureland from an invasive plant species— *Prosopis juliflora*. Yet the Il Chamus never abandoned their pastoral practices while adapting to economic, environmental, and political forces.

Little, Aboud, and Lenachuru's research revealed that formal education had mixed results. During the past twenty-five years, households that invested in both their male and female children's education benefited in that many found salaried and wage-paying employment. In times of drought, family members who are wage earners contribute financially to food security; they can purchase necessary food items and reduce the risk of famine. The researchers also found that the Il Chamus with postsecondary educations (mostly men) had larger livestock holdings than others. They used their incomes to purchase animals and to avoid selling livestock at distressed prices in order to buy food during droughts.

Little and colleagues emphasize that it is critical to distinguish between the effects of formal education on income and food security and its effects on pastoralism as a way of life. Access to secondary education has had a marked cultural impact on Il Chamus pastoralists. Elderly family members noted that the more education their children had, the less they understood the ways of traditional pastoralists. The more highly educated children wanted to put up fences, privatize shared rangelands, and hire laborers to manage the family's livestock holdings. The elders recognized that going to school and tending livestock do not go hand in hand; the time investment needed to do each is too demanding.

Formal education has nevertheless been successful in augmenting the pastoral activities of the Il Chamus. Graduates can compete successfully for salaried employment and thereby provide their households with food security without having to rely on dryland farming. In addition, educated pastoralists can seek out markets that pay higher prices for their livestock, a practice not traditionally considered. When pastoralists do not have to sell their animals in order to survive, they can wait for favorable market prices.

The researchers recommend that school calendars follow the wet and dry seasons, so that households do not have to choose between an education and herding and agricultural practices. Future policy makers will need to recognize local pastoral traditions while they design educational programs to improve the welfare of the pastoralists and their ability to manage in a historically drought-prone environment.

QUESTIONS FOR FURTHER THOUGHT

1. What are some of the influences that increased access to secondary education has on traditional pastoral practices?

2. What policy recommendations should come out of this research with respect to increasing opportunities for formal education?

Critical to any culture's survival is meeting the society's basic needs, and for the most part this involves access to food and drinkable water. In one form or another, every culture has a system for procuring food: growing it, raising it, trading for it, and even shopping for it. The pattern for obtaining one's food is known as a *subsistence strategy*. As we know, not all food-getting systems or subsistence strategies are equitable. Within societies and between societies, some people have greater access to more food than others. We see examples of extremes in access or lack of access in countries where people are severely malnourished or dying of starvation, while in other countries people are dying from overconsumption and obesity, which has become a global epidemic.

All societies (whether small-scale or highly complex) have at their disposal a limited amount of vital resources, such as land, water, livestock, machines, food, and labor. This simple fact requires all societies to consider how to allocate scarce resources, produce needed items, distribute them, and develop consumption patterns that contribute to an adaptive strategy that enables them to survive in their environment. In other words, every society, if it is to survive, must develop systems of production, distribution, and consumption.

In all parts of the world, both culture and the environment influence the traditions that are passed on from one generation to the next in terms of how food is obtained, what is considered food and how it is eaten, and who gets to eat and when. There are some regions of the world where people produce nonfood items for trade to purchase their food, such as growing tobacco, cotton, or trees for timber. In most Western countries, the majority of people are not tied to the land or to the sea for their subsistence strategy; they are not likely to be involved in the actual production of their sustenance. In other words, they shop for their food as modern-day hunter-gatherers of the supermarkets. People can choose from a wide selection of food items, many from different parts of the world, thanks to globalization, food preservation, transportation systems, and storage facilities.

In this chapter we will examine five food-getting strategies and the various ways in which they are influenced by technology and the environment. As you know, culture is at the heart of what makes each society different, and it is culture that influences what different peoples eat as well as how they go about obtaining food in the environment in which they live.

Human Adaptation

Anthropologists, particularly those who specialize in environmental anthropology, have always had an interest in how humans adjust to their natural environments. They want to know how a particular environment influences people and their culture, and conversely how the culture (and people's activities) influences the physical environment (Sutton and Anderson 2009). Throughout history the various patterns of subsistence have had an impact on the environment, and culture has enabled people to adapt to changing conditions. Some anthropologists refer to this as *cultural ecology*, which was introduced by Julian Steward (1963).

When we speak of human adaptation to a particular environment, we are referring to two types of adaptation: *cultural* and *biological*. Cultural responses to cold climates include "technological" solutions such as building fires, using animal skins as clothing and blankets, and seeking refuge from the elements in caves or constructed dwellings. And let's not forget using wood fires, coal-burning stoves, and gas and electric heating systems for keeping warm. Humans who live in cold climates also engage in certain behaviors that are adaptive. They tend to eat more food, particularly fats and carbohydrates, especially during the colder months; they engage in greater amounts of activity securing food and getting fuel for heat, which increases their internal body temperature; and they curl up when sleeping to reduce the surface area of exposure and resulting heat loss. However, some would say many cultures have gone soft with today's access to modern housing, heating and cooling systems, hot and cold running water, and refrigerated food storage containers. Members of these cultures now have a hard time going without such conveniences, which is especially noted when there are long power outages.

A number of studies by environmental anthropologists document highly successful adaptations to the environment among contemporary societies, and archaeological evidence demonstrates successful land management in prehistoric societies. According to Kevin Krajick (1998), archaeological research in southern Peru indicates that the Incas used conservation practices such as irrigation canals, terracing, and tree planting to build a highly efficient agricultural system in the Peruvian highlands. Archaeologists and geologists have found that between 2000 B.C. and 100 A.D., pre-Incan people had over-farmed the land, causing severe soil erosion and degradation. Core soil samples indicate that by the time the Incas took over the area, alder trees were beginning to proliferate, soil was less eroded, and seeds from maize began to appear. Terraces were built by people who hauled soil to the hillsides from the valley and riverbeds below. And the Incas built a 31.2-mile canal system that provided water to hillside cultivators from streams and lakes located at higher altitudes. Researchers have suggested (based on both archaeological evidence and written accounts after the Spanish conquest in the early 1500s) that the Incas practiced agroforestry by purposefully planting trees and managing them as part of the agricultural system.

As one more example of the usefulness of anthropological research data, some of the ancient Incan farming practices are being revived by contemporary residents of the area. Since 1995, local Peruvian farmers have rebuilt the terraces, reconstructed the canal system, and put 160 hectares of land under cultivation. Preliminary reports suggest that crops are growing well and using less fertilizer than is required in other areas. One of the major grains produced by the Incas was quinoa. Today quinoa and a variety of Inca potatoes are found in Western supermarkets. Clearly the Incas had hundreds of years to develop an agricultural system that maximized the utility of the land without degrading it. This example illustrates how people in the past provide lessons for people in the present.

Environment and Technology

Which food-getting strategy is developed by a given culture depends, in large measure, on the culture's environment, technology, and way of life. The relationship between the physical environment and food-getting methods is not tidy. For example, people could reside in a rural area with fantastic soils conducive to good farming, but choose to rely on a grocery store as their food source. We also know that the earth cannot easily be divided into neat ecological zones, each with its own unique and mutually exclusive climate, soil composition, vegetation, and animal life. Geographers often divide the earth's land surface into categories, including grasslands, deserts, tropical forests, temperate forests, polar regions, and mountain habitats. Some of these environments are particularly hospitable to the extent that they support a number of modes of food acquisition. Others are more limiting in the types of adaptations they permit. Anthropologists generally agree that the environment does not determine food-getting patterns but rather sets broad limits on the possibilities, especially when we consider that culture defines what is considered a food item. For example, among some cultures in Africa, Asia, and Latin America, insects such as grasshoppers, grubs, and termites are regular fare or snack foods, whereas in other cultures these items are not considered food but something that ought to be avoided.

In part it is technology—a part of culture—that helps people adapt to their specific environment. In fact the human species enjoys a tremendous adaptive advantage over all other species precisely because it has developed a wide range of technological solutions to the problems of survival. In many cases, cultures with complex technologies have gained greater control over their environments and their food supplies. Many societies with simple technologies also adapt ingeniously to their natural surroundings, and they may do so with fewer negative consequences to their environments (like the Inca mentioned above).

The specific mode of food getting is influenced by the environment itself and its interface with a people—both their culture and their technology. To illustrate, the extent to which a hunting-and-gathering society is able to procure food depends not only on the sophistication of the society's tools but also on the abundance of plant and animal life in the environment and the society's definition of what is edible and how to process it into something people will consume. Similarly the productivity of irrigation agriculture varies according to the society's technology, environmental factors such as the availability of water, and the natural nutrients in the water and in the soil. These environmental factors set an upper limit on the productivity of any given food-getting system and the size of the population it can support. Cultural ecologists call this limit the environment's **carrying capacity** (Glossow 1978; Sutton and Anderson 2009).

A natural consequence of exceeding the carrying capacity is damage to the environment, such as killing off too much game or depleting the soil of its nutrients for growing crops and raising animals. Societies cannot easily increase their food-getting productivity beyond the carrying capacity. Thus, if a society is to survive, it must meet the fundamental need of producing or procuring enough food and water to keep its population alive while not exhausting its natural resources.

Major Food-Getting Strategies

The main forms of food procurement (hunting and gathering, horticulture, pastoralism, and intensive agriculture, which has expanded into industrial agriculture) are not mutually exclusive because most human societies use more than one strategy. Where this is the case, however, one form usually predominates. Moreover, in each category we can expect to find considerable variation largely because of differences in environment, historical experiences, technology, and cultural preferences. These food-getting categories are presented in Figure 6.1 and explored in more detail in the following sections.

Hunting-and-Gathering Societies

Hunting and gathering (also known as *food collecting* or *foraging*)—as compared to food producing—involves the search for wild plants and

FIGURE 6.1
Features of the major food-procurement categories

	Foragers	Horticulturalist	Pastoralist	Intensive agriculturists
Also known as:	Hunters and gatherers	Slash and burn, shifting cultivation, swidden	Herders	Industrial agriculture
Population size	Small	Small/Moderate	Small	Large
Permanency of settlement	Nomadic (or semi-)	Generally sedentary	Nomadic (or semi-)	Permanent
Surpluses	Minimal	Minimal	Moderate	Usual
Trade	Minimal	Minimal	Moderate	Very important
Labor specialization	None	Minimal	Minimal	Highest degree
Class differences	None	Minimal	Moderate	Highest degree

© Cengage Learning 2013

animals that exist in the natural environment. People have been hunting, gathering, and fishing for the majority of the time they have been on earth. It was not until the **neolithic revolution**—approximately ten thousand years ago—that humans for the first time produced their food by means of horticulture or animal husbandry (B. Smith 1998). With the emergence of food production and population expansion into many regions of the earth, the reliance on hunting and gathering as the only means of a group's subsistence has been marginalized.

Even though most societies have become food producers, a handful of societies in the world today are still hunters and gatherers. Some hunter-gatherers are known to be food collectors; they live in differentiated environments that require them to exploit specific food resources and often store them in bulk (Binford 1980). Others are known as food foragers, and they reside in undifferentiated environments that do not require them to store food; their knowledge of when and where to go to obtain food items was traditionally sufficient to sustain them. Foraging and collecting societies vary widely in other cultural features and are found in a wide variety of environments (semideserts, tropical forests, and polar regions).

Despite the considerable variation among contemporary foragers and collectors (hunters and gatherers), it is possible to make the following three generalizations about most of them. First, hunting-and-gathering societies have low population densities. They have quotas or limits so that they do not overexploit their resources. Living below the carrying capacity of their environment has enabled such populations to reside in particular habitats for millennia. Second, hunting-and-gathering societies are usually nomadic or seminomadic. By and large, they move periodically from place to place in search of wild animals and vegetation, and usually they do not recognize individual land rights. Third, contemporary hunting-and-gathering peoples occupy the remote and marginally useful areas of the earth, including the Alaskan tundra, the Kalahari Desert, the Australian Outback, and the Ituri Forest of central Africa. It is reasonable to suggest that these food-gathering, hunting-and-fishing societies, with their simple technology, have been forced into these marginal habitats by food producers, with their more complex technologies.

The association of hunting and gathering with an absence of social, political, and economic complexity is an accurate portrayal of the remaining hunting-and-gathering societies; most are small-scale, unspecialized, egalitarian, and decentralized. However, archaeologists have found prehistoric societies that in all likelihood had considerably more social complexity (Price and Brown 1985). In the 1960s some anthropologists (Marshall Sahlins, Richard Lee) suggested that certain food-gathering groups were well off despite inhabiting some very unproductive parts of the earth.

Historically known foragers

Historically Known Foragers (Hunter-Gatherers)

1 Eskimos or Inuit	7 Plains Indians	13 Okiek
2 Subarctic Indians	8 Amazon Basin Hunter-Gatherers	14 Hadza
3 Northwest Coast Indians	9 Gran Chaco Indians	15 San
4 Plateau Indians	10 Tehuelche	16 Native Australians
5 California Indians	11 Fuegians	17 Maori
6 Great Basin Indians	12 "Pygmies"	18 Toala

19 Agta	25 Vedda
20 Punan	26 Kadar
21 Kubu	27 Chenchu
22 Semang	28 Birhor
23 Andaman Islanders	29 Ainu
24 Mlabri	30 Chukchi

Hunter-gatherers such as the Ju/'hoansi traditionally identify a wide range of plants and animals as food, which enables them to adapt to a challenging environment. Their knowledge of their environment and of what is edible, such as these mongongo nuts, is key to their survival.

Marshall Sahlins (1968) described hunters and gatherers as representing the "original affluent society." Hunters and gatherers, he argued, spent little time working, had all the food they needed, and enjoyed considerable leisure time. Although many scholars today take issue with this formulation, considerable evidence suggests that foragers are capable of adapting to harsh environments with creativity and resourcefulness (Sutton and Anderson 2009). Perhaps we can get a better idea of how foragers and collectors procure their food by examining two very different contemporary groups—the Ju/'hoansi of present-day Namibia and the Inuit of the Arctic region—in greater detail.

THE JU/'HOANSI OF THE KALAHARI REGION One of the best-studied foraging societies, the Ju/'hoansi, inhabit the northwestern part of Africa in the Kalahari Desert, which straddles Namibia, Botswana, and Angola. In 1963, when Richard Lee first visited the Dobe Ju/'hoansi, he observed that three-quarters of them lived in camps, surviving on what they hunted and gathered from their surrounding environment as well as what they gleaned from their pastoralist neighbors—the Herero and Tswanna, who kept small herds of cattle and goats. Since the Ju/'hoansi lived in a desert environment, they had to keep moving in order to keep eating, since food and water resources were sparse (R. Lee 2007). Food-procuring activities were divided between men and women. Women collected 60 to 80 percent of the food (by weight) in the form of roots, nuts, fruits, and other edibles and occasionally snared small game; men hunted medium and large animals and occasionally brought back gathered items. The Ju/'hoansi's most important single food item was the mongongo nut, which accounted for about half of their diet. Nutritionally, the mongongo, which is found in abundance all year long, contains five times more calories and ten times more protein per cooked unit than cereal crops. Unlike people in other arid regions, however, the Ju/'hoansi did not have any periods of plenty and they had no way of storing food supplies. When food shortages occurred, the Ju/'hoansi adapted by relying on networks among their local groups to reduce their risk of starvation.

Even though the terms *affluence* and *abundance* tend to be relative, Richard Lee (1968) presented convincing evidence that the Ju/'hoansi were not teetering on the brink of starvation. In fact their food-gathering techniques were both productive and reliable. A measure of Ju/'hoansi affluence noted in the 1960s was their selectivity in taking foods from the environment. If they had indeed been on the brink of starvation, they would have exploited every conceivable source of food. But, in fact, they ate only about one-third of the edible plant foods and regularly hunted only 17 of the 223 local species of animals known to them (R. Lee 1968). Lee estimated that the average Ju/'hoansi adult spent twelve to nineteen hours per week in the pursuit of food, which left a good deal of time for such leisure activities as resting, visiting, and entertaining visitors. With the major group values of sharing and reciprocity, security for the Ju/'hoansi was ensured by giving rather than hoarding, because during hard times people could cash in on their accumulated obligations.

By the mid-1970s, the Ju/'hoansi had adopted many of the lifeways of the neighboring peoples. Many families had begun to plant fields and keep goats, two agricultural pursuits that had been unheard of just a decade earlier. Traditional grass huts were replaced by more substantial semipermanent mud structures. They began to substitute manufactured clothing for their traditional skin garments. Bows and arrows were still made, but were primarily sold to tourists rather than used in hunting. All of these changes were accompanied by a major infusion of cash and consumer goods into Ju/'hoansi society.

Along with these changes in material culture, John Yellen (1990) found that the Ju/'hoansi began to place less emphasis on intimacy, sharing, and interdependence. The spatial layout of the camps changed from a circular arrangement with the doors facing one another to a linear layout that gave families greater privacy; the distance between huts increased; and the hearth, which traditionally had been a focal point of socializing, was moved inside each hut rather than located outside. Yellen also found increased hoarding of material goods purchased with the new-found cash, and as they accumulated more possessions, the Ju/'hoansi became less mobile and less willing to continue their seminomadic, foraging lifestyle. The major impetus for the relatively sudden changes in culture was not disenchantment with the foraging lifestyle but rather the civil war in the region, which forced some Ju/'hoansi into settlements.

The introduction of money, commodities, and wage labor expedited the process of culture change within the Ju/'hoansi culture. By the early years of the twenty-first century, the majority of the Ju/'hoansi obtained most of their food by raising small domestic livestock, tending small gardens, participating in government food programs, and purchasing items at food stores. Located in their territory are trading markets, boreholes, schools, health clinics, and airstrips. And, of course, changes in their means of livelihood have resulted in other changes in their way of life (R. Lee 2003, 2007; J. Yellen 1990). For example, the Ju/'hoansi who live in //Nhoq'ma village at Nhoma in the Tshumkwi are playing host to tourists. Neil Digby-Clarke (2007) reports that the owners of a nearby lodge and safari outfit have developed a close relationship with the Ju/'hoansi. In 2000 they entered into an exclusive agreement with the village at //Nhoq'ma, and in 2003 they built a tent camp for tourists and donated it to the villagers. Digby-Clarke describes the tourist accommodations as "five luxury double tents, complete with en-suite facilities." The community generates revenue from this arrangement. In 2005 the villages received a total of N$105,000 (Namibian dollars), and in 2006 the amount increased to N$130,000 generated by two hundred tourists visiting the Ju/'hoansi. The Ju/'hoansi are embarking on ecotourism, an environmentally sensitive approach to cultural tourism.

THE INUIT The traditional Inuit of the Arctic region existed in a delicate balance with their environment. Living in the barren Arctic and sub-Arctic regions stretching from Greenland in the east to Alaska in the west, the Inuit have had to adapt to a climate of bitterly cold temperatures, short summers, and a terrain almost devoid of vegetation. Traditionally they were hunters and fishermen living off of animal life. They hunted for whales, walruses, caribou, seals, polar bears, and birds, supplementing

their diet with seaweed. They spent part of the year on the move, searching for food, and then part of the year at a central, more permanent camp. The Inuit divided the year into three hunting seasons, each revolving around a single animal: the seal, the caribou, and the whale.

Understanding the seasonal migratory patterns of animals was central to the Inuits' subsistence strategy. During the harsh winter months, when the sea is completely frozen over, the Inuit relied heavily on seal hunting. To maximize their chances for successful seal hunting, the Inuit often organized themselves into large communities of up to sixty people from several distantly related, extended families. Inuit hunters waited patiently, sometimes for hours, for a seal to surface and be killed. Seal meat was first shared through reciprocal exchanges within kinship lines and then among others in the community to ensure that no one went hungry. Following the whaling season in April and May, the Inuit turned their attention to other forms of food collection. As the ice began to break up, game became more plentiful, and the Inuit hunted caribou with bows and arrows and fished for salmon and trout with pronged spears. During these summer months, people tended to live in smaller groups and their social interaction was less intense. Thus the Inuit adapted to their environment by organizing their economic and social lives around the availability of different types of game and the strategies required for hunting them.

Much of what we have described about traditional Inuit hunting and fishing practices has changed over the last several decades. Most contemporary Inuit live in villages, hunt with guns rather than spears and harpoons, and use snowmobiles rather than dogsleds. Some live in houses with modern conveniences such as telephones and TVs, and a growing number of Inuit are engaged in wage employment. Even though they may eat imported foods, the Inuit still practice traditional hunting and gathering. Today's twenty-first-century Inuit hunters use ice floe maps,

© B&C Alexander/ArcticPhoto

Although the Inuit from Nunavut, Canada, have been using snowmobiles for more than a half century, they face new challenges as they adapt to the influences of global warming.

regularly updated by the European Space Agency, for tracking the rapidly changing ice edge conditions that determine where wildlife is most likely to be found. More recently the Inuit have worked to protect their traditional ways and to maintain their subsistence lifestyle. In 1999 the Canadian government created a new territory called Nunavut ("our land" in the Inuit language) for the Inuit. The new territory is 1.2 million square miles—twice the size of Alaska and larger than all of western Europe. It sustains a population of about twenty-seven thousand. The creation of Nunavut gives the Inuit a measure of control over their own lives and an opportunity to preserve their traditional culture.

FISHERMEN OF THE TWENTY-FIRST CENTURY Although hunting and gathering has been largely replaced by food production, there remains one very important form of hunting that many world economies depend on—that is, fishing. Today's commercial fishermen are equipped with Global Positioning System (GPS) technology to locate large schools of fish, high-tech equipment, and strong synthetic nets that are invisible to fish. Despite their enormous technological advantages, modern fishermen may very well become victims of their own success. The rivers, lakes, and oceans of the world, which not too long ago seemed inexhaustible, produce only a limited number of fish. In the northwest Atlantic Ocean, where commercial fishing boats from Europe and Asia have fished the waters off the coast of the United States and Canada, the carrying capacity has been exceeded. By the 1960s the cod stock had declined so dramatically from overfishing that the governments of the United States and Canada extended their exclusive fishing rights to 200 nautical miles from shore. Although this kept foreign fishing vessels out of the area, it encouraged the proliferation of domestic fishermen. Fish stocks are shrinking and future stocks are in jeopardy because fish populations cannot sustain themselves at the current rate of extraction.

Industrial commercial fishing—the last form of big-time "hunting"— illustrates the traditional dilemma of hunting-and-gathering people. Value is placed on the quantity and frequency of fish caught and traded on an international scale among strangers. As the public demand for wild-caught seafood increases and fishermen become more efficient hunters, they run the risk of destroying their food supply and, in the process, eliminating biodiversity and ruining the health of their ecosystem. As with so many aspects of the global economy, overfishing of waters has had more negative consequences for some segments of the world's population than for others. Since fish populations in the Northern Hemisphere have been drastically reduced by commercial fishing interests in the United States, Canada, Japan, Russia, and northern Europe, many fishing companies from the developed world have moved south of the equator to the oceans around Africa and South America

Human and environmental interfaces have direct consequences not only for the survival of fish species but also for those whose livelihoods depend on fishing. As a boat passes through heavily oiled marsh near Pass a Loutre, Louisiana, on May 20, 2010, we can clearly see the immediate impact of the oil spill. The future of the wildlife, the fishermen, and others remains in question.

and are fishing within the 200-mile limits of independent countries. Most are there legally, but a growing number of commercial fishing companies are harvesting these waters illegally.

We have described the connection between fishermen and their environment and how globalization is forcing fishing vessels to exploit waters all over the world to meet the public's increasing demand for wild-caught seafood. Other human and environmental interactions also have direct consequences not only for the survival of fish species but also for those who make their livelihoods from fishing. For example, on April 20, 2010, one of BP's oil-drilling platforms exploded and collapsed forty miles off the Gulf Coast of Louisiana, with huge quantities of oil gushing into the water. This environmental crisis affected marine life, coastal marshes, wildlife, the livelihoods of fishermen and their families, the coastal tourism industry, and the cultural traditions of coastal peoples. The future of the multigenerational fishing families and all those connected to the fishing industry hangs in a delicate balance; many interviewed by the media feared that they will lose their way of life and that the environment will not recover during their lifetime.

Food-Producing Societies

Approximately ten thousand years ago, humans made a revolutionary transition from subsisting exclusively on what they obtained naturally from the environment to producing food (the domestication of plants and animals). For reasons that are still not altogether clear, humans began to cultivate crops and keep herds of animals as sources of food. That is, humans were able to *produce* food and they no longer had to rely solely on what existed naturally in the environment. This shift from hunting and gathering to producing food, known as the *neolithic revolution,* occurred in several different areas of the world independently. The earliest known plant and animal domestication occurred around ten thousand years ago in the Middle East in the region called the Fertile Crescent, including parts of Jordan, Israel, Syria, southeastern Turkey, northern Iraq, and western Iran. The first domesticated animal and plant species were dogs, sheep, goats, wheat, and barley.

Domestication of crops and livestock developed independently outside of the Fertile Crescent. By nearly ten thousand years ago, villagers in northern China were raising millet, and people farther south were growing rice (Loewe and Shaughnessy 1999). Archaeologists have found evidence for the emergence of plant and animal domestication in sub-Saharan Africa around five thousand years ago. Archaeologists believe the people in central Mexico cultivated squash, chilies, beans, and a variety of millet by five thousand years ago. Corn was developed as early as seven thousand years ago from a wild grass called teosinte. Indians throughout North and South America eventually came to depend on corn, also known as maize, for much of their food, even though some of their other grains were more nutritious. And between three thousand and seven thousand years ago, the first cultivated potato appeared in southern Peru and northeastern Bolivia (B. Smith 1998).

A number of theories have been suggested to explain why the neolithic revolution occurred. Although no definitive explanation has emerged, most archaeologists agree that the shift to food production was a response to certain environmental or demographic conditions, such as variations in rainfall or population pressures. It is reasonable to suggest that most of the early hunter-gatherers did not rush to adopt agriculture. Cultivating requires a greater expenditure of labor than

The Fertile Crescent

© Cengage Learning 2013

does hunting and gathering, and it usually produces a less varied (and less interesting) diet. It is likely that food production came about serendipitously and resulted in feeding an increasing number of people who could no longer be sustained by hunting and gathering alone. It also may have met people's desire to stay in one place rather than migrating on a seasonal or as-needed basis.

CHANGES RESULTING FROM FOOD PRODUCTION What made the neolithic revolution so revolutionary was that it produced the world's first population explosion. Even though early neolithic communities were small, they were far larger than any others in human prehistory. Throughout the Near East, Egypt, and Europe, thousands of skeletal remains have been unearthed from the neolithic period (10,000 to 5,500 years ago) compared to only a few hundred from the entire paleolithic period, even though the paleolithic lasted hundreds of times longer than the neolithic.

Food production led to a dramatic increase in population. As we pointed out, hunter-gatherers had built-in limits or quotas on what they could extract from the natural environment. Overextraction would destroy their natural food sources. Cultivators, in contrast, could increase their food supply (and thus support larger populations) by sowing more seeds, managing soil nutrients, and building irrigation systems. As cultivators increased the amount of land under cultivation, they came to rely on their children for help, and consequently family size increased. And, in the end, the neolithic revolution started the gradual trend toward a more settled way of life.

The cultivation of crops also brought about other important cultural changes. For example, cultivating can potentially generate more food per unit of land than hunting-and-gathering activities. Increased yields may have allowed farmers to store more food for times of scarcity, trade with others, and enable other members to specialize in non–food-producing activities. People could for the first time become specialists, inventing and manufacturing the tools and machinery needed for a more complex social structure. Once some people were liberated from the food quest, they were able to make new implements such as the plow, pottery storage containers, metal objects, the wheel, stone masonry, and improved hunting and fishing technology. These inventions and others resulted from an increase in labor specialization, which led to the second revolution: the emergence of civilization.

The importance of changes brought about by the neolithic revolution cannot be overestimated. The introduction of agriculture and animal husbandry ten thousand years ago set humankind on a radically different evolutionary path. Although it enabled humans to move toward civilization (urban societies), the industrial revolution, and eventually the global information age, the neolithic also had its downside. Recent discoveries by paleopathologists (physical anthropologists who study disease among ancient peoples) suggest that the transition to early agriculture from a hunting-and-gathering subsistence strategy actually led to a decline in overall health. To illustrate, skeletal remains of hunter-gatherers from Greece and Turkey at the end of the ice age (approximately twelve thousand years ago) indicate that the average height was five feet nine inches for men and five feet five inches for women, but by five thousand years ago, the predominantly agricultural people from the same region were appreciably shorter (averaging five feet three inches for men and just five feet for women), indicating a nutritional decline. Findings from the excavation of burial mounds in the Illinois and Ohio River valleys also point to negative health consequences for populations that turned to maize cultivation in the twelfth century. When compared with foragers who preceded them, maize farmers had a 50 percent increase in tooth enamel defects (hypoplasia) caused by malnutrition, four times the incidence of iron deficiency anemia, and a 300 percent increase in bone lesions indicative of infectious disease (M. N. Cohen and Armelagos 1984). With the rise of agriculture in the area, the average life expectancy dropped from twenty-six to nineteen years.

Early farmers paid a high price for their newfound food-getting strategy. First, early farmers were limited in the number of crops they could plant and still have time to hunt and gather items to balance their diet. They ran the risk of serious malnutrition or even starvation if those crops failed. Second, the increased population densities brought people into closer contact with one another and consequently made everyone more susceptible to both parasitic and infectious diseases. And finally, food production had dramatic social effects. The egalitarianism of traditional hunting-and-gathering societies was replaced by increasing social inequality and other problems such as poverty, crime, war, aggression, and environmental degradation. Thus, even though the transition to food production is seen as a defining moment in human evolution, it certainly had some negative consequences.

HORTICULTURE Horticulture—also known as *subsistence agriculture* or *small-holder agriculture*—is small-scale, low-intensity farming on small plots. It involves the use of basic hand tools such as the hoe and the digging stick rather than plows and other machinery driven by animals or engines. Because horticulturalists produce low yields, which are consumed directly by the household, not much of a surplus is generated. Some horticulturalists raise domesticated animals, such as pigs or chickens, for both food and prestige. Horticultural societies, such as the Yanomamo, who live in the Amazon Basin of Venezuela and Brazil, are known to supplement their diet with occasional hunting and gathering of wild plants and animals (Chagnon 1992). Still other horticultural groups, such as the Samoans, supplement their crops with protein derived from fishing, while the Miskitos, indigenous people of coastal Nicaragua, fish and raise small domesticated livestock along with their horticultural practices. In Central America, Mayan horticulturalists augment their crops (corn, beans, squash, pumpkins, and chili peppers) with fruit-bearing trees such as papaya, avocado, and cacao.

A major technique of horticulturalists, especially those who live in tropical regions of the world, is **shifting cultivation**, sometimes called **swidden cultivation** or the **slash-and-burn method**. This technique involves clearing the land by manually cutting down the growth, burning it, and planting in the burned area. The ash residue serves as a fertilizer; however, soil nutrients are usually depleted within a few years. The land then lies fallow until the natural vegetation is restored, or it may be abandoned altogether. Slash-and-burn cultivating can eventually destroy the environment if fields are not given sufficient fallow time. In such cases the forests may be replaced by grasslands or the soil may be depleted of nutrients, which results in poverty for the farmers. Even though slash-and-burn cultivation involves rotating the areas that are

An Indian boy in Venezuela assists his family in slash-and-burn agriculture by setting fire to an old garden. The ash from the fire will restore the soil's fertility for the next growing season.

farmed, it does not necessarily follow that horticulturalists also move their homes.

The slash-and-burn system cannot support the high population densities that can be sustained by intensive agriculture because most of the land must be left fallow at any given time. However, some slash-and-burn farmers produce abundant harvests of tropical forest products without destroying the land. To illustrate, R. Jon McGee (1990) found that the Lacandon Maya of Chiapas, Mexico, grow more than forty different crops in their cleared fields (*milpas*). By spreading many crops over a *milpa*, the Lacandon are imitating both the diversity and the dispersal patterns found in the natural primary forest. Their tiered approach to farming mirrors the layers of vegetation in the tropical forest. For example, corn, beans, squash, and tomatoes are intercropped at ground level. Well above the surface crops are bananas and oranges, and root crops such as manioc and sweet potatoes are cultivated below the ground's surface. McGee points out that this form of slash-and-burn horticulture is efficient because the typical Lacandon Mayan family can feed itself while working fewer than half the days in a year.

The governments of many developing countries are interested in transforming traditional economies (such as slash-and-burn horticulture) into world market economies, thereby attracting foreign capital, providing wage-paying jobs, and raising a country's gross national product. These government officials in parts of Africa, Asia, and South America argue that by restricting (or prohibiting altogether) slash-and-burn horticulture, overall productivity will be increased, people will eat better and be healthier, and the export economy will grow. However, a major problem in these efforts to transform traditional horticulture has been that government officials often have different value assumptions from the local farmers whose culture they are trying to change. To illustrate, Jeffrey Brewer's (1988) study of small-scale horticulturalists in Indonesia demonstrated that government programs started with the assumption that wet rice agriculture is preferable to slash-and-burn cultivation because of its high return *per unit of land*. The local Indonesian horticulturalists, however, preferred their traditional slash-and-burn technique because of its relatively high return *per unit of labor*. Local farmers, in other words, preferred their traditional methods because they did not require as much labor and made fewer demands on their time. They valued their leisure time more than larger yields. This is extremely important ethnographic information for government planners because it will enable them to either scale down their costly efforts to eliminate slash-and-burn horticulture or design alternative programs that take the local values into account.

In another example, rural horticulturalists in Honduras were asked to shift from subsistence production—growing food to feed their family—to the production of chili peppers for the export market. The farmers did not support this initiative because, in their minds, chili peppers did not feed their families. It did not make sense to them to stop producing crops that fed their families and instead produce cash crops and then use the income to buy food to feed their families. Outsiders looking on may want to consider what is culturally valued; sometimes what outsiders value or believe is progress is not desired by members of the local community.

Today we find horticulture practiced among backyard gardeners and those who have transformed their yards into edible landscapes. Relying primarily on their own labor to plant and harvest for home consumption, these gardeners are providing families with fresh, homegrown produce. Horticulture still exists as a subsistence strategy in South and Central America as well as in certain areas of Central Africa, Southeast Asia, and Melanesia. It continues to work well where people have access to land on which to raise crops and livestock.

PASTORALISM Like horticulture, **pastoralism** first appeared in the neolithic period. This subsistence pattern, sometimes referred to as *animal husbandry,* involves herding, breeding, and using domesticated animals such as camels, cattle, goats, horses, llamas, reindeer, sheep, and yaks. Pastoralism is most frequently practiced in areas of the world where the terrain, soil, or rainfall is inadequate for agriculture but provides sufficient vegetation for livestock to graze. Pastoralism is generally associated with geographic mobility because herds must be moved periodically to exploit seasonal pastures and water sources (Barfield 1993; Sutton and Anderson 2009).

Anthropologists differentiate between two types of movement patterns among pastoralists: transhumance and nomadism. A third form of pastoralism found in industrial societies is known as sedentary ranching and dairy farming. **Transhumance** is the seasonal movement of livestock between upland and lowland pastures. Among pastoral groups that practice transhumance, there is a base location where the elders, women, children, and lactating animals reside and a herding camp for adolescent boys and young adult men to raise the nonlactating animals. This division of labor and residence helps to lessen the pressures placed on available pasturelands. **Nomadism** is the migration of whole villages that relocate when their animals need new pastures. The availability of water and pasture, government restrictions, and the demands of other food-getting strategies (such as cultivation) influence the cultural patterns of pastoral people. Even though some anthropologists lump all pastoralists in a single subsistence strategy, pastoralism is not a unified phenomenon.

A general characteristic of nomadic pastoralists is that they take advantage of seasonal variations in pasture so as to maximize the food supply of their herds. The Kazaks of Eurasia, for example, keep their livestock at lower elevations during the winter, move to the foothills in the spring,

Because this group of East African pastoralists treat land as belonging to everyone in society, you are unlikely to find any "No Trespassing" signs here.

and migrate to the high mountain pastures during the summer. Such seasonal movement provides optimal pasture and avoids climatic extremes that could negatively affect the livestock. Moving their animals at different times of the year avoids overgrazing and enables pastoralists to raise considerably more livestock than they could if they chose not to migrate.

The consensus among anthropologists is that pure pastoralists—those who get all of their food from livestock—are either extremely rare or nonexistent. Because livestock alone cannot meet all the nutritional needs of a population, most pastoralists need some grains to supplement their diets. Many pastoralists either combine the keeping of livestock with some form of cultivation or maintain regular trade relations with neighboring agriculturalists. Moreover the literature is filled with examples of nomadic pastoralists who produce crafts for sale or trade or find other wage-paying work. Thus many pastoralists have long engaged in nonpastoral activities, but they have always considered animal husbandry to be their identity and their livelihood.

It is clear that in pastoral societies livestock play a vital economic role not only as a food source but in other ways as well. Melville Herskovits (1924), an anthropologist who worked among East African pastoralists, found that cattle served three purposes, from which he derived the term *cattle complex*. First, cattle were an economic asset with a utilitarian purpose. Cattle were a source of food; their milk, blood, and meat were shared and sold; their dung was used for fertilizer, house building, and fuel; their urine was used as an antiseptic; their bones were used for tools and artifacts; their skins were used for clothing and shelter; and their strength provided a means of transportation or traction. Second, cattle had a social function, played a symbolic role, and were important status symbols: Large herds conveyed status to families or enabled sons to secure a wife (or wives). Livestock often influenced the social relationships among people in pastoral societies. For example, an exchange of livestock between the families of the bride and groom was required in many pastoral societies before a marriage was legitimized. In the event of an assault or a homicide, in some societies livestock was given to compensate the victim's family as a way of restoring normal social relations. The sacrifice of livestock at the grave sites of ancestor-gods was a way in which people kept in touch with their deities. Third, farmers were attached to their cattle; cattle were valued and adorned. In fact, among the Nuer, young boys were named after a favorite animal in their family's herd. These and other social uses of livestock remind us that domesticated animals in pastoral societies not only serve as the major food source but also are intimately connected to other parts of the culture, such as the systems of marriage, social control, and religion.

A modern form of pastoralism is practiced by cattle and sheep ranchers in western North America, Australia, New Zealand, Argentina, and a few other areas of the world. These ranchers do not identify themselves as subsistence pastoralists, but rather as businessmen who produce a commodity for national and international markets. These business ranchers use mechanized equipment such as trucks, airplanes, and helicopters to round up their animals. They are risk takers: They know that their livelihoods may be jeopardized by theft, diseases, or other natural disasters or the size of their herds may double in a few years and make them rich.

INTENSIVE AGRICULTURE Intensive agriculture (intensive cultivation) is today's most prevalent subsistence pattern. It relies on large-scale production practices that result in much more food being produced per acre than with other subsistence patterns, and it supports larger populations. Intensive farming methods began about five thousand years ago as the human population grew beyond the environment's carrying capacity using horticulture and pastoralism. Intensive agriculture is characterized by the use of the plow, draft animals, or machinery to plow, fertilize, and irrigate. The system is designed to produce a surplus, and as a consequence of increased productivity, there is an increase in the human carrying capacity. Cultivators who invested their time and energy in a piece of land developed the notion of property rights and established permanent settlements.

Archaeologists contend that the first intensive agricultural societies were the ancient civilizations in Egypt, Mesopotamia (now Iraq and eastern Syria), India and Pakistan, northern China, Mesoamerica, and western South America (Sutton and Anderson 2009). Today intensive agriculture is the primary food-production pattern in all developed nations except those that are too arid or too cold for any form of farming. Over the last century, large-scale agricultural techniques spread rapidly throughout the world with the introduction of farm machinery, seed varieties, and commercially produced fertilizers, pesticides, and herbicides. This essentially resulted in the industrialization of farming in the richer nations (discussed below).

There is a price for this greater productivity, however, because intensive agriculture requires a large investment of both labor and capital. First, in terms of labor, agriculturalists devote hours of hard work to prepare the land. In hilly areas the land is terraced and maintained, and irrigation systems may involve drilling wells, digging trenches, or building dikes. All of these activities increase the land's productivity enormously but are extremely labor intensive. Second, intensive agriculture, as compared to horticulture, requires a much greater investment of capital in plows (which must be maintained), mechanical pumps (which can break down), draft animals (which can become sick and die), and farm inputs such as fuel, fertilizers, seeds, and other needs.

Intensive agriculture is closely associated with both higher levels of productivity and more settled communities. In fact, not until early horticultural societies had developed more intensive forms of agriculture could civilizations exist (that is, urban societies). Surplus crops produced by farmers were sold in village markets. Some of these market centers increased in population over time and became towns and eventually cities. People were liberated to engage in activities other than food production. New occupations emerged, such as merchants, craftsmen, professional soldiers, priests, rulers, and bureaucrats. Structural changes became more apparent as societies became more stratified (that is, marked by greater class differences). Political and religious hierarchies evolved to manage the economic surpluses and mediate among the different socioeconomic classes. Eventually state systems of government (complete with bureaucracies, written records, taxation, a military, and public works projects) were established. These structural changes would not have occurred without the development of a reliable system of food production that could sustain a larger population. Intensive agricultural production provided both the opportunity and the commodities and forever changed the course of history in many parts of the world.

INDUSTRIAL AGRICULTURE As we have seen, the domestication of plants and animals followed by the intensification of agriculture had revolutionary consequences for food production. A third major revolution in our capacity to feed ourselves occurred several hundred years ago with the industrial revolution. **Industrialization** in food production relies on technological sources of energy. Water and wind power (harnessed by waterwheels and windmills) were used in the early stages of the industrial period, but today industrial agriculture uses motorized equipment such as tractors and combines (powered by fossil fuels and biodiesel). The science of biochemistry has been applied to modern agriculture to produce fertilizers, pesticides, herbicides, and high-yielding seed varieties, all of which increase the yields of food and nonfood commodities (for example, cotton and tobacco).

Industrialized agriculture requires heavy machinery and many pieces of farm equipment for the annual corn harvest, a process that is no longer a family enterprise on some farms.

Farmers operating in industrialized societies today have a wealth of new technology at their disposal to increase productivity. Industrial farmers now use the Internet to access a wide range of agricultural information—from equipment sales to pesticide use to marketing opportunities. Moreover new systems of gathering weather information help farmers manage their crops. Other farmers equip their grain-harvesting combines with transmitters that allow a GPS satellite to track their exact position in their fields at any given time (Friedman 1999a). The sophisticated technology now available enables farmers to keep records on how much they harvest from each acre of land as well as the precise crop variety, water level, and fertilizer that will produce the highest possible yield on each parcel of land. This high-tech farm management is good for the environment because it uses fertilizer more economically, and it is good for the farmer because it increases the overall yield per unit of land. With all of this information at their fingertips, farmers are able to assess their risk and react quickly to protect their crops and inform their buyers or consumers about how their crops are responding.

Industrial agriculture requires complex systems of market exchange because of its highly specialized nature, the high yields produced, and the distance some crops travel before they are eaten or manufactured into something edible. Moreover, within the past several decades, industrial agriculture has witnessed even more changes with the dramatic expansion of agribusiness—large-scale agricultural enterprises that involve the latest technology and a sizable salaried workforce. Most industrial farmers engage in monoculture, the production of a single commodity on vast acreage. Some Canadian, U.S., South American, Asian, and African farmers have become experts at producing single commodities (corn, soybeans, wheat, tea, coffee, pineapples, bananas, wheat, tobacco, cotton, or flowers) rather than a wide variety of products for subsistence. With the income earned from the sale of the monoculture commodities, industrial farmers purchase food items for their households.

A recent consequence of this form of agribusiness is the demise of small-scale farms that used mainly family labor. Corporate farms have replaced farmers with wage workers—displaced farmers or immigrant farm workers who are paid low wages—to keep the "new" industrial farm working at optimum efficiency. Where we find large-scale export agriculture we tend to find transnational corporations controlling the farming enterprise. Many plantations are owned by multinational corporations such as Dole Food Company and Chiquita Brands International. In fact, today Kenya is one of the leading exporters of roses to Europe, while Colombia and Ecuador are the leading exporters of bananas to the United States.

Gradually the developed world is becoming more concerned with the agriculture and food system, the environment, and personal health. In some regions of the United States and Europe, the number of small-scale farmers and farmers' markets has been increasing. Their success comes as a result of people supporting a local food system and wanting to buy food that has not traveled too far from field to plate. Community projects are strengthening ties between food consumers and food producers (Goodall 2005). In fact the International Slow Food Movement that Carlos Petrini established in 1986 in Italy now has tens of thousands of members who want to help preserve traditional ways of farming, protect heritage animals, and promote native seed varieties along with traditional recipes. These shifting interests in food and food production help smaller farmers hold on to their land and their way of life.

While industrial agriculture has produced farms of enormous size and productivity, these changes have come at a high cost. For modern North Americans to have a wide variety of foods in their diets, which are frequently eaten out of season or year round, additional expenses are incurred for the processing, transporting, and marketing of these foods. The average food product purchased at a U.S. supermarket has traveled nearly 1,500 miles before a consumer takes it home (Pirog 2003). In addition, industrial agriculture has been responsible for considerable environmental destruction. For example, in various parts of the world, the water tables are lowered, water fauna have been destroyed by pesticides, aquifers are contaminated by leaching chemicals, soil is salinized from over-irrigation, and the air has been polluted by crop spraying. And, as if this were not enough, the twenty-first century is witnessing a proliferation of genetically modified seeds for corn, soybeans, and cotton. The long-term use of these seeds may have harmful effects on traditional seed varieties (Shiva 2000; J. Smith 2003). Although more people are being fed from industrial agriculture today, the litany of the negative effects of agriculture is almost endless. In fact, Jared Diamond (1987) has described agriculture as "the worst mistake in the history of the human race."

Out in the Real World: Niche Marketing for Local Commercial Fishermen

Commercial fishing has long been a critical part of North Carolina's coastal heritage and local economy. Early fishing communities were established several hundred years ago. Fishing families worked the waters, built boats, made nets, and sold and traded seafood. Many of the descendants of these families still live in the area; however, few have been able to continue the legacy as full-time fishermen. Today quintessential fishing communities along Carteret County's coastline struggle to maintain a viable fishing industry. While no one thing explains the decline of the fishing industry, a collection of events and conditions makes it impossible for local commercial fishermen to sustain their livelihood through fishing.

One applied anthropologist (your author Susan Andreatta) conducted interviews with fishermen and learned that they have weathered storms, hurricanes, and government regulations. However, she also found out that today's fishermen encounter additional pressures such as high fuel prices, shark bites on nets, turtles squashing crab cages, and loss of markets in which to sell their catch. Competition from imported seafood has displaced fresh, local seafood, and changes in the environment, government policy, and market conditions have negatively affected not only the local fishing industry but also those people who own or are employed at fish houses, fish processors, and local restaurants as well as drivers of refrigerated seafood trucks.

In 2006 Andreatta embarked on a multiyear applied project designed to help Carteret County fishermen increase their seafood sales. The project focused on creating a direct marketing program that would educate residents and visitors to seek out and purchase local seafood and expand these niche marketing opportunities. She worked with members of the fishing community, who in 2006 trademarked *Carteret Catch*™, a branding program with a logo to identify seafood caught by commercial fishermen from Carteret County.

Drawing on participatory action research, Andreatta involved fishermen, members of *Carteret Catch*™, and others working in the industry in developing an alternative social marketing approach to influence a behavioral change (Van Willigen 2002). They wanted consumers to more easily recognize and purchase local seafood.

The inspiration for a direct-marketing strategy for the fishing industry came from Andreatta's work with local farmers in North Carolina— in particular, she worked with small-scale farmers who relied on farmers' markets and community-supported agriculture (CSA) plans to sell their local produce. CSAs are direct-marketing arrangements in which families or individuals prepay a farmer in the winter for fresh produce they will receive when the harvest is available. This early payment helps the farmer buy seeds and maintain the farm at a time when no funds are coming in. These prepaying people share the risk and the bounty with the farmer. From this direct-marketing approach for farmers emerged community-supported fisheries (CSFs) for fishermen (Andreatta and Parlier 2010).

To help sustain the local fishing industries, the public was encouraged to prepay for a season of locally caught fish in the form of a CSF, to buy directly from fish house dealers or from roadside vendors known to sell local seafood, and to frequent restaurants known to purchase local seafood. The *Carteret Catch*™ branding program combined with CSF arrangements helped the public to identify which roadside stands, fish houses, and restaurants served local seafood. The public plays an important role in sustaining local fisheries by choosing where they spend their money and in this case what seafood they purchase.

By 2010 CSFs and branding programs expanded into other coastal areas in North Carolina, Maine, New Hampshire, South Carolina, Australia, and Nova Scotia (Andreatta, Nash, and Bath-Martin 2011). In addition one fish retailer and member of *Carteret Catch*™ began transporting seafood to Duke University in Durham, North Carolina. This retailer now has members signed up for a weekly distribution and a waiting list for others interested in joining. CSFs have started a new trend in the state as the public seeks to support local fishermen and eat local seafood.

QUESTIONS FOR FURTHER THOUGHT

1. How are community-supported agriculture arrangements different from community-supported fishing arrangements?

2. What ideas do you have to help small farmers and fishermen maintain their subsistence strategy? What suggestions do you have to protect the environment for farmers and fishermen?

SUMMARY

1. For any society to survive, it must develop strategies and technologies for procuring or producing food from its environment. Five major food-procurement strategies are hunting and gathering, horticulture, pastoralism, intensive agriculture, and industrial agriculture.

2. Though lacking high levels of technology, many small-scale societies have made successful adaptations to their natural environments—hence their long-time survival.

3. The success of various food-getting strategies depends on the interaction between a society's technology and its environment. Environments influence rather than determine food-getting practices. The level of technology that any society has at its disposal is critical to adapting and using the environment.

4. Carrying capacity is the maximum number of people a particular society can support given the available resources. Permanent damage to the environment usually results if a culture exceeds its carrying capacity.

5. Hunting and gathering, the oldest form of food getting, relies on procuring foods that are naturally available in the environment. Approximately ten thousand years ago, people for the first time began to domesticate plants and animals; this transition is called the neolithic revolution.

6. Compared to societies with other food-getting practices, hunting-and-gathering societies tend to have low-density populations, are nomadic or seminomadic, live in small social groups, and occupy remote, marginally useful areas of the world.

7. Horticulture, a form of small-scale plant cultivation, relies on simple technology and produces low yields for home consumption with little or no surpluses. The slash-and-burn method of cultivation involves clearing the land by burning the vegetation and then planting seeds in the fertile ash residue.

8. Pastoralism, keeping domesticated livestock as a source of food, is usually practiced in areas of the world that are unable to support any type of cultivation. Pastoralists are most often nomadic or seminomadic, and they have regular contact with farmers as a way of supplementing their diet.

9. Intensive agriculture, a more recent phenomenon than horticulture, uses technology such as irrigation, fertilizers, and mechanized equipment to produce high crop yields capable of supporting large populations. Intensive agriculture is usually associated with permanent settlements, cities, high levels of labor specialization, and the production of surpluses to be sold or traded in a market.

10. Industrial agriculture relies on high levels of energy and technology (such as tractors and combines), inputs, high-yielding seeds, a mobile labor force, and a complex system of markets.

KEY TERMS

Health care workers in the Congo dress appropriately when working with patients who have highly infectious and lethal diseases such as Ebola.

© REUTERS/MSF/Pascale Zintzen/HO/Landov

CHAPTER 7

Kinship, Marriage, and Family

KINSHIP AND FAMILY PATTERNS HELP LOCAL VILLAGERS SLOW DOWN THE SPREAD OF INFECTIOUS DISEASES

Epidemics, the widespread occurrences of infectious disease, have killed millions of people over time, even when some of the outbreaks might have been prevented. Epidemics of the plague, smallpox, measles, cholera, typhoid, malaria, tuberculosis, West Nile virus, SARS, HIV/AIDS, and Ebola have shaped human history. So how can anthropologists help to prevent the outbreak of some infectious diseases?

Two anthropologists who have been working as medical anthropologists give an account of their experiences in *Ebola, Culture and Politics: The Anthropology of an Emerging Disease* (2008). A husband-and-wife team, Barry and Bonnie Hewlett (Bonnie is also a nurse) describe working in Uganda, Sudan, Gabon, and the Congo during and shortly after outbreaks of Ebola hemorrhagic fever. The Ebola virus is not new to Africa nor are deaths from this infectious disease.

From a *biomedical* perspective, Ebola hemorrhagic fever is known to kill 50–90 percent of its victims within seven days after infection. There are no treatments, pills, or vaccines for this disease, and worse yet, researchers do not know its origin. The suspected cause is direct contact with blood secretions or organs of infected persons or animals. "Transmission from game animals often occurs in African rural areas because domesticated meat is generally not available, and game meat is an important source of protein" (Hewlett and Hewlett 2008: 4). In the Congo the government banned the consumption of game meat as a way to prevent the spread of the Ebola virus.

As long-time ethnographers in Africa, the Hewletts brought cultural knowledge to their approach to developing a *biocultural* model (also known as an *ethnomedical* perspective) to explain how local villagers define Ebola and what strategies they use to cope with the disease. The Hewletts looked for cross-cultural patterns in the spread of Ebola and its implications for families, villages, and even countries. They also looked at the initiatives of national governments and international health care providers. By living in local villages, the Hewletts were able to obtain data through open-ended, semistructured interviews, focus groups, and unstructured discussions with as many people as possible who had a vested interest in efforts to control Ebola. They contacted men and women who were at risk, those who were suffering from the disease, and those who had survived, as well as nurses, doctors, and local healers involved in treating the disease.

It is from speaking with such a wide range of people that the Hewletts were able to develop intricate cultural models about the decision-making processes involved in the treatment of infected family members (2008: 34). From this biocultural approach, their research revealed a wide range of local beliefs about what Ebola is, how it is transmitted, how to treat it, and who should be treated. Some people blamed sorcery for the illness; others thought local healers spread the disease; and still others believed that sharing infected game such as gorilla or monkey meat contributed to the outbreaks.

The Hewletts were able to see patterns of behavior that contributed to exposure to Ebola. Most important, they found that local people already were doing things to manage the outbreaks. Local people isolated those who were infected or limited their contacts, kept children away from them, and sought treatment and advice from local healers as well as government health personnel. Infectious killing diseases are always present. The work of the Hewletts pointed out the need for outside health care providers and for national governments to work with local healers to define Ebola and develop ways to manage or control these epidemics.

QUESTIONS FOR FURTHER THOUGHT

1. What can we learn from a biocultural perspective of the Ebola virus?

2. What issues should outsiders consider when working cross-culturally on health-related matters?

In all known societies, people recognize a certain number of relatives who make up the basic social group generally called the family. This is not to imply, however, that all societies view the family in the same way. In fact humans have developed a wide variety of family types. To most middle-class North Americans, the family includes a husband and a wife and their children. To an East African herdsman, the family includes hundreds of kin related through both blood and marriage. Among the Hopi, the family is made up of a woman and her husband and their unmarried sons and married daughters, along with the daughters' husbands and children. Kinship is at the heart of social structure; it defines who our relatives are and are not. Whom a person marries, where he or she lives, from whom a person inherits property, and status all depend on the person's place within the kinship system. In all societies, it might not be an exaggeration to say that kinship relations are tantamount to social relations.

This chapter will examine the variety of family types found throughout the world as well as the practice of marriage that leads to the formation of families and the kinship systems that bind them together. An applied anthropologist may start out with a keen understanding of kinship and family, as the Hewletts did in the opening example, but then observe village life change dramatically in the face of extreme circumstances such as the spread of the Ebola virus. Thus one should keep in mind that the traditional social structures described in this chapter may be disrupted by epidemics, political violence, or other natural or human crises.

Whether we are considering small- or large-scale societies, kinship systems are important because they help people adapt to interpersonal and environmental challenges. Kinship systems are adaptive because they provide a plan for aligning people and resources in strategic ways. They set limits on sexual activity and on who can marry whom, they establish the parameters of economic cooperation between men and women, and they provide a basis for proper child-rearing. Moreover kinship systems often provide a mechanism for sharing certain pieces of property (such as land or cattle) that cannot be divided without being destroyed. Beyond the limits of the immediate family unit, kinship systems extend one's relationship to a much wider group of people. To illustrate, membership in a small, local group of kin enables an individual to draw on more distant kinsmen for protection or economic support during difficult times. Also, when small family groups are confronted with large-scale projects, they often recruit cooperative labor from among existing groups of extended kinsmen.

Kinship Defined

Kinship refers to the relationships—found in all societies—that are based on blood or marriage. Those people to whom we are related through birth or blood are our **consanguineal relatives**; those to whom we are related through marriage are our **affinal relatives**. Each society has a well-understood system of defining relationships between these different types of relatives. Every society, in other words, defines the nature of kinship interaction by determining which kin are more socially important than others, the terms used to classify various types of kin, and the expected forms of behavior between them.

The term **fictive kinship** is used for relationships that are determined by neither blood nor marriage. For example, the process of adoption creates a set of relationships between the adoptive parents and child that have all of the expectations of relationships based on descent or marriage. Often close friends of the family are referred to as *aunt* or *uncle,* even though they have no biological or marital relationship. And, of course, the godparent–godchild relationship, which carries with it all sorts of kinship obligations, often involves people who do not share blood or marriage connections. These examples remind us that it is possible to have kinship-like relationships without an actual biological or marital connection.

Using Kinship Diagrams

Although all societies have kinship systems, the definitions of the relationships between kin vary widely from one group to another. In different societies people with the same biological connection may be defined and

FIGURE 7.1
Kinship diagram symbols

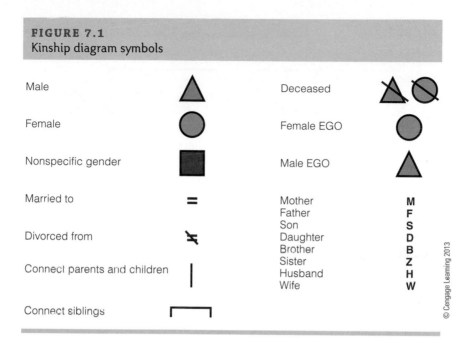

Male	▲	Deceased	▲ ⊘
Female	◯	Female EGO	◯
Nonspecific gender	■	Male EGO	▲
Married to	=	Mother	M
		Father	F
		Son	S
Divorced from	✗	Daughter	D
		Brother	B
Connect parents and children	❘	Sister	Z
		Husband	H
		Wife	W
Connect siblings	⌐¬		

© Cengage Learning 2013

labeled differently and are expected to behave differently toward one another. Before trying to sort out the complexities of different kinship systems, it will be helpful to introduce a form of shorthand used by cultural anthropologists in analyzing kinship systems.

As a way of simplifying kinship systems, anthropologists use kinship diagrams rather than relying on verbal explanations alone. In this standardized notational system, all kinship diagrams are viewed from a central point of reference (called *EGO*), the person from whose perspective we are tracing the relationships. All kinship diagrams use the symbols in Figure 7.1.

Starting with our point of reference (EGO), we can construct a hypothetical family diagram, as in Figure 7.2 on the next page. We refer to all of the people in the diagram with the following symbols:

1. Father's sister (FZ)
2. Father's sister's husband (FZH)
3. Father's brother's wife (FBW)
4. Father's brother (FB)
5. Father (F)
6. Mother (M)
7. Mother's sister's husband (MZH)
8. Mother's sister (MZ)
9. Mother's brother (MB)

FIGURE 7.2
Generic kinship diagram

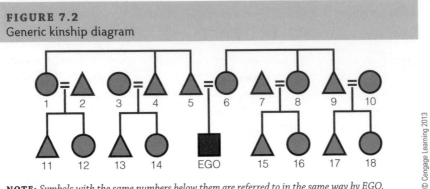

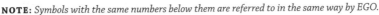

NOTE: *Symbols with the same numbers below them are referred to in the same way by EGO.*

© Cengage Learning 2013

10. Mother's brother's wife (MBW)
11. Father's sister's son (FZS)
12. Father's sister's daughter (FZD)
13. Father's brother's son (FBS)
14. Father's brother's daughter (FBD)
15. Mother's sister's son (MZS)
16. Mother's sister's daughter (MZD)
17. Mother's brother's son (MBS)
18. Mother's brother's daughter (MBD)

Principles of Kinship Classification

No kinship system in the world uses a different term for every single relative. Instead all kinship systems group relatives into certain categories, refer to them by the same term, and expect people to behave toward them in a similar fashion. How a particular society categorizes relatives depends on which principles of classification it uses.

In some kinship systems—our own being a good example—distinctions between kin depend on generation. Mothers, fathers, and their siblings are always found in the first ascending generation, immediately above EGO; sons, daughters, nieces, and nephews are always one generation below EGO in the first descending generation; grandmothers and grandfathers are always two generations above EGO; and so forth.

The Formation of Descent Groups

Kinship systems play an important role in helping people sort out how they should behave toward various relatives. In anthropological terms **kinship systems** encompass all of the blood and marriage relationships that help people distinguish among different categories of kin, create rights and obligations among kin, and serve as the basis for the formation of certain types of kin groups. Some societies make distinctions among kinship categories based on whether people are related by blood (consanguineal kin) or through marriage (affinal kin). To illustrate, we distinguish between sons and sons-in-law and between sisters and sisters-in-law. However, we do not distinguish between mother's brother (a blood relative) and mother's sister's husband (an affinal relative), both of whom we call *uncle*.

Anthropologists also use the narrower term **descent** to refer to a person's kinship connections traced back through a number of generations. The rules of descent often provide the basis for the formation of social groups. Descent group members have a strong sense of identity, often share communally held property, provide economic assistance to one another, and engage in common civic and religious ceremonies. Descent groups serve as a mechanism for inheriting property and political office, regulating marriages, and structuring primary political units.

Rules of descent may be divided into two distinct types. The first is **unilineal descent**, whereby people trace their ancestry through either the mother's line or the father's line, but not both. Unilineal groups that trace their descent through the mother's line are called *matrilineal* descent groups; those tracing their descent through the father's line are called *patrilineal* descent groups. The second type of descent is **multilineal descent**, which is traced through both females and males and includes *ambilineal* descent and *bilateral* descent. Because descent is traced in mainstream North America according to the bilateral principle, many Euro-Americans have difficulty understanding unilineal descent.

Unilineal Descent Groups

For societies that rely on kinship groups to perform most of their social functions (such as marriage, dispute settlement, and religious ceremonies), unilineal descent groups provide a social organization with unambiguous roles and statuses. Because a person becomes a member of a unilineal descent group by birth, it is clear to which group one belongs. A person has no questions about her or his rights of inheritance, prestige, and social roles, including who may marry whom. Approximately 60 percent of all kinship systems found in the world are based on the unilineal principle.

PATRILINEAL DESCENT GROUPS Patrilineal descent is by far the more common of the two types of unilineal descent. It is practiced on all of the major continents and in a wide range of societies, including Native American groups (such as the Ojibwa and Dene), some East African farmers and pastoralists, the Kapauku Papuans of the New Guinea Highlands, and traditional Chinese. In societies with patrilineal descent groups, a person is related through the father, father's father, and so forth. In other words, a man, his own children, his brother's children (but not his sister's children), and his son's children (but not his daughter's children) are all members of the same descent group. Females must marry outside their own patrilineages, and the children a woman bears belong to the husband's lineage rather than to her own.

We will use traditional China to illustrate patrilineages because China is by far the largest patrilineal society in the world. The Chinese family, at least ideally, was made up of the patrilineage, comprising a man, his wife or wives, his sons, daughters-in-law, grandchildren, and great-grandchildren. When a son reached marriageable age, the extended family provided a wife for him. In most cases the wives came from other unrelated families, but sometimes Chinese couples adopted unrelated infant girls for the express purpose of providing future brides for their sons. Sons stayed with the patrilineage while females transferred to the husband's patrilineage, which helps to explain the Chinese preference for males. The residence pattern was patrilocal (see below), in which the wives lived with and became part of the husband's lineage. As in any patrilineal society, inheritance passed from the father to his son(s) and grandson(s).

In the United States and much of western Europe, parents are expected to give priority to the needs of their children. But in the Chinese family, the reverse is true: It is the children who have the major obligation to the family. Children must show deference, respect, and obedience to their parents for as long as the parents are alive. Children are obligated to provide for the comfort of their aging parents and, even after their death, must attend to the parents' spiritual needs through ceremonies of ancestor worship. Sons feel pressure to perpetuate their father's lineage by producing sons of their own.

MATRILINEAL DESCENT GROUPS In a **matrilineal descent** system, a person belongs to the mother's descent group, which comprises a woman, her siblings, her own children, her sisters' children, and her daughters' children. Matrilineal descent groups make up about 15 percent of the unilineal descent groups found among contemporary societies. They are found in several areas of the world, including some northern Native Americans (such as the Navajo, Hopi, Cherokee, and Iroquois), the Truk and Trobriand Islanders of the Pacific, and the Bemba and Ashanti in Africa.

It is important not to confuse matrilineal descent with **matriarchy,** in which the women in a society have more authority and decision-making prerogatives than the men. In most cases where matrilineal descent is practiced, men retain the lion's share of the power and authority.

To illustrate, in a patrilineal society a man passes his property and hereditary political office to his own son, whereas in a matrilineal society property and office pass from a man to his sister's son. In fact, in a matrilineal society the most important male relationship a man has is with his sister's son (or mother's brother).

A good example of a matrilineal society is the Zuni people of New Mexico, one of the best-described and most typical groups among the western Pueblos. The Zuni are divided into thirteen matrilineal clans, each comprising several lineages. The household, which is the essential economic unit, is composed of a woman or a group made up of the grandmother, her sisters, and their daughters who are descended through females. Because the Zuni practice matrilocal residence, husbands live with their wives and their wives' matrilineal kin. The women are the permanent residents of the house and are bound together by their joint care of all the sacred objects in the house.

This Zuni grandmother and granddaughter from New Mexico practice matrilineal descent.

Just as wives are viewed as strangers or outsiders in the traditional Chinese extended family, so are the husbands in the Zuni family. Husbands divide their energy and allegiances between their wife's matrilineage and that of their mothers and sisters. When important ceremonial activities need to be conducted, it is the married brothers (presently married and living with the matrilineages of their wives) who return to perform them at their mother's house. The men perform economic roles for their wives but ritual roles for their own matrilineages. The Zuni man who has the highest prestige is not the wealthiest in a material sense but rather the one who performs ceremonial roles with his family's religious fetishes.

Multilineal Descent Groups

Some societies have kinship systems that are not based on the unilineal principle. Anthropologists call these multilineal descent groups and classify them into two basic types: ambilineal descent and bilateral descent. Some societies practice a form of descent in which kinship is traced both matrilineally and patrilineally. In such societies an individual belongs to both the mother's and the father's lineages. Descent under such a system is matrilineal for some purposes and patrilineal for others. For example, movable property such as small livestock or agricultural produce may be inherited from the mother's side of the family, whereas nonmovable property such as land may be inherited from the father's side.

AMBILINEAL DESCENT In societies that practice **ambilineal descent**, parents have a choice of affiliating their children with either kinship group. Compared with unilineal systems, which restrict one's membership to either the mother's or the father's group, ambilineal systems are more flexible because they allow for individual choice concerning group affiliation. In some cases the parents are expected to choose the group with which their children will eventually affiliate. Other systems allow the individual to move continuously through life from one group to another, provided he or she affiliates with one descent group at a time. Still other systems permit overlapping membership with a number of groups at the same time. As a general rule, however, the greater the flexibility in membership, the weaker the group's loyalties, cohesiveness, and impact on the lives of its members.

BILATERAL DESCENT In societies (such as mainstream U.S. society) that practice **bilateral descent**, a person is related equally to both the mother's and the father's sides of the family. A bilateral system tends to be symmetrical to the extent that what happens on one side of the kinship diagram also happens on the other side. In other words, the grandparents, aunts, uncles, and cousins are treated equally on both sides of the family. Bilateral systems create links from both sides of the family but usually include only close kin from a few generations.

The kinship group recognized in a bilateral system is known as the *kindred*—a group of closely related relatives connected through both parents to one living relative. In bilateral systems no two individuals (except siblings) have the same kindred because it is based on a network of relatives. Moreover kindreds cannot perform the same functions— such as joint ownership of property, common economic activities, regulation of marriage, or mutual assistance—as unilineal groups. This loosely structured network of relatives works particularly well in a society that highly values individuality, personal independence, and geographic mobility.

Bilateral descent is adaptive for small-scale foraging societies, such as the Ju/'hoansi of Botswana and Namibia, but for different reasons than those found in economically complex societies. In small-scale societies that are geographically mobile and have scarce resources, bilateral descent enables people to make claims on a large set of kinsmen who may be dispersed over a wide area. They are able to draw on their kindred during times of need, which offers a type of social security. Even though people may be both givers and receivers of assistance from relatives, over the long run this is an efficient and effective adaptive strategy.

Residence Patterns: Where Do Wives and Husbands Live?

In the same way that all societies establish rules of descent, they also set guidelines regarding where married couples will live. When two people marry in the United States, it is customary for the couple to take up residence in a place of their own, apart from the relatives of either spouse. This residence pattern is known as *neolocal residence* (that is, a new place). Most societies prescribe that newlyweds will live in the same household with or close to relatives of the wife or the husband. There are five types of residence patterns:

- **Patrilocal residence:** The married couple lives with or near the relatives of the husband's father.
- **Matrilocal residence:** The married couple lives with or near the relatives of the wife.
- **Avunculocal residence:** The married couple lives with or near the husband's mother's brother.
- **Ambilocal (bilocal) residence:** The married couple has a choice of living with either the relatives of the wife or the relatives of the husband.
- **Neolocal residence:** The married couple establishes an independent place of residence away from the relatives of either spouse.

To a significant degree, residence patterns are linked to the types of kinship systems in any society. For example, there is a reasonably close correlation between **patrilocal residence** and patrilineal descent and between matrilocal residence and matrilineal descent. To be certain, residence patterns do not *determine* kinship ideology, but social interaction between important categories of kin is easier if those kin live in close proximity to one another.

Marriage and the Family

Even though we use the terms *family* and *marriage* routinely, their meanings are ambiguous. Because social scientists and laypeople alike use these terms indiscriminately, it will be helpful to define them in more detail. A family is a social unit characterized by economic cooperation, the management of reproduction and child-rearing, and common residence. Family members, both adults and children, recognize certain rights and obligations toward one another. Marriage can be defined as a series of customs that formalize the relationship between adult partners within the family. Marriage is a socially approved union between two or more adult partners that regulates the sexual and economic rights and obligations between them.

A same-sex couple is legally married at the Arlington Street Church in Boston, Massachusetts.

Although many Westerners assume that marriage takes place only between men and women, others recognize same-sex marriage as being legitimate. In parts of West Africa, for example, a successful woman merchant, who may already be married to a man, may take a wife to help with the domestic duties while she is at work (Vallely 2010). Among the Nandi of Kenya, a woman may marry a woman (female husband) when the female bride's father has only daughters and no male heirs. Under such conditions the female husband arranges for a male consort to father children biologically for her bride.

Until very recently same-sex couples could not legally marry anywhere in the world. In a limited number of countries today, however, same-sex marriage has been legalized and thus protected under the law in the same way as heterosexual unions. The Netherlands was the first country to legalize same-sex marriage in April 2001, followed by Belgium, three Canadian provinces (British Columbia, Ontario, and Quebec), Spain, South Africa, Norway, and Sweden. In the United States, many same-sex couples are still fighting for the right to legally marry, but same-sex marriage is now legal in certain states (New Hampshire, Massachusetts, Connecticut, Iowa, Vermont, New York, and Washington, DC).

Marriage and the Family: Functions

The functionalist school of anthropologists, represented by Bronislaw Malinowski and Alfred Radcliffe-Brown, sought to understand how the parts of a culture contributed to the well-being of the society. Following some of the early functionalist research, we can better understand how the formation of families through marriage serves important functions for the societies in which they operate. One function is to create fairly stable relationships between men and women that regulate sexual mating and reproduction. A second social function of marriage is to provide a mechanism for regulating the sexual division of labor that exists to some extent in all societies. For reasons that are both biological and cultural, men in all societies perform some tasks and women perform

The family, such as this one in China, provides a structured environment that supports and meets the needs of children.

others. Likewise, marriage usually brings about domestic relationships that facilitate the exchange of goods and services.

Third, marriage creates family relationships that provide for the material, educational, and emotional needs of children. Unlike most other animal species, human children depend on adults for the first decade or more of their lives for their nourishment, shelter, and protection. Moreover human children require adults to provide the many years of cultural learning they need to develop into fully functioning members of the society. Even though it is possible for children to be reared largely outside a family unit (as is done on the kibbutzim of Israel), in most societies marriage creates a set of family relationships that provide the material, educational, and emotional support children need for their maturation.

Mate Selection: Who Is Out of Bounds?

Every society known to anthropology has established for itself rules that regulate mating (sexual intercourse). The most common form of prohibition is mating with certain types of kin who are defined by the society as being inappropriate sexual partners. The prohibition on mating with certain categories of relatives is known as the **incest taboo**. Incest taboos are different from rules that prohibit marrying certain kinsmen. Although incest taboos and rules prohibiting marrying certain kin often coincide with each other, it cannot be assumed that they always coincide.

The most universal form of incest taboo involves mating between members of the immediate (nuclear) family—that is, mothers and sons, fathers and daughters, and brothers and sisters—although there are several notable yet limited exceptions. For political, religious, or economic reasons, members of the royal families among the ancient Egyptians, Incas, and Hawaiians were permitted to mate with and marry their siblings, although this practice did not extend to the ordinary members of those societies. The incest taboo invariably extends beyond the scope of the immediate or nuclear family, however. In some, but not all, states in the United States, people are forbidden by law from mating with their first cousins. In some non-Western societies, the incest taboo may extend to large numbers of people on one side of the family but not on the other. For example, a man is permitted (even encouraged) to mate with and marry the daughter of his mother's brother (a first cousin or a *cross cousin;* see page 183) but is strictly prohibited from doing so with the daughter of his mother's sister (also a first cousin or a *parallel cousin;* see page 183). Given that incest taboos are universally found throughout the world, anthropologists have long been interested in explaining their origins and persistence.

Mate Selection: Whom Should You Marry?

As we have seen, every society defines a set of kin with whom a person is to avoid marriage and sexual intimacy. Beyond this notion of incest, people in all societies are faced with rules either restricting their choice of marriage partners or strongly encouraging the selection of certain people as highly desirable mates. These are known as rules of **exogamy** (marrying outside of a certain group) and **endogamy** (marrying within a certain group).

Rules of Exogamy

Because of the universality of the incest taboo, all societies have rules about marrying outside a certain group of kin. These are known as rules of exogamy. In societies such as the United States and Canada, the exogamous group extends only slightly beyond the nuclear family. It is considered either illegal or inadvisable to marry one's first cousin and, in some cases, one's second cousin, but beyond that one can marry other more distant relatives and encounter only mild disapproval. In societies that are based on unilineal descent groups, however, the exogamous group is usually the lineage, which can include hundreds of people, or even the clan, which can include thousands of people who are unmarriageable. Thus, when viewed cross-culturally, rules of exogamy based on kinship do not appear to be based on the closeness of blood ties.

Rules of Endogamy

In contrast to exogamy, the rule of endogamy requires a person to select a mate from within one's own group. Hindu castes in traditional India, for example, are strongly endogamous, believing that to marry below one's caste will result in serious ritual pollution. In addition to caste, endogamy may be applied to other social units, such as to the village or local community, as was the case among the Incas of Peru, or to racial groups, as was practiced in the Republic of South Africa for much of the twentieth century.

Even though there are no strongly sanctioned legal rules of endogamy in the United States, people often marry within their own group based on class, ethnicity, religion, and race. General social segregation by class, coupled with parental and peer pressure to "marry your own kind," results in a high level of endogamy in complex Western societies such as the United States.

Arranged Marriages

In Western societies, with their strong emphasis on individualism, mate selection is largely a decision made jointly by the prospective bride and groom. Aimed at satisfying the emotional and sexual needs of the individual, the choice of mates in Western society is based on such factors as physical attractiveness, emotional compatibility, and romantic love. Even though absolute freedom of choice may be influenced by social class, ethnicity, and religion, individuals in most contemporary Western societies are free to marry anyone they please.

In many societies, however, the interests of the families are so strong that marriages are **arranged**. Family members of the prospective bride and groom handle the negotiations, and for all practical purposes, the decision of whom one will marry is made primarily by one's parents or other influential relatives. In certain cultures, such as parts of traditional Japan, India, and China, future marriage partners are betrothed while they are still children. All such cases of **arranged marriage**, wherever they may be found, are based on the cultural assumption that because marriage is a union of two kin groups rather than merely two individuals, it is far too significant an institution to be based on something as trivial as physical attractiveness or romantic love.

Arranged marriages are often found in societies that have elaborate social hierarchies; perhaps the best example is Hindu India. Indian arranged marriages are further reinforced by other traditional Indian values and beliefs. Fathers, it was traditionally held, sinned if they failed to marry off their daughters before puberty. For centuries Hindu society has viewed females as lustful beings who tempt males with their sexual favors. Thus a girl had to be married at an early age to protect herself and the reputation of her family, as well as the men who might become sinners.

As a result of this belief, in certain parts of India girls marry at a very young age. Although the average age at marriage for females in India has been rising modestly over the past thirty years, the practice of child marriage is still widespread. According to UNICEF's "State of the World's Children—2009 Report," 47 percent of India's women aged twenty to twenty-four were married before the legal age of eighteen, and the rate was even higher (56 percent) in rural areas. The report concluded that four of every ten child marriages (under eighteen years of age) in the world occur in India. Even though the Indian government passed a law in 1978 setting the minimum age of marriage for females at eighteen, the law has been largely unenforced owing to cultural conservatism and the sheer size of the Indian population.

Anthropologist Serena Nanda (1992) reminds us that arranging marriages in India is serious business. In addition to making certain that a mate is selected from one's own caste, parents are careful to arrange marriages for their children that take into consideration such factors as level of education, physical attractiveness, compatibility with future in-laws, and level of maturity.

In many cases today, however, matchmaking family members are being rendered obsolete by an explosion of matrimonial websites. Would-be brides and grooms from India (as well as Indians living abroad) can go to websites with URLs such as Asianmatches.com, Suitablematch.com, and Matrimonials.com, where they can search for the ideal partner according to language, religion, caste, level of education, occupation, and even height, complexion, or astrological sign. By participating in these electronic matchmaking services, Indian young people are essentially agreeing with the traditional notion of arranged marriages but asking for (and getting) more input into the process. These new high-speed matrimonial websites greatly expand the pool of potential candidates, increase the amount of information that is available for prescreening, and give the bride and groom more time to make up their minds. Traditional Indian parents are willing to move to "assisted marriages" largely because they are more efficient and are likely to lead to what both parents and children want: strong, long-lasting marriages between compatible partners and compatible families. In fact many parents today are searching these matrimonial websites on behalf of their unmarried sons and daughters.

Even though mate selection in North America generally is a matter of individual choice, many singles are not opposed to seeking help. Internet matchmaking services used by North Americans focus on dating, romance, and finding the right relationship, with marriage as a more distant goal. Online dating services have millions of subscribers and generate hundreds of millions of dollars in revenue each year. They have become a normal part of the singles scene for people of all ages. One of the leading online matchmaking services is eHarmony, which, according to a Harris survey, was responsible for about 2 percent of all marriages in 2007—or nearly 120 weddings a day (Tierney 2008).

Preferential Cousin Marriages

A somewhat less coercive influence on mate selection than arranged marriages is found in societies that specify a preference for choosing certain categories of relatives as marriage partners. A common form of preferred marriage is **preferential cousin marriage**, which is practiced in one form or another in most of the major regions of the world. Some kinship systems distinguish between two different types of first cousins: cross cousins and parallel cousins. **Cross cousins** are children of siblings of the opposite sex— that is, one's mother's brothers' children and one's father's sisters' children. **Parallel cousins**, on the other hand, are children of siblings of the same sex (the children of one's mother's sisters and one's father's brothers). In societies that make such a distinction, parallel cousins, who are considered family members, are called *brother* and *sister* and thus are excluded as potential marriage partners. Cross cousins are not thought of as family members, but are considered by some societies as preferred marriage partners, because such a union maintains the ties between kin groups established by the marriages that took place in the preceding generation.

The Levirate and Sororate

Individual choice also tends to be limited by another form of mate selection that requires a person to marry the husband or wife of deceased kin. The **levirate** is the custom whereby a widow is expected to marry the brother (or some close male relative) of her dead husband. Usually any children fathered by the woman's new husband are considered to belong legally to the dead brother rather than to the actual father. This custom serves as a form of social security for the widow and her children and preserves the rights of the husband's family to her future children. The levirate, practiced in a wide variety of societies in Oceania, Asia, Africa, and India, is closely associated with placing a high value on having male heirs so that a man's lineage will not die out. In recent times this practice is coming under question because of unintended consequences related to the spread of HIV/AIDS and outmigration in search of employment.

The **sororate**, which comes into play when a wife dies, is the practice of a widower marrying the sister (or some close female relative) of his deceased wife. If the deceased spouse has no sibling, the family of the deceased is under a general obligation to supply some equivalent relative as a substitute. For example, in societies that practice the sororate, a widower may receive, as a substitute wife, the daughter of his deceased wife's brother.

Number of Spouses

In much the same way that societies have rules regulating whom one may or may not marry, they have rules specifying how many mates a person may or should have. Cultural anthropologists have identified three major types of marriage based on the number of spouses permitted: **monogamy** (the marriage of one man to one woman at a time), **polygyny** (the marriage of a man to two or more women at the same time), and **polyandry** (the marriage of a woman to two or more men at the same time).

Monogamy

The practice of having only one spouse at a time is so widespread in the United States and Canada that most people have great difficulty imagining any other marital alternative. For most North Americans, sharing a spouse is unthinkable. Any person who chooses to take more than one marriage partner at a time is in direct violation of conventional norms, most religious standards, and the law.

Interestingly, many societies that practice monogamy circumvent the notion of lifelong partnerships by either permitting extramarital affairs (provided they are conducted discreetly) or practicing **serial monogamy** (taking a number of different spouses one after another rather than at the same time). In fact serial monogamy is common in the United States, Canada, and much of western Europe.

Polygyny

Even though monogamy is widely practiced in the Western world, the overwhelming majority of world cultures do not share a monogamous tradition. Polygyny is practiced widely in traditional India and China and remains a preferred form of marriage throughout Asia, Africa, and the Middle East. There are numerous references to polygyny in the Old Testament of the Bible.

Although North America is adamantly monogamous, the practice of having more than one wife at a time does exist, particularly in the state of Utah. Although the Church of Jesus Christ of Latter-Day Saints outlawed polygyny in 1890, the practice persists on a small scale by those who have left the church and started their own religions. Officially polygyny is prohibited by both the church and the state of Utah, but violations are generally not prosecuted. Some people practice polygyny today because of its deep-seated religious significance. Others practice it because they consider it a desirable lifestyle choice.

Many cultures that practice polygyny today are small-scale societies with small populations. Even in societies where polygyny is most intensively practiced, one would not expect to find more than 35 percent of the men actually having two or more wives. Polygyny in these societies is the *ideal*, not the usual, form of marriage. There are a number of reasons most men in polygynous societies never acquire more than one wife. First, any marriage requires the approval and financial support of kinsmen, and this support is not always easy to obtain. Second, in some polygynous societies, it is considered inappropriate for men of low rank to seek additional wives, so a certain segment of the males are restricted to being monogamous. And third, the management of two or more wives and their children within a household requires administrative skills. In fact, in some African societies, the word for *co-wife* is derived from the root word for *jealousy*.

Polyandry

Polyandry, the mirror image of polygyny, is the marriage of a woman to two or more men at the same time. A much rarer form of plural marriage than polygyny, polyandry is found in fewer than 1 percent of the societies of the world, most notably in Tibet, Nepal, and India. Polyandry may be fraternal (where the husbands are brothers) or nonfraternal.

Perhaps the best-known case of polyandry was found among the Toda of southern India, who practiced the fraternal variety. Traditionally when a woman married a man, she also became the wife of all of his brothers, including even those who had not yet been born. Marriage privileges rotated among the brothers. Even though all of the brothers lived together with the wife in a single household, there was little competition or sexual jealousy. When the wife became pregnant, paternity was not necessarily ascribed to the biological father (genitor) but was determined by a ceremony that established a social father (pater), usually the oldest brother. Today these customs are changing slowly among the Toda. With fewer early marriages, girls are able to get an education and further their dreams rather than marrying and bearing children at an early age. Some girls now work in embroidery factories. Neighboring communities have taken over the Todas' land, thus limiting their ability to raise buffalo and grain, which was the work that Toda men did to care for their families.

Economic Considerations of Marriage

Most societies view marriage as a binding contract between at least the principal partners and in many cases between their families. The contract specifies the transfer of certain rights between the parties involved—legal rights to children and rights of the spouses to each other's economic goods and services. Often the transfer of rights is accompanied by the transfer of some type of economic consideration. These transactions, which may take place either before or after the marriage, can be divided into three categories: bridewealth, bride service, and dowry.

Bridewealth

Bridewealth is the compensation given upon marriage by the family of the groom to the family of the bride. Although bridewealth is practiced in most regions of the world, it is perhaps most widely found in Africa. Bridewealth is paid in a wide variety of currencies, but in almost all cases the commodity used for payment is highly valued in the society. For example, traditionally reindeer were given as bridewealth by the reindeer-herding Chukchee, sheep by the Navajo of the American southwest, and cattle by the pastoral Maasai and Nuer of eastern Africa. Marriage payments took the form of blankets for the Kwakiutl of the Pacific northwest and mats for the Fiji of Oceania.

Since the mid-twentieth century, bridewealth has become "monetized" (that is, money is becoming the typical medium of exchange). The transition from subsistence-based to cash-based economies has profoundly affected bridewealth practices. Traditionally bridewealth was an exchange of (often valuable) commodities from the groom's lineage to the bride's lineage. Because traditional bridewealth solidifies long-term ties between two entire lineages, the bride and groom did not benefit directly from the exchange. When bridewealth becomes tied to money that can be earned by the individual prospective groom, however, the close interdependence of family members becomes much less important.

Just as the commodities used in bridewealth transactions vary considerably, so does the amount of the transaction. To illustrate, a poor Nandi man of Kenya can obtain a bride with no more than a promise to transfer one animal to the bride's father. Yet a suitor from the Jie tribe of Uganda normally transfers fifty head of cattle and one hundred head of small stock (sheep and goats) to the bride's family before the marriage becomes official. The higher the bridewealth, as found among the Jie, the greater the chance the couple will stay together because of family pressure. Large bridewealth payments tend to make the negotiations between the two families more flexible and consequently more cordial. When the bridewealth is low, the addition or subtraction of one item becomes highly critical and is likely to create hard feelings between the two families.

The monetization of bridewealth in Oceania among the people of the Fiji Islands and Papua New Guinea is an indication that they view marriage increasingly as a financial transaction. According to Richard Marksbury (1993), people are postponing marriage until a later age, marriage payments are being used for personal fulfillment rather than redistributed among a wide range of kin, men are incurring serious debts in their attempt to meet their payments, marriages are becoming less stable, and traditional husband-wife roles are changing.

Cultural anthropologists consider bridewealth a rational and comprehensible part of traditional systems of marriage. For example, bridewealth was seen as security or insurance for the good treatment of the wife, as a mechanism to stabilize marriage by reducing the possibility of divorce, as a form of compensation to the bride's lineage for the loss of her economic potential and her childbearing capacity, as a symbol of the union between two large groups of kin, and as a mechanism to legitimize traditional marriages in much the same way that a marriage license legitimizes Western marriages.

Bride Service

In societies that have considerable material wealth, marriage considerations take the form of bridewealth paid in various commodities. But, because people in many small-scale societies cannot accumulate capital goods, men often give their labor to the bride's family instead of material goods; this is **bride service**. In some cases bride service is practiced to the exclusion of property transfer; in other cases it is a temporary condition, and the transfer of some property is expected at a later date. When a man marries under a system of bride service, he often moves in with his bride's family, works or hunts for them, and serves a probationary period of several weeks to several years.

Bride service is likely to be found in nomadic foraging societies such as the traditional Ju/'hoansi of southwestern Africa. According to Janice Stockard (2002: 28–29), Ju/'hoansi men select husbands for their daughters based largely, but not exclusively, on the hunting skills of the prospective groom. Suitors must demonstrate considerable hunting expertise before they are eligible to marry because the father-in-law will depend on the daughter's husband to provide him with adequate supplies of meat through a prolonged period of bride service.

Dowry

In contrast to bridewealth, a **dowry** is goods or money transferred in the opposite direction—from the bride's family to the groom or to the groom's family. The dowry is always provided by the bride or the bride's family, but the recipient of the goods varies from one culture to another. In some societies the dowry was given to the groom, who then had varying rights

Slovakian women are carrying dowry objects, which a bride receives from her family as her inheritance and brings with her into her new matrimonial home.

to dispose of it. In rural Ireland the dowry was given to the father of the groom in compensation for land, which the groom's father subsequently bequeathed to the bride and groom. The dowry was then used, wholly or in part, by the groom's father to pay the dowry of the groom's sister. The dowry is confined to Eurasia, most notably in medieval and renaissance Europe and in northern India.

More often than not, the dowry was not given to the husband but was something that the bride brought with her into the marriage. In traditional society in Cyprus, the dowry often consisted of a house or other valuable property. If the husband mistreated his wife or if the marriage ended in divorce, the woman was entitled to take the dowry with her. The dowry in this sense, very much like bridewealth, functioned to stabilize the marriage by providing a strong economic incentive not to break up.

Divorce

Just as all cultures have established a variety of ways of legitimizing marriages, they also have many ways of dealing with separation and **divorce**, the formal dissolution of a marriage. The divorce arrangements throughout the world vary widely according to the reasons for the divorce and how easy or difficult it is to get divorced. Although marriages break down in all societies, some societies are reluctant to officially sanction divorce and some even forbid it. At the other extreme, a Hopi woman in Arizona could divorce her husband quite easily by simply putting his belongings outside the door.

Family Structure

Cultural anthropologists have identified two fundamentally different types of family structure. The *nuclear* family is based on marital ties, whereas the *extended* family, a much larger social unit, is based on blood ties among three or more generations of kin.

The Nuclear Family

The **nuclear family** is a two-generation family formed around the marital union and the children. Even though the nuclear family to some degree is part of a larger family structure, it remains an autonomous and independent unit. That is, the everyday needs of economic support, child care, and social interaction are met within the nuclear family itself rather than by a wider set of relatives. In societies based on the nuclear family, it is customary for the couple to live apart from both sets of parents (neolocal residence). The nuclear family is most likely to be found in societies where geographic mobility is common. This certainly is the case in the United States and Canada.

In addition to being found in highly industrialized societies, the nuclear family is found in certain societies at the other end of the technological spectrum. In some foraging groups that live in environments with meager resources (such as the Inuit of northern Canada and the traditional Shoshone of Utah and Nevada), the nuclear family is the basic food-collecting unit. Thus both U.S. society and some small-scale food-collecting societies have adopted the nuclear family pattern because of their need for geographic mobility.

The Extended Family

An **extended family** consists of two or more nuclear families that are linked by blood ties. Most commonly this takes the form of a married couple living with one or more of their married children in a single household or homestead and under the authority of a family head. Such extended families, which are based on parent-child linkages, can be either patrilineal or matrilineal. It is also possible for extended families to be linked through sibling ties, consisting of two or more married brothers and their wives and children.

When a couple marries in a society with extended families, the newlyweds are not expected to establish a separate and distinct family unit. Instead, for example, the young couple may take up residence in the homestead of the husband's father (or the wife's mother), and the husband continues to work for his father, who also runs the household. Moreover most of the personal property in the household is not owned by the newlyweds but is controlled by the husband's father. Eventually the father will die or retire and allow the younger men to assume positions of leadership and power within the extended family. Unlike the nuclear family, which lasts only one generation, the extended family can last for an indefinite number of generations.

Kinship and the Modern World

Of all aspects of human societies, kinship systems are the most intimate and long-lasting set of social relationships a person will experience. Based as they are on birth and marriage, they create social ties that are often close and emotional. Kinship groups often involve strong bonds of obligation, security for their members, and moral coercion to adhere to social norms. We cannot assume, however, that these well-integrated kinship groups have remained unchanged in the face of external pressures such as urban migration, poverty, unemployment, and a host of other hardships. Moreover kinship systems are constantly changing through contact with external forces, such as industrializing economies, colonization and decolonization, intrusions by missionaries, and cultural diffusion in general.

The study of kinship, marriage, and family has always presented a challenge to students of anthropology. Unless they are born into a family that has kept careful records of its history, most people have little knowledge of their ancestors beyond three or four generations. Within the last decade, however, the revolution in information technology has made it possible for people to reconstruct their genealogies many generations into the past. There are online sites that enable people to find information about long-forgotten family members. The site that has the largest family database is Ancestry.com, which for a fee provides access to digitized records on immigration, births, marriages, and deaths.

The task of understanding kinship systems has been made even more complex because of such phenomena as transnational adoptions, gay and lesbian families, and new *reproductive technologies,* such as sperm banks, in vitro fertilization (IVF), and surrogate motherhood. For example, technology is available to create an embryo in a laboratory by combining a husband's sperm with an egg from a woman other than his wife and then implanting the embryo into the uterus of a surrogate mother who will carry the baby for nine months. When the baby is born, the original sperm-donating husband and his wife will raise the child as their own. Who is the mother? Is it the woman who donated the egg (the genetic mother)? Is it the woman who carried the child and gave birth to it (the gestational mother)? Or is it the woman who will raise the child (nurturing/social mother)? A number of difficult court cases have dealt with disputes involving children conceived through various reproductive technologies. These technologies create dilemmas for our legal system, our ethical and moral standards, and our basic vocabulary of kinship and family.

Some parts of the world are experiencing a crisis of overpopulation. Globally the average fertility rate is 3.1 births per women, but the rates range from 1 to 7. Some national campaigns to reduce population increases have adopted aggressive family-planning policies, such as limiting the number of children per household (China) or reducing the number of births through sterilization (India).

Western Europe, however, is experiencing the opposite problem—a crisis of underpopulation. The modern Italian family is experiencing a low birth rate, with an average of one child. Demographers and politicians are increasingly worried about low birth rates because this means that the population is no longer able to replace itself. In response to the declining birth rate, the Italian government ran a media blitz encouraging people to have larger families.

Anthropologist Elizabeth Krause conducted fieldwork in central Italy, where she explored the trend toward having small families and the implications it has for society, politics, economics, and culture. In *A Crisis of Births: Population Politics and Family-Making in Italy*, Krause (2004) describes how she lived in the industrial-agricultural province of Tuscany for two years with her husband and five-year-old. A number of questions guided her research, and she explored both what contributed to Italy's declining birth rate and what its consequences were for the society at large.

The younger Italian generations see a small family, with one or two children, as the ideal.

Herbert Scholpp/GlowImages.com

As part of her fieldwork experience, Krause worked in a family-operated workshop for a sweater factory, sewing on buttons. By getting involved in the community, she was able to gain a real appreciation of working families and of families in different social and economic classes. Krause discovered that a small family had become a symbol of the post-war era for the upwardly mobile; it was an indication of changing gender relations and identities. The older generation of Italians had a different perspective on family and family size than the younger generations did. And Krause found that the low fertility rate was accompanied by struggles in male-female relationships. Both men and women were carving out new identities and figuring out what it means to be Italian, European, and modern. Therefore, by examining economics, gender roles, division of labor, the concept of work, immigration, racism, and nationalism, as well as emotions, feelings, and expectations, Krause gained new insights into the Italian family and family-making.

From an applied perspective, these research findings contribute to approaches taken by demographers and politicians with respect to family-planning initiatives designed to increase a country's birth rate. As Krause (2005: 67) points out, "Family-making is not merely about reproducing babies, but it is also about producing the material goods and wages, as well as the care and nurturing, that make for a viable family." People who fear that immigrants will reproduce at a faster rate and alter the old social and class structures of Italian society are overlooking the contemporary Italian cultural context that figures prominently in current family-making beliefs and practices.

QUESTIONS FOR FURTHER THOUGHT

1. How does the trend of Italians having small families play out at different levels of society?

2. What impact does changing family size have on gender relationships and gender identity in a society?

SUMMARY

1. Although kinship relations are more important in some societies than in others, kinship is the single most important aspect of social structure in all societies. Kinship is based on both consanguineal (blood) and affinal (marriage) relationships.

2. All kinship systems group relatives into certain categories, call them by the same term, and expect people to behave toward these relatives in similar ways. How a particular culture categorizes its relatives varies according to different principles of classification, such

as generation, marriage, relative age, sex of the connecting relative, and side of the family.

3. Many societies have rules of descent that affiliate people with different sets of kin. In unilineal descent people trace their ancestry through either their mother's or their father's line. Patrilineal descent affiliates a person with the father's kin group; matrilineal descent affiliates a person with the mother's kin group.

4. In multilineal descent people trace their ancestry through both the mother's and the father's sides of the family. People who practice ambilineal descent may choose to affiliate their children with either the mother's or the father's kin group. In bilateral descent a person is related equally to both the mother's and the father's sides of the family.

5. Because of the vast ethnographic variations found in the world, the terms *family* and *marriage* are not easy to define. Anthropologists define a family as a social unit whose members cooperate economically and manage reproduction and child-rearing. Marriage, the process by which families are formed, is a union between adult partners.

6. All societies have rules governing the number of spouses a person can have. Different societies may emphasize monogamy (having one spouse at a time), polygyny (a man having more than one wife at a time), or polyandry (a woman having more than one husband at a time).

7. In many societies marriages involve the transfer of some type of economic consideration in exchange for rights of sexual access, legal rights over children, and rights to each other's property. These economic considerations involve such practices as bridewealth, bride service, and dowry.

8. All societies have guidelines regarding where a married couple should live after they marry. The couple can live with or near the husband's relatives (patrilocal), the wife's relatives (matrilocal), the husband's mother's brother (avunculocal), or the relatives of either the wife or the husband (ambilocal). Or the husband and wife can form a new residence of their own (neolocal).

9. Reproductive technologies (such as in vitro fertilization and surrogate motherhood) that have become available in recent decades raise legal, ethical, and definitional challenges for understanding the nature of kinship.

KEY TERMS

affinal relatives 170
ambilineal descent 176
ambilocal residence 177
arranged marriage 181
avunculocal
  residence 177
bilateral descent 176
bride service 187
bridewealth 186
consanguineal
  relatives 170
cross cousins 183
descent 173

divorce 188
dowry 187
endogamy 180
exogamy 180
extended family 189
fictive kinship 170
incest taboo 179
kinship system 172
levirate 183
matriarchy 174
matrilineal descent 174
matrilocal residence 177
monogamy 184

multilineal descent 173
neolocal residence 177
nuclear family 189
parallel cousins 183
patrilineal descent 173
patrilocal residence 177
polyandry 184
polygyny 184
preferential cousin
  marriage 183
serial monogamy 184
sororate 183
unilineal descent 173

CHAPTER 8

Sex, Gender, and Sexuality

SON PREFERENCE: NEW REPRODUCTIVE TECHNOLOGIES AND FAMILY-BUILDING STRATEGIES IN INDIA

In some cultures such as India and China there is a preference for having sons instead of daughters. The populations of these two countries are the highest in the world, and their governments have imposed restrictions on family size. China officially has a one-child policy, and the Indian government supports slowing down population growth and sponsors media campaigns advocating the benefits of a small family. In the late 1990s, the Indian government revised its national policy to promote reproductive health and make contraceptive methods more easily available. Now new uses of reproductive technologies have emerged to not only monitor a pregnancy but also assist families in making decisions about how many children to have. We must ask: What cultural reasons are there for preferring one sex over the other? Why do sons have an advantage over daughters?

Applied anthropologist Sunil Khanna went to India to study sex preference and gender roles. He was curious why sons are preferred and daughters neglected, and he wanted to better understand why some families (and physicians) use reproductive technology, specifically ultrasound, to identify the sex of a fetus and seek selective abortions of female fetuses. Something was going on because parents were creating gender inequality by increasing the number of males, and Khanna wanted to know why.

Khanna conducted his ethnographic research in an agrarian village community, Shahargaon, that was undergoing modernization and urbanization. He reports in *Fetal/Fatal Knowledge: New Reproductive Technologies and Family-Building Strategies in India* (2010) that, because of modernization, sons were no longer needed in agriculture. Nevertheless son preference intensified because sons added prestige and status to the family by becoming economic and political assets. Sons were given better education, health care, and opportunities to improve their lives, while daughters were considered economic liabilities. In fact, daughters were seen as an expense because a family had to save for a daughter's wedding dowry and in the end the daughter would move away to live with the husband's family (*patrilocality*) where her work would benefit the husband's family, not the bride's parents.

Since the 1990s Shahargaon residents have had access to free contraceptives and family planning services at a state-funded primary health clinic (PHC), which offers prenatal and postnatal care. New reproductive technologies, specifically ultrasound and amniocentesis, are offered to measure human growth and detect developmental abnormalities. These technologies are now being used to determine the sex of the fetus. In fact, billboards and newspaper advertisements promote the use of ultrasound as a way to avoid having unwanted daughters. Nevertheless not all of the local physicians at the PHC support this selective use of reproductive technology. Recent data indicate that the total population of the village is growing, but at a slower rate, and the sex ratio continues to favor males at an alarming rate. Data from 1993, 1999, and 2003 indicated a steady decline in the number of females compared to the number of males, while the overall population in the village increased by 17 percent (from 782 in 1993 to 938 in 2003). The sex ratio of children (newborn to six years old) indicated a decline in the number of girls from 710 (per 1,000 boys) in 1993 to 597 in 2003. Clearly families are making cultural choices about the use of reproductive technologies with respect to family-building strategies and son preference.

QUESTIONS FOR FURTHER THOUGHT

1. What role does government play in population control?

2. Why does a preference for sons exist in India—and, in particular, in the village of Shahargaon?

One need not be a particularly keen observer of humanity to recognize that men and women differ physically in important ways. What is the reason for these physical differences, and how are they expressed within a culture? And how do these differences affect men and women across different cultures? Within anthropology we draw on *both* biology *and* cultural traditions to explain the differences between men and women (Mascia-Lees and Black 2000). From a biological perspective, we can examine the physical differences through an evolutionary framework. Evolutionary theories fall into four categories: male strength, male aggression, male bonding, and women's childbearing hypotheses. Biology and evolutionary theory help to explain why men on average are taller and have considerably greater body mass than women as well as the differences between men's and women's sex organs, breast size, hormone levels, body hair, and muscle/fat ratios (Brettell and Sargent 2005). Some men have greater physical strength because of their larger hearts and lungs and greater muscle mass. At the most basic level, biology informs us that men and women differ genetically, with women having two X chromosomes and men having both an X and a Y chromosome. Unlike humans, some animals (such as mice and pigeons) manifest no visible sexual differences between males and females. Because of the significant physiological differences in humans, however, we are **sexually dimorphic**.

In rare instances the X and Y chromosomes have incomplete separations and the result is hermaphroditism, where an individual has both male and female sexual characteristics. One of the more controversial examples is the eighteen-year-old female runner from South Africa who won the gold medal in the 800-meter event in the 2009 World

Championships in Athletics. Her sex was questioned, and extensive laboratory tests confirmed that she has both male and female sex organs but a female identity. What is brought into question is what it means to be male and female from a physical and cultural perspective.

Most researchers can agree on the physiological (genetically based) differences between men and women, but there is considerably less agreement on the extent to which these differences actually cause differences in behavior or in the way men and women are treated in society (Brettell and Sargent 2005). These lines of questioning focus on a society's practices that contribute to how men and women are socialized into culturally appropriate roles and behavior.

As in so many other aspects of behavior, the nature-nurture debate is relevant in the area of behavioral differences between men and women. In other words, do men and women behave differently because of their genetic predisposition or because of their culture? During the twentieth century, ethnographers showed that the definitions of femaleness and maleness vary widely from society to society. Because of significant cultural variability in behaviors and attitudes between the sexes, most anthropologists now prefer to speak of *gender differences* rather than *sex differences* (Mascia-Lees and Black 2000). The term **sex** refers to the biological or genetic differences between males and females. **Gender** refers to "the socially constructed roles, behaviors, activities and attributes that a given society considers appropriate for men and women" (World Health Organization 2009).

Although the use of the term *gender* acknowledges the role that culture plays, it is not always possible to determine the extent to which culture or biology determines behavioral or attitudinal differences between the sexes. What we can say, however, is that biological differences influence (or set broad limits on) social definitions of maleness and femaleness to varying degrees. To illustrate, the fact that only women can give birth provides a basis for a particular set of attitudes and behaviors for women, and this results in some cultures socializing women to be nurturing and have life-giving qualities. Likewise, because of their greater body mass, men in some cultures are encouraged to be courageous, aggressive, and warlike. Nevertheless, as we will see, many different social definitions of **masculinity** and **femininity** are found throughout the world.

Margaret Mead's (1935) classic study of sex and temperament in three New Guinea cultures illustrates the range of gender variation found among the Arapesh, Mundugumor, and Tchambuli. Mead found that, among the Arapesh, both men and women were cooperative, nonaggressive, and responsive to the needs of others—all traits that most Westerners consider to be feminine. In contrast, both genders among the Mundugumor were expected to be fierce, ruthless, and aggressive.

Among the Tchambuli, there was a complete reversal of the male-female temperaments considered usual in our own society; that is, females were the dominant, impersonal partners who were aggressive food providers, whereas males were less responsible, more emotionally dependent, more preoccupied with art, and spent more time styling their hair and gossiping about the opposite sex. Mead argued that if those temperaments that we regard as traditionally feminine (that is, nurturing, maternal, and passive) can be held as a masculine ideal in one group and can be frowned on for both sexes in another, then we no longer have a basis for saying that masculinity and femininity are biologically based. Although Mead's work has been criticized in recent years for its subjectivity, it nevertheless demonstrates the enormous variability in gender roles across cultures.

Cross-cultural studies further complicate our understanding of gender. Mainstream U.S. culture recognizes two genders, male and female, which marginalizes other gender alternatives, such as *transgender* (someone who was assigned a sex, usually at birth, but has a different gender identity) and *androgynous* (a person who does not fit cleanly into a society's typi-cal masculine and feminine gender roles and may share a combination of masculine and feminine characteristics). People who are uncomfortable with anything other than two genders tend to explain everything else away as being abnormal or even curable. However, some cultures not only accommodate the ambiguities of these gender alternatives but also see them as legitimate or, in some cases, powerful. Third-gender individuals are well established in the Native American literature, particu-larly in the Plains between the Great Lakes and California. According to Charles Callender and Lee Kochems (1983), at least 113 Native Ameri-can groups provided a third gender as a legitimate social alternative. Also known as Two-Spirits, these are both females and males who adopt some of the roles and traits of the opposite gender. To illustrate, the Lakota of the northern Plains had transgendered men called *winkte,* who possessed both masculine and feminine spirits; the Zuni of the southwestern United States recognized as fully legitimate members of society a third gender that they called *We'wha;* and the Cheyenne had a similar transgender category called *hemanah* (literally "half-woman, half-man"), who often accompanied war expeditions in ceremonial roles as noncombatants. In all of these cases, people became transgendered through spiritual calling, individual inclination, or parental selection—where parents were involved in selecting their child's sexual orientation.

Another interesting example is the male/female Hijra in Hindu India. A combined male/female role is a major theme in Hindu art, religion, and mythology. For example, androgynous people and impersonators of the opposite sex are found widely in Hindu mythology among both humans

This Hijra man, who presents himself as being "like a woman" is an example of the socially constructed basis for sexuality.

and their deities. These same themes are played out in parts of contemporary India. For example, Serena Nanda (1990) describes a festival that takes place in Tamil Nadu, in south India, in which the Hijras are transformed. During the festival the Hijras identify with Krishna, who is a deity that changes form from male to female. The Hijras become the wives and then the widows of Koothandavar, a male deity. With the Hijras dressed in their finest clothes and jewelry, the ritual reaffirms their identification with Krishna.

The Hijras of Hindu India are significant because they provide an example of a society that tolerates a wider definition of gender than is found in our own society. The Hijras, who undergo an emasculation rite, present themselves as being "like women," or female impersonators. In fact their "emasculation rite," involving voluntary castration, indicates their high level of commitment to this special gender category. The Hijras do not function sexually as men, claim to have no sexual feelings for women, dress in women's clothing, wear women's hairstyles, and even walk and carry themselves as women do. Clearly the Hijras are neither male nor female in the conventional sense of the terms, but they are seen as a special, even sacred, gender group.

Human Sexuality

As we have said, anthropologists pride themselves on being holistic in their approach to understanding a people's culture. As such, anthropology has a long history of documenting the sexual practices of Western and non-Western peoples. From this early work on **human sexuality**, which was formally recognized as an area of study in 1961 when the AAA held a session on the topic at its national meeting, anthropologists have been amassing data on sexual practices and incorporating these practices into their ethnographic accounts.

There is wide interest in human sexuality. Culture teaches us what kinds of sexual feelings and practices are normal and natural in one's society and goes so far as to prescribe which ones are considered deviant, inappropriate, and unlawful. To be sure, gathering ethnographic information on human sexuality is delicate. First, because sexual activity in all societies is a private matter, it is off limits to anthropological observation. Second, when anthropologists have interviewed people about sexuality, they tend to confine their questions to more objective matters such as number of sexual partners, frequency of sexual intercourse, and acceptance of premarital sexual activity. Anthropologists today look back at findings from research on human sexuality conducted prior to the 1970s and recognize a strong male bias, since most anthropologists were males who had access to predominantly male informants. Fortunately times have changed; in more recent ethnographic studies, both sexes are portrayed with greater representation and a more balanced picture of human sexuality.

Today anthropologists studying human sexuality have become more interested in explaining why there is such diversity in gender roles across cultures. Perhaps the most fundamental generalization that has emerged is that human sexuality varies widely from culture to culture. In other words, we find enormous variations throughout the world in the sexual behaviors permitted or encouraged before marriage, outside marriage, and within marriage. This cross-cultural variation in human sexuality raises interesting theoretical and methodological questions, especially for how one may go about organizing fieldwork or developing applied health-related anthropology projects, such as addressing the transmission of HIV/AIDS.

When examining variations in male or female homosexuality, anthropologists distinguish between *sexual preference* and *sexual activity*. It is possible to engage in homosexual activity while maintaining a heterosexual preference, and conversely it is possible to live in a heterosexual marriage and have homosexual preferences. In the United States, the cultural definition of male and female homosexuality does not distinguish between preference and activity. Rather it is assumed that a man or woman who engages voluntarily in homosexual activity does so because of a dominant same-sex preference. The normative view of homosexuality in the United States today remains generally negative. This is most clearly illustrated in the ongoing debates over the legal recognition of same-sex marriages, gay men and women serving in the military, and same-sex adults adopting children.

When living in countries that have greater sexual freedom, gays, lesbians, and bisexuals from the Middle East practice their homosexuality more openly and without fear of reprisals. For example, the large Muslim population in Berlin has the opportunity to attend an event called Gayhane, a monthly dance club event for Arab and Turkish gays and lesbians (Kulish 2008). This event allows gays and lesbians from the Middle East to merge their cultural and sexual identities. These immigrants may still face discrimination in Berlin for both their ethnicity and their sexual orientation, but at least they are not being put to death "in the worst, most severe way" for their homosexual lifestyles.

So we are left with the big question: Why do some countries have sexual freedom and others do not? At the simplest level, one can say it is because of culture. However, we need to broaden this notion of culture to include religion and politics. For example, in some societies it is their interpretation of their religion or belief system that governs their sexual behaviors. In societies that link their belief system with their political system, it is possible to establish laws governing sexual behavior and sexuality. There is no clear pattern to answer why it is culturally permissible to engage in homosexual acts in one country and it is unlawful in another, or to explain the degree to which a crime of engaging in a homosexual act is punished in different societies.

Gender Roles

All societies make some distinctions between what men are expected to do and what women are expected to do. In some societies **gender roles** are rigidly defined, but in others the roles of men and women overlap considerably. For instance, gender roles include the kinds of work assigned to men and women, the familial roles that people play, the leadership positions assigned to men and women in the home and outside of the home, and the roles men and women are assigned in ritual practices. Despite the universality of gender roles, there is variation in the division of labor by gender, although cultures of the world do share some general patterns in the ways in which they divide tasks between women and men. To illustrate, in most cases it is primarily men who engage in warfare, trap and kill large animals, clear land, build houses, and fish at sea. Women, on the other hand, are more likely to tend crops, gather wild fruits and plants, trap and kill small animals (including fish in lakes and streams), prepare food, care for children, collect firewood, clean house, launder clothing, and carry water. A number of tasks are performed by both men and women, such as tending small domesticated animals, making utilitarian products (pottery and baskets), milking animals, planting and harvesting crops, and collecting shellfish.

Some roles (such as hunting for men and child care for women) are closely associated with gender. In contemporary ethnographies of hunter-gatherers, researchers frequently describe the role of men as the hunters of large game, but both men and women might be the hunters of small game, such as with the Ju/'hoansi of the Kalahari. On the other side of the equation, child care is an overwhelmingly female activity, but in some cases men make substantial contributions, such as among the Navajo of the American Southwest.

Gender Stratification

It is generally recognized that the status of women varies from one society to another. In some East African pastoral societies, women are in a clearly subordinate position in their social relationships with men. In other societies, such as the Ju/'hoansi, the relationships between the genders are more egalitarian. Social scientists generally agree that **gender stratification** exists to some degree in all societies, but there is considerably less agreement about how one measures the relative status of men and women because gender stratification involves a number of different components that may vary independently of one another. It is now recognized that there are many important indicators of women's status, including economic, power, prestige, autonomy, and ideological dimensions. To illustrate, when considering the relative status of women in any society, one needs to look at the roles women play, the value society places on their contributions, their legal rights, whether and to what degree they are expected to be deferential to men, their economic independence, and the degree to which they decide on the major events of their lives, such as marriage, profession, and childbearing, among other factors.

The multidimensional nature of women's status was illustrated by Martin Whyte's (1978) comparative study of ninety-three societies, which identified fifty-two status dimensions found in the anthropological literature. Interestingly all of these status dimensions varied independently of one another. In other words, no single cluster or complex of variables of women's status varied consistently from culture to culture. To illustrate, women in certain West African societies, because of their influence in the marketplace, have an appreciable amount of economic independence, but they nevertheless remain subordinate to their husbands in most other respects. Thus determining the status of women is difficult because it is not a one-dimensional phenomenon.

Another difficulty in ascertaining the status of women is that it is not static. In some societies the relative status of men and women fluctuates along with political changes. For example, during the reign of the Shah of Iran, Iranian women's roles kept pace with modernization.

During the 1960s and 1970s, increasingly large numbers of Iranian women abandoned the rules of **purdah** (domestic seclusion and veiling), obtained higher educations, and gained entry into traditionally male professions. With the return of religious and cultural fundamentalism after the Shah was ousted, however, women were forced back under the veil and resumed traditional female roles by order of the Ayatollah. In fact, their life and death depended on their adherence to the new order. Since the American invasion of Afghanistan in 2001, changes have been occurring for Afghan women. The new Afghan constitution extends equality to women, yet it is mostly the urban women rather than the rural women who benefit from the new opportunities. In the historic elections of 2005, women registered and voted. In addition, 68 of the 249 seats in the lower parliament are reserved for women. In the 2009 election, women candidates ran for president and vice president. Although major strides are being made, Afghan women still need greater access to education and health care.

Yet another complicating factor in determining the status of women can occur even before birth. Hindu society in northern India is among the most highly stratified along gender lines. India as a whole, and particularly northern India, has enormously skewed sex ratios due to the widespread

© Jalil Rezayee/epa/Landov

Burkas and veils remain common attire for women in rural and urban areas of Afghanistan. Prior to a 2009 election, this Afghan woman shows her voter card at a voter registration center in Herat, Afghanistan.

neglect of girls' health care and nutrition (Khanna 2010). As we saw in the chapter-opening scenario, in northern India sons are more highly valued than daughters because a son provides status and prestige to his parents, while a daughter requires a costly dowry to marry and will live with her husband's family, providing no benefit to her own parents. Sex ratios have become even more skewed in recent years with the widespread use of ultrasound equipment to determine sex prenatally. The incidence of abortions of female fetuses has increased so rapidly in the last several decades that the female population of some rural villages has been reduced by nearly 25 percent. And even for those women who live to adulthood, many face impoverished widowhood or dowry death.

Although it is possible to identify societies where gender distinctions are kept to a minimum, there is overwhelming evidence that women are subordinate to men in many critical areas of life. From time to time women in various cultures have wielded considerable power, such as the Iroquois of the American Northeast and the Hopi of the American Southwest, but there is little ethnographic or archaeological evidence for matriarchy—women's rule or domination over men (Bamberger 1974). It is, however, possible to find societies that the people themselves describe as matriarchies—where women exert considerable power without dominating males (or ruling them in a political or economic sense) to the same degree that men dominate women in many patriarchal societies. For example, among the Minangkabau of West Sumatra, Indonesia, females and males interact more like partners than competitors. The foundation of gender relationships among the Minangkabau is their central philosophical notion of *adat*: People, animals, and wildlife should be nurtured so that society will be strong. This emphasis on nurturing tends to favor cooperation and the maternal in everyday life rather than competition and male dominance. According to Peggy Sanday (2004), on ceremonial occasions women in Minangkabau society are addressed by the term reserved for the mythical queen, and symbolically the maternal is viewed as the spiritual center and the foundation of the society. Moreover women exert considerable power in everyday social life. Women control land inheritance, husbands reside in their wives' residences, and in the event of divorce, the husband gathers his belongings and leaves. Yet, despite the central role of women in society, this is hardly an example of matriarchy. Rather neither men nor women rule in Minangkabau society because decision making is based on consensus and cooperation.

Despite such examples as the Minangkabau, we find that women, to one degree or another, tend to be excluded from the major centers of economic and political power and control in most societies. Moreover the roles women play as mothers and wives invariably carry with them fewer prerogatives and lower prestige than male roles. Although to speak of **universal male dominance** would be an oversimplification, the evidence does suggest a general **sexual asymmetry** among most cultures of the world in the allocation of power and influence, particularly in the economic and political spheres.

This sexual asymmetry is so pervasive that some anthropologists have attributed it to biological differences between men and women, such as greater size, strength, and physical aggressiveness. Ernestine Friedl (1978), however, argued that men tend to dominate not because of biological traits but rather because they control the distribution of scarce resources. Irrespective of who produces the goods, Friedl contended, the people who *control* the allocation of resources (usually men) possess the currency needed to create and maintain powerful political alliances and obligations. Using examples from a number of societies, Friedl demonstrated how men dominate in those societies in which women have little or no control over the allocation of scarce resources and, conversely, how women with some control of resources have achieved greater equality.

Gender inequality, however, is not a unified phenomenon; it takes many different forms in different societies. For example, sexual violence against women can take many forms—from individual rape to collective gang rape, to other forms of abuse including verbal abuse. Acts of sexual aggression and dominance against women have always occurred; sometimes these acts have been organized and other times they have been spontaneous (Brettell and Sargent 2005; Rylko-Bauer, Whiteford, and Farmer 2009). The record of sexual violence is at times disguised as prostitution, which remains today a huge and global industry. In postindustrial countries gender inequity is creating disparities in access to formal education, employment, health care, and finances. We will discuss some of the varieties of these gender disparities next.

Education

Women throughout the world have made progress toward equal educational enrollment, but huge gaps remain. Two-thirds of all the illiterate people in the world today are women. More than 70 percent of women aged twenty-five and older in sub-Saharan Africa, southern Asia, and western Asia are illiterate (World Bank 2011). There are more illiterate women than men in every major region of the world. Even though world literacy has been on the rise in recent decades, it has risen faster for men than for women, thereby widening the gender gap. In developing countries such as Pakistan, India, Yemen, and Afghanistan, the large literacy gap between men and women is most often related to poverty and access to education. Where high levels of poverty are coupled with gender discrimination, women and girls are the ones who are marginalized. Efforts are being made, however, by individuals and non-profit organizations to reduce the gender disparities, especially through education programs.

Employment

The percentage of women in the world's workforce has increased in the last several decades, due largely to economic necessity. However, the world's women, particularly in developing countries, are concentrated in the lowest-paid occupations and receive lower pay and fewer benefits than men. Women are also more likely to work part time, have less seniority, and occupy positions with little or no upward mobility. Moreover an increasing number of women in Asia, Africa, and South America are being pushed into the informal economy: small-scale, self-employed trading of goods and services. Some of the activities associated with the informal economy—such as street vending, beer brewing, and prostitution—are outside the law. All of this has led to the impoverishment of women worldwide, a phenomenon known as the **feminization of poverty**. It is now estimated that between 60 and 70 percent of all people living in poverty throughout the world are women, and the inequities are increasing (Martin 2008). To illustrate, the number of women living in poverty increased disproportionately to the number of men during the past decade, in part from the growing number of female-headed households (single women). Moreover the increasing feminization of poverty was particularly acute in poorer, developing countries and for minority women living in wealthier, more industrialized nations (Wright 2006).

Reproductive Health

A third area in which the world's women have not fared as well as men is reproductive health. Although most women in the developed world control the number of children they have, in some parts of the world there is pressure to have small families, as in Europe and China (Krause 2004). In other parts of the world there is pressure to have large numbers of children, and women on average have four or five children. In certain countries with particularly high birthrates (such as Malawi, Mali, Yemen, Ethiopia, and the Ivory Coast), the average woman bears more than seven children in her lifetime (Holloway 2007; MacFarquhar 1994). Pregnant women in developing countries face risks that include malnutrition and a lack of trained medical personnel to deal with high-risk pregnancies. In fact it has been estimated that pregnant women in developing countries are eighty to six hundred times more likely to die of complications of pregnancy and birthing than are women in the industrialized world (Holloway 2007).

A related health issue for women is the extent to which gender inequalities make them more vulnerable to HIV/AIDS. Women's economic dependence on men, as well as the threat of violence against wives and girlfriends, may make them unable to protect themselves. In many parts of the world, it is unacceptable for a woman to say no to unwanted or unprotected sex. A study conducted in Zambia (Urdang 2001) revealed how vulnerable wives are to HIV/AIDS and other diseases sexually transmitted by their husbands. Fewer than one in every four women, according to the study, believed that they could refuse to have sex with their husbands, even if the husband had been unfaithful and was infected. Similarly anthropologist Richard Lee (2007) attributes the low incidence of HIV/AIDS among the Ju/'hoansi of Namibia and Botswana to, among other factors, the traditional high status of women and their relative gender equality. Because the typical Ju/'hoansi wife tends to be relatively empowered, she is more likely to insist that her husband wear a condom and, should he refuse, to not have sex with him. In addition, social customs are so restrictive in some countries that often young women are denied access to information about the dangers of HIV/AIDS and how best to protect themselves. It is little wonder that in societies where women have relatively little control over their own sexual behavior, the incidence of this deadly disease is much higher for young women than it is for their male counterparts.

Finance

The women of the world are also at a disadvantage in obtaining credit from financial institutions (Waring 1989, 2004). According to World Bank estimates, 90 percent of the more than half billion women living in poverty around the world do not have access to credit. Loans as small as $100 would go a long way in helping women to start their own small businesses, which could substantially improve their economic conditions. But both private lenders and aid organizations, by and large, have not made even this level of credit available to women. A notable exception is Grameen Bank in Bangladesh, the world's best-known microlender, which for four decades has made small-business loans to the poorest segments of Bangladesh society. By March 2008 Grameen Bank had made 7.5 million loans, 97 percent to women, who used the modest loans to turn their operations into viable businesses. Extending this type of credit to impoverished women has proved to be an excellent investment. First, World Bank data show that women repay their loans in 98 percent of the cases, as compared with 60–70 percent for men. Second, the World Bank has found that credit given to women has a greater impact on the welfare of the family because women tend to spend their money on better nutrition and education for their children—areas given lower priority by male borrowers (Barua 2006).

Thus it is clear that women throughout the world continue to carry a heavy burden of inequality. Although they make up half of the world's population, women do approximately two-thirds of the work, earn one-tenth of the world's income, and own less than 1 percent of the world's property. Even in the wake of some political and economic advances, women in many parts of the world are falling further behind their male counterparts.

Gender inequality does not necessarily depend on how wealthy a country is. The United Nations has developed an indicator of progress toward equality for women called the Gender Empowerment Measure (GEM), which assesses gender inequality in three main areas: (1) political participation and decision-making power (i.e., parliamentary seats), (2) economic participation and decision-making power, and (3) power over economic resources (i.e., income). A score of 1.0 indicates equality between men and women. As is apparent in Table 8.1, Norway, Australia, Iceland, Canada, and Ireland score the highest on the GEM, while Niger, Afghanistan, Sierra Leone, Central African Republic, and Mali have the lowest scores. Note that the United States ranks 13 among 182 countries in the world.

TABLE 8.1 Countries with the Highest and Lowest Ranks on the Gender Empowerment Measure

COUNTRY	RANK
Norway	1
Australia	2
Iceland	3
Canada	4
Ireland	5
Netherlands	6
United States	13
Mali	178
Central African Republic	179
Sierra Leone	180
Afghanistan	181
Niger	182

© Cengage Learning 2013

Source: UNDP 2009 Report on Gender Empowerment Measure, http://hdr.undo.org/en/media/ HDR_2009_EN_Table_K.pdf.

Gender Ideology

Generalized male dominance is buttressed by a **gender ideology**, which we define as a system of thoughts and values that legitimizes gender roles, statuses, and customary behavior. In religion women are often excluded categorically by gender ideology from holding major leadership roles or participating in certain ceremonies. In some African societies, men's physical well-being is thought to be jeopardized by contact with a woman's menstrual discharge. In Bangladesh and some African cultures, men are associated with the right side and women with the left side, a dichotomy that also denotes purity-pollution, good-bad, and authority-submission. Even in the area of food production, foods procured by men (such as meat from the hunt) are often more highly valued than those procured by women (such as roots, nuts, and berries), even though the latter foods are the major source of nutrition. In many parts of the world, women are treated legally as minors in that they are unable to obtain a driver's license, bank account, passport, or even birth control device without the consent of their husbands or fathers. One particularly effective ideological mechanism for keeping women in a subordinate position is found among the Luo of western Kenya, whose creation myth (no doubt originated and perpetuated by men) blames women for committing the original sins that resulted in the curse of work for men.

In many parts of the world, such as India and China, the devaluation of women starts early in life. The birth of a son is often cause for rejoicing, but the birth of a daughter is met with silence. In some patrilineal societies, boys are more highly valued because they will contribute to the longevity of the lineage, whereas their sisters will produce children for their husbands' lineage. Because parents often assume that sons will provide for them in their old age, they are much more likely to give sons preferential treatment for education and careers. However, over time the preference for sons in China and India has created such a lopsided ratio of boys to girls that economists project there may be as many as 30 million to

Although they assume a subordinate position in their family lives, some African women are able to gain considerable power, authority, and autonomy by virtue of their economic activities, as with this vegetable vendor in Ethiopia.

© Dominic Harcourt-Webster/Robert Harding Picture Library

40 million more men than women of marriageable age in each country by 2020. In societies where girls are less valued, they are not able to financially support either their own parents or their husband's family later in life because they were often denied access to schooling, medical facilities, and nutritious diets. To be certain, there are some societies that prefer female children (in East Africa, Pakistan, and New Guinea), but the dominant practice is a preference for male children.

A study that illustrates the complexity of gender ideology was conducted by Sandra Barnes (1990) among Yoruba women in Lagos, Nigeria. Female subordination among the Yoruba can best be described as contextual or situational. That is, women subordinate themselves in some contexts by showing great deference to their husbands and to male family elders, employers, and public officials, but in other situations (such as market activity) they are independent, assertive, and powerful. Thus we see a basic paradox in Yoruba society: Although female subordination is clearly the norm, particularly in family affairs, it is widely held that women can, and even should, strive for powerful positions in the worlds of economics and politics. Barnes explains the apparent paradox in terms of homeownership. Because of their success in the markets, women are able to attain high status by owning a home, and once they become homeowners, they are able to carry that status over into the realm of politics and public affairs.

Exploitation Caused by Gender Ideology

In some parts of the world, gender ideology is so biased toward males that females can suffer dire consequences. For example, large numbers of females are missing in census counts. It has been estimated (Sen 2001) that the countries of China and India together have more than 80 million fewer females than would be expected. In most countries, including the United States and Canada, women slightly outnumber men (approximately 105 women for every 100 men). But in India and China, where traditionally there has been a strong gender bias against females, the sex ratio strongly favors males. In China, for example, the government reported (Yardley 2005) that the sex ratio had reached 119 boys for every 100 girls. This imbalance is caused by poorer nutrition and medical care for females, selective abortions, and the underreporting or hiding of female births. Demographers predict that in twenty years China could have 40 million bachelors unable to find a wife. However, despite government efforts to provide incentives for girl babies (such as free tuition for girls and annual pensions for elderly people who have only daughters), there remains a strong cultural preference, particularly in rural areas, for male children.

A particularly malignant manifestation of **male gender bias** in northern India is **female infanticide**, the outright killing of female babies

(Khanna 2010). Sons are much more desirable than daughters because they are considered economic assets. They are needed for farming, they are more likely to be employed for wages, they receive marriage dowry, and because they don't leave home when they marry, they can support the parents in their later years.

There are also more subtle forms of female child abuse, such as sustained **nutritional deprivation**, which, though perhaps not fatal, can retard learning, physical development, and social adjustment (Rose 1994). Sunil Khanna (2010) reports that in his home country of India gender bias against girls leads to significant differences in weight-for-age statistics for boys and girls younger than five years of age. Barbara Miller (1993) found considerable evidence of this less direct form of gender exploitation. For example, the sex ratio of children being admitted to hospitals is at least two to one in favor of boys, an imbalance caused by the sex-selective child care practices of the parents. These studies indicate how gender ideology can lead to a lethal form of gender exploitation.

Another graphic form of gender exploitation is female genital cutting (FGC), also known as female circumcision. Amnesty International estimates that more than 130 million women worldwide have had their childhood or early adolescence interrupted by a traumatic operation in which a girl's genitalia (labia and clitoris) are either partially or completely removed surgically. Although this practice, customary in large parts of Africa and the Middle East, has been condemned by international medical and human rights groups, it is thought that more than two million FGCs are still performed every year, which is equivalent to four procedures performed every minute worldwide. These operations are typically performed with crude and unsterile instruments, without benefit of anesthesia, and with little or no protection against infection. The practice is justified by traditionalists on the grounds of protecting a girl's chastity and thus the family's honor, promoting cleanliness, repressing a girl's sexual desires, and reducing the likelihood of rape. It has long been known, however, that the operation itself poses severe medical risks for women. Moreover a large-scale medical study (Rosenthal 2006) concluded that FGC raises by 50 percent the likelihood that mothers or their newborns will die during childbirth. There is, in other words, an increasing amount of evidence from many sources that millions of girls worldwide continue to be subjected to pain, psychological trauma, infection, death, and compromises to their reproductive health to an extent that their brothers are not.

Widespread abuse of women in other cultures is deeply disturbing and shocking, but we should not assume that equally appalling gender-based violence does not occur in our own culture. Both physical violence, in the form of wife battering and homicide, and sexual assault against women are pervasive and direct consequences of extreme gender ideology. Sexual and physical violence against women has been, and continues to be, a serious problem in the United States and around the world. Lori Heise, Mary Ellsberg, and Megan Gottemoeller (1999) reported that around the world at least one in three women has been beaten, coerced into having sex, or otherwise abused during her lifetime.

Most violence against women in the United States occurs not in a dark alley but in the home. According to the American Medical Association (2002), nearly one-quarter of all women in the United States (more than 12 million) were abused by a former or current partner during their lifetime. Because many women still do not define a sexual assault by their husband as a rape, it is likely that many such assaults go unreported, and consequently these findings must be considered low estimates. With data like these, it is little wonder that Richard Gelles (quoted in Roesch 1984) has suggested that, with the exception of the police and the military, the family is the most violent institution in the United States.

Physical violence against women by a husband or intimate partner is the result of gender ideology and occurs in our own culture as well as in many other cultures around the world.

From a cross-cultural perspective, it is clear that domestic violence against women exists in all parts of the world. For example, the United Nations (UNFPA 2005) cites studies from around the world on the most pervasive form of gender-based violence: abuse by a husband or intimate partner. Survey results indicate that the number of women who have been physically assaulted by an intimate partner range from a low of 10 percent to a high of 69 percent.

Gender in the United States

When we think of traditional gender roles in the United States, two words usually come to mind: *breadwinner* and *housewife*. According to this traditional view, males, who are often characterized as logical, competitive, goal oriented, and unemotional, were responsible for the economic support and protection of the family. Females, on the other hand, with their warm, caring, and sensitive natures, were expected to restrict themselves to child-rearing and domestic activities: preparing meals, cleaning the house, collecting wood and water, working in kitchen gardens, and doing a variety of other tasks to support the household.

This traditional view of gender roles in the United States was valid for only a relatively brief period in our nation's history, however—from roughly 1860 through the 1950s. Kingsley Davis and Wilbert Moore (1988: 73) called the years from 1860 to 1920 the "heyday of the breadwinner system"; they identified 1890 as its peak because less than 3 percent of native-born married women in the United States worked outside the home at that time.

Although women may not be called *breadwinners,* working is not new to them. Women have always worked both inside and outside the home, especially minority and lower-class women. Before industrialization, pioneer women were fully productive contributors to the rural homestead. With the start of the industrial revolution, minority and lower-class women started working outside the home while still caring for their own homes.

With the rise of industrialization in the late nineteenth century, the nation's economy shifted from agriculture to manufacturing. This rapid industrialization was revolutionary because it tended to separate work life from family life. Unlike work on the family farm, factory work could not be easily combined with child-rearing and domestic tasks. As women became more confined to the home, their direct contribution to economic production decreased. As men's and women's spheres were separated, the terms *breadwinner* and *housewife* became entrenched in our vocabulary. Interestingly, we have retained this view of separate spheres for men and women into the twenty-first century even though the forces of change that eroded that separation were under way by the early 1900s. From the 1910s through the early 1920s, young, middle-class women joined the workforce outside the home, and it went largely unnoticed until the Great Depression. Then, with the high rate of unemployment, most people opposed women working because they saw it as women taking jobs from unemployed men.

It is true that men entered the workforce in greater numbers than women during the twentieth century, but we must not assume that women did not also make significant contributions to factory production. This is particularly true of poor and working-class women, minority women, immigrant women, and single mothers. Several factors contributed to the entry of women into the workforce. First, as industrialization became more complex, more clerical workers were needed, and most of them were women. Second, as infant mortality rates fell, women bore fewer children, thereby increasing the number of years they could work outside the home. Third, many women gravitated toward the textile industry because they were thought to possess greater manual dexterity than men and therefore to be more adept at sewing clothes. Fourth, World War II helped galvanize women's role in the workplace. The government launched a propaganda campaign with the fictional character "Rosie the Riveter." Rosie was considered an ideal female worker: efficient, loyal, patriotic, and pretty (Yellin 2004). Fifth, the rising divorce rate forced many women to support themselves and their children without the financial aid of a spouse. Sixth, the development of infant formula enabled many women to work outside the home without jeopardizing the nutritional needs of their infants. And, finally, periodic economic downturns drove an increasing number of women to join the workforce because two salaries were often needed to make ends meet.

Today both men and women are in the paid labor force, with approximately 74 percent of men and 60 percent of women participating. The percentage of women working outside the home has changed dramatically over the past four decades. Specifically, the proportion of working women over sixteen years of age rose from about 50 percent in 1970 to 58.9 percent in 2010 (U.S. Department of Labor 2010). The figure had been higher, but the current high unemployment rate nationally, which hovers between 9.0 and 10.0 percent, makes it difficult for people who want work to find employment. It is important to point out that employed married women, particularly those with children, often carry a **double workload** by both working for wages and being primarily responsible for housework and child care.

Another characteristic of the wage sector of the U.S. economy is its high rate of **occupational segregation** along gender lines. Despite decades of legislation aimed at reducing gender discrimination in the workplace, the majority of both men and women continue to work in gender-segregated occupations. Most women in the United States work as clerk/secretaries, hairdressers, sales clerks, food service workers, health care personnel, and child care workers, all relatively low-paying jobs. More than 90 percent of nurses, 80 percent of librarians, and 70 percent of teachers are women. At the other end of the spectrum, women make up only 1 percent of corporate CEOs, 6 percent of partners in private law firms, and 8 percent of state and federal judges (U.S. Department of Labor 2010). In addition men tend to dominate supervisory positions, even in areas where a majority of the workers are women. This occupational segregation is even more pronounced for minority women because gender segregation is aggravated by race. Despite these data illustrating occupational segregation, in the last several decades women have made considerable inroads into some high-status professions, such as medicine. According to the American Medical Association (2008), the proportion of women physicians increased from 7.6 percent in 1970 to 27.8 percent in 2006.

Although an increasing number of women are entering professions that require advanced education, such as law, medicine, and engineering, occupations associated with low prestige and low income still have higher proportions of women. Poverty in the United States has become feminized just as it has in other parts of the world. For example, more than half of all female-headed families with children are living below the poverty line—a poverty rate that is approximately four times higher than the poverty rate for two-parent families. The feminization of poverty is particularly acute when we look at minorities. Whereas 45 percent of White, female-headed families live in poverty, approximately 70 percent of families headed by African American or Hispanic women are officially living in poverty. A number of factors have contributed to the feminization of poverty in the United States in recent decades: the continued involvement of women in low-paying jobs; the additional responsibilities for child-rearing; the relative lack of women in political and policy-making positions; and women's limited access to education, skills training, financial credit, and health care.

As we look back on our discussion of gender stratification in the United States, it seems fairly obvious that in time the gap between men and women will narrow. The cost of gender stratification is high for both men and women, with the perpetuation of inequality in the workplace as well as at home. One can recognize that the culturally constructed male and female roles and statuses in the United States have negative consequences. For example, men in the United States have higher mortality rates than women at all ages and for most of the fifteen leading causes of death. They abuse their bodies with drugs, alcohol, and tobacco more than women. And men engage in certain professions that carry higher risks, such as mining, construction, and deep-sea fishing.

Women continue to adapt to the changing times in the twenty-first century. They are making choices that influence their home and family life as well as their place in the workforce. For example, American women are marrying later in life, staying in school longer, delaying childbirth, and having fewer children than in earlier years. More women are choosing to continue working while balancing the traditional parenting role. Gender discrimination persists and at its worst is coupled with fighting battles for equal pay for equal work. In terms of health, women generally have more work-related cases of carpal tunnel syndrome, tendonitis, infectious and parasitic diseases, and anxiety and stress disorders compared to men. Although working women still face the demands of a heavy workload balancing family, jobs, and possibly sexual harassment at the workplace, women have made great strides in the workplace. Nevertheless we should see continued efforts for gender equity by both men and women at home *and* in the workplace in twenty-first-century American culture.

Out in the Real World: Assisting Afghan Women in Health Care and Education

World organizations are intervening to help Afghan women gain access to formal education and basic health care. In a country that has strong views on the differences between women and men, how should outside groups go about working in the rural communities?

Afghanistan is a strict Muslim country, and it is culturally unacceptable for women, primarily in rural areas, to visit with men who are not family members. Since the fall of the Taliban in late 2001, the position of Afghan women has been gradually changing. In fact, under the new Afghan constitution, "the citizens of Afghanistan—whether man or woman—have equal rights and duties before the law." Urban women are no longer forced to wear the *burka*, a head-to-toe covering that conceals a woman's body and face from men, and some women have returned to work; women have even been appointed to some government positions. Nevertheless women are still repressed in rural areas, where families do not allow them, regardless of age and kinship, to participate in public life. They are denied basic education and health care, and many are forced into marriages. Due to the lack of health care, particularly obstetric care, and education, Afghanistan is one of the most dangerous places to bear children. One in sixty-two Afghan women die from pregnancy-related causes, whereas only one in 4,800 women in the United States die from pregnancy-related causes. On average an Afghan woman gives birth seven times, so the risk

Afghan girls attend a lesson at a school in Sarkani village.

© Oleg Popov/Reuters/Landov

of complications is much higher than for a woman in the United States, who averages two births. Moreover the average life expectancy for Afghan women is forty-four years.

A non-governmental organization (NGO), Women for Women International has established literacy programs that have taught 5,000 women to read and write and have trained 2,500 women in basic health and birthing practices. Women for Women International has developed programs to provide access to education, employment, and health care for women. By working within the context of a culture, the NGO has helped women to make a difference for themselves, for one another, and for their families.

QUESTIONS FOR FURTHER THOUGHT

1. Why is having a sensitive cross-cultural understanding of gender important when working in Afghanistan?

2. What kinds of applied projects can you think of that might assist rural Afghan communities?

3. What cultural and ethical considerations does one need to consider before engaging in any kind of planned development in another country?

SUMMARY

1. The word *gender* refers to the way members of the two sexes are perceived, evaluated, and expected to behave. Although biology sets broad limits on definitions of gender, there is a wide range of ideas about what it means to be feminine or masculine.

2. In very general terms, there is considerable uniformity in sex roles throughout the world. Men engage in warfare, clear land, hunt animals, build houses, fish, and work with hard substances; women tend crops, prepare food, collect firewood, clean house, launder clothes, care for children, and carry water.

3. The status of women is multidimensional, involving such aspects as the division of labor, the value placed on women's contributions, economic autonomy, political power, legal rights, and the extent to which women control the everyday events of their lives.

4. Gender ideology is used in most societies to justify universal male dominance. Deeply rooted values about the superiority of men, the ritual impurity of women, and the preeminence of men's work are often used to justify the subjugation of women. However, women have demonstrated that they do not perceive themselves in the same ways they are portrayed in these (largely male) gender ideologies.

5. In some societies gender ideologies are so extreme that females suffer serious negative consequences, such as female infanticide, female genital cutting, female nutritional deprivation, rape, and spouse abuse.

6. The economy of the United States is characterized by a high rate of occupational segregation along gender lines. Not only are occupations gender segregated, but women tend to earn considerably less than men. Moreover there has been a trend in recent decades toward the feminization of poverty around the world due to unequal access to education and the higher-paying skilled jobs.

KEY TERMS

double workload 215

female infanticide 211

femininity 198

feminization of
  poverty 207

gender 198

gender ideology 210

gender roles 202

gender stratification 203

human sexuality 200

male gender bias 211

masculinity 198

nutritional
  deprivation 212

occupational
  segregation 215

purdah 204

sex 198

sexual asymmetry 206

sexual dimorphism 197

universal male
  dominance 205

A local chief in Kaduna, Nigeria.

Brian Ward/Photo Researchers, Inc.

CHAPTER **9**

Political Organization and Social Control

221

MONOLINGUALISM AND HOMELAND SECURITY

Cross-cultural misunderstandings can occur whenever people from different cultural backgrounds get together. This happens among ordinary people and heads of state as well as government bureaucrats. In February 2004 in the Portland, Oregon, airport, seven members of the Moroccan Parliament were detained for several hours by employees of the Transportation Security Administration (TSA) due to an unintentional language mix-up.

The visitors, part of a goodwill tour, were searched and interviewed by FBI agents before they boarded the plane. At the gate, however, one member of the delegation realized that he had left a carry-on bag at a terminal coffee shop. When he returned after retrieving the bag, authorities refused to allow him to board the plane and, in fact, the pilot ordered the other six members off the plane for further questioning and inspection. TSA employees were alarmed when they discovered documents written in Arabic containing several references to 911.

Because the TSA officials could not read Arabic and the Moroccan delegation had no fluency in English, it took a while before the incident was resolved. As it turned out, the group's hosts in Dallas had given them instructions to dial 911 if they needed assistance. Here, then, was an unfortunate incident, caused by a lack of linguistic/cultural knowledge on the parts of both the foreign visitors and U.S government employees, which did nothing to foster international understanding between Morocco and the United States.

QUESTIONS FOR FURTHER THOUGHT

1. What is racial/ethnic profiling? Do you think the TSA authorities used profiling in this situation?

2. Is there any way this unfortunate incident could have been avoided?

3. Can you think of other cross-cultural misunderstandings that have occurred with international travelers?

As mentioned in the discussion of cultural universals in Chapter 2, all societies, if they are to remain viable over time, must maintain social order. Every society must develop a set of customs and procedures for making and enforcing decisions, resolving disputes, and regulating the behavior of its members. Every society must make collective decisions about its environment and its relations with other societies and about how to maintain social order at home. This chapter will explore the political and social foundations of collective decision making and maintenance of social order by discussing such topics as political organization, law, power, authority, political integration, social control, and conflict resolution (Kurtz 2001; Lewellen 2003).

When most North Americans think of politics and social control, a number of familiar images come to mind:

- Political leaders such as presidents, governors, mayors, and commissioners
- Complex bureaucracies employing thousands of civil servants
- Legislative bodies ranging from the smallest town council to the U.S. Congress
- Formal judicial institutions that comprise municipal, state, and federal courts
- Law enforcement bodies such as police departments, national guard units, and the armed forces
- Political parties, nominating conventions, and secret-ballot voting

All of these are formal mechanisms that our own society uses for making and enforcing political decisions as well as coordinating and regulating people's behavior. Some small-scale societies in the world have none of these things—no elected officials, legislatures, judges, formal elections, armies, or bureaucracies. We should not conclude from this, however, that such societies do not have some form of political organization. As we shall discover in this chapter, all societies have customary procedures for decision making, conflict resolution, and social control.

Types of Political Organization

The term *political organization* refers to the way in which power is distributed within a society so as to control people's behavior and maintain social order. All societies are organized politically, but the degree of specialization and the formal mechanisms vary considerably from one society to another. Societies differ in their political organization based on three important dimensions:

1. The extent to which political institutions are distinct from other aspects of the social structure; for example, in some societies political structures are barely distinguishable from economic, kinship, or religious structures.
2. The extent to which legitimate **authority** is concentrated in specific political roles.
3. The level of **political integration**—that is, the size of the territorial group that comes under the control of the political structure.

These three dimensions are the basis for classifying societies into four fundamentally different types of political structure: band societies, tribal societies, chiefdoms, and state societies (Service 1978). Although some societies do not fit neatly into a single category, this fourfold scheme can help us understand how different societies administer themselves and maintain social order.

Our discussions of all four types of political organization are written using the "ethnographic present"—that is, describing a culture as it was in an earlier time (e.g., prior to contact with a colonizing power). Thus we need to remember that there are no pure bands, tribes, or chiefdoms in the world today. Rather these nonstate forms of political organization have had more complex state political systems superimposed on them.

Band Societies

The least complex type of political structure is the **band society**, characterized by small and usually nomadic populations of food collectors. Although the size of a band can range from twenty to several hundred individuals, most bands are made up of between thirty and fifty people. The actual size of a particular band is directly related to its food-gathering methods; that is, the more food a band has at its disposal, the larger the number of people it can support. Although bands may be loosely associated with a specific territory, they have little or no concept of individual property ownership of land or livestock, and they place a high value on sharing, cooperation, and reciprocity. Band societies have very little role specialization and are highly egalitarian, with few differences in status and wealth. Because this form of political organization is so closely associated with foraging, it is generally thought to be the oldest form of political organization.

Band societies share four traits:

1. Because bands are composed of a relatively small number of people who are related by blood or marriage, a high value is placed on "getting along" with one another.

2. Band societies have the least amount of political integration; that is, the various bands are independent of one another and are not part of a larger political structure.

3. In band societies political decisions are often embedded in the wider social structure. Because bands are composed of kin, it is difficult to distinguish between purely political decisions and those that we would recognize as family, economic, or religious decisions.

4. Leadership roles in band societies tend to be very informal. There are no specialized political roles or leaders with designated authority. Instead leaders in band societies are often, but not always, older men who are respected for their experience, wisdom, good judgment, and knowledge of hunting.

The Ju/'hoansi of the Kalahari exemplify a band society with a *head-man* (a person, nearly always a man, in many small-scale societies who functions as a leader but has little or no coercive authority). Although the position of headman is hereditary, the actual authority of the headman is limited. The headman coordinates the movement of his people and usually walks at the head of the group. He chooses the sites of new encampments and has first pick of location for his own house site. But beyond these limited perks of office, the Ju/'hoansi headman receives no other rewards. He is not responsible for organizing hunting parties, making artifacts, or negotiating marriage arrangements. These activities fall to the individual members of the band. The headman is not expected to be a judge of his people, but he can be called upon for his experience and wisdom to suggest resolutions to problems. Moreover he has no more material possessions than anyone else. As Lorna Marshall (1965: 267) so aptly put it when referring to the Ju/'hoansi headman: "He carries his own load and is as thin as the rest."

Tribal Societies

Whereas band societies are usually associated with food collecting, **tribal societies** are found most often among food producers (horticulturalists and pastoralists). Because plant and animal domestication is far more productive than foraging, tribal societies tend to have populations that are larger, denser, and somewhat more sedentary than bands. Tribal societies are similar to band societies in several important respects, however. Both are egalitarian to the extent that there are very few marked differences in status, rank, power, and wealth. In addition tribal societies, like bands, have local leaders but no centralized leadership. Leadership in tribal societies is informal and not vested in a centralized authority. A man is recognized as a leader by virtue of certain personality traits such as wisdom, integrity, intelligence, and concern for the welfare of others. Although tribal leaders often play a central role in formulating decisions, they cannot force their will on a group. In the final analysis, decisions are arrived at through group consensus.

The major difference between tribes and bands is that tribal societies have certain **pan-tribal mechanisms** that cut across and integrate all the local segments of the tribe into a larger whole. These mechanisms include tribal associations such as clans, age grades, and secret societies. Pan-tribal associations unite the tribe against external threats. These integrating forces are not permanent political fixtures, however. Most often the local units of a tribe operate autonomously. The integrating mechanisms come into play only when an external threat arises. When the threat is eliminated, the local units return to their autonomous state. Even though these pan-tribal mechanisms may be transitory, they

Tribal societies, such as the Samburu of Kenya, have certain pan-tribal mechanisms, such as clans and age organizations, that serve to integrate the tribe as a whole.

nevertheless provide wider political integration in certain situations than would ever be possible in band societies.

In many tribal societies, the kinship unit known as the clan serves as a pan-tribal mechanism of political integration. The *clan* is defined as a group of kin who consider themselves to be descended from a common ancestor, even though individual clan members cannot trace, step by step, their connection to the clan founder. Clan elders, although they do not hold formal political offices, usually manage the affairs of their clans (settling disputes between clan members, for example) and represent their clans in dealings with other clans.

The pastoral Nuer of the southern Sudan are a good example of a tribal form of political organization (Evans-Pritchard 1940). The Nuer, who number approximately three hundred thousand people, have no centralized government and no government functionaries with coercive authority. Of course there are influential men, but their influence stems more from their personal traits than from the force of elected or inherited office. The Nuer, who are highly egalitarian, do not readily accept authority beyond the elders of the family. Social control is maintained by segmentary lineages, in that close kin are expected to come to the assistance of one another against more distantly related people.

The term *tribe* has carried with it a generally negative connotation in the Western world for the past several centuries. During the colonial period of the nineteenth century, the term *tribal,* often equated with "uncivilized," was used to disparage any group that had no centralized hierarchical authority.

Chiefdoms

As we have seen, in band and tribal societies, local groups are economically and politically autonomous, authority is decentralized, and populations tend to be generally egalitarian. Moreover roles are unspecialized, populations are small, and economies are largely subsistent in nature. But as societies become more complex—with larger and more specialized populations, more sophisticated technology, and growing surpluses—their need for more formal and permanent political structures increases. In such societies, known as **chiefdoms**, political authority is likely to reside with a single individual, acting alone or in conjunction with an advisory council.

Chiefdoms differ from bands and tribes in that chiefdoms integrate a number of local communities in a more formal and permanent way. Unlike bands and tribes, chiefdoms are made up of local communities that differ from one another in rank and status. Based on their genealogical proximity to the chiefs, nobles and commoners hold different levels of prestige and power. Chiefships are often hereditary, and the chief and his or her immediate kin constitute a social and political elite. Rarely are chiefdoms unified politically under a single chief; more often they are composed of several political units, each headed by its own chief.

Chiefdoms also differ from tribes and bands in that chiefs are centralized and permanent officials who have higher rank, power, and authority than others in the society. Unlike band or tribal headmen, chiefs usually have considerable power, authority, and in some cases wealth. Internal social disruptions are minimized in a chiefdom because the chief usually has authority to make judgments, punish wrongdoers, and settle disputes. Chiefs usually have the authority to distribute land to loyal subjects, recruit people into military service, and assign laborers to public works projects.

Chiefs are also intimately related to the economic activities of their subjects through the redistributive system of economics. Subjects give food surpluses to the chief (not uncommonly at the chief's insistence), which the chief then redistributes through communal feasts and doles. This system of redistribution through a chief serves the obvious *economic* function of ensuring that no people in the society go hungry. It also serves the important *political* function of providing the people with a mechanism for expressing their loyalty and support for the chief.

The precolonial Hawaiian political system of the eighteenth century embodied the features of a typical chiefdom. According to Elman Service (1975), Hawaiian society, covering eight islands, was layered into three basic social strata. At the apex of the social hierarchy were the *ali'i*, major chiefs believed to be direct descendants of the gods; their close relatives often served as advisors or bureaucrats under them. The second echelon, known as the *konohiki,* were less important chiefs who were often distant relatives of the *ali'i.* And finally the great majority of people were commoners, known as *maka 'ainana.* The major chiefs and their subordinates wielded considerable power and authority over the general population because they had responsibility for the allocation of water for irrigation, communal labor, dispute settlement, and recruiting men for warfare.

State Societies

The **state system of government** is the most formal and most complex form of political organization. A *state* can be defined as a hierarchical form of political organization that governs many communities within a large geographic area. States collect taxes, recruit labor for armies and civilian public works projects, and have a monopoly on the right to use force. They are large bureaucratic organizations made up of permanent institutions with legislative, administrative, and judicial functions. Whereas bands, tribes, and (to a lesser degree) chiefdoms have political structures based on kinship, state systems of government organize their power on a supra-kinship basis. That is, a person's membership in a state is based on his or her place of residence and citizenship rather than on kinship affiliation. Over the past several thousand years, state systems of government have taken various forms, including Greek city-states; the Roman Empire; certain traditional African states such as Bunyoro, Buganda, and the Swazi; theocratic states (governments headed by clerical leaders considered to be divinely guided) such as ancient Egypt; and modern nation-states such as Germany, China, Canada, and the United States.

State systems of government are characterized by a high degree of role specialization and hierarchical organization. Many of the specialized political roles are played out in legislative bodies, such as the German Bundestag in Berlin.

© Brooks Kraft/Corbis

The authority of the state rests on two important foundations. First, the state holds the exclusive right to use force and physical coercion. Any act of violence not expressly permitted by the state is illegal and consequently punishable by the state. Thus state governments make written laws, administer them through various levels of the bureaucracy, and enforce them through mechanisms such as police forces, armies, and national guards. The state needs to be continuously vigilant against threats both from within and from without to usurp its power through rebellions and revolutions. Second, the state maintains its authority by means of ideology. For the state to hold on to power over the long run, there must be a philosophical understanding among the citizenry that the state has the legitimate right to govern. In the absence of such an ideology, it is often difficult for the state to maintain its authority by means of coercive force alone.

State systems of government, which first appeared about 5,500 years ago, are found in societies with complex socioeconomic characteristics. For example, state systems of government are supported by intensive agriculture, which is required to support a large number of bureaucrats who are not producing food. This fully efficient food-production system gives rise to cities, considerable labor specialization, and a complex system of internal distribution and foreign trade. Because the considerable surpluses produced by intensive agriculture are not distributed equally among all segments of the population, state societies are socially stratified. That is, forms of wealth such as land and capital tend to be concentrated in the hands of an elite, who often use their superior wealth and power to control the rest of the population. Moreover the fairly complex laws and regulations needed to control a large and heterogeneous population give rise to the need for some type of writing, record keeping, and a system of weights and measures.

State systems of government are characterized by a large number of **specialized political roles**. Many people are required to carry out very specific tasks, such as law enforcement, tax collection, dispute settlement, recruitment of labor, and protection from outside invasions. These political/administrative functionaries are highly specialized and work full time to the extent that they do not engage in food-producing activities. These permanent political functionaries are highly stratified or hierarchical. At the apex of the administrative pyramid are those with the greatest power—kings, presidents, prime ministers, governors, and legislators—who enact laws and establish policies. Below them are descending echelons of bureaucrats responsible for the day-to-day administration of the state. As is the case in our own form of government, each level of the bureaucracy is responsible to the level immediately above it.

Not only are the political structures of state societies stratified and hierarchical, but so are the entire societies themselves. Stratified state societies are characterized by considerable inequality in terms of power, wealth, and prestige. The political, economic, and social inequality in stratified societies is both permanent and formally recognized by the members of the society. Some people—and, indeed, entire groups of people—have little or no access to the basic resources of the society, while others have considerable access. Various groups in stratified societies are noticeably different in social position, wealth, lifestyle, access to power, and standard of living. The unequal access to rewards is generally inheritable from one generation to the next.

Social scientists generally recognize two different types of stratified societies: those based on class and those based on caste. The key to understanding this fundamental distinction is **social mobility**. In **class** systems, a certain amount of upward and downward social mobility exists. In other words, an individual can change his or her social position dramatically within a lifetime. An individual, through diligence, intelligence, and good luck, could go from rags to riches; conversely, a person born to millionaire parents could wind up as a homeless street person (Newman 1999). **Caste** societies, on the other hand, have little or no social mobility. Membership in a caste is determined by birth and lasts throughout one's lifetime, although this is changing in certain situations in India. Whereas members of a class society are able to elevate their social position by marrying into a higher class, caste systems allow marriages only within one's own caste.

Another important distinction is how statuses (positions) within each type of society are allocated. Class systems are associated with an **achieved status**, whereas caste systems are associated with an **ascribed status**. Achieved statuses are those that the individual chooses or at least has some control over. A person attains an achieved status as a result of her or his personal effort, such as graduating from college, marrying someone, or taking a particular job. In contrast, a person is born into an ascribed status and has no control over it. Statuses based on such criteria as sex, race, and age are examples of ascribed statuses.

It is important to bear in mind that stratified societies cannot all be divided neatly into either class or caste systems. In general, class systems are open to the extent that they are based on achieved statuses and permit considerable social mobility, and caste systems tend to be closed to the extent that they are based on ascribed statuses and allow little or no social mobility, either up or down. Having made these conceptual distinctions, however, we must also realize that in the real world, class and caste systems overlap. Most stratified societies contain elements of both class and caste.

CLASS SOCIETIES Even though the boundaries between social strata in a class society are not rigidly drawn, social inequalities nevertheless exist. A social class is a segment of a population whose members share similar lifestyles and levels of wealth, power, and prestige. The United States is a good example of a class society. In some areas of the United States, such as coal-mining towns in Appalachia, there may be only two classes: the haves and the have-nots. More often, however, social scientists identify a number of social classes: capitalist (upper), upper middle, middle, working,

working poor, and underclass (Bensman and Vidich 1987; Gilbert 2008).

Our national mythology includes the belief that the United States offers a good deal of social mobility. Yet studies of social class in the United States have shown that most people remain in the class into which they are born and marry within that class as well. Members of the same social class share not only similar economic levels but also similar experiences, educational backgrounds, political views, memberships in organizations, occupations, and values. In addition, studies of social class have shown, not surprisingly, that members of a social class tend to associate more often with one another than with people in other classes. In other words, a person's life chances, though not determined, are very much influenced by social class.

In stratified societies, different groups, ranging from the homeless to the upper class, have different levels of power, prestige, and wealth. In the United States over the past four decades, the gap between those at the top and those at bottom has widened.

CASTE SOCIETIES In contrast to class societies, those that are based on caste rank their members according to birth. Membership in castes is unchangeable, people in different castes are segregated from one another, social mobility is virtually nonexistent, and marriage between members of different castes is strictly prohibited.

Caste societies, wherever they may be found, have certain characteristics in common. First, caste membership is directly related to economic issues such as occupation, workloads, and control of valuable resources. The higher castes have a monopoly on high-status occupations, control the allocation of resources to benefit themselves, and avoid engaging in difficult or low-status work. In short, the higher castes have more resources and do less. Second, members of the same caste share the same social status largely because of their strong sense of caste identity, residential and social segregation from other castes, and uniformity of lifestyles. Third, caste exclusiveness is further enhanced because each caste has its own set of secret rituals, which tend to intensify group awareness. Fourth, the higher castes are generally most interested in maintaining the caste system for the obvious reason that they benefit from it the most.

Caste societies are found in a number of regions of the world, such as among the Rwandans in Central Africa, but the best-known—and certainly the best-described—example of the caste system is in Hindu India. Hinduism's sacred Sanskrit texts rank all people into four categories, called **varnas**, which are associated with certain occupations. According to a Hindu myth of origin (see Mandelbaum 1970), the four major varnas originated from the body of primeval man. The highest caste, the Brahmins (priests and scholars), came from his mouth; the Kshatriyas (warriors) emanated from his arms; the Vaishyas (tradesmen) came from his thighs; and the Shudras (cultivators and servants) sprang from his feet. These four castes are hierarchically ranked according to their ritual purity. Below these four castes—and technically outside the caste system—is still another category called the Untouchables or, literally, outcasts. The Untouchables, who are confined to the lowest and most menial types of work, such as cleaning latrines and leather-working, are considered so impure that members of the other four castes must avoid all contact with them. Today this lowest caste prefers the term **Dalit**, which means literally the "crushed" or "oppressed" people. Even though caste inequities were explicitly prohibited by the Indian constitution of 1950, caste still plays an important role in the lives of most Indians in the twenty-first century.

THE MODERN NATION-STATE In recent times the word *state* has often been combined with the word *nation* to form the entity called a *nation-state*. Although these two words are often used interchangeably in everyday conversation, they are two distinct concepts. On the one hand, a **nation** is a group of people who share a common symbolic identity, culture, history, and often religion. A **state**, on the other hand, is a particular type of political structure distinct from a band, tribal society, or chiefdom. When combined, the term *nation-state* refers to a group of people sharing a common cultural background that is unified by a political structure that they all consider legitimate and that is not a band, tribe, or chiefdom.

Although this is a fairly tidy definition, few of the nearly two hundred so-called nation-states in the world today actually fit the definition. This is largely because few such entities have populations with homogeneous cultural identities. For example, the United Kingdom comprises England, Wales, Scotland, and Northern Ireland. We sometimes refer to the United Kingdom as England, but the Welsh, Scots, and Irish, clearly do not regard themselves as English in their language, tradition, or ethnicity. The collapse of the Soviet Union gave rise to a dozen new nation-states, including Belarus, Ukraine, Georgia, Azerbaijan, and Moldova. And of course many of the newly independent African nation-states represented in the United Nations since the 1960s have enormous ethnic heterogeneity.

Variations in Political Structures

In the preceding sections we have looked at four fundamentally different types of political systems. This fourfold scheme, though recognized by some anthropologists, is not universally accepted. For example, in a classic study of political systems in Africa, Meyer Fortes and E. E. Evans-Pritchard (1940) distinguished between only two types of structures: state systems and **headless societies**. Others (E. Cohen and Eames 1982) recognize three major forms of political structure: simple, intermediate, and complex. Such differences in the way various ethnologists have conceptualized political structures should serve as a reminder that all of these schemes are ideal types. That is, not all of the societies in the world fit neatly into one box or another. Instead of discrete categories, in reality there is a continuum with bands (the simplest form) at one extreme and states (the most complex form) at the other. Thus, whether we use two, three, or four major categories of political organization, we should bear in mind that the political systems of all societies vary along a continuum on a number of important dimensions. To illustrate, as we move from left to right (bands through tribes and chiefdoms to states), gradations occur, as shown in Figure 9.1. The variations in political structures are accompanied by corresponding variations in other aspects of world cultures, as shown in Figure 9.2.

FIGURE 9.1
Variations in political aspects of world cultures

	Bands	Tribes	Chiefdoms	States
Degree to which political institutions are distinct from kinship	Indistinguishable			Distinct
Level of political integration	Local group			Many groups
Specialized political roles	Informal leadership			Highly specialized
	Temporary			Permanent
Degree of political coerciveness	Little/none			Complete
Conflict resolution	Informal			Formal and informal

© Cengage Learning 2013

FIGURE 9.2
Variations in socioeconomic aspects of world cultures

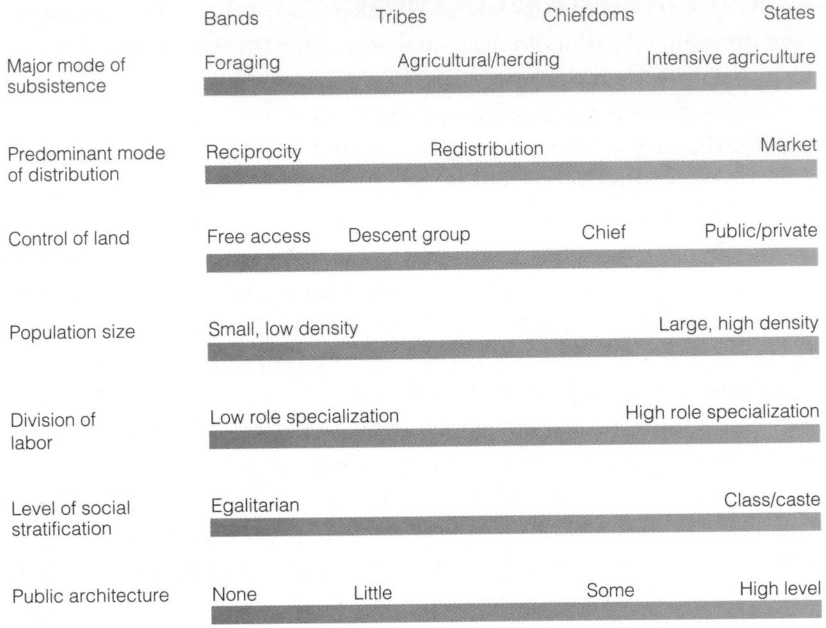

	Bands	Tribes	Chiefdoms	States
Major mode of subsistence	Foraging	Agricultural/herding	Intensive agriculture	
Predominant mode of distribution	Reciprocity	Redistribution		Market
Control of land	Free access	Descent group	Chief	Public/private
Population size	Small, low density		Large, high density	
Division of labor	Low role specialization		High role specialization	
Level of social stratification	Egalitarian			Class/caste
Public architecture	None	Little	Some	High level

© Cengage Learning 2013

Social Control

As the preceding section explained, political structures vary from very informal structures such as bands at one extreme to highly complex state systems of government at the other extreme. Whatever form of political organization is found in a society, however, it must inevitably address the issue of **social control**. In other words, every society must ensure that most of the people behave in appropriate ways most of the time. Statelike societies, such as our own, have a wide variety of formal mechanisms to keep people's behavior in line, including written laws, judges, bureaucracies, prisons, execution chambers, and police forces. At the other extreme, small-scale band societies, such as the Inuit or Ju/'hoansi, have no centralized political authority but nevertheless maintain social order among their members through informal mechanisms of social control. In fact, because of the effectiveness of these non-governmental mechanisms of social control (discussed below), people deviate from acceptable behavior considerably less in most band societies than in societies that have more elaborate and complex forms of political organization.

Every society has defined what it considers to be normal, proper, or expected ways of behaving. These expectations, known as **social norms**, serve as behavioral guidelines that help the society work smoothly. To be certain, social norms are not adhered to perfectly, and in fact there is a certain amount of deviance from them in all societies. But most people in any given society abide by the norms most of the time. Moreover social norms take a number of different forms, ranging from etiquette to formal laws. Some norms are taken more seriously than others. On one hand, all societies have certain social expectations of what is proper, but such behavior is not rigidly enforced. To illustrate, although it is customary in the United States for people to shake hands when being introduced, a person's refusal to shake hands does not constitute a serious violation of social norms. The person who does not follow this rule of etiquette might be considered rude but would not be arrested or executed. On the other hand, some social norms (such as those against grand larceny or murder) are taken very seriously because they are considered absolutely necessary for the survival of the society.

Social scientists use the term **deviance** to refer to the violation of social norms. It is important to keep in mind that deviance is relative, however. What people in one culture consider to be deviant is not necessarily considered deviant in other cultures. In other words, it is not the act itself but rather how people define the act that determines whether it is deviant. To illustrate, suicide among middle-class North Americans is considered to be unacceptable under any conditions. In traditional Japan, however, the practice of *hara-kiri*, committing ritual suicide by disembowelment, was considered in traditional times the honorable thing to do for a disgraced nobleman. Thus, whereas ritual suicide was normative for the Japanese nobleman, it is considered deviant for a businessperson in Montreal or Miami.

All social norms, whether trivial or serious, are sanctioned; that is, societies develop patterned or institutionalized ways of encouraging people to conform to the norms. These **sanctions** are both positive and negative because people are rewarded for behaving in socially acceptable ways and punished for violating the norms. **Positive sanctions** range from a smile of approval to being awarded the Congressional Medal of Honor. **Negative sanctions** include everything from a frown of disapproval to the death penalty.

Social sanctions may also be formal or informal, depending on whether a formal law (legal statute) has been violated. To illustrate, if a woman in a restaurant is talking in a voice that can be easily overheard by people at nearby tables, she will probably receive stares from the other diners. But if she starts yelling at the top of her lungs in the restaurant, she will probably be arrested for disturbing the peace or disorderly conduct. The difference, of course, is that in the first case the woman isn't breaking the law, but in

FIGURE 9.3

Continuum of social norms in the United States

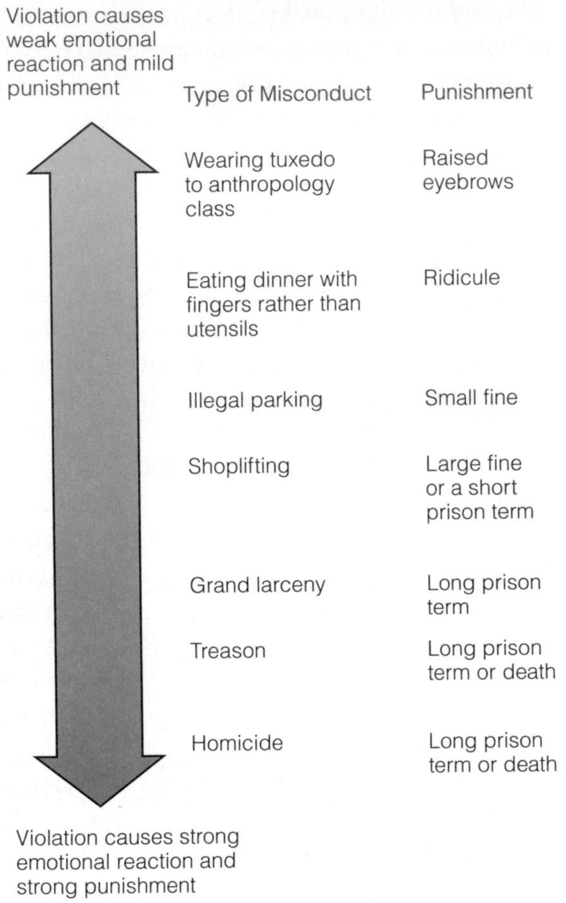

Violation causes
weak emotional
reaction and mild
punishment

Type of Misconduct	Punishment
Wearing tuxedo to anthropology class	Raised eyebrows
Eating dinner with fingers rather than utensils	Ridicule
Illegal parking	Small fine
Shoplifting	Large fine or a short prison term
Grand larceny	Long prison term
Treason	Long prison term or death
Homicide	Long prison term or death

Violation causes strong
emotional reaction and
strong punishment

© Cengage Learning 2013

the second case she is. Figure 9.3 shows a continuum of social norms and sanctions in U.S. society.

Just as the types of social norms found in any society vary, so do the mechanisms used to encourage people to adhere to those norms. For most North Americans, the most obvious forms of social control are the formal or institutionalized ones. When asked why we tend to behave ourselves, we probably think of formal laws, police forces, courts, and prisons. We don't rob the local convenience store, in other words, because if caught, we are likely to go to prison.

Most of our "proper" behavior is probably governed by less formal, and perhaps less obvious, mechanisms of social control. In band and tribal societies that lack centralized authority, informal mechanisms of social control may be all that exist. It should be emphasized, however, that this distinction between formal and informal mechanisms does not imply that informal means of social control exist only in band and tribal societies. Although societies with complex political organizations (state societies in particular) are best known for written laws and courts, they also rely on an appreciable number of informal mechanisms of social control.

Compared to complex state organizations, bands and tribes have little that appears to be *governmental* in the Western sense of the term. These small-scale political systems have been described as *headless* societies or "tribes without rulers" (Middleton and Tait 1958). In the absence of formal governmental structures, how do these headless societies maintain social order? The following three sections examine mechanisms of social control that are found (1) universally in all types of societies, from band through state systems; (2) only in small-scale societies such as bands and tribes; and (3) only in complex, heterogeneous, and hierarchical state systems.

Mechanisms of Social Control in All Types of Societies

SOCIALIZATION Every society, if it is to survive, must pass on its social rules and norms from one generation to another. It seems obvious that people cannot conform to the social norms unless they learn them. Thus all societies have some system of **socialization**, which involves teaching the young what the norms are and that they should not be violated. In other words, not only do people live in societies, but societies live in people. People learn their social norms with a certain degree of moral compulsion. We learn, for example, that in North America people wear clothes in public and that we should do so as well. Usually we internalize our social norms so effectively that we would never consider violating them. Some social norms—such as not appearing nude in public—are so thoroughly ingrained in us through socialization that the thought of violating them is distasteful and embarrassing. Other social norms do not have the same level of moral intensity, such as driving under the speed limit or maintaining good oral hygiene. But as a general rule, when people learn the norms of their society, they are at the same time internalizing the moral necessity to obey them.

PUBLIC OPINION One of the most compelling reasons for not violating social norms is **public opinion** or social pressure. In general, people from all parts of the world wish to be accepted by the other members of their society. Most people fear being rejected or criticized by their friends or neighbors. This strong desire to be liked is reflected in comments such as "Don't do that! What will the neighbors think?" Of course, it is impossible to determine how many people are deterred from violating the social norms by fear of negative public opinion. At the same time, we can cite many examples of how societies use social pressure (or what is called "strategic embarrassment") very deliberately to keep people in line. Indeed gossip, ostracism, rumor, sarcasm, and derision are powerful corrective measures for reforming social behavior. For example, some city and county governments in the United States print the names of tax delinquents in the local newspaper in an attempt to embarrass them into paying their taxes. In colonial America the stocks and pillory were excellent examples of using public opinion to control people's behavior. Someone who was caught breaking the social norms (such as committing adultery or stealing) was confined to the stocks or pillory, which, not coincidentally, was always located in the center of town. Even though long confinements were physically very uncomfortable, the realization that all of your friends, relatives, and neighbors would see you and know of your crime was by far the greater punishment.

SUPERNATURAL BELIEF SYSTEMS A powerful mechanism of social control in all types of societies is **supernatural belief systems**—belief in supernatural forces such as gods, witches, and sorcerers. People will refrain from antisocial behavior if they believe that some supernatural (suprahuman) force will punish them for it. Of course it is impossible to determine how many norms are *not* violated because people fear supernatural retribution, but we have to assume that the belief in supernatural sanctions acts as a deterrent to some degree. Nor is it necessary to prove that the gods, for example, will punish social deviants. If people believe that "god will get them" for doing something wrong, the belief itself is

Many people in the world, including members of this Christian church, tend to conform to social norms out of a strong belief in supernatural forces.

usually enough to discourage the deviant behavior. This is certainly the case in Western religions (Judeo-Christian), which teach about atonement for one's sins, Judgment Day, and heaven and hell, which are the ultimate positive and negative sanctions. In small-scale societies there are other forms of supernatural belief systems (such as ancestor worship, sorcery, and witchcraft) that are equally effective social mechanisms for controlling people's behavior.

Belief in **witchcraft**, which is common in some small-scale societies, discourages people from engaging in socially deviant behavior. In many societies where witchcraft is practiced, people reject the idea that misfortunes are the result of natural causes. If crops fail or large numbers of people die, the usual explanation is that someone has been practicing witchcraft. In societies that believe in witchcraft, a deviant runs the risk of being labeled a witch, and fear of being accused of witchcraft strongly encourages conformity. For example, in colonial America, nonconformists, freethinkers, and others who didn't conform to expected behavioral norms were driven from their communities for allegedly being witches. Jean La Fontaine (1963: 217) notes how witchcraft serves as a mechanism of social control among the Bantu-speaking Bagisu of East Africa:

> Witchcraft beliefs act as a form of social control in discouraging behavior that is socially unacceptable. In Bagisu the eccentric is branded a witch. . . . Children grow up with the realization that the stigma of nonconformity is dangerous; too great a departure from the norms of everyday conduct will attract the suspicion of others and lead to isolation and eventual destruction.

Mechanisms of Social Control in Small-Scale Societies

CORPORATE LINEAGES Corporate lineages play an important role in most small-scale societies. **Corporate lineages** (which can number in the hundreds) are kinship groups whose members often live, work, play, and pray together. Property is controlled by the lineage, people derive their primary identity from the group, and even religion (in the form of ancestor worship) is a lineage matter. Acting like a small corporation, the lineage has a powerful impact on the everyday lives of its members and can exert considerable pressure on people to conform to the social norms.

One means by which a corporate lineage exerts control over its members is economic. All important property, such as land and livestock, is controlled by the elders of the corporate lineage. Often property is allocated on the basis of conformity to societal norms. Those who behave as the society expects them to behave are likely to receive the best plots of land and use of the best livestock. Conversely those who violate social norms are likely to be denied these valuable economic resources.

Corporate lineages, to some degree, also act as mechanisms of social control because of their scale. Corporate lineages serve as localized communities, numbering from several hundred to several thousand relatives. Because members of the lineage have frequent and intense interaction with one another on a daily basis, it is virtually impossible for anyone to maintain her or his anonymity. People's lives are played out in such close proximity to one another that everyone knows what everyone else is doing. To illustrate, a man who wants to engage in socially inappropriate behavior (such as having an extramarital affair) would think twice because it would be difficult, if not impossible, to keep it a secret. By way of contrast, it is considerably easier to have an extramarital affair and remain undetected in a large city. Thus the small scale of corporate lineage communities tends to inhibit social deviance because it is much more difficult for people to get away with breaking the rules.

Marriage in corporate lineage societies also plays a role in social control. Marriage is regarded primarily as an alliance between two lineages—that of the bride and that of the groom—and only secondarily as a union between two individuals. In many cases the marriage is legitimized by bridewealth (the transfer of property, often livestock, from the kin group of the groom to the kin group of the bride). When a man wants to get married, he cannot pay the bridewealth himself because he does not have personal control over property. Like the rest of his relatives, he has limited rights and obligations to property such as cattle. If marriage cattle are to be transferred, the prospective groom must convince a number of his kin to give up their limited use of cows. If the prospective groom has a reputation for violating the social norms, it is unlikely that he will get permission to transfer the cows. Thus the members of a corporate lineage, through their collective capacity to control marriage, have considerable power to coerce people to behave appropriately.

SONG DUELS Just as societies differ in the incidence of crime, they also differ in the way they handle disputes and crimes. One example of a formal mechanism for resolving disputes was found among the Inuit of Canada, Alaska, and Greenland. Because the Inuit had little property due to their nomadic way of life, conflicts rarely arose over violation of property rights. However, disputes often arose between men over the issue of wife stealing. A man would attempt to steal the wife of a more prominent man as a way of elevating his own standing within the community. One common way of punishing wife stealing among the Inuit was to murder the wife stealer. In fact Knud Rasmussen (1927) found that all of the men he studied had been a party to a murder, either as the murderer or as an accessory, and invariably these murders stemmed from allegations of wife stealing. However, there were alternative ways to resolve disputes over wife stealing. One was to challenge the alleged wife stealer to a **song duel**, a derisive song contest, which was fought with song and lyrics rather than with weapons. The plaintiff and defendant, appearing in a public setting, chided each other with abusive songs especially composed for the occasion. The contestant who received the loudest applause emerged the winner of this "curse by verse" song duel. Interestingly, the resolution of the conflict was based not on a determination of guilt or innocence but on one's verbal dexterity.

INTERMEDIARIES Some societies use **intermediaries** to help resolve serious conflicts. The Nuer of the African Sudan are a case in point (Evans-Pritchard 1940). Even though the Nuer political system is informal and decentralized, one role in the society—the **Leopard-Skin Chief**—is, to a degree, institutionalized. In the absence of any formal system of law courts to punish serious crimes such as murder, the Leopard-Skin Chief serves as a mediator between the victim's family and the family of the murderer. When a homicide occurs, the murderer, fearing the vengeance of the victim's family, takes sanctuary in the home of the Leopard-Skin Chief. In an attempt to prevent an all-out feud, the Leopard-Skin Chief tries to negotiate a settlement between the two families. His role is to work out an equitable agreement whereby the murderer's family will compensate the victim's family with some form of property settlement (say, forty head of cattle) for the loss of one of its members. These animals will be used as bridewealth for the lineage to obtain a wife for one of its members. It is thought that the sons from such a marriage will fill the void left by the murder victim.

If either side becomes too unyielding, the Leopard-Skin Chief can threaten to curse the offending party. The Leopard-Skin Chief does not decide the case, however. Rather he is only an intermediary, with no authority to determine guilt or force a settlement between the parties. Intervening on behalf of the public interest, he uses his personal and supernaturally sanctioned influence to bring the disputing parties to some type of settlement of their dispute.

MOOTS: INFORMAL COURTS Found in many African societies, moots are a highly effective mechanism for resolving conflicts. **Moots** are informal airings of disputes involving kinsmen and friends of the litigants. These adjudicating bodies are ad hoc, with considerable variation in composition from case to case. Moots generally deal with domestic disputes, such as mistreating a spouse, disagreeing about an inheritance, or not paying debts.

Anthropologist James Gibbs (1963) describes in considerable detail the moot system as found among the Kpelle, a Mande-speaking group of rice cultivators in Liberia and Guinea. Gibbs found that moots differ from the more formal court system that is administered by district chiefs in Kpelle society. First, unlike the more formal court system, moots are held in the homes of the complainants rather than in public places. Second, all parties concerned (**council of elders**, litigants, witnesses, and spectators) sit very close to one another in a random and mixed fashion. This seating arrangement is in marked contrast to more formal (Western) courts, which physically separate the plaintiff, the defendant, the judge, and the jury. Third, because the range of relevance in moots is very broad, the airing of grievances is more complete than in formal courts of law. Fourth, whereas in formal courts the judge controls the conduct of the proceedings, in moots the investigation is more in the hands of the disputants themselves. Fifth, moots do not attempt to blame one party unilaterally but rather attribute fault in the dispute to both parties. Finally, the sanctions imposed by the moot are not so severe that the losing party has grounds for a new grudge against the other party. The party found to be at fault is assessed a small fine, is expected to give the wronged party a token gift, and is required to make a public apology.

Unlike more formal court systems—including those in our own society—moots do not separate the guilty party from society by incarceration. Just the opposite is true. Moots attempt to *reintegrate* the guilty party back into the community, restore normal social relations between the disputing parties, and achieve reconciliation without bitterness and acrimony. The ritualized apology given by the guilty party symbolizes the consensual nature of the resolution and its emphasis on healing the community rather than simply punishing the wrongdoer.

OATHS AND ORDEALS Another way of resolving conflicts—particularly when law enforcement agencies (such as governments) are not especially strong—is through religiously sanctioned methods such as oaths and ordeals. An **oath** is a formal declaration to some supernatural power that what you are saying is truthful or that you are innocent. Although they can take many different forms, oaths almost always are accompanied by a ritual act, such as smoking a peace pipe, signing a loyalty document, or swearing on the Bible (as in our courts of law). Because some believe that to swear a false oath could lead to supernatural retribution, oaths can be effective in determining guilt or innocence.

An **ordeal** is a dangerous test used to determine guilt. If the accused passes the test, it is believed that a higher supernatural force has determined that the party is innocent; if he or she fails, the gods have signaled the party's guilt. In some African societies, an accused person is expected to plunge his hand into a pot of boiling water, lift out a hot stone, and then put his hand into a pot of cold water. The hand is then bandaged and examined the following day. If the hand is blistered, the accused is deemed guilty; if not, his innocence is proclaimed. To Westerners steeped in the principles of the physical sciences, such an approach to determining guilt or innocence seems mystical at best. But there is often more information being gathered than meets the untrained eye. For example, those in charge of conducting the ordeal prepare the accused psychologically to take the proceedings seriously. They explain in considerable detail how the ordeal works; they may put their own hands in the water briefly to show how the innocent are protected from blistering. During these preliminaries to the actual physical ordeal, the person administering the ordeal is looking for nonverbal behaviors of the suspect that may indicate probable guilt: signs of excessive anxiety such as muscle tension, perspiration, or dilation of the pupils. Based on an assessment of these nonverbal signs of anxiety, the ordeal administrator may alter such factors as the length of time the suspect's hand stays in the water, which, in turn, may affect the outcome of the ordeal.

Mechanisms of Social Control in State Societies

As we have noted, *all* societies use informal mechanisms of social control to some degree. Western cultures rely heavily on such mechanisms as socialization, public opinion, and religious sanctions to encourage people to maintain the social order by behaving appropriately. Often, however, these informal mechanisms are not sufficient to maintain the desired level of conformity to the norms. The violation of social norms often results in disputes among people in the society. When such disputes become violent conflicts (such as theft, assault, or homicide), we call them **crimes**. Because societies face the possibility of violent conflict erupting among their members, they need to develop explicit mechanisms to address and, it is hoped, resolve the conflicts.

Although no society in the world is free from crime, the incidence of crime varies considerably from society to society. It appears that crime is more likely to occur in large, heterogeneous, stratified societies than in small-scale societies. For example, the crime rate in U.S. cities is approximately ten times higher than in rural areas. Several logical arguments support this finding. First, as mentioned in the discussion of corporate lineages, people in small-scale societies have little or no anonymity, which makes getting away with a crime more difficult. Second, because people in small-scale societies know most of the other people, they are more likely to be concerned with negative public opinion. Third, the heterogeneous character of populations in large-scale, complex state societies means that there are many groups with different, and sometimes conflicting, interests. Finally, the fact that large-scale societies are almost always stratified into classes or castes means that the lower strata of the population may feel blocked from upward mobility and consequently may be more likely to want to violate the rights of those in the more privileged strata.

A characteristic of state systems of government is that they have a monopoly on the use of force. Through a system of codified laws, the state both forbids individuals from using force and determines how it will use force to require citizens to do some things and prevent them from doing others. These laws, which are usually in written form, are established by legislative bodies, interpreted by judicial bodies, and enforced by administrators. When legal prescriptions are violated, the state has the authority, through its courts and law enforcement agencies, to fine, imprison, or even execute the wrongdoer. To suggest that the state has a monopoly on the use of force does not mean that only the government uses force, however. State systems of government constantly have to deal with unauthorized uses of force, such as crime (violent disputes between individuals or groups), **rebellion** (attempts to displace the people in power), and **revolution** (attempts to overthrow the entire system of government).

The system of codified laws used to resolve disputes and maintain social order in complex societies is different from other types of social norms. Legal anthropologist E. Adamson Hoebel (1972) identified three basic features of **law**. Although his definition of *law* goes beyond the type of law found in Western societies, it certainly applies to that type of law as well.

1. Law involves the legitimate use of physical coercion. Law without the force to punish or deprive is no law at all, although in most cases force is not necessary because the very threat of force or compulsion acts as a sufficient deterrent to antisocial behavior.

2. Legal systems allocate official authority to privileged people who are able to use coercion legitimately.

3. Law is based on regularity and a certain amount of predictability; that is, because laws build on precedents, new laws are based on old ones.

Legal systems in complex societies have different objectives from systems of conflict resolution found in other societies. The objective of the Nuer Leopard-Skin Chief and the Kpelle moots, for example, was to compensate the victim and to reestablish harmony among the disputants and consequently peace within the community. Law enforcement and conflict resolution in complex societies, in contrast, tend to emphasize punishment of the wrongdoer, which often takes the form of incarceration or, in some cases, death. In other words, the legal system is not aimed at either compensating the victim or reintegrating the offender back into the community.

This fundamental difference in legal philosophy has played itself out in a number of conflicts around the world. In the case of the tribal violence that started in the mid-1980s in northern Uganda, the International Criminal Court at The Hague indicted rebel leaders in 2005 for killing innocent civilians. Local leaders in Uganda, however, wanted to use age-old rites designed to have the defendants admit publicly to their atrocities, pay a reasonable compensation to the victims, and then make amends with the total community. The traditional solution, based on a powerful capacity to forgive, emphasizes peace, healing between the parties, and reintegration of the wrongdoers back into the community. While the Ugandan government supports the efforts of the International Criminal Court, it has also adopted the traditional notion of forgiveness and healing as one of its strategies to restore peace to the country. Since 2000 an amnesty program has led thousands of rebels to lay down their arms, admit publicly to their misdeeds, and be welcomed back into the society. Using these traditional African philosophies of justice and law in Uganda is very similar to the work of the Truth and Reconciliation Commission (headed by Bishop Desmond Tutu) used to heal racial hatred and distrust after decades of the apartheid system in South Africa (Lacey 2005: 1).

© REUTERS/Chip East

Archbishop Desmond Tutu served as co-chair of the Truth and Reconciliation Commission, which used traditional African philosophies of law and justice to heal racial hatreds and distrust after decades of segregation in South Africa.

The incompatibility of customary law and Western law presented legal challenges for newly independent countries beginning in the early 1960s. When Western governments (such as the British, French, Portuguese, Belgians, and Spanish) administered colonies in the nineteenth and twentieth centuries, they invariably imposed their own laws on the local people, which were often at odds with local customary laws. As the colonial period came to an end during the 1960s and 1970s, many newly independent governments needed to develop legal systems based on their own customs and traditions rather than on those of the former colonial powers. This proved to be a formidable task, given the considerable ethnic diversity in the new countries.

One such former colony was the country of Papua New Guinea, which won its independence in 1975. With a population of 3.5 million, Papua New Guinea was home to approximately 750 mutually unintelligible languages and at least that many customary legal systems (Scaglion 1987: 98). The government of this newly independent country was faced with the daunting task of identifying the legal principles of these diverse customary legal systems and reconciling them into a new national legal system. To accomplish this, the parliament established the Law Reform Commission, which sponsored the Customary Law Project (CLP). Headed by legal anthropologist Richard Scaglion of the University of Pittsburgh, the CLP conducted research on local customary laws in order to determine how, and to what extent, they might serve as the basis for a national legal system.

Collecting this database of customary laws (made up of hundreds of detailed case studies) made two important practical contributions to the emerging legal system of Papua New Guinea. First, this legal database was immediately useful to lawyers searching out legal precedents for their ongoing court cases. Second, the database helped to identify, and subsequently alleviate, certain problems arising from a conflict between customary laws and the existing national legal system. To illustrate, in the area of family law, polygyny was perfectly permissible under customary law but was strictly forbidden under existing statutory law. Drawing on the database of case studies, the Law Reform Commission, in conjunction with the legislative and judicial branches of the government, drafted and passed a family bill that formally recognized the legality of customary marriages and provided for polygyny under certain circumstances.

Out in the Real World: Should Anthropologists Work for the Military?

As we have tried to show throughout this textbook, cultural anthropology has been applied successfully to a number of professional areas such as medicine, education, and business. The one professional area that has had the least collaboration with anthropology has been the military. This has become painfully obvious in our twenty-first-century wars in Afghanistan and Iraq, which have revealed just how uninformed our soldiers on the ground and our national security leadership are regarding the social and cultural realities of our adversaries. This lack of cross-cultural knowledge on the part of the military has been due to two concurrent trends over the past forty years. First, the U.S. military/national security establishment has almost completely ignored the field of cultural anthropology—the discipline that focuses on understanding cultural differences and similarities. And, second, cultural anthropologists have avoided working with the military out of fear of jeopardizing their ethical responsibility to protect the lives of the people they study.

Since 2007, however, the U.S. military has made a deliberate attempt to include anthropology and anthropologists in its training programs and strategic planning. To illustrate, officers and enlistees in the Air Force are now taking courses in comparative religion, cultures, and philosophies because they are becoming increasingly more engaged with the civilian populations where they are stationed. Moreover the Pentagon has appropriated $40 million for a program to embed anthropologists and other social scientists with combat units in Iraq and Afghanistan. According to one commander of a unit working with anthropologists, the unit's combat operations were reduced by 60 percent in the first seven months, enabling soldiers to focus more on improving security, health care, and education for the local population. More meetings with local leaders and residents—with increased cross-cultural understanding—meant that troops were able to help the local people meet their everyday needs rather than forcefully entering their homes in search of insurgents. In other words, the recently acquired cross-cultural communication skills of U.S. troops have enabled them to begin to win the hearts and minds of the local people they were trying to protect.

Although applying anthropological data, theory, insights, and values to military personnel sounds both logical and humane, some professional anthropologists have stridently opposed the Pentagon's inclusion of anthropology. A group of professional anthropologists called the Network of Concerned Anthropologists have asked both anthropology students and faculty to pledge that they will refuse to cooperate with the military's counterinsurgency efforts. They reason that if you believe that the United States is engaged in an unprincipled, brutal, and unjust "preemptive war" in Iraq, then you should not contribute your cross-cultural expertise to helping the military win the war. If you do collaborate with the military, the argument goes, you will be using your knowledge (given to you by the local population through fieldwork) to harm or even kill those who trusted you and shared their culture with you.

On the other side of the issue are those anthropologists who contend that to boycott the military would be a great loss, not just to the military and the United States but also to anthropology and the countries we are occupying. Whether we approve or disapprove of the wars, these proponents suggest, U.S. actions in Iraq and Afghanistan are a reality. If these countries are to survive, and hopefully thrive, in the future, the United States and its allies must adopt more enlightened policies based on anthropological insights. Richard Shweder (2007), professor of anthropology at the University of Chicago, sums up this position:

> The real issue . . . is not whether the military should know more rather than less about other ways of life—of course it should know more. The real issue is how our profession is going to begin to play a far more significant educational role in the formation of foreign policy, in the hope that anthropologists won't have to answer some patriotic call late in a sad day to become an armed angel riding the shoulder of a misguided American warrior.

QUESTIONS FOR FURTHER THOUGHT

1. What specific roles have cultural anthropologists played with the U.S. military in Afghanistan and Iraq?

2. Where do you stand on this contemporary social issue? Should anthropologists be employed with the U.S. military and, if so, to what extent?

3. What are the ethical responsibilities that anthropologists (working with the military) have to the people they have studied?

SUMMARY

1. All societies have political systems to manage public affairs, maintain social order, and resolve conflict. The study of political organization involves topics such as the allocation of political roles, levels of political integration, concentrations of power and authority, mechanisms of social control, and means for resolving conflict.

2. Political anthropologists generally recognize four fundamentally different forms of political organization based on amounts of political integration and specialization of political roles: bands, tribes, chiefdoms, and states.

3. Band societies have the least political integration and role specialization. They are most often found in foraging societies and are associated with low population densities, distribution systems based on reciprocity, and egalitarian social relations.

4. Tribal societies are most commonly found among horticulturalists and pastoralists. With larger and more sedentary populations than are found in band societies, tribally based societies have certain pan-tribal mechanisms that cut across a number of local segments and integrate them into a larger whole.

5. Chiefdoms have a more formal and permanent political structure than is found in tribal societies. Political authority in chiefdoms rests with a single individual, acting either alone or with the advice of a council. Most chiefdoms, which tend to have distinct social ranks, rely on feasting and tribute as a major way of distributing goods.

6. State systems—with the greatest amount of political integration and role specialization—are associated with intensive agriculture, market economies, urbanization, and complex social stratification. States, which first appeared about 5,500 years ago, have a monopoly on the use of force and can make and enforce laws, collect taxes, and recruit labor for military service and public works projects.

7. Some social control mechanisms are found in all forms of political structure, from bands through states. These include socialization, public opinion, and supernatural belief systems.

8. In the absence of formal mechanisms of government, many small-scale societies maintain social control by means of corporate lineages, song duels, intermediaries, moots, and oaths and ordeals.

9. State societies, which have a monopoly on organized force, rely primarily, but not exclusively, on formal mechanisms of social control, such as laws and courts.

KEY TERMS

achieved status 230
ascribed status 230
authority 223
band societies 224
caste 230
chiefdoms 227
class 230
corporate lineages 239
council of elders 242
crime 243
Dalit 232
deviance 235
headless societies 233
intermediaries 241
law 244

Leopard-Skin Chief 241
moots 241
nation 232
negative sanctions 235
oath 242
ordeal 242
pan-tribal
  mechanisms 225
political integration 223
positive sanctions 235
public opinion 237
rebellion 244
revolution 244
sanctions 235
social control 234

social mobility 230
social norms 234
socialization 237
song duel 240
specialized political
  roles 229
state 232
state system of
  government 228
supernatural belief
  systems 238
tribal societies 225
varnas 232
witchcraft 239

A Hindu religious pilgrim prays in Varanasi, India.

CHAPTER 10
Supernatural Beliefs

RELIGIOUS FREEDOM IN FLORIDA

Sultaana Freeman, a thirty-four-year-old Islamic resident of Winter Park, Florida, had no difficulty getting a Florida driver's license in February 2001 despite having insisted (on religious grounds) that her picture be taken behind a veil. Several months after September 11, however, officials from the Florida Department of Motor Vehicles changed their minds and informed Freeman that in order to keep her license she would need a new photo showing her entire face. She subsequently gave up her driver's license and then sued the state to get it reinstated (Canedy 2002; Pristin 2002). Here is a clear case of a conflict between a person's right to be true to her religion (Islam requires that she shield her face in public) and the government's need to maintain public safety by being able to identify a person in a traffic stop.

The state argued that law enforcement officials need a full-face photo in order to verify one's identity, which is, after all, why driver's licenses have photos. Admittedly, after September 11, this need for public safety and security took on greater urgency when it was assumed that there was a strong relationship between some religious beliefs and acts of terrorism.

On the other side of the issue, lawyers for Freeman argued that forcing her to have a full-face picture is unreasonable and subjective and violates her freedom of religion. It was pointed out that Florida statutes do not prohibit a person from being veiled in photos for driver's licenses. Moreover Florida's Religious Restoration Act explicitly states that laws that burden the exercise of religion must have a compelling government purpose. Lawyers for Freeman claimed that the state had no such compelling purpose because their client was open to providing fingerprints, DNA, or other information that could be used to verify her identity. It was patently unfair, they argued, to expect Freeman to have to choose between her religious beliefs and the convenience of having a valid driver's license.

QUESTIONS FOR FURTHER THOUGHT

1. If you were the judge in this civil case, how would you rule?

2. Can you think of other minority groups in the United States whose religious beliefs have run counter to the legal system?

Beginning in the nineteenth century, religion was studied from a scientific, rather than just a theological, perspective. For example, in *The Elementary Forms of Religious Life*, French sociologist Emile Durkheim (2001) argued that religion enables people to transcend their individual identities and to see themselves as part of a larger collective. Another social scientist, Max Weber, analyzed religion as it relates to economic institutions. In his classic study, *The Protestant Ethic and the Spirit of Capitalism*, Weber (1958) claimed that the Protestant faith supported the rise of capitalism in Western societies. And, of course, Karl Marx, studying religion from a non-theological perspective, linked organized religions with social inequality by suggesting that religion was a tool for oppressing the lower classes.

The scientific study of religion since the nineteenth century has been interpreted by some as the beginning of the end for organized religion. Yet the analysis of religion by social scientists has not caused people to abandon their religions in great numbers. To be certain, some religious groups in different parts of the world have lost followers, but others have gained adherents in recent decades, particularly fundamentalist groups (both at home and abroad). For example, long before 9/11 the world witnessed a rise in Islamic fundamentalism in such places as Saudi Arabia, Iran, and Egypt; the recent governments in Israel have been elected largely by the growing number of Jewish fundamentalists; and the most dramatic growth in church affiliation in the United States in the last several decades has been among various fundamentalist (evangelical) churches, such as the Assembly of God and the Church of God in Christ. Thus the scientific study of religion has hardly inhibited these particular religious movements, and in fact their "anti-science" stance on many contemporary issues might suggest that a scientific view of the world has contributed to their growth.

Cultural anthropologists have devoted considerable attention to analyzing religion since they began to make direct field observations of peoples of the world. Although anthropologists have not always agreed on how to interpret different religious systems, all would agree that the many religious practices found throughout the world vary widely from one another. These religious systems might involve sacrificing animals to ancestor-gods, using a form of divination called ordeals to determine a person's guilt or innocence, or submitting oneself to extraordinary pain as a way of communicating directly with the deities (Lehmann and Myers 1993).

Defining Religion

The forms of religion vary enormously, but all are alike to the extent that they are founded on a belief in the supernatural. For our purposes in this chapter, we shall define **religion** as a set of beliefs in supernatural beings and forces directed at helping people make sense of the world and solve important problems. Because human beings are faced with a series of

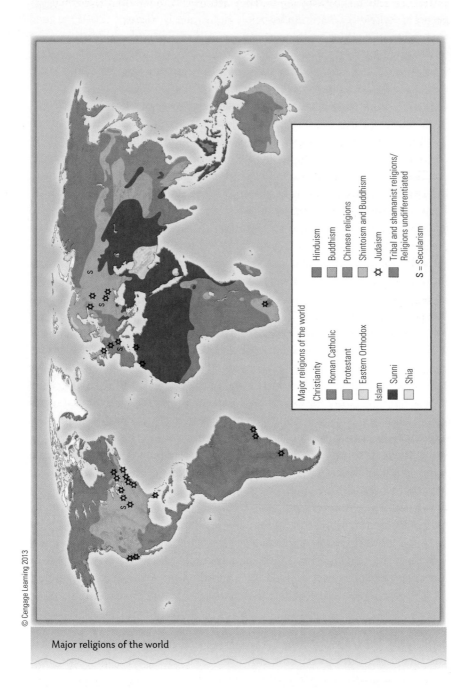

Major religions of the world

Major religions of the world

Christianity
Roman Catholic
Protestant
Eastern Orthodox
Islam
Sunni
Shia

Hinduism
Buddhism
Chinese religions
Shintoism and Buddhism
Judaism
Tribal and shamanist religions/
Religions undifferentiated

S = Secularism

important life problems that cannot all be resolved through the application of science and technology alone, they attempt to overcome these limitations by appealing to or manipulating supernatural forces.

Anthropologists have long observed that all societies have a recognizable set of beliefs and behaviors that can be called religious. According to George Murdock's (1945) widely quoted list of cultural universals, all societies have religious rituals that appease supernatural forces, sets of beliefs concerning what we would call the soul or human spirit, and notions about life after death.

To be certain, nonreligious people can be found in all societies. But when we claim that religion (or a belief in the supernatural) is universal, we are referring to a cultural phenomenon rather than an individual one. For example, we can find individuals in the Western world who do not believe personally in supernatural forces such as deities, ghosts, demons, or spirits. Nevertheless these people are part of a society that includes a set of religious beliefs and practices to which many (perhaps a majority) of the population adhere.

Because religion, in whatever form it may be found, is often taken very seriously and passionately by its adherents, there is a natural tendency for people to see their own religion as the best while viewing all others as inferior. Westerners, for example, often use science, logic, and empirical evidence (for example, through the study of biblical texts) to bolster and justify their own religious practices. Nevertheless science and logic are not adequate to either establish the inherent validity of Western religious beliefs or demonstrate that non-Western religions are false. In other words, no religion is able to demonstrate conclusively that its deities can work more miracles than those of other religions, although some certainly try. The central issue for anthropologists is not to determine which religion is better or more correct but rather to identify the various religious beliefs in the world as well as how they function, to what extent they are held, and the degree to which they affect human behavior.

Defining *religion* is difficult because anthropologists disagree on how to distinguish between religious and nonreligious phenomena. In some societies religion is so thoroughly embedded in the total social structure that it is difficult to distinguish religious behavior from economic, political, or kinship behavior. To illustrate, when a Kikuyu elder sacrifices a goat at the grave of an ancestor-god, is he engaging in religious behavior (he is calling for the ancestor-god to intervene in the affairs of the living), economic behavior (the meat of the sacrificed animal will be distributed to and eaten by members of the kinship group), or kinship behavior (kin will have a chance to express their group solidarity at the ceremonial event)?

Such a ritual sacrifice performs all of these functions at the same time. In highly specialized societies, such as our own, people tend to divide human behavior into what, at least for them, are logical categories: social, economic, political, religious, educational, and recreational, for example. Because many small-scale, less specialized societies do not divide human behavior into the same categories used in Western society, it is often difficult for Westerners to recognize those aspects of human behavior that we think of as purely religious.

Another difficulty in defining religion and the supernatural is that different societies have different ways of distinguishing between the natural world and the supernatural world. In our own society, we reserve the term *supernatural* for phenomena we cannot explain through reason or science. Other societies, however, do not divide the world into natural and supernatural arenas. For example, the Nyoro of Uganda have a word for sorcery that means "to injure another person by the secret use of harmful medicines or techniques" (Beattie 1960: 73). Sorcery in Nyoro society can take different forms. Placing a person's body substances (such as pieces of hair or fingernail clippings) in an animal horn and putting the horn on the roof of the person's house with the intention of causing that person harm is an act of sorcery in Nyoro society, but so is putting poison into an enemy's food or drink.

Given our own Western dichotomy between the natural and the supernatural, we would interpret these two acts as substantially different. We would see the first act as an attempt to harm another person by the use of magic. If the intended victim died, Western law courts would never hold the perpetrator culpable, for the simple reason that it could not be proven scientifically that placing the magical substances on the roof was the cause of the death. Westerners would view the poisoning as premeditated murder, however, because it could be determined scientifically (that is, through an autopsy) that the poison did cause the person to die. This illustration should remind us that not all societies share our Western definition of the supernatural. It is precisely because of this difference in viewing the natural and supernatural worlds that Westerners have so much difficulty understanding non-Western religions, which they usually consider irrational or contradictory.

Another source of confusion when we try to define religion is our inability to separate supernatural beliefs from other aspects of culture. People often claim to be acting in the name of their religion, but in fact they are using their religion to support or reject other (nonreligious) features of their culture. For example, we often think of such policy issues as opposition to abortion, gay marriage, Darwin's theory of evolution, and stem cell research as being part of the philosophy of evangelical Christianity. But it is certainly possible—and definitely demonstrable—to believe in the central core of evangelical Christianity (e.g., personal conversion and the full authority of the Bible) without rejecting abortion, Darwinian evolution, or gay marriage. In fact evangelical Christianity is making significant headway in various urban ministries throughout the country, from San Francisco to New York City, among well-educated members of the creative class who express just the opposite positions on these social issues. For example, Rev. Timothy J. Keller has been wildly successful at growing his Redeemer Presbyterian Church in Manhattan to four thousand members over the last two decades. He appeals to all sorts of urban professionals—from designers to university students—because his sermons are literary and intellectual. He replaces the traditional "hellfire and brimstone" with well-reasoned sermons quoting such sources as C. S. Lewis and the liberal newspaper *The Village Voice*. Keller (along with other urban evangelical ministers) has been successful because he understands the difference between the core evangelical (religious) message and a number of contemporary sociocultural issues on which Jesus and the Bible had nothing to say (Luo 2006). Thus there seems to be a

Evangelist Rev. Timothy J. Keller thrives in Manhattan by embracing the city and identifying with its culture.

growing number of Christian evangelicals in the United States who refuse to put conservative politics at the heart of their Christian ideology.

Religion and Magic

Anthropologists who study supernatural beliefs cross-culturally have long been fascinated by the relationship between religion and magic. Whereas some anthropologists have emphasized the differences between these two phenomena, others have concentrated on their similarities. It is important to examine both the similarities and the differences because, even though religion and magic can be found operating separately, most often they are found in some combined form. Religion and magic share certain features. Because both are systems of supernatural belief, they are nonrational; that is, they are not susceptible to scientific verification. In other words, whether religious or magical practices actually work cannot be empirically demonstrated. Rather, such practices must be accepted as a matter of faith. Moreover people turn to both religion and magic—at least in part—as ways of coping with the anxieties, ambiguities, and frustrations of everyday life.

On the other hand, magic and religion differ in important respects. First, religion deals with the major issues of human existence, such as the meaning of life, death, and one's spiritual relationship with deities. In contrast, magic is directed toward specific, immediate problems, such as curing an illness, bringing rain, or ensuring safety on a long journey. Second, religion uses prayer and sacrifices to appeal to or petition supernatural powers for assistance. Magicians, on the other hand, believe they can control or manipulate nature or other people by their own efforts. Third, religion by and large tends to be a group activity, whereas magic is more individual. Fourth, whereas religion is usually practiced at a specified time, magic is practiced irregularly in response to specific and immediate problems. Fifth, religion usually involves officially recognized functionaries such as priests, whereas magic may be performed by a wide variety of practitioners who may or may not be recognized within the community as having supernatural powers.

Despite these five differences, in actual practice elements of religion and magic are often found together. In any religion, for example, there is a fine line between praying for God's help and coercing or manipulating a situation to bring about a desired outcome. Also it is not at all unusual for a person to use elements of both religion and magic simultaneously. To illustrate, a soldier about to enter combat may ask for divine protection through prayer while carrying a lucky rabbit's foot (a magical charm). Following the lead of nineteenth-century anthropologist Sir James Frazer, modern-day anthropologists distinguish between two types of magic: imitative magic and contagious magic. **Imitative magic** is based on the principle "what you do is what you get." The religion of voodoo contains some elements of imitative magic. The idea behind a voodoo doll is that by doing harm to the doll (such as sticking it with pins, burning it, or throwing it into the ocean), you will be able to magically harm the person the doll represents. **Contagious magic** is the notion that an object that has been in contact with a person retains a magical connection to that person. The strongest magical connection exists between a person and something that has been a part of his or her body, such as hair, nail clippings, or teeth. Those who practice contagious magic believe that a person can be harmed by evil magicians if they can obtain any of these former body parts. In some parts of East Africa, economic development projects designed to build latrines to improve sanitation have been unsuccessful because people are fearful of defecating in a place where one's feces could be obtained by an evildoer.

Magic involves the manipulation of supernatural forces for the purpose of intervening in a wide range of human activities and natural events. Magic is used ritualistically in some societies to ensure the presence of game animals, to bring rain, to cure or prevent illness, or to protect oneself from misfortune. Magic, however, can also be (and often is) directed to cause evil. In some societies it is believed that certain people called witches or sorcerers use supernatural powers to bring harm to people. Because these forms of "negative magic" hold such fascination for Westerners, it is instructive to examine them in greater detail.

Voodoo practitioners conduct a nocturnal ceremony of healing over a footbridge in New Orleans, Louisiana.

Although the terms *witchcraft* and *sorcery* are sometimes used synonymously, cultural anthropologists distinguish between them. As practiced in a wide variety of societies throughout the world, **witchcraft** is an inborn, involuntary, and often unconscious capacity to cause harm to other people. On the other hand, **sorcery**, which often involves the use of materials, potions, and medicines, is the deliberate use of supernatural powers to bring about harm. Some societies have specialized practitioners of sorcery, but in other societies anyone can practice sorcery. Because sorcery involves the use of certain physical substances, the evidence for its existence is easily found. Witchcraft, by contrast, is virtually impossible to prove or disprove because there is no visible evidence of its existence.

Whereas sorcery involves the use of material substances to cause harm to people, witchcraft, it is thought, relies solely on psychic power (that is, thoughts and emotions). In other words, witches can turn their anger and hatred into evil deeds simply by thinking evil thoughts. How witches are conceptualized varies widely from society to society, but in all cases witches are viewed negatively. Witches are generally seen as being unable to control the human impulses that normal members of society are expected to keep in check. For example, they are perceived to have insatiable appetites for food, uncontrollable hatred, and perverted sexual desires. The Mandari in the southern Sudan believe that witches dance on their victims' graves. The Lugbara of Uganda tell of witches who dance naked, which for them is the ultimate social outrage. The Ganda and Nyoro of Uganda believe in witches who eat corpses. Among the Kaguru of Tanzania, witches are believed to walk upside down, devour human flesh, commit incest, and in general flout the rules and constraints of normal society. In many parts of the world, witches are associated with the night, which separates them from normal people, who go about their business during the daytime. Moreover witches are often associated with certain animals, such as bats, rats, snakes, lizards, or leopards, that are black, dangerous, and nocturnal.

Functions of Religion

Anthropological studies of religion are no longer dominated by the search for origins. More recent studies have focused on how religious systems *function* for both the individual and the society as a whole. Because religious systems are so universal, it is generally held that they must meet a number of important needs at both personal and societal levels. Yet it should be obvious to most religious practitioners that supernatural powers don't always work as effectively as the practitioners think they should. For example, we pray to God for the recovery of a sick friend, but the friend dies nevertheless; a ritual specialist conducts a rain dance, but it still doesn't rain; or the living relatives sacrifice a goat at the grave site of the ancestor-god but still are not spared the ravages of the drought. Although supernatural beings and forces may not always perform their requested functions (that is, bring about supernatural events), they do perform less obvious functions for both the individual and the society as a whole. These latent functions, as they are called by Robert Merton (1957), fall into two broad categories: social and psychological.

Social Functions of Religion

One of the most popular explanations for the universality of religion is that it performs important functions for the overall well-being of the society of which it is a part. Let's consider three such social functions of religion: social control, conflict resolution, and reinforcement of group solidarity.

SOCIAL CONTROL One very important social function of religion is its use as a mechanism of social control. Through both positive and negative sanctions, religion tends to maintain social order by encouraging socially acceptable behavior and discouraging socially inappropriate behavior. Every religion, regardless of the form it takes, is an ethical system that prescribes proper ways of behaving. When social sanctions (rewards and punishments) are backed with supernatural authority, they become more compelling. Biblical texts, for example, are very explicit about the consequences of violating the Ten Commandments. Because of their strong belief in ghostly vengeance, the Lugbara of Uganda scrupulously avoid engaging in any antisocial behavior that would provoke the wrath of the ancestor-gods. Hindus in India believe that violating prescribed caste expectations will jeopardize their progress in future reincarnations.

Religious beliefs and behaviors serve as mechanisms of social control for reasons other than fear of divine retribution. Michael McCullough and Brian Willoughby (2009), psychologists at the University of Miami, have investigated the notion that a sincere belief in religion gives people greater internal control, resistance to temptation, and hence adherence to societal norms. A review of the scholarly research over the past century reveals that devoutly religious people generally do better in school, have longer life spans, and have more satisfying marriages. But McCullough and Willoughby were interested in learning whether these findings could be explained by an increase in self-control. They found that brain scan studies reveal that praying, reading holy texts, and meditating (three religious activities) stimulate two parts of the brain associated with the self-regulation of attention and emotions. In another study conducted in 2003, people who were subliminally exposed to religious words (like *God* and *Bible*) were slower to recognize words associated with temptation, such as *alcohol* and *pornography*. Although McCullough and Willoughby reviewed research conducted largely on Western and Christian populations, evidence from research conducted in the non-Western world is consistent with their main conclusion: There is a close correlation between religious beliefs and practices, on the one hand, and self-control, conscientiousness, and adherence to social norms on the other.

From an anthropological perspective, it is irrelevant whether these supernatural forces really do reward good behavior and punish bad behavior. Rather than concern themselves with whether supernatural forces work the way they are thought to, anthropologists are more interested in whether people actually believe in the power of the supernatural forces. After all, it is belief in the power of the supernatural sanctions that determines the level of conformity to socially prescribed behavior.

CONFLICT RESOLUTION Another social function of religion is the role it plays in reducing the stress and frustrations that often lead to social conflict. In some societies, for example, natural calamities such as epidemics or famines are attributed to the evil deeds of people in other villages or regions. By concentrating on certain religious rituals designed to protect themselves against outside malevolence, people avoid the potential disruptiveness to their own society that might occur if they took out their frustrations on the evildoers. Moreover disenfranchised or powerless people in stratified societies sometimes use religion as a way of diffusing the anger and hostility that they might otherwise direct against the total social system. To illustrate, in his study of separatist Christian churches in the Republic of South Africa, Bengt Sundkler (1961) showed how small groups of Black South Africans—who had been systematically excluded from the power structure by apartheid—created the illusion of power by manipulating their own religious symbols and forming their own unique churches. By providing an alternative power structure, these breakaway Christian churches served to reduce conflict in South Africa by diverting resentment away from the wider power structure.

Sundkler's interpretation of separatist churches in South Africa is similar to Marx's nineteenth-century interpretation of religion as the opiate of the masses. As an economic determinist, Marx claimed that religion, like other institutions, reflects the underlying modes of production in the society. The purpose of religion, according to Marx, was to preserve the economic superstructure that allowed the upper classes (bourgeoisie) to exploit the working classes (proletariat). By focusing people's attention on the eternal bliss awaiting them in heaven, religion diverts their attention from the misery of their lives in the here and now. In other words, religion blinds working people to the fact that they are being exploited by the ruling class. As long as the working class focuses on the afterlife, they are not likely to heed Marx's advice to revolt against their oppressors. Thus religion is a societal mechanism to reduce conflict between differing economic subgroups.

REINFORCEMENT OF GROUP SOLIDARITY A third social function of religion is to intensify the group solidarity of those who practice it. Religion enables people to express their common identity in an emotionally charged environment. Powerful social bonds are often created among people who share the experiences of religious beliefs, practices, and rituals. Because every religion or supernatural belief system has its own unique structural features, those who practice it share in its mysteries, whereas those who do not are excluded. In short, religion strengthens a person's sense of group identity and belonging. And, of course, as people come together for common religious experiences, they often engage in other nonreligious activities as well, which further strengthens the sense of social solidarity.

The role of organized religion in creating and maintaining group solidarity is particularly important in immigrant populations. To illustrate, recent Korean immigrants to the United States, even those who are not particularly religious, often join a Korean Christian church as a way of establishing instant social networks with other Korean immigrants. According to Charles Ryu:

> In America, whatever the reason, the church has become a major and central anchoring institution for Korean immigrant society. Whereas no other institution supported the Korean immigrants, the church played the role of

anything and everything—from social service, to education, to learning the Korean language: a place to gather, to meet other people, for social gratification, you name it. The way we think of church is more than in a religious connotation. . . . Your identity is tied so closely to the church you go to. I think almost 70 to 80 percent of Korean Americans belong to church. . . . Living in American society as a minority is a very difficult thing. You are nobody out there, but when you come to church, you are somebody. (1992: 162–63)

Psychological Functions of Religion

In addition to promoting the well-being of the society, religion functions psychologically for the benefit of the individual. Anthropologists have identified two fundamentally different types of psychological functions of religion: a cognitive function, whereby religion provides a mental framework for explaining parts of our world that we do not understand, and an emotional function, whereby religion helps to reduce anxiety by prescribing some straightforward ways of coping with stress.

COGNITIVE FUNCTION In terms of its mental/intellectual function, religion is psychologically comforting because it helps us explain the unexplainable. Every society must deal with imponderable questions that have no definitive logical answers: When did life begin? Why do bad things happen to good people? What happens to us when we die? Even in societies like our own—where we have, or think we have, many scientific answers—many questions remain unanswered. A medical pathologist may be able to explain to the parents of a child who has died of malaria that the cause of death was a bite by an infected anopheles mosquito. But that same pathologist cannot explain to the grieving parents why the mosquito bit their child and not the child next door. Religion can provide satisfying answers to such questions because the answers are based on supernatural authority.

Unlike other life forms, humans have a highly developed desire to understand themselves and the world around them. But because human understanding of the universe is so imperfect, religion provides a framework for giving meaning to events and experiences that cannot be explained in any other way. Religion assures its believers that the world is meaningful, that events happen for a reason, that there is order in the universe, and that apparent injustices will eventually be rectified. Humans have difficulty whenever unexplained phenomena contradict their worldview. One of the functions of religion, then, is to enable people to maintain their worldview even when events seem to contradict it.

EMOTIONAL FUNCTION The emotional function of religion is to help individuals cope with the anxieties that often accompany illnesses, accidents, deaths, and other misfortunes. Because people never have complete control over the circumstances of their lives, they often turn to religious ritual in an attempt to maximize control through supernatural means. In fact the less control people feel they have over their own lives, the more they are likely to practice religion. The fear of facing a frightening situation can be at least partially overcome by believing that supernatural beings will intervene on one's behalf; shame and guilt may be reduced by becoming humble and pious in the face of the deities; and during times of bereavement, religion can be a source of emotional strength.

People perform religious rituals as a way of invoking supernatural beings to control the forces over which they feel they have no control. The rituals take different forms throughout the world. To illustrate, the Trobriand Islanders perform magico-religious rituals for protection before a long voyage; to protect their gardens, men in parts of New Guinea put leaves across their fences, believing that the leaves will paralyze the arms and legs of any thief who raids the garden; and in Nairobi, Kenya, some professional football teams reportedly hire their own ritual specialists to bewitch their opponents. In addition to providing peace of mind, such religious practices may actually have a positive *indirect* effect on the events they are intended to influence. For example, even if their witchcraft doesn't work, football players are likely to play more confidently if they believe they have a supernatural advantage. This ability to act with confidence is a major psychological function of religion.

Although most North Americans think of themselves as highly scientific, on many occasions we too use supernatural forces to ensure that our activities will have a successful outcome. For example, anthropologist George Gmelch (1994b) described how professional baseball players use ritual to try to influence the outcome of a game:

> To control uncertainty Chicago White Sox shortstop Ozzie Guillen doesn't wash his underclothes after a good game. The Boston Red Sox's Wade Boggs eats chicken before every game (that's 162 meals of chicken per year). Ex-San Francisco Giant pitcher Ron Bryant added a new stick of bubble gum to the collection in his bulging back pocket after each game he won. Jim Ohms, my teammate on the Daytona Beach Islanders in 1966, used to put another penny in the pouch of his supporter after each win. Clanging against the hard plastic genital cup, the pennies made an audible sound as the pitcher ran the bases toward the end of a winning season

In some cases Western governments use non-Western spiritual practices when it is politically expedient to do so. In 1998 the Transit Authority of Portland, Oregon, proudly unveiled its light rail system, featuring the Washington Park Station, which, at 260 feet below ground, was the deepest subway station in the United States. However, members of local Asian communities in Portland were appalled because the tunnel ran under a cemetery, which, they claimed, disturbed the spirits of the dead and created a dangerous situation for the train riders. In fact the Asian groups cited several above-ground traffic accidents as having been caused by the angry spirits of the dead. In response to these very real concerns of the Asian community, Transit Authority officials brought in a group of Lao Buddhist monks who performed rituals to appease the dead spirits. Even though transit officials were ribbed for allowing these Eastern rituals to be performed in the subway tunnel, they did ease the minds of local Asians and restored their confidence in the local transit system (D'Antoni and Heard 1998).

Mark "The Bird" Fidrych, a pitcher for the Detroit Tigers, practiced ritualistic magic before each game by patting and talking to the pitcher's mound.

© Bettmann/Corbis

Types of Religious Organization

Like other aspects of culture, religion takes a wide variety of forms throughout the world. To bring some order to this vast diversity, it is helpful to develop a typology of religious systems based on certain common features. One commonly used system of classification, suggested by Anthony Wallace, is based on the level of specialization of the religious personnel who conduct the rituals and ceremonies. Wallace (1966) identified four principal patterns of religious organization based on what he calls cults. Wallace uses the term **cult** in a general sense to refer to forms of religion that have their own set of beliefs, rituals, and goals. This analytical and nonjudgmental use of the term *cult* should not be confused with the more popular, and pejorative, definition used to refer to an antisocial religious group that brainwashes its members before leading them to mass suicide. The four forms of religious organization Wallace identified are individualistic cults, shamanistic cults, communal cults, and ecclesiastical cults. According to Wallace's typology, these cults form a scale. Societies with ecclesiastical cults also contain communal, shamanistic, and individualistic cults; those with a communal form also contain shamanistic and individualistic cults; and those with shamanistic cults also contain individualistic cults. Although it is likely that societies with only individualistic cults could have existed in earlier times, there are no contemporary examples of such religious systems.

TABLE 10.1 Characteristics of the Four Types of Religious Organization

	ROLE SPECIALIZATION	SUBSISTENCE PATTERN	EXAMPLE
Individualistic	No role specialization	Food collector	Crow vision quest
Shamanistic	Part-time specialization	Food collector/pastoralism/horticulture	Tungus shamanism
Communal	Groups perform rites for the community	Horticulture/pastoralism	Totemistic rituals
Ecclesiastical	Full-time specialization in hierarchy	Industrialism	Christianity and Buddhism

© Cengage Learning 2013

Sources: Adapted from Anthony F. C. Wallace, Religion: An Anthropological View *(New York: Random House, 1966).*

Wallace's four types correspond roughly to different levels of socioeconomic organization. In a very general way, individualistic and shamanistic cults are usually associated with food-collecting societies, communal cults are usually found in horticultural and pastoral societies, and ecclesiastical cults are characteristic of more complex industrialized economies. However, this association between forms of religious organization and socioeconomic types is only approximate at best because there are some notable exceptions. For example, certain American Plains Indians and some aboriginal Australians had communal forms of religion even though they were food collectors and lived in bands. See Table 10.1 for a summary of the four types of religious organization.

Individualistic Cults

Individualistic cults have no religious specialists and represent the most basic level of religious structure according to Wallace's typology. Each person has a relationship with one or more supernatural beings whenever he or she has a need for control or protection. Because individualistic cults do not make distinctions between specialists and laypersons, all people are their own specialists, or as Marvin Harris has put it, these cults are a type of do-it-yourself religion (Harris and Johnson 2003: 266). Even though no known societies rely exclusively on the individualistic form of religion, some small-scale band societies practice it as a predominant mode.

The **vision quest**, a ritual found among traditional Plains Indian cultures, is an excellent example of the rituals practiced by an individualistic cult. During traditional times it was expected that, through visions, people would establish a special relationship with a spirit that would provide them with knowledge, power, and protection. Sometimes these visions came to people through dreams or when they were by themselves. More often, however, the individual had to purposefully seek out the visions through such means as fasting, mutilating their bodies, smoking or ingesting hallucinogenic substances, and spending time alone in an isolated place.

A person would go on a vision quest if he or she wanted to gain special power to excel as a warrior, to restore one's honor after being tormented by a bully or jilted by a lover, or to acquire knowledge about a future course of action. For example, a Crow warrior would go to a place that was thought to be frequented by supernatural spirits. There he would strip off his clothes, smoke, and abstain from drinking and eating. He might even chop off part of a finger or engage in other types of self-inflicted torture for the sake of getting the spirits' attention. Crow visions took a variety of forms but usually had several elements in common. First, the visions usually came in the form of a spirit animal, such as a bison, eagle, or snake. Second, the vision seeker gained some special knowledge or power. Third, the vision often appeared on the fourth day of the quest—four being a sacred number for the Crow. Finally, the animal spirit adopted the quester by functioning as his or her own protector spirit.

Shamanistic Cults

In addition to having individualistic cults, all contemporary societies operate at the shamanistic level. Shamanistic societies are found in arctic and subarctic regions, Siberia, Tibet, Mongolia, parts of Southeast Asia, and widely throughout the South American rain forests. **Shamans** are part-time religious specialists who are thought to have supernatural powers by virtue of birth, training, or inspiration. They use these powers for healing, divining, and telling fortunes during times of stress, usually in exchange for gifts or fees. **Shamanistic cults** represent the simplest form of religious division of labor because, as Wallace (1966: 86) reminds us, "The shaman in his religious role is a specialist; and his clients in their relation to him are laymen." The term *shaman,* derived from the Tungus-speaking peoples of Siberia (Service 1978), encompasses many different types of specialists found throughout the world, including medicine men and women, diviners, spiritualists, palm readers, and magicians.

Shamans are generally believed to have access to supernatural spirits that they contact on behalf of their clients. The reputation of a particular shaman often rests on the power of the shaman's "spirit helpers" (usually the spirits of powerful, agile, and cunning animals) and her or his ability to contact them at will. Shamans contact their spirits while in an altered state of consciousness brought on by smoking, taking drugs, drumming rhythmically, chanting, or dancing monotonously. Once in a trance, the shaman, possessed with a spirit helper, becomes a medium or spokesperson for that spirit. While possessed, the shaman may perspire, breathe heavily, take on a different voice, and generally lose control over his or her own body. Even though Westerners often view shamans as con artists, in their own societies they are seen as a combination of holy person, doctor, and social worker. In many respects traditional shamans in non-Western

A Mayan shaman from Mexico prays with the help of a crucifix.

societies are not appreciably different from professional channelers in the United States, who speak on behalf of spirits for their paying clients.

In shamanistic societies, it is believed that everyday occurrences are intimately connected to events in the spirit world. The shaman's role is to enter an altered state of consciousness, allow his or her soul to travel to the spirit world, seek out the causes of earthly problems, and then coerce, beg, or do combat with the spirits to intervene on behalf of the living. Inuit shamanism provides a good example of how shamans are thought to work. Most Inuit believe that water mammals are controlled by an underwater female spirit who occasionally withholds animals when Inuit hunters behave immorally. One of the most challenging tests for an Inuit shaman is to travel to the watery underworld to convince the spirit to release the seals and walruses so they can be hunted again.

How an individual actually becomes a shaman varies from society to society. In many societies shamans achieve their power through a series of initiations or ordeals imposed by the spirits of the underworld. Even after acquiring shamanistic power by doing battle with the spirits, a shaman may lose those hard-won powers through subsequent unsuccessful battles with the spirits. In some societies it is possible to become a shaman by having a particularly vivid or powerful vision in which spirits enter the body. In other societies one can become a shaman by serving as an apprentice under a practicing shaman. Among the Tungus of Siberia, mentally unstable people who experience bouts of hysteria are the most likely candidates for shamanism because hysterical people are thought to be the closest to the spirit world (Service 1978). In societies that regularly use hallucinogenic drugs, almost any person can achieve the altered state of consciousness needed for the practice of shamanism. For example, Michael Harner (1973) reports that among the Jivaro Indians of the Ecuadorian Amazon, who use hallucinogens widely and have a strong desire to contact the supernatural world, about one in four men is a shaman.

Communal Cults

Communal cults—which involve a more elaborate set of beliefs and rituals—operate at a still higher level of organizational complexity. Groups of ordinary people (organized around clans, lineages, age groups, or secret societies) conduct religious rites and ceremonies for the larger community. These rites, which are performed only occasionally or periodically by nonspecialists, are considered to be absolutely vital to the well-being of both individuals and the society as a whole. Even though these ceremonies may include specialists such as shamans, orators, or magicians, the primary responsibility for the success of the ceremonies lies with nonspecialists, who at the conclusion of the ceremony return to their everyday activities. Examples of communal cults are the ancestral ceremonies among the traditional Chinese, puberty rites found in sub-Saharan African societies, and totemic rituals practiced by aboriginal peoples of Australia.

Communal rituals fall into two broad categories: rites of passage, which celebrate the transition of a person from one social status to another, and rites of solidarity, which are public rituals that foster group identity and group goals and have explicit and immediate objectives, such as calling on supernatural beings or forces to increase fertility or prevent misfortune.

RITES OF PASSAGE Rites of passage are ceremonies that mark a change in a person's social position. These ritualistic ceremonies, which have religious significance, help both individuals and the society deal with important life changes, such as birth, puberty, marriage, and death. Rites of passage are more than ways of recognizing certain transitions in a person's life, however. When a person marries, for example, he or she not only takes on a new status but also creates an entire complex of new relationships. Rites of passage, then, are important public rituals that recognize a wider set of altered social relationships.

According to Arnold Van Gennep (1960), all rites of passage, in whatever culture they may be found, tend to have three distinct ritual phases. The first phase, separation, is characterized by the stripping away of the old status. In the second phase, the individual is in a transitional stage, cut off from the old status but not yet integrated into the new status. Because this transitional stage is associated with danger and ambiguity, it often involves the endurance of certain unpleasant ordeals as well as the removal of the individual from normal, everyday life for a certain period of time. The third and final phase involves the ritual incorporation of the individual into the new status. Ethnographic data from all over the world have supported Van Gennep's claim that all rites of passage involve these three phases.

These three ritual phases are well demonstrated in the rites of adulthood practiced by the Kikuyu of Kenya, who initiate both girls and boys (Middleton and Kershaw 1965). The Kikuyu, like other traditional East African societies, practice initiation ceremonies as a way of ensuring that children will become morally and socially responsible adults. Despite some regional variations, the Kikuyu initiation rite includes certain rituals that conform to Van Gennep's threefold scheme.

Kikuyu initiation into adulthood involves a physical operation—circumcision for males and clitoridectomy for females. Days before the physical operation, the initiates go through rituals designed to separate them from society and their old status and place them in close relationship to god. First, the initiates are adopted by an elder man and his wife; this event symbolically separates them from their own parents. Second, the initiates spend the night before the circumcision singing and dancing in an effort to solicit the guidance and protection of the ancestor-gods. Third, the initiates have their heads shaved and anointed, symbolizing the loss of the old status. And finally, they are sprayed with a mixture of honey, milk, and medicine by their adoptive parents in another separation ritual, which John Middleton and Greet Kershaw (1965) call the ceremony of parting.

As Van Gennep's theory suggests, the second (transition) phase of the Kikuyu initiation ceremony is a marginal phase filled with danger and ambiguity. The initiates undergo the dramatic and traumatic circumcision or clitoridectomy as a vivid symbolization of their soon-to-be assumed responsibility as adults. Both male and female initiates are physically and emotionally supported during the operation by their sponsors, who cover them with cloaks as soon as the operation is completed. Afterward the initiates spend four to nine days in seclusion in temporary huts (*kiganda*), where they are expected to recover from the operation and reflect upon their impending status as adults.

The third and final phase of Kikuyu initiation rituals involves the incorporation of the initiate (with his or her new status) back into the society as a whole. At the end of the seclusion period, the new male adults have certain ceremonial plants put into the large loops in their earlobes (a form of body mutilation practiced during childhood), symbolizing their newly acquired status as adult men. This phase of incorporation (or reintegration) involves other rituals as well. The men symbolically put an end to their transition stage by burning their *kiganda*; their heads are again shaved; they return home to be anointed by their parents, who soon thereafter engage in ritual intercourse; they ritually discard their initiation clothing; and they are given warrior paraphernalia. Once these incorporation rituals have been completed, the young people become full adults with all of the rights and responsibilities that go along with their new status.

RITES OF SOLIDARITY The other type of communal cult is directed toward the welfare of the community rather than the individual. These **rites of solidarity** permit a wider social participation in the shared concerns of the community than is found in societies with predominantly shamanistic cults. A good example of a cult that fosters group solidarity is the ancestral cult, found widely throughout the world. Ancestral cults are based on the assumption that, after death, a person's soul continues to interact with and affect the lives of her or his living descendants. In other words, when people die, they are not buried and forgotten but rather are elevated to the status of ancestor-ghost or ancestor-god. Because these ghosts, who are viewed as the official guardians of the social and moral order, have supernatural powers, the living descendants practice certain communal rituals designed to induce the ancestor-ghosts to protect them, favor them, or at least not harm them.

Like many of their neighboring cultures in northern Ghana, the Sisala believe that their ancestor-ghosts are the guardians of the moral order. All members of Sisala lineages are subject to the authority of the lineage elders. Because the elders are the most important living members of the group, they are responsible for overseeing the interests and harmony of the entire group. Though responsible for group morality, the elders have no direct authority to punish violators. The Sisala believe that the primary activity of the ancestor-ghosts is to punish living lineage members who violate behavioral norms. To be specific, ancestor-ghosts are thought to take vengeance on any living members who steal from their lineage mates, fight with their kin, or generally fail to live up to their family duties and responsibilities. Eugene Mendonsa described a specific case that graphically illustrates the power of ancestral cults among the Sisala:

> At Tuorojang in Tumu there was a young man named Cedu. He caught a goat that was for the ancestor of his house . . . , and killed it to sell the meat. When the day came for the sacrifice, the elders searched for the goat so they could kill it at the *lele* shrine. They could not find it, and asked to know who might have caught the goat. They could not decide who had taken the goat, so they caught another and used it for the sacrifice instead. During the sacrifice, the

elders begged the ancestors to forgive them for not sacrificing the proper goat. The elders asked the ancestors to find and punish the thief. After the sacrifice, when all the elders had gone to their various houses, they heard that Cedu had died. They summoned a diviner to determine the cause of death, and found that Cedu had been the thief. The ancestors had killed him because he was the person who stole the goat that belonged to the ancestors. (1985: 218–19)

This case illustrates the Sisala belief in the power of the ancestor-ghosts to protect the moral order. When a breach of the normative order occurs, the elders conduct a communal ritual petitioning the ghosts to punish the wrongdoer. As with other aspects of religion, the anthropologist is not concerned with whether the diviner was correct in determining that Cedu died because he had stolen the goat. Instead the anthropologist is interested in the communal ritual and its immediate social effects: It restored social harmony within the lineage and served as a warning to others who might be thinking of stealing from their lineage members.

Ecclesiastical Cults

The most complex form of religious organization, according to Wallace, is the **ecclesiastical cult**, which is found in societies that have state systems of government. Ecclesiastical cults can be found in societies with a pantheon of several high gods (such as traditional Aztecs, Incas, Greeks, or Egyptians) and in those with essentially monotheistic religions (such as Buddhism, Christianity, Islam, or Judaism). Ecclesiastical cults are characterized by full-time professional clergy, who are formally elected or appointed and devote all or most of their time to performing priestly functions. Unlike shamans, who conduct rituals during times of crisis or when their services are needed, these full-time priests conduct rituals that occur at regular intervals. (For a list of the sizes of the major ecclesiastical religions in the world today, see Table 10.2.)

In addition, these priests are part of a hierarchical or bureaucratic organization under the control of a centralized church or temple. Often, but not always, these clerical bureaucracies are either controlled by the central government or closely associated with it. In many ecclesiastical cults, the prevailing myths and beliefs are used to support the supremacy of the ruling class. In fact, it is not unusual for the priests to be part of that ruling

TABLE 10.2 Number and Percent of Adherents of Major World Religions

RELIGION (PERCENT)	NUMBER OF ADHERENTS (MILLIONS)
Christianity (33)	2,100
Islam (21)	1,500
No religious preference (16)	1,100
Hindu (14)	900
Chinese traditional (6)	394
Buddhism (6)	376
Primal-indigenous/African traditional (6)	400
Other (1.5)	100
Sikh	23
Judaism	14
Bahai	7
Jainism	4.2

© Cengage Learning 2013

Source: *National and World Religion Statistics, 2010 (www.adherents.com).*

class. Because of this close association between the priesthood and polit-
ico-economic institutions, women have not traditionally played very active roles as priests. This is another important difference between priests
and shamans, for at least as many women as men are practicing shamanism throughout the world. Even in modern, complex societies, women are
particularly active as mystics, channelers, palm readers, astrologers, and
clairvoyants.

In societies with ecclesiastical cults, there is a clearly understood
distinction between laypersons and priests. Laypersons are primarily responsible for supporting the church through their labor and their financial contributions. Priests are responsible for conducting religious rituals
on behalf of the lay population, either individually or in groups. Whereas
the priests serve as active ritual managers, the lay population participates
in rituals in a generally passive fashion.

Although ecclesiastical cults have enormous control over people's
lives, they have not wiped out other forms of religion. Inuits, many of
whom have converted to Christianity, for example, may continue to con-
sult a shaman when ill; Africans from Tanzania often continue to worship
their ancestors despite being practicing Roman Catholics; and in our own
society many people have no difficulty consulting a palmist, a psychic,
or an astrologer even though they adhere to one of the large, worldwide,
monotheistic religions.

We certainly do not need to go very far from home to see examples of
ecclesiastical organizations. The United States has hundreds of religious

This priest in California is a full-time religious specialist who works within the hierarchical organization of the Roman Catholic Church.

denominations and approximately a quarter of a million separate congregations. Most people in the United States think they understand the nature of religious institutions around them, but there are probably more misconceptions and stereotypes about religion than about any other area of American life. Most people would be surprised to learn that church membership in the United States has grown, not declined, steadily over the last several hundred years. According to Roger Finke and Rodney Stark (2005: 23), only 17 percent of the population in 1776 claimed church membership; by the start of the Civil War, the number had grown to 37 percent; by the mid-1920s, it had leaped to 58 percent; and by the early 1990s, 69 percent claimed church affiliation. According to a Gallup Poll conducted in 2003, 65 percent of adults in the United States claimed to be a member of a church or synagogue (Newport 2004). Even though most Americans think of themselves as living in a secular society, religion is highly valued in the United States, particularly in comparison with other Western, industrialized nations.

An extensive survey published in 2010 by the Pew Forum on Religion & Public Life details religious affiliation in the United States and explores the shifts that are taking place in the U.S. religious landscape. Based on a sample of more than 35,000 Americans aged eighteen and older, the survey concludes that religious affiliation in the United States is both very diverse and extremely fluid. See Table 10.3 for the religious affiliations of those questioned in the survey.

Religion: Continuity and Change

By examining the various functions of religion, we can see that religion is a conservative force in a society. In a general sense, religions support the status quo by keeping people in line through supernatural sanctions, relieving social conflict, and providing explanations for unfortunate events. Moreover some of the major world religions, through both

TABLE 10.3 Religious Affiliation in the United States

RELIGION	PERCENT
Evangelical Protestant	26.3
Catholic	23.9
Mainline Protestant	18.1
Unaffiliated	16.1
Historical Black churches	6.9
Mormon	1.7
Jewish	1.7
Jehovah's Witnesses	0.7
Buddhist	0.7
Muslim	0.6
Hindu	0.4
Other world religions	0.3
Other faiths	1.2
Don't know/refuse	0.8

© Cengage Learning 2013

Source: Pew Forum on Religion & Public Life, U.S. Religious Landscape Survey, 2010 (http://religions. pewforum.org).

philosophical convictions and political interpretations, have tended to retard social change. To illustrate, orthodox Hindu beliefs, based on the notion that one's present condition in life is based on deeds done in past lives, have had the effect of making people so fatalistic that they accept their present situations as unchangeable. Such a worldview is not likely to bring about major revolutions, or even minor initiatives for change. Likewise, on a number of issues facing the world's population, Catholicism has taken highly conservative policy positions. For example, the 1968 papal decree by Pope Paul VI opposing all forms of artificial birth control makes it very difficult for developing nations to control their population growth. Conservative Muslims have taken a strong stand against the introduction of new values and behaviors, particularly from the Western world.

However, religion has also played a major role in global social change over the past several decades. For example, the Catholic Church, allied with the Solidarity Movement, played a pivotal role in bringing about the downfall of the Communist government in Poland in 1989. By burning themselves alive on the streets of Saigon during the 1960s, Buddhist priests in Vietnam were a powerful force in stimulating antiwar sentiment in the United States, which eventually led to the withdrawal of U.S. troops. In South America during the 1970s and 1980s, a militant form of Catholicism known as **liberation theology** merged Catholic theology with activism for social justice for the poor. Catholic priests and nuns, often without the support or approval of their own church authorities, engaged in various projects designed to help the poor raise themselves up from the lowest echelons of society. Closer to home, African American churches in the United States, with their strong theme of struggle against bondage and oppression, have long played a role in social change. Well before the civil rights movement of the 1960s, Black churches were headquarters and rallying places for protestors and community activists. Indeed, for the past 150 years, African Americans have used the moral authority of their churches and mosques to push for racial justice and social change.

Under certain circumstances religion can play an important role in transforming a society. At times certain societies have experienced such high levels of stress and strain that the conservative functions of religion could not hold them together. Instead new religions or sects sprang up to create a new social order. Different terms have been used in the literature to describe these new religious forces for social change, including **nativistic movements** among Native Americans, **cargo cults** in Melanesia, **separatist Christian churches** in southern Africa, **mahdist movements** in the Muslim world, and **millenarian movements** in Christian areas of the world.

Anthropologists call all of these religious movements, with their aim of breathing new life and purpose into the society, **revitalization movements**, a term first coined by Anthony Wallace (1966). The common thread running through them is that they tend to arise during times of cultural stress brought about by rapid change, foreign domination, and perceived deprivation. Because these three conditions are often associated with colonialism, many revitalization movements have appeared in societies that have been under colonial domination.

As we have seen in earlier chapters, the IT revolution in general and the Internet in particular are having enormous effects on our economic, social, and political lives. How will information technology affect our religious lives? Although it is too early to answer this question definitively, we are already seeing a rapidly growing number of religious organizations posting their own websites and chat rooms. It is now possible to spread your own religious ideas cheaply, instantaneously, and all over the world. In much the same way that radio and television extended the reach of religious ideas, the Internet is accelerating the notion of religion no longer being confined by the walls of a church. Are we headed for a new type of "churchless religion" in which cyber-churches and virtual congregations replace the face-to-face interaction found in traditional churches, mosques, synagogues, and temples?

Global Changes in World Religions

In much the same way that markets have been globalizing over the past decade, the revolution in information and communications has had far-reaching effects on the various ecclesiastical religions of the world. For much of the twentieth century, most North Americans who identified with a particular religion adhered to a fairly straightforward set of religious beliefs and practices. People practiced Islam, Christianity, Buddhism, or Judaism, and it was relatively easy to predict what set of beliefs they held. As the twentieth century came to a close, however, many people were practicing a hodgepodge of beliefs. It has been reported (Lamont-Brown 1999) that as many as 40 million people in Japan are now practicing "new religions," which involve blending the two major religions in Japan (Buddhism and Shintoism) with elements of Confucianism, shamanism, animism, ancestor worship, Protestantism, and Catholicism. Traditional world religions, and even denominations of Christian religions, are cross pollinating at a rapid rate. As one observer noted:

> Jews flirt with Hinduism, Catholics study Taoism, and Methodists discuss whether to make the Passover seder an official part of worship. Rabbi Zalman Schachter-Shalomi, a prominent Jewish scholar, is also a Sufi sheik, and James Ishmael Ford, a Unitarian minister in Arizona, is a Zen sensei, or master. The melding of Judaism with Buddhism has become so commonplace that marketers who sell spiritual books, videotapes, and lecture series have a name for it: "JewBu." (L. Miller 1999: 1)

It is difficult to tell whether this cross-fertilization of religious beliefs and practices will be a short-term phenomenon or a more permanent condition of the world's ecclesiastical religions. In any event it is a fairly serious dilemma for the leaders of world religions, who see this intermingling as a threat to their identity.

Not only are people blending elements of more than one religion, but decades of Christian proselytizing are actually changing the geographic distribution and centers of power in some world religions such as Christianity. Over the past half century, Christianity has experienced a major shift in power and influence from the long-established churches of Europe and North America to the so-called "Global South" (Africa, South America, and South Asia). For decades European Christian churches have been losing membership and have faced considerable difficulties recruiting priests. Christian church membership in the developing world, however, has been booming during this same period. For example, whereas there were 10 million Christians in Africa in 1900, there are more than 360 million today. South America now boasts 560 million Christians, while south Asia has 313 million (Steinmetz 2004). In fact, Christianity has become so widely practiced in the "godless" country of China (approximately 50 million adherents) that

Chinese authorities in June 2006 pulled *The Da Vinci Code* off movie screens nationwide as a concession to Chinese Catholic groups.

Along with the blending and geographic redistribution of religious beliefs, in the age of globalization certain religious ideas and practices are working their way into the secular world of international business. For tens of generations, Indians from all segments of society have sought guidance from mystics and astrologers who claim to predict the future by analyzing numbers or studying the alignments of the stars and planets. Today there is growing evidence that these traditional supernatural practices are being used in the offices of multinational corporations to help make decisions concerning strategic planning, mergers, and hiring. Some Indian mystics are specialists in *vaastu* (similar to the Chinese belief in *feng shui*), which seeks to ensure good fortune through proper interior design. It is not at all uncommon for Indian high-tech corporations to hire such mystic specialists to review architectural plans prior to the construction of new corporate facilities. Film producers in Bollywood (India's counterpart to Hollywood) often seek the advice of numerologists, who claim that one's destiny is largely determined by numbers and their configurations, before making a final decision on a film's title or date of release. A person's astrological sign may even be a factor in whether a person is hired. The line between science and supernatural beliefs is becoming increasingly blurred (Lakshmi 2004).

In some countries the nonreligious changes occurring in the global economy are bringing about fundamental changes in their own traditional religious practices. To illustrate, although Indians have practiced yoga for centuries, many middle-class Indians, whose twenty-first-century jobs are putting increased pressure on their time, feel that the practice of traditional yoga is too complex and time-consuming. Today followers of Swami Ramdev practice a modified form of yoga with twelve thousand others in Jawaharlal Nehru Stadium in New Delhi, India. By concentrating on breath control, which is only one aspect of traditional yoga, the Swami claims that practitioners of his "yoga made easy" will remain healthy in mind and body. This is a very appealing message for people caught up in the pressures of the twenty-first-century global economy (Kumar 2005).

We have heard a good deal in recent years about the outsourcing of manufacturing and high-tech jobs from Canada and the United States to India. Less known, however, is that due to a shortage of priests in North America, local Catholic parishes are sending Mass Intentions (requests for masses said for a sick relative, the remembrance of deceased kin, or a prayer offering for a newborn) to India. Catholic priests in India (who have more time than North American priests and need the money) are now conducting the masses on behalf of North American Catholics after receiving the requests via e-mail (Rai 2004). Thus here is a dramatic illustration of how, in this age of globalization, we are outsourcing not only jobs to India but also our religious rituals.

For the past several decades, medical anthropology in the United States has been the most rapidly growing area of applied anthropology. Medical anthropologists have helped develop systems of medical knowledge and patient care by focusing their cross-cultural lens on the relationship between health and supernatural beliefs, doctor–patient relationships, the integration of alternative and mainstream medical practices, and the interaction of social, environmental, and biological factors that influence health and sickness. For half a century, research in medical anthropology has demonstrated that, when medical caregivers are working with culturally different patients, culture is a critical variable in the diagnosis and treatment of illnesses. Specifically, the effective treatment of immigrant patients in Chicago or Toronto must take into account the patients' (culturally constructed) beliefs and customary practices about their bodies, their bodily processes, and the nature and causes of illness. These findings are now being taken seriously by the Western medical establishment. Hospitals, medical clinics, and the doctors and nurses who treat culturally different patients are today using these cross-cultural data to modify some of their standard operating procedures.

Some hospitals and clinics operating in U.S. cities with significant immigrant populations have been taking into account (from day one) the supernatural beliefs that people bring with them to a medical setting. To illustrate, a hospital in Brooklyn, New York, postponed the official opening of a new clinic for Chinese immigrants by 24 hours. Although the clinic was set to open on April 24, 2006, hospital officials were informed that, according to the Chinese belief in numerology, the number 24 is considered "unlucky." By simply waiting until April 25 (a more auspicious date), officials ensured that most of their Chinese patients would feel more positive about visiting the clinic. Clearly a clinic will not be able to serve its Chinese patients if those patients are reluctant to use the clinic because they fear it is a place of bad fortune (Confessore 2006: 37).

In addition to the date of the official opening, clinic officials must be sensitive to other traditional Chinese beliefs in order to reduce patient anxiety, which can retard or even prevent recovery from illnesses. For example, because Chinese associate the color white with death, the clinic designers took the culturally appropriate measure of painting the walls shades of pink and yellow. Moreover chefs in the hospital's kitchens have learned to make rice porridge, a widely favored Chinese "comfort food." Had this hospital opened a clinic for immigrants from the Middle East rather than China, they would have applied anthropological insights by facing their patients' beds east (toward Mecca), so they could pray comfortably five times a day as their faith requires; by ensuring that male doctors do not examine female patients; and by not touching patients with their left hands.

Some readers might object to these modifications as pandering to immigrant patients. After all, these ethnocentric observers would argue, if "those people" choose to get sick in the United States, they darn well better expect to do things our way! But such short-sighted super-patriotism misses the point. The primary mission of health care professionals is to restore health to those who are ill as quickly and efficiently as possible. It has been demonstrated, time and again, by medical anthropologists that unless health professionals both understand and take into account the supernatural beliefs of all their patients, whatever medical strategies are employed will be less than fully successful. It makes no sense, from a medical perspective, to try to argue your patients out of their beliefs and accept yours. That simply is not going to happen. Medical practitioners are finally beginning to accept a basic truth taught by medical anthropologists—that understanding and accommodating the supernatural beliefs of culturally different patients are absolutely essential for providing them with the best possible health care.

QUESTIONS FOR FURTHER THOUGHT

1. Do Westerners associate any number(s) with bad luck?

2. Can you think of any other ethnic groups in the United States or Canada whose cultural or religious beliefs conflict with conventional Western medical practices?

3. Do you think that the hospital in Brooklyn was pandering to the superstitions of the local Chinese population? Why or why not?

SUMMARY

1. Although all cultures have supernatural beliefs, these beliefs take widely varying forms from society to society. It is often difficult to define supernatural belief systems cross-culturally because different societies have their own ways of distinguishing between the natural and the supernatural.

2. The anthropological study of religion does not attempt to determine which religions are better than others or which gods are able to work the most miracles per unit of time. Rather cultural anthropologists concentrate on describing the various systems of religious belief, how they function, and the degree to which they influence human behavior.

3. Religion differs from magic in that it deals with big issues such as life, death, and god, whereas magic deals with more immediate and specific problems. Whereas religion asks for help through prayer, magic is a direct attempt to control and manipulate supernatural forces.

4. Witchcraft and sorcery are two supernatural belief systems that cause harm to people. Whereas sorcery involves the deliberate attempt to cause people misfortune through the use of certain material substances, witchcraft is an inborn and generally involuntary capacity to work evil.

5. Religion performs certain social functions. It enhances the overall well-being of the society by serving as a mechanism of social control, helping to reduce the stress and frustrations that often lead to social conflict, and intensifying group solidarity.

6. Religion also performs certain psychological functions, such as providing emotional comfort by helping to explain the unexplainable and helping a person cope with the stress and anxiety that often accompany illness or misfortune.

7. Following the scheme suggested by Wallace, the four types of religious organization are individualistic cults, shamanistic cults, communal cults, and ecclesiastical cults. These types of religion vary roughly with increasing levels of socioeconomic complexity. Individualistic cults are associated with food-collecting societies, and ecclesiastical cults are found in highly industrialized societies.

8. The most basic form of religious organization is the individualistic cult, characterized by an absence of religious specialists. The vision quest of certain Native American cultures is an example of an individualistic cult's religious practices.

9. Shamanistic cults involve the least complex religious division of labor. Shamans are part-time religious specialists who, it is believed, help or cure their clients by intervening with supernatural powers while in an altered state of consciousness.

10. In communal cults ordinary people conduct religious ceremonies for the well-being of the community. Examples of communal cult ceremonies are the rites of passage (such as circumcision ceremonies) found widely throughout sub-Saharan Africa and the ancestral cults that foster group solidarity among members of a kinship group.

11. Ecclesiastical cults, which are found in societies with state systems of government, are characterized by full-time professional clergy who are usually organized into a hierarchy.

12. Revitalization movements—religious movements aimed at bringing new life and energy into a society—usually occur when societies are experiencing rapid cultural change, foreign domination, or perceived deprivation. Revitalization movements have taken a number of different forms, including nativistic movements, cargo cults, and millenarian movements.

13. Religion has played an important role in global social change through liberation theology (whereby Catholic priests and nuns work for social reform and justice for the poor) and religious nationalism (whereby religious beliefs are merged with government institutions).

14. In the last twenty-five years, some significant changes have occurred in world religions, such as the blending of elements of different religions, the geographic redistribution of centers of power, and the spread of certain religious ideas and practices into such areas as the conduct of global business.

KEY TERMS

cargo cults 276
communal cults 269
contagious magic 258
cult 265
ecclesiastical cults 272
imitative magic 258
individualistic cults 266
liberation theology 276
magic 258

mahdist movements 275
millenarian movements 276
nativistic movements 276
religion 253
revitalization movements 276
rites of passage 269

rites of solidarity 271
separatist Christian churches 276
shamanistic cults 267
shaman 267
sorcery 259
vision quest 266
witchcraft 259

"Raven Steals the Sun" by Tlingit glass artist Preston Singletary. The raven in Tlingit mythology is a benevolent trickster who stole the sun from an ancient chief, thereby bringing light into the world.

CHAPTER 11

Art

MUSIC AND URBAN REVITALIZATION IN BRAZIL

Who would have thought that music could be the motivating force behind the social and economic revitalization of an urban community with more than five thousand people? Carlinhos Brown, a singer, songwriter, and percussionist, was born and raised in the Candyall neighborhood of Salvador, Brazil (Santos 2009). Candyall (pronounced *kahn-djee-all*) was a blighted neighborhood with a high rate of unemployment, unpaved streets, low average income, deteriorating homes, and sewage running in the streets. After becoming one of Brazil's best known musicians, Brown wanted to use his reputation and his relative affluence to pull his old neighborhood up from poverty and despair. In 1994 he started by building a music school in Candyall for local children who had dreams of success but little opportunity to learn music or develop skills. While the school has graduated a sizable number of successful musicians over the years, Brown has leveraged that success by encouraging local residents to join a community-based civic association aimed at rejuvenating the neighborhood. Over the past decade, the community organization has built and renovated more than 250 homes and has convinced the city to build a local health clinic, install proper sewer lines, and supply a public source of water. In short, Carlinhos Brown has used his music, his reputation, and his personal resources to restore neighborhood pride and dignity and to make Candyall a cool place to live.

QUESTIONS FOR FURTHER THOUGHT

1. Are you aware of any other examples of efforts to economically develop neighborhoods or communities through the use of music or the arts?

2. What were some of the personality traits of Carlinhos Brown that enabled him to rejuvenate his old neighborhood of Candyall?

Artistic expression is one of the most distinctive human characteristics. No group of people known to cultural anthropologists spends all of its time in the utilitarian pursuit of meeting basic survival needs. In other words, people do not hunt, grow crops, make tools, and build houses purely for the sake of sustaining themselves and others. After their survival needs are met, all cultures, even technologically simple ones, decorate their storage containers, paint their houses, embroider their clothing, and add aesthetically pleasing designs to their tools. They compose songs, tell riddles, dance creatively, paint pictures, make films, and carve masks. All of these endeavors reflect the human urge for self-expression and aesthetic pleasure. It would be hard to imagine a society without art, music, dance, and poetry. As the study of cultural anthropology reminds us, artistic expression is found in every society and aesthetic pleasure is felt by people everywhere (Coote and Shelton 1992).

What Is Art?

For centuries, people from a variety of disciplines—including philosophers, anthropologists, politicians, art historians, and professional artists themselves—have proposed definitions of *art*. George Mills (1957: 17) suggested that "definitions (of art) vary with the purposes of the definers." To illustrate, the artist might define art in terms of the creative process, the politician's definition would emphasize the communicative aspects of art that could mobilize public opinion, the art historian or knowledgeable collector would focus on the emotional response art produces, and the cultural anthropologist might define art in terms of the role or function it plays in religious ceremonies. Nevertheless, despite these diverse definitions, any definition of art, if it is to have any cross-cultural comparability, must include most, but not necessarily all, of the following five basic elements:

1. The artistic process should be creative, playful, and enjoyable and need not be concerned with the practicality or usefulness of the object being produced.

2. From the perspective of the consumer, art should produce some type of emotional response, either positive or negative.

3. Art should be **transformational**. An event from nature, such as a cheetah running at full speed, may be aesthetically pleasing in that it evokes a strong emotional response, but it is not art. It becomes art only when someone transforms the image into a painting, dance, song, or poem.

4. Art should communicate information by being representational. In other words, once the object of art is transformed, it should make a symbolic statement about what is being portrayed.

5. Art implies that the artist has developed a certain level of technical skill not shared equally by all people in a society. Some people have more highly developed skills than others because of the interplay of individual interests and opportunities with genetically based capacities.

Centuries of debate by reasonable people have failed to produce a universally agreed-upon definition of art. Although we will not presume to establish a universal definition, it will be useful, for the purposes of this chapter, to suggest a working definition based on the five elements just listed. Thus art is both the process and the products of applying certain skills to any activity that transforms matter, sound, or motion into a form that is deemed aesthetically meaningful by people in a society.

By using these five features, we can include a wide variety of artistic activities in our definition of art. In all societies people apply imagination, creativity, and technical skills to transform matter, sound, and movement into works of art. The various types of artistic expression include the graphic or plastic arts—such as painting, carving, weaving, basket making, and sculpting out of clay, metal, or glass; the creative manipulation of sounds and words in such artistic forms as music, poetry, and folklore; and the application of skill and creativity to body movement that gives rise to dance. It should be pointed out that these three neatly defined categories of artistic expression sometimes include forms that are not familiar to Westerners. To Westerners the graphic and plastic arts include such media as painting and sculpture, but in the non-Western world people may also include the Nubians' elaborate body decoration (Faris 1972), Navajo sandpainting (Witherspoon 1977), and the Inuits' body tattooing (Birket-Smith 1959). Moreover some activities that in our own society have no particular artistic content may be elevated to an art form in other societies. The Japanese tea ceremony is an excellent case in point.

Every society has a set of standards that distinguish between good art and bad art or between more and less satisfying aesthetic experiences. In some societies, such as our own, what constitutes good art is determined largely by a professional art establishment made up of art critics, museum and conservatory personnel, professors of art, and others who generally make their living in the arts. Other societies may not have professional art establishments, and their artistic standards tend to be more democratic in that they are maintained by the general public. Thus the decoration on a vase, the rhythm of a song, the communicative power of a dance, and the imagery of a painting are subject to the evaluation of artists and non-artists alike.

Differences in Art Forms

Many Western people view art from other, less complex societies as being "primitive" because it does not adhere to our culture's notion of what constitutes good art. Western art is displayed in museums and galleries with the name of the artist prominently featured. When we visit exhibitions of African or Polynesian art in Western museums, however, the artist is not even identified by name. Instead the viewer is given a rather elaborate description of where the piece comes from, the materials and techniques used to make it, the function it performs, how it might reflect other aspects of the local culture, and the name of the Western collector who purchased it. According to Sally Price (2001), this practice of identifying the collector rather than the artist is a not-so-subtle way of saying that the value of the art object is determined more by who bought it than by who made it. Despite attempts by art historians to perpetuate the use of the term *primitive*, we do not use it in this book because of its misleading connotations of both inferiority and evolutionary sequencing. Instead we use the term *small-scale* to describe egalitarian societies that have small populations, simple technologies, and little specialization of labor.

One difference between art from small-scale societies and art from complex societies stems from the lifestyles and settlement patterns in these two types of societies. Because small-scale societies tend to be foragers, pastoralists, or shifting cultivators with nomadic or seminomadic residence patterns, the art found in these societies must be highly portable. It is not reasonable to expect people who are often on the move to develop an art tradition comprising large works of art, such as larger-than-life sculptures or large painted canvases. Instead art in small-scale societies is limited to forms that people leave behind on rock walls or cliffs or forms that they can take with them easily, such as performing arts (song, dance, and storytelling); body decoration (jewelry, body painting, tattooing, and scarification); and artistic decorations on practical artifacts such as weapons, clothing, and food containers.

The second significant difference in the art of small-scale societies and complex societies stems from their different levels of labor specialization. As societies began to develop increasingly more specialized roles following the neolithic revolution (about ten thousand years ago), some segments of the population were freed from the everyday pursuits of providing food. The subsequent rise of civilizations was accompanied by the emergence of full-time specialists, such as philosophers, intellectuals, literati, and aesthetic critics, whose energies were directed, among other things, at distinguishing between good art and bad art. The standards of aesthetic judgment have become explicit and elaborately defined by specialists in more complex societies. To be certain, small-scale societies have aesthetic standards, but they are less elaborate, more implicit, and more widely diffused throughout the entire population.

As a general rule, as societies become more specialized, they also become more highly stratified into classes with different levels of power, prestige, and wealth. The aesthetic critics responsible for establishing artistic standards in complex societies are invariably members of the upper classes or are employed by them. Thus, a third contrast in the art of small-scale and complex societies is that art in complex societies is associated with the elite. Not only are those who set the standards often members of the elite, but "high" art in complex societies often is owned and controlled by the upper classes. Moreover, in some complex societies, art both glorifies and serves the interests of the upper classes. In contrast,

In complex societies, artistic standards are defined by full-time specialists such as curators, art professors, and professional critics—many of whom are associated with institutions like the Art Institute of Chicago.

because small-scale societies are more egalitarian, art tends to be more democratic in that all people have roughly equal access to it.

In addition to these three fundamental differences, art in small-scale societies is often utilitarian in nature—for example, the elaborate carvings on hunting weapons, the intricate woven rugs of the Navajo, and the fetishes carved by the Zuni in the American Southwest. Although we can observe connections between art and, say, religion in our own society, in small-scale societies art is used in many other areas of culture. In fact, because art is such an integral part of the *total* culture, many small-scale societies do not even have a word for art. That is, because art pervades all aspects of peoples' lives, they do not think of art as something separate and distinct. One example, sandpainting as practiced in Navajo culture, is as much religion, myth, and healing as it is art. According to Dorothy Lee, Navajo sandpaintings are created as part of a ceremony that

> brings into harmony with the universal order one who finds himself in discord with it. . . . Every line and shape and color, every relationship of form, is the visible manifestation of myth, ritual and religious belief. The making of the painting is accompanied with a series of sacred songs sung over a sick person. . . . When the ceremonial is over, the painting is over too; it is destroyed; it has fulfilled its function. (1993: 13)

The Functions of Art

To gain a fuller understanding of art, we must move beyond our working definition to examine the roles art plays for both people and societies. The very fact that artistic expression is found in every known society suggests that it functions in some important ways in human societies. The various functions of art can be divided into two basic types: how artistic elements function for the psychological well-being of the individual and how they function for the well-being and continuity of the society as a whole.

Emotional Gratification for the Individual

Quite apart from whatever benefits art may have for the total society, it is generally agreed that art is a source of personal gratification for both the artist and the viewer. It would be hard to imagine a world in which people engaged only in pursuits that met their basic survival needs. Although people devote most of their time and energy to meeting those needs, it is equally true that all people derive some enjoyment from art because it provides at least a temporary break from those practical (and often stressful) pursuits. After the crops are harvested, the African horticulturalist has time to dance, tell stories, and make or view pieces of art. Likewise, as a diversion from their workaday lives, many Westerners seek gratification by attending a play, a concert, or a museum. No doubt, it was this personal gratification derived from art that prompted Richard Selzer (1979: 196) to comment: "art . . . is necessary only in that without it life would be unbearable."

The psychologically beneficial functions of art can be examined from two perspectives: that of the artist and that of the beholder. For the artist the creative process releases emotional energy in a very concrete or visible way—for instance, by painting, sculpting, writing a play, or performing an interpretive dance. Artists, at least in the Western world, are viewed as living with a creative tension that, when released, results in a work of art. This release of creative energy also brings pleasure to the artist to the extent that she or he derives satisfaction from both the mastery of techniques and the product itself.

From the perspective of the viewer, art can evoke pleasurable emotional responses. For example, works of art can portray events, people, or deities that conjure up positive emotions. The symbols used in a work of art can arouse a positive emotional response. The viewer can derive pleasure from being dazzled by the artist's virtuosity. These pleasurable responses can contribute to the mental well-being of art viewers by balancing the stresses in their everyday lives.

However, it is also possible for art to have the opposite effect by eliciting negative emotions. The artistic process, if not successful from the artist's point of view, can result in increased frustration and tension. Moreover any art form is capable of eliciting disturbing or even painful emotions that can lead to psychological discomfort for the viewer.

Social Integration

In addition to whatever positive roles it may play for the individual, art contributes to the maintenance and longevity of the society in which it is found. As functionalist anthropologists remind us, art is connected to other parts of the social system. One need only walk into a church, synagogue, or temple to see the relationship between art and religion. Moreover art has been used in many societies to evoke positive opinions of systems of government and individual political leaders.

Through various symbols, art communicates a good deal about the values, beliefs, and ideologies of the culture of which it is a part. The art

Photo © JackRamsdale.com. Section A-23 for Mural Arts Program

The "Peace Wall," created by the Mural Arts Program of Philadelphia, is an example of how art can help a community bridge cultural differences among its members.

forms found in any given society reflect the major cultural themes and concerns of the society. To illustrate, prominent breasts on female figures are a major theme in much of the wood sculpture from West Africa. This dominant theme reflects a very important social value in those West African societies: having children. Somewhat closer to our own cultural traditions, much of the art in Renaissance Europe reflected religious themes central to Christianity. Thus certain forms of graphic arts help to integrate the society by making the dominant cultural themes, values, and beliefs more visible. By expressing these cultural themes in a tangible way, art ultimately functions to strengthen people's identification with their culture by reinforcing those cultural themes.

The intimate interconnectedness of art and religious life is well illustrated in Bali (Indonesia), a culture with a long and rich tradition of dance and music. The large number of ceremonies that occur annually on the Bali-Hindu calendar involve elaborate displays and performances designed to attract the gods and please the people. Various life-cycle events such as births and funerals are celebrated by special orchestras with music and dance. Some musical instruments, thought to be the gift of the gods, are considered so sacred that they can only be displayed, not actually played. According to one Balinese expert: "Music and dance are spiritual musts. The arts are an invitation for the gods to come down and join the people. There is a very physical contact with the unseen, with the ancestors . . . that makes the people in the village very happy" (Charle 1999: 28).

Art helps to strengthen and reinforce both social bonds and cultural themes. For example, cultural values are passed on from generation to generation using the media of song and dance. As part of the intense education in African bush schools, various forms of dance are used to teach proper adult attitudes and behaviors to those preparing for initiation. The role of music in education is well illustrated by Bert, Ernie, Kermit, and the other characters of *Sesame Street*, who sing about values such as cooperation, acceptable forms of conflict resolution, the fun of learning, and race relations. Music also can be used to solidify a group of people. Any history of warfare is woefully incomplete without some mention of the role that martial music played to rally the people against the common enemy.

Social Control

A popular perception of artists and their works in the Western world is that they are visionary, nonconformist, and anti-establishment. Although this is often true in contemporary Western societies, much art found in other societies (and indeed in our own Western tradition in past centuries) reinforces the existing sociocultural system. For example, art can help instill important cultural values in younger generations, coerce people to behave in socially appropriate ways, and buttress the inequalities of the stratification system in a society.

Art contributes to the status quo by serving as a mechanism of social control. Art historians generally recognize that art has a strong religious base, but they have been less cognizant of the role art plays in other cultural domains. A notable exception is Roy Sieber (1962), an art historian who has demonstrated how wooden masks serve as agents of social control in several tribal groups in northeastern Liberia. The Mano generally believed, for example, that the god-spirit mask embodied the spiritual forces that actually control human behavior. The death of a high-status man was marked by a wooden death mask carved in his honor. A crude portrait of the deceased, the death mask was thought to be the ultimate resting place of the man's spirit.

Through the medium of these pieces of art, the spirits were thought to be able to intervene in the affairs of the living. Specifically, the masks played an important role in the administration of justice. When a dispute arose or a crime was committed, the case was brought before a council of wise and influential men who reviewed the facts and arrived at a tentative decision. This decision was then confirmed (and given supernatural force) by one of the judges who wore the death mask, thus concealing his own identity. Therefore, in addition to whatever other functions these artistically carved masks played among the Mano, they served as mechanisms of social control within the criminal justice system.

Art also plays an important role in controlling behavior in more complex societies. In highly stratified societies, state governments sponsor art in order to instill obedience and maintain the status quo. In some early civilizations, for example, state-sponsored monumental architecture—such as pyramids and cathedrals—was a visual representation of the astonishing power of both the gods and the rulers. Most people living in these state societies would think twice before breaking either secular or religious rules when faced with the awesome power and authority represented in these magnificent works of art.

Particularly in modern times, the state may use art to control (or at least influence) people's behavior in more subtle ways. For example, in present-day China, the music played on state-controlled radio is purposefully chosen to soothe rather than to provoke. In keeping with its desire to build a "harmonious society," Chinese authorities play only light and upbeat music, with such themes as romance, diligence, and "it's not so bad being poor but happy." You will hear no angry rap music, protest songs, or heavy rock tunes on state-monopolized radio in China today. The purpose of music is to lull the masses into passivity, rather than to arouse any negative or inharmonious sentiments (French 2007).

Preserving or Challenging the Status Quo

By serving as a symbol for social status, art contributes to the preservation of the status quo. To one degree or another, all societies make distinctions between different levels of power and prestige. As societies become more highly specialized, systems of stratification become more complex, and the gap widens between the haves and the have-nots. Power is expressed in different ways throughout the world, including the use of physical force, control over political decisions, and accumulation of valuable resources. One particularly convincing way to display one's power is symbolically through the control of valuable items in the society. The accumulation of such practical objects as tools would not be a particularly good symbol of high prestige because everyone has tools and because one hardly needs an overabundance of everyday practical objects. The accumulation of art objects, however, is a much better symbol of high prestige because art objects are unique, not commonly found throughout the society, and often priceless.

Art is associated with status symbols in many societies that have ranked populations. For example, virtually all the art in ancient Egyptian civilizations was the personal property of the pharaohs. The high status of the hereditary king of the Ashanti of present-day Ghana is symbolized by a wide variety of artistic objects, the most important of which is the Golden Stool. In the Western world, many public art galleries are filled with impressive personal collections donated by powerful, high-status members of society (Getty, Hirshhorn, and Rockefeller, among others).

Art is a force for preserving the status quo, but it is also often used in the opposite way—as a vehicle of protest, resistance, and even revolution. A number of artists have attempted, through their own artistic media, to raise the consciousness of their oppressed countrymen in order to bring about changes in the political and social structure. For example, Marjorie Agosin (1987) documented the case of the Chilean *arpilleristas*, who told the story of political oppression on scraps of cloth. These courageous artists were considered such a threat to the established government that they were eventually banned in their own country. In Chile during the Pinochet regime, local artists painted murals under the cover of night depicting scenes of government oppression, only to have them removed by the military police the next morning.

Graphic and Plastic Arts

Graphic and plastic arts include a number of forms of expression and a wide variety of skills. Although the Western notion of **graphic** and **plastic arts** usually refers to painting, sculpture, print making, and architecture, the anthropological definition also includes such art forms as weaving, embroidery, quilting, tailoring, jewelry making, and tattooing and other forms of body decoration. In some societies one form of art, such as wood carving, may be highly developed, and others, such as painting or metalworking, may be nonexistent.

The analysis of these art forms is further complicated because different cultures use different materials and technologies depending, in part, on what materials are available locally. Whereas Native Americans of the Northwest Coast are well known for their carvings of wood, other cultures use horn, bone, ivory, or soapstone. In some small-scale societies, the nature of people's ceramic art is determined by the availability of locally found clays, such as the micaceous clay pots indigenous to the Taos Pueblo of New Mexico. Often the level of technology influences whether a culture uses metals such as gold, silver, and bronze in its art traditions.

Not only do different art traditions draw on different materials, techniques, and media, but the nature of the creative process also varies cross-culturally. To illustrate, in the Western tradition, the practice of commissioning a piece of art is quite common. For a fee, portrait artists use their creative talents to paint realistic (and usually flattering) likenesses of their prominent clients. However, it is not likely that a client could commission an Inuit artist to carve a walrus from a piece of ivory. According to the

© Nikreates/Alamy

Art comes in many forms—some utilitarian and others not. Here a man weaves a rug in Rajasthan, India.

Inuit notion of the creative process, that would be much too willful, even heavy handed. Whereas the Western artist is solely responsible for painting the canvas or molding the clay in an act of will, the Inuit carver never forces the ivory into any uncharacteristic shapes. The Inuit artist does not create but rather helps to liberate what is already in the piece of ivory. Edmund Carpenter describes the Inuit's notion of the role of the artist:

> As the carver holds the unworked ivory lightly in his hand, turning it this way and that, he whispers, "Who are you! Who hides there!" And then: "Ah, Seal!" He rarely sets out to carve, say, a seal, but picks up the ivory, examines it to find its hidden form and, if that's not immediately apparent, carves aimlessly until he sees it, humming or chanting as he works. Then he brings it out: seal, hidden, emerges. It was always there: he did not create it, he released it; he helped it step forth. (1973: 59)

Of all the forms of art in the world, the graphic and plastic arts have received the greatest amount of attention from cultural anthropologists. This is understandable because until recently the analysis of the plastic and graphic arts was the most manageable. Before the development of such data-gathering technology as sound recorders, motion pictures, and camcorders, analyzing music and dance was difficult. The graphic and plastic arts, however, produce objects that are tangible and can be removed from their cultural contexts, displayed in museums, and compared with relative ease. Moreover a painting or a sculpture has a permanence not found in music, dance, or drama.

Music

We often hear the expression "music is the universal language." By this people mean that even if two people do not speak each other's language, they can at least appreciate music together. But like so many popular sayings, this one is only partially true. Although all people do have the same physiological mechanisms for hearing, what a person actually hears is influenced by his or her culture. Westerners tend to miss much of the richness of Javanese and Sri Lankan music because they have not been conditioned to hear it. Whenever we encounter a piece of non-Western music, we hear it (process it) in terms of our own culturally influenced set of musical categories involving scale, melody, pitch, harmony, and rhythm. And because those categories are defined differently from culture to culture, the appreciation of music across cultures is not always ensured. To illustrate this point, Mark Slobin and Jeff Titon tell a story about a famous Asian musician who attended a symphony concert in Europe during the mid-nineteenth century:

> Although he was a virtuoso musician in his own country, he had never heard a performance of western music. The story goes that after the concert he

was asked how he liked it. "Very well," he replied. Not satisfied with this answer, his host asked (through an interpreter) what part he liked best. "The first part," he said. "Oh, you enjoyed the first movement?" "No, before that!" To the stranger, the best part of the performance was the tuning up period. (1984: 1)

Ethnomusicology

The cross-cultural study of music is known as **ethnomusicology**, a relatively new field that involves the cooperative efforts of both anthropologists and musicologists (Nettl and Bohlman 1991). Ethnomusicology has made rapid progress due to developments in high-quality recording equipment needed for basic data gathering. Slobin and Titon (1984) identified four major concerns of ethnomusicology:

1. *Ideas about music:* How does a culture distinguish between music and nonmusic? What functions does music play for the society? Is music viewed as beneficial or harmful to the society? What constitutes beautiful music? On what occasions should music be played?

2. *Social structure of music:* What are the social relationships between musicians? How does a society distinguish between various musicians on the basis of such criteria as age, gender, race, ethnicity, and education?

3. *Characteristics of the music itself:* How does the style of music in different cultures vary (scale, melody, harmony, and timing)? What different musical genres are found in a society (lullaby, sea chantey, hard rock, and so on)? What is the nature of musical texts (words)? How is music composed? How is music learned and transmitted?

4. *Material culture of music:* What musical instruments are used in a culture? Who makes the musical instruments, and how are they distributed? How are musical tastes reflected in the instruments used?

As these areas of interest indicate, ethnomusicology is concerned with both the structure and techniques of music and the interconnections between music and other parts of the culture. Yet, during the course of cross-cultural studies of music, ethnomusicologists have been torn between two approaches. At one extreme, they have

© J. Harp/Robertsstock.com

Ethnomusicologists would be interested in studying both the music of this Ukrainian bandura player and how the music reflects the wider culture of which it is a part.

TABLE 11.1 Comparison of Music from Egalitarian and Stratified Societies

EGALITARIAN SOCIETIES/SIMPLE ECONOMICS	STRATIFIED SOCIETIES/COMPLEX ECONOMICS
Repetitious texts	Nonrepetitious texts
Slurred articulation	Precise articulation
Little solo singing	Solo singing
Wide melodic intervals	Narrow melodic intervals
Non-elaborate songs (no embellishments)	Elaborate songs (embellishments)
Few instruments	Large number of instruments
Singing in unison	Singing in simultaneous intervals

© Cengage Learning 2013

searched for musical universals—elements found in all musical traditions. At the opposite extreme, they have been interested in demonstrating the considerable diversity found throughout the world. Bruno Nettl (1980: 3) describes this tension: "In the heart of the ethnomusicologist there are two strings: one that attests to the universal character of music, to the fact that music is indeed something that all cultures have or appear to have . . . and one responsive to the enormous variety of existing cultures."

All ethnomusicologists—whether their background is in music or cultural anthropology—are interested in the study of music in its cultural context. Alan Lomax and his colleagues (1968) conducted one of the most extensive studies of the relationship between music and other parts of culture. Specifically they found some broad correlations between various aspects of music and a culture's level of subsistence. Foraging societies were found to have types of music, song, and dance that were fundamentally different from those of more complex producers. By dividing a worldwide sample of cultures into five different levels of subsistence complexity, Lomax found some significant correlations. For example, differences emerged between egalitarian, small-scale societies with simple subsistence economies and large-scale, stratified societies with complex systems of production (see Table 11.1).

Dance

Dance has been defined as purposeful and intentionally rhythmical nonverbal body movements that are culturally patterned and have aesthetic value (Hanna 1979: 19). Although dance is found in all known societies, the forms it takes, the functions it fulfills, and the meanings attached to it vary widely from society to society. In some societies dance involves considerable energy and body movement, whereas in other societies it is much more restrained and subtle. Because the human body is capable of a wide variety of postures and movements, which body parts are active and which postures are assumed differ from one dance tradition to another. In some African societies (such as the Ubakala of Nigeria) drums are a necessary part of dance, whereas in others (such as the Zulu) they are not. Dancing alone is the expected form in some societies, but in others it is customary for groups to dance in circles, lines, or other formations. Yet, whatever form dance takes in any culture, it remains a persuasive form of communication that blends body movements with both emotions and cognition. As Judith Hanna (2005: 11) reminds us: "Both dance and verbal language have vocabulary (locomotion and gestures in dance), grammar (ways one movement can follow another), and semantics (including symbolic devices and spheres for encoding feelings and ideas)."

Moreover the relative value of dance as an art form varies widely from one society to another. To illustrate, the government of the small country of Cuba supports dance in a number of visible ways, making Cuba one of the great dance nations of the world. For example, Cuba is the venue for a number of important international dance festivals, and in fact many world-class dancers come to Cuba to study dance. The professional dancers of the Ballet Nacional de Cuba enjoy high status at home and international acclaim when performing abroad. And free dance education is available to any child from kindergarten through university. Now compare this high level of public promotion of all forms of dance in Cuba with the situation just ninety miles to the north in the United States. The overwhelming majority of adults in the United States have never attended a fully staged ballet, a contemporary dance performance, or even a ballroom dance competition. Despite the fact that the physical conditioning required of professional dancers often exceeds that of other professional athletes, dance in the United States is generally thought of as a female, or an effeminate, profession. And despite the recent popularity of reality-based dance shows on TV (*Dancing with the Stars* and *So You Think You Can Dance*), government officials (from the courts to the National Endowment for the Arts) expend an enormous amount of time and energy trying to determine whether certain dance forms are too sexual, involve too much nudity or semi-nudity, or encourage inappropriately close contact between partners (Hanna 2005).

Functions of Dance

As with other forms of artistic expression, the functions of dance are culturally variable. Dance is likely to function in different ways both between and within societies. Dance often performs several functions simultaneously within a society, but some functions are more prominent than others. To illustrate, dance can function psychologically by helping people cope more effectively with tensions and aggressive feelings; politically by expressing political values and attitudes, showing allegiance to political leaders, and controlling behavior; religiously by various methods of communicating with supernatural forces; socially by articulating and reinforcing relationships among members of the society; and educationally by passing on cultural traditions, values, and beliefs from one generation to the next.

Dance and Other Aspects of a Culture

Lomax and his colleagues (1968) demonstrated quite graphically how dance is connected to other aspects of a culture. Specifically their research shows how dance reflects and reinforces work patterns. By examining more than two hundred films, they were able to find a number of similarities between work styles and dance styles. The Netsilik Eskimos (Inuit) provide an interesting—and not atypical—example. For the Netsilik dancing consists of solo performances that take place during the winter in a large communal igloo. Lomax describes the dance in considerable detail:

> One after another, the greatest hunters stand up before the group, a large flat drum covered with sealskin in the left hand, a short, club-like drumstick in the other. Over to the side sit a cluster of women chanting away as the hunter drums, sings, and dances. The performer remains in place holding the wide stance used by these Eskimos when they walk through ice and snow or stand in the icy waters fishing. Each stroke of the short drumstick goes diagonally down and across to hit the lower edge of the drum and turn the drumhead. On the backstroke it strikes the other edge, reversing the motion, which is then carried through by a twist of the left forearm. The power and solidity of the action is emphasized by the downward drive of the body into slightly bent knees on the downstroke and the force of trunk rising as the knees straighten to give full support to the arm on the upstroke. The dance consists largely of these repeated swift and strong diagonal right arm movements down across the body. (1968: 226–27)

Many of the postures and motions in Netsilik dance are the very ones that are necessary for successful seal hunting in an Arctic environment. The Netsilik seal hunter may wait patiently and silently for hours over a hole in the ice before a seal appears. When it does, the hunter's harpoon flies instantly and powerfully in a single stroke diagonally across the chest. Thus the stylistic movements in Netsilik dance are essentially identical to those used in their everyday hunting activities. The qualities of a good hunter—speed, strength, accuracy, and endurance—are portrayed and glorified in dance. In other words, as part of their leisure activity, hunters, through the medium of dance, re-dramatize the essentials of the everyday subsistence activities that are so crucial for their survival.

Film: A Recent Art Form

When Americans think of film as an art form, instinctively they imagine American filmmaking legends such as Steven Spielberg, Robert Altman, and Francis Ford Coppola. However, many countries in all parts of the world have long and rich traditions of filmmaking as an art form. For example, Ingmar Bergman in Sweden, Sergei Eisenstein in Russia, and Akira Kurosawa in Japan all made world-class films during the twentieth century. The continent of Africa (from Cape Verde to Cape Horn) has a rich tradition of filmmaking; since 1981 it has supported its own annual international film festival in Mogadishu, Somalia, exclusively for African films. And with China emerging as an economic superpower in the twenty-first century, its rapidly growing film industry has moved away from films glorifying the state to films (by such world-renowned directors as Jia Zhangke and Li Yang) highlighting the negative aspects of China's entry into modern capitalism and global markets.

The latest territory to receive critical acclaim for filmmaking is Nunavut, the new homeland of the Inuit people carved out of the landmass of Canada in 1999. Until this century, the only connection between the Inuit people and filmmaking was Robert Flaherty's documentary *Nanook of the North*, a silent film about the Inuit made in 1922. Eight decades later an Inuit filmmaker named Zacharias Kunuk, using all Inuit actors and crew, made a feature-length film in the native language of the Inuit (Inuktitut). The film, *Atanarjuat: The Fast Runner*, while providing ethnographic insights into traditional Inuit culture, is more than just another documentary about a vanishing way of life. Based on an ancient Inuit folk epic, *Atanarjuat* uses Inuit actors to tell a powerful and compelling story in the ancient words of their traditional language. Shot over a period of six months, the film portrays the movement of the seasons, which so thoroughly influence Inuit daily life. Capturing on camera a number of different hues of black and white, Kunuk manages to reveal complex psychological motives behind the actions of his mythical characters, whose story up until now had always been conveyed in oral tradition. *Atanarjuat* won the "best first feature film" award at the Cannes International Film Festival in 2001, just two years after the founding of the Inuit self-governing territory.

While Hollywood studios have been making big-budget films for decades, filmmakers in Mumbai, India (colloquially known as "Bollywood"), have made far more films than Hollywood over the decades and have won the hearts and minds of a much larger audience. Bollywood films are devoured not only by a potential audience of a billion people at home, but also by the millions of Indians living in the United States, the United Kingdom, Europe, the Middle East, and elsewhere. These films have been dubbed into other languages, including French, Russian, and Mandarin Chinese.

Far more people see films made in Bollywood (India) than in Hollywood (California).

© Aamir Khan Productions/Singh Sachdev, Hardeep/The Kobal Collection

The popularity of Bollywood films rests on their story lines, which have been called "pre-cynical" (Mehta 2004). Unlike their Hollywood counterparts, which tend to be edgy and ambiguous when dealing with such topics as love, family, and patriotism, Indian films are melodramatic and always celebrate true love, courage, devotion to country, and, above all, motherhood. Moreover most Bollywood films are musicals that last as long as three and a half hours, with as many as a dozen "big production" song-and-dance numbers. Even though many Americans have heard of these Indian-made films, few have actually seen one, unless they happen to be Indians living in the United States. For most Americans these films are overly optimistic and overly sentimental for the coffeehouse crowd and certainly too sedate for American men, who generally prefer to watch things being blown up. Even though Indian films are very popular among the several million Indian Americans living in the United States, it remains to be seen whether Bollywood will make as much of an inroad into mainstream U.S. cinema as Indian engineers and computer scientists have made into Western technology industries.

Art: Continuity and Change

Like all other aspects of culture, the various forms of expressive arts (graphic and plastic arts, music, dance, and verbal arts) are subject to both internal and external forces of change. Anyone who has ever taken a course on the history of twentieth-century American art, for example, knows that unique schools of painting (with their own distinctive styles, materials, and themes) emerge, become prominent, and eventually die out and become part of history. To illustrate, the Ashcan School (Edward Hopper and Arthur Davies) of 1908–1918 featured scenes of urban realism; the 1920s and 1930s witnessed the Art Deco style, characterized by straight lines and slender forms; abstract expressionists during the 1940s, such as Jackson Pollock and Willem de Kooning, emphasized spontaneous personal expression over more conventional artistic values; minimalism, popular in the 1950s, emphasized pure, simple, and reduced forms; and finally the pop art of Andy Warhol and Roy Lichtenstein in the 1960s used images from mass media, advertising, and popular culture in ironic ways.

In the early centuries of American art, painting styles and approaches were relatively stable, often lasting for several decades. In the absence of high-speed transportation and communication technology, different artistic traditions were not able to diffuse very rapidly. The late twentieth century, however, witnessed many more changes than had occurred in the two preceding centuries.

Rapid and dramatic changes occurred in the art world even before the term *globalization* became fashionable. Nowhere is this truer than in the area of glass sculptural art during the last half century. In the early 1960s, advances in small-furnace technology—along with the pioneering efforts of Harvey Littleton in the United States and Erwin Eisch in Germany—brought the art of glassmaking out of the factory and into the artist's studio. In a little more than four decades, many new techniques of glassblowing, casting, constructing, and lampworking diffused rapidly throughout the world. American artist Dale Chihuly traveled to Venice in 1969, Venetian master Lino Tagliapietra traveled to the Pilchuck Glass School in Seattle, and the influential Czech glass artists Stanislav Lebenski and Jaraslava Brychtova traveled all over the world. This frenzy of cross-fertilization since the 1960s has produced a worldwide art movement that now numbers more than five thousand studio glass artists.

The growth of the glass art movement over the last four decades is noteworthy not only for its scale and global distribution, but also because of its prominence in the art world and in the marketplace. To illustrate, single pieces of glass art (which would fit on an ordinary end table in one's living room) by contemporary artists such as Lino Tagliapietra or William Morris sell for $60,000 and upward. Larger pieces (such as Chihuly chandeliers or Morris's life-sized pieces from his "Man Adorned" series) retail for between $300,000 and $800,000 each.

The possibilities in the twenty-first century for cross-fertilization of artistic traditions are increasing. Art exhibits today travel around the world rather than remaining in galleries or museums for centuries on end as they did in the past. Similarly, in the area of music, both rock stars and symphony orchestras go on world tours, performing in front of audiences all over the globe. We have seen British pop artist Sting record fusion music with Cheb Mami from Algeria and the rock group Killing Joke collaborate with Maori singer and poet Hinewehi Mohi. More recently the 2011 Grammy award for "Best Pop Collaboration" was awarded for the song "Imagine" to Herbie Hancock, Pink, and India.Arie of the United States, Seal and Jeff Beck from the United Kingdon, Konono No°1 from the Democratic Republic of the Congo, and Oumou Sangaré of Mali. According to anthropologist Renata Rosaldo: "Cultural artifacts flow between unlikely places, and nothing is sacred, permanent, or sealed off " (Jenkins 2001: 89).

And, finally, we are beginning to see how a particular society adopts new art forms from other parts of the world and infuses them with its own traditional cultural content. *Indian Idol,* like its American counterpart, is a talent competition with unknown Indian singers of Western pop music. A new and very popular TV show produced in Abu Dhabi, United Arab Emirates (UAE), uses the same glamorous sets and big-budget productions, but rather than scantily clad singers competing with Western love ballads, the contestants compete in an elaborate style of Bedouin poetry popular among the Gulf States but virtually unknown in the rest of the Arab world (Fattah 2007). Not only has the success of the show (entitled *Poets of Millions*) spawned similar shows in other Islamic countries such as Egypt and Lebanon, but it is catapulting the UAE to cultural leadership in the Arab world. No longer is the UAE considered to be an ultra-conservative, oil-wealthy country with no popular culture of its own. In the twenty-first century, the UAE is transforming its traditional art forms and dialects into forms that can be understood and appreciated in other parts of the Arab world and beyond. And, interestingly, this repackaging of traditional art from the UAE for both internal and external consumption is occurring in a country that is planning to spend $10 billion to build and operate branches of the Guggenheim and the Louvre museums.

Out in the Real World: Anthropologist-Turned-Detective Finds Stolen African Statues

In 1985 Monica Udvardy, a cultural anthropologist from the University of Kentucky, was conducting field research among the Mijikenda people on the Kenya coast. During the course of her research, Udvardy took a photograph of a local man standing in front of two traditional wooden statues (known as *vigango*) erected to appease the ancestor-spirits and to honor and protect his two deceased brothers. When Udvardy returned several months later to give the man a copy of the photo, he told her that the two statues in the photo had been stolen and asked for her help in trying to locate them. Before leaving Kenya, Udvardy searched curio shops in some of the tourist-oriented towns in hopes of finding the purloined statues, but she did not locate them.

Then, fourteen years later in 1999, while attending the African Studies Association meetings in Philadelphia, Udvardy was startled to see one of the missing statues in a slide presentation given by Linda Giles on some of the artifacts from the Museum at Illinois State University. Udvardy, in collaboration with Giles, then began to research how the statue made its long journey from the coast of Kenya to the museum in Illinois. In the process of their sleuthing, the two scholars tracked down 294 other *vigango* in nineteen museums in the United States, among which was the second stolen statue from the 1985 photograph.

It was determined that most of these 294 *vigango* were brought into the United States by a single art dealer from Los Angeles, who claimed to have purchased the statues legitimately from tourist shops in Mombasa, Kenya. He sold these statues to private collectors and to museums for as much as $5,000 each. The most generous interpretation of the art dealer's behavior is that he was unaware of the cultural and religious significance of these *vigango*, which, he claimed, he bought and sold as nothing more than works of art. But no self-respecting Mijikenda adult would ever erect a statue to the spirits in honor of dead relatives and then sell it for money. This would be as absurd as a person in the United States ripping the headstone from the grave of her or his deceased mother and selling it to get a little extra cash. Anyone who understood the cultural significance of *vigango* in Mijikendo society would immediately realize that such a statue in a tourist shop in Mombasa would have had to be stolen.

In February 2006 the National Museums of Kenya requested that museum officials in Illinois return the *vigango* to the original family owners in eastern Kenya. Because the original photograph, coupled with Udvardy's investigations, provided solid evidence that the statue had been stolen, museum officials agreed to return the supernatural statue to its rightful owners. Hampton University Museum in Virginia, where the second stolen statue in the photograph resided, also agreed to return the stolen *vigango*.

In June 2007 a repatriation ceremony was held by the National Museums of Kenya at the ancestral home of the family that had lost the statues twenty-two years earlier. This ceremony marked the first time in history that stolen artifacts were returned from the United States. The media attention surrounding this event raised global awareness of the theft of *vigango* and other cultural property from non-Western countries. The rest of the world is finally beginning to understand the devastating impact that global trafficking of African artifacts has on local communities. In fact, art dealers in the United States have voluntarily returned an additional nine *vigango* to Kenya. Here, then, is another example of how original anthropological fieldwork, along with years of sleuthing and investigating, led to the solution of a real-life societal problem—namely, the return of stolen sacred objects to their rightful owners (Lacey 2006; Udvardy and Giles 2008).

1. Is it rare for stolen artifacts to become part of a museum's permanent collection, or is it fairly common?

2. Should those museums that have *vigango* as part of their holdings return them to the Mijikenda people of East Africa?

3. Does the government of Kenya have a responsibility to prevent the sale and exportation of *vigango* and similar spiritual artifacts?

SUMMARY

1. Although there is no universal definition of *art,* for purposes of this chapter we define *art* as the process and products of applying certain skills to any activity that transforms matter, sound, or motion into a form that is deemed aesthetically meaningful to people in a society. The creative process of making art should be enjoyable, produce an emotional response, be transformational, convey a message, and involve a certain level of skill on the part of the artist.

2. The forms of artistic expression discussed in this chapter are the graphic and plastic arts (such as painting, sculpting, and weaving), music, dance, and film.

3. In contrast to the art found in small-scale societies, the art of more complex societies is more permanent, has more elaborate and explicit standards of evaluation, and is associated with the elite.

4. Art contributes to the well-being of both the individual and the society. For the individual, art provides emotional gratification to both the artist and the beholder. For the society, various forms of art strengthen and reinforce both social bonds and cultural themes, promote social control, and serve as a symbol of high status, particularly in complex societies.

5. Ethnomusicologist Alan Lomax suggests that the music traditions in small-scale societies differ from those in more complex societies in that the former are characterized by more repetitive texts, slurred articulation, little solo singing, non-embellished songs, few instruments, and singing in unison.

6. Like other forms of art, dance has many different forms and functions. Moreover dance is intimately connected to other aspects of culture, as illustrated by the Netsilik (Inuit).

7. Like all other aspects of culture, forms and styles of art change over time. Despite the Internet and the IT revolution (which has accelerated the sharing of art across cultures), cultures do not appear to be surrendering their unique forms of artistic expression.

KEY TERMS

dance 296	graphic arts 293	transformational 285
ethnomusicology 295	plastic arts 293	

An elderly Chinese man in traditional nineteenth-century clothing uses technology from the twenty-first century.

CHAPTER **12**

Global Challenges and the Role of Applied Anthropology

A CLOSING LETTER TO STUDENTS

Congratulations on working your way through this textbook! We opened Chapter 1 with a letter to you explaining this book's "applied perspective" and what you might hope to gain from it. We said that this not only is a brief (yet comprehensive) textbook introducing you to the field of cultural anthropology, but also is designed to show how the research findings, theories, methods, and insights of cultural anthropology can be useful in your everyday personal and professional lives. The real-life relevance of cultural anthropology has been highlighted in two special features of the text: (1) real (not hypothetical) chapter-opening scenarios and (2) chapter-ending case studies on how the insights of cultural anthropology have been used in the real world to address human and societal challenges.

Now that you have had nearly a semester to familiarize yourself with both the scope and relevance of cultural anthropology, we want to conclude the book with this capstone chapter that will focus on two major concerns. First, we will identify some of the major global challenges of the twenty-first century for all peoples of the world, including (but not limited to) climate change, the survival of indigenous peoples, environmental degradation, sustainable economic development, the spread of world health pandemics, and the widening gap between the rich and the poor. And second, we will explore how cultural anthropologists are contributing to the resolution of many of these global problems.

As we have seen, anthropological insights can be helpful (and in many cases essential) in solving social problems. Basic cultural information certainly is useful to help us avoid breakdowns in communication when interacting with people from different cultural or subcultural backgrounds, both at home and abroad. In addition, cross-cultural competency can be valuable in meeting your professional objectives, whether you choose a career in medicine, business, education, law, architecture, counseling, public administration, criminal justice, marketing, or just about any other area we could imagine. And, as we shall see in this chapter, anthropologists are helping to address many of the global challenges of the twenty-first century. Anthropologists are making a difference by drawing on the same data, insights, methods, and theories that you have been studying this semester.

The purpose of this letter is to make sure that you have fully understood how important cultural anthropology can be to the future of your personal lives, your neighborhoods, your towns, your states, your nation, and the planet itself. Not only should you appreciate the importance of understanding culture to operate effectively in cross-cultural situations , but you should know cultural anthropology well enough to be able to communicate it to your parents and friends (who still may be wondering why you are not taking only courses in business management and finance) and also to your future employers, no matter what field you actually enter.

As we have tried to show throughout this text, the discipline of anthropology looks at humans, wherever they may be found, from earliest prehistory up to the present. Because of the enormous time frame it has carved out for itself, anthropology is able to observe both long-term and short-term sociocultural trends. To illustrate, because archaeologists have looked at cultural development over the last several thousand years, they have been able to identify some major cultural trends or transformations, such as the neolithic revolution, the rise of urban societies, and the industrial revolution. Cultural anthropologists, who focus on contemporary cultures and societies of the world, are constantly looking at more recent and, by definition, more short-term sociocultural trends and developments. These include post–World War II trends such as world immigration patterns; the rise of religious fundamentalism; rapid urbanization in Africa, Asia, and Latin America; the spread of world health pandemics such as AIDS; environmental degradation; and the widening gap between the rich and the poor throughout the world.

Because anthropologists have identified these recent trends, they are often asked to predict where these trends will lead humankind in the future and what effects they will have on the human condition. Anthropologists, like the members of any other profession, have no special powers of prediction. They cannot tell us, with any degree of certainty, what the global cultural mosaic will look like at the end of the twenty-first century. What anthropologists *are* able to do, however, is document the recent trends and changes, and then predict how things might be in the future, *provided these changes continue on their present course*. How the world actually looks ninety years from now will depend on natural phenomena, such as earthquakes, over which humans have little control, as well as on purposeful actions taken by people and their governments. It is impossible to predict how either will affect current sociocultural trends. The best anthropologists can do is to describe the recent trends so as to enable people in the future to reinforce the beneficial trends and take action to slow down or reverse the more deleterious trends.

The less affluent countries are not alone in facing the many daunting challenges mentioned above. To one degree or another, these are *global problems* for all nations, rich and poor alike. We are not suggesting that people from affluent nations are suffering the consequences of these global problems as much as people from poor nations do, but wealthy nations have a real stake in helping to ameliorate these pressing global issues. Unless some of the more egregious inequities and injustices between rich and poor nations are addressed, the affluent nations will continue to grapple with political instability, global pandemics, and military interventions. The problems that face former colonies and other poor nations are global issues that cannot be ignored by any nation because they affect the very sustainability of humankind.

The world of the new millennium poses a number of major challenges. These include, but are not limited to, global health problems, the widening gap between poor and wealthy nations (and between poor and wealthy people *within* these nations), demographic shifts both between and within nation-states, environmental destruction, the depletion of the world's natural resources, the need for cleaner and more sustainable sources of energy, children's need for quality education and health care, and the injustices inflicted on the world's indigenous peoples and other vulnerable populations. In one way or another, all of these global issues are both interrelated and have their origins in nineteenth- and twentieth-century industrialization and colonialism. For the remainder of this final chapter, we want to look at three of these major global challenges in some detail: (1) sustainable economic development in the developing world, (2) the cultural survival of indigenous populations, and (3) global environmental challenges. We will describe each of these global problem areas in its contemporary context and then discuss how anthropologists are addressing these challenges in their research and policy recommendations.

In keeping with the theme of this textbook, we want to reiterate that cultural anthropologists bring a good deal to the table in addressing today's global challenges. First, because cultural anthropologists rely so heavily on direct research (participant-observation) at the grassroots level, they are in the best position to observe the impact of global changes on people's lives. In other words, unlike economists, anthropologists are studying the real consequences of colonialism, industrialization, and rapid globalization on real people rather than focusing on such impersonal "leading indicators" as GNP and demographic shifts. Second, because anthropologists take a holistic approach, they tend to look for those interconnections between the parts of local societies that other specialists (such as agronomists, development planners, and other social scientists) might miss. And finally, since anthropologists work from a comparative and cross-cultural perspective, it is likely that they will be aware of how similar peoples in different parts of the world are dealing with these global challenges.

Sustainable Economic Development for Marginalized Peoples

Today's countries can be roughly divided into two broad categories: the haves and the have-nots. This dichotomy is sometimes characterized as the industrialized versus the non-industrialized worlds, or the developed versus the developing worlds. There is considerable disagreement about the reasons for these differences, but no one can deny the vast differences in material wealth between the richest nations (such as Canada, Switzerland, the United States, and Japan) and the poorest nations (such as Chad, Mozambique, Ethiopia, and Bangladesh). The income of the average American is 342 times greater than the income of the average person in Burundi. (See Table 12.1.) Enormous disparities can also be seen in noneconomic measures. The life expectancy is seventy-seven years in Norway but only forty-seven years in Burkina Faso. The infant mortality rate in Mali is 168 per one thousand live births, whereas in Finland it is only 6.

How did the contemporary world become so uneven in economic development? Social scientists have offered differing interpretations, but they usually boil down to one of two competing theories. One broad

TABLE 12.1 Per Capital Gross National Income (reported in 2011 based on 2010 data)

TEN RICHEST NATIONS	PER CAPITA GNI
Norway	$85,380
Luxembourg	$75,510
Switzerland	$70,350
Denmark	$58,980
Sweden	$49,930
Netherlands	$49,720
Finland	$47,170
United States	$47,140
Ireland	$40,990
United Kingdom	$38,540
TEN POOREST NATIONS	
Guinea Bissau	$540
Uganda	$490
Ethiopia	$380
Niger	$360
Sierra Leone	$340
Eritrea	$340
Malawi	$330
Ethiopia	$280
Liberia	$190
Congo, Democratic Republic	$180
Burundi	$160

© Cengage Learning 2013

Sources: World Bank Atlas (http://data.worldbank.org/indicator/NY.GNP.PCAP.CD).

theory explains these vast differences in economic development in terms of the inherent sociocultural differences between the rich and the poor. Often called **modernization theory**, this model is based on a dichotomy of traditional versus modern that serves not only as an attempted description of reality but also as a planning strategy for bringing about economic development in less developed nations. The modern nations are associated with high levels of technology, industrialization, scientific rationality, formal education, efficient bureaucratic governments, strong market economies, punctuality, religious pluralism, low birth and death rates, upward mobility based on merit, rapid change, plans for the future, and a decline in the extended family. Traditional nations, on the other hand, have fewer of these characteristics. Modernization theory posits that in order for developing nations to become developed, they must become more modern by taking on more of the "modern" characteristics listed above. The process of economic development occurs through the mechanism of foreign aid from the wealthy nations to the less developed nations.

The modernization theory of economic development suffers from ethnocentric assumptions. First, modernization theorists assume that all people in the world ought to gladly embrace all of the economic, cultural, and social changes inherent in "becoming modern." Second, they clearly overestimate the extent to which some non-Western people resist modernization, in large part because they ignore the many creative adaptations these people have made for centuries. Third, and perhaps most important, proponents of modernization theory assume that traditional people will be better off if they become modern. Because becoming modern is progressive, it is widely held that it must be beneficial. Modernization theorists assume that the advantages of becoming modern—such as higher incomes and standards of living—are universally beneficial. Even though becoming modern also involves giving up much of one's traditional culture, modernization theorists see it as a small price to pay in exchange for the obvious benefits.

Whereas 168 of every thousand children in Mali die in infancy, only 6 of every thousand die in Finland.

© B&C Alexander/ArcticPhoto

The other major theory to explain the disparities between rich and poor has been called the **world systems theory**. According to this theory, the rich and poor nations of the world are not fundamentally different because of innate cultural features but rather because of how they have operated within the world system. The wealthy countries of the world have achieved high levels of development by exploiting other regions, plundering their natural resources, using their people as cheap sources of labor, and dominating their markets. In 1884 at the Conference of Berlin, European powers carved up the entire continent of Africa. The French took large parts of West Africa; the British controlled Nigeria, the Gold Coast, Kenya, Uganda, and the Rhodesias; the Portuguese got Angola and Mozambique; and the tiny country of Belgium took control of the mineral-rich Congo, an area seventy-six times larger than itself. These nineteenth-century industrializing nations of Europe set up plantations and mining operations in their colonies, exploited cheap African labor, exported some of their own excess people to the colonies, and then sold many of their finished products back to the Africans they claimed to be helping.

Whereas Europeans actually took political control over their colonies, the United States chose to establish commercial influence through its corporations, mostly in Central and South America. Whether we are talking about corporate imperialism or outright colonialism, however, the consequences were the same: The exploitation of people and resources by the dominant powers (by exporting capital gains and keeping "developing nations" in continual debt) impeded the economic growth of the subordinate nations. Thus, according to the world systems theory, economic development is not the result of specific cultural characteristics but instead occurs when one group purposefully increases its own wealth at the expense of others.

The present debate in development anthropology revolves around the question of whether rising incomes and standards of living always have a positive effect on all parties concerned. Modernization theorists answer this question affirmatively, but a number of studies over the past several decades have strongly suggested that economic growth and development do not always improve people's lives. Some have even suggested that economic progress (as defined by rising wages, increased GNI, and so on) actually has lowered the quality of life for many non-Western people. Despite the best intentions of international development agencies, multimillion-dollar foreign aid projects have often resulted in greater poverty, longer working hours, overpopulation, poorer health, more social pathology, and environmental degradation (Bodley 2007, 2008).

Contrary to conventional thinking, many of the anticipated benefits of economic development have turned out to be illusory or downright detrimental. For example, attempts to engage non-Western people in programs of planned economic development often result in an increase in the incidence of disease for four reasons. First, many of the more modern lifestyles that people adopt bring new diseases associated with the industrialized world. For example, as early as the 1970s, Charles Hughes and John Hunter (1972) and Ian Prior (1971) found that rapid cultural change was followed by dramatic increases in the incidence of diseases such as diabetes, heart disease, obesity, hypertension, gout, and high blood pressure in areas where these conditions previously had been unknown. Second, the incidence of certain bacterial or parasitic diseases increases precipitously in areas experiencing rapid cultural change. To illustrate, the construction of dams and irrigation systems in the Sudan as part of the Azande development scheme created ideal breeding conditions for the snail larva that causes schistosomiasis, one of Africa's most deadly diseases. Third, environmental degradation caused by drilling for oil and gas, mining, and industrial pollution presents a host of health threats to people in developing nations. As Alicia Fentiman (2009) has suggested, Nigerian fishing people in the Niger Delta face contaminated drinking water, skin disorders from bathing in oil-polluted water, and respiratory diseases from oil flares as a direct result of oil drilling by the Shell Oil Company. And fourth, health problems in the developing world are further aggravated by the rapid urbanization that often accompanies economic development. People crowding into cities looking for employment have more exposure to contagious diseases, which are made even worse by poor nutrition and unsanitary living conditions.

Programs of economic development often lead to changes in people's dietary habits. In some cases these dietary changes are voluntary to the extent that some new foods, associated with powerful outsiders, are status symbols. But, more often than not, diets change because of circumstances associated with the objectives of economic development that are beyond the control of the local people. For example, in an attempt to grow more cash crops (which help to raise wages and bring in foreign exchange capital), non-Western people often divert time and energy from growing their normal food crops. The result is that they spend much of their hard-earned cash on foods that are both costly and nutritionally inferior in order to feed their families.

This was the case among Brazilian farmers who made the transition from growing food crops to growing sisal, a cash crop used in the production of rope (Gross and Underwood 1971). Although the farmers spent most of their income on food, they could not provide adequate nutrition for their families. The study showed that the children of sisal workers were particularly at risk because most of the food went to the adults so they could maintain the strength needed for their strenuous work. These children of sisal workers, owing to their caloric deficiencies, experienced slower growth rates. In addition to physical retardation, improper nourishment can lead directly to a reduced mental capacity and a lowered resistance to infection.

Not only do people who are caught up in economic development often eat less food, but they also eat food that is worse for them than their traditional diets. Often these foods, purchased rather than homegrown, are low in minerals, vitamins, fiber, and protein but high in sugar, sodium, and saturated fats. The lack of vitamins and minerals leads to an increased incidence of nutritionally related diseases, and the lack of protein may cause kwashiorkor (protein malnutrition), the leading cause of death in Africa and other parts of the developing world. The marked increase in sugar consumption by non-Western people has led to both a rapid and dramatic deterioration of dental health (Bodley 2008) and alarmingly high rates of obesity and diabetes among the world's poor.

Economic development programs have had deleterious effects on sizable segments of the target populations. Not only is health negatively affected, but other unfortunate (and usually unanticipated) consequences also occur. The natural environment is often degraded, families break down, social problems increase, and support systems disintegrate. In most cases economic development brings with it higher productivity, lower prices for goods and services, and a rising standard of living; however, higher productivity eventually may lead to fewer jobs due to automation or outsourcing. Automobiles in developing countries get better and more affordable, but as cars become more prevalent, the roads become jammed with traffic, the air is more polluted, and people waste more time stuck in traffic. Economic development brings higher living standards, but stress, anxiety, and clinical depression become more prevalent. E-mail is cheap and fast, but users must deal with the spam messages that arrive each day. Cell phones are convenient, but cell-phone owners are virtually never out of contact with the office. SUVs may be comfortable and seemingly safer owing to their size, but they cause more traffic fatalities, increase a nation's dependency on Middle Eastern oil, and are the newest twenty-first-century symbol of the principle of "power without responsibility." Biotechnology may increase people's life expectancy, but it also may leave them dependent on costly synthetic drugs.

To be certain, some segments of non-Western populations benefit from programs of economic development, but large numbers or even the majority wind up worse off than they would have been if the development efforts had never begun. To point out these negative consequences, however, is not to suggest that we should abandon foreign assistance programs or stop trying to increase people's access to material resources. The negative results occur most often when development programs are introduced without the full participation and understanding of the people they are designed to help. They are, in other words, "top-down" programs that fail to involve the local people in planning and administration and, even worse, do not understand the cultures of the people who are supposed to benefit from the program.

Specifically, what sociocultural information can anthropologists provide to assist economic development efforts? For example, if a development agency wants to resettle a group of nomadic cattle herders onto farmland so that they can become agriculturalists, the agency will need to know the answers to a number of *cultural* questions in order to assess (1) how best to meet the program's objectives or (2) whether they should attempt the project at all. To illustrate, the following questions about nomadic pastoralists—routinely asked by anthropologists—are only a few of the many that need answers:

- How are resources shared and distributed in the community?
- What material goods are highly valued, and how are they related to other nonmaterial aspects of the culture?
- How is labor divided according to age and gender?
- Do household tasks change according to the season of the year?
- What is the composition of the family (the basic economic unit)?
- Are there significant differences in family composition throughout the society?
- How stratified (in terms of wealth, power, and prestige) is the society?
- How is decision-making power distributed? Are some groups or individuals systematically excluded from positions of power?

If we take seriously the notion of the systemic nature of culture, then we must assume that a change in one part of the system is likely to bring about changes in other parts. It is only when development planners understand the nature of those parts, and how they are interrelated, that they can anticipate what some of the negative consequences may be and thus take steps to mitigate or avoid them. And since cultural anthropologists are the ones *on the ground* studying the cultures of those local populations targeted for sustainable development projects, it is only logical that anthropologists be intimately involved in the design, administration, and evaluation of sustainable development projects.

The literature on development anthropology is filled with examples of *good* development projects and *bad* ones or—put another way—those that have been largely beneficial to local people and those that have caused more harm than good. Good programs of sustainable development are those that are initiated from within the country and culture(s) rather than imposed by some well-meaning, but often short-sighted, international development agency. One recent sustainable economic development program was started by the not-for-profit organization called PhytoTrade Africa, established in 2002 as a trade association in southern Africa for natural products made from indigenous plants used in the food, drink, and cosmetic industries (Cox 2008). PhytoTrade Africa represents private-sector businesses, development agencies, and individuals in an effort to alleviate poverty, protect biodiversity, and develop economically successful industries that are ethical, environmentally friendly, and sustainable. The organization accomplishes its goals in three key ways: by identifying and developing new products, by developing world markets for these new products, and by nurturing the local African harvesters and producers.

One of the major products PhytoTrade has identified and is bringing to world markets is the harvestable fruit of the baobab tree, which grows naturally and abundantly throughout southern and eastern Africa. PhytoTrade partners with local fruit distribution companies (such as the Baobab Fruit Company of Senegal) that agree to purchase their fruit only from those local suppliers who meet their health and processing standards. Thus local individuals and families harvest the baobab fruit and sell it at a fair market price to local or regional distribution companies.

The fruit of the baobab tree is becoming a popular food product because it has a number of desirable features. Traditionally it was used as a highly nutritious and tasty snack for children; a dietary supplement for pregnant women; medicine to relieve stomachaches, fevers, and malaria; and, when hydrated, a refreshingly tangy drink similar to lemonade. It is exceptionally nutritious, containing high levels of antioxidants, essential minerals such as calcium, potassium, iron, and magnesium, and twice as much vitamin C as an orange. In a study by the United Nations, a solution of water and baobab powder was found to be a more effective remedy for dehydration in children than the standard remedies used by the World Health Organization. Today baobab fruit powder is being used in a wide variety of food and drink products sold internationally, including smoothies, juices, breakfast cereals, cereal bars, snacks, ice cream, yogurt, jams, sauces, marinades, specialty teas, and health supplements.

Why do anthropologists and development experts consider this a good economic development project?

- The baobab fruit industry in southern Africa is an excellent example of "economic development from within." Rather than an already-established industry imported from the developed world,

PhytoTrade Africa is a company that is starting local sustainable industries using fruit from Baobab trees, such as this one in Tanzania.

this new source of jobs and income is based on a traditional product grown in their own backyards, and, as a result, much of the profits stay with the local people.

- Since baobab trees in Africa are plentiful, large, mature, and extremely resilient, fruit harvesters do not have to worry about possible crop failures.
- The development of a baobab fruit industry requires little or no capital investment on the part of the local harvesters, who are the primary beneficiaries of the entire enterprise.
- Becoming a harvester requires no special set of skills. Anyone with two hands and a large sack can harvest the plentiful fruit of the baobab tree.
- Because PhytoTrade sets a fair market price for the fruit, local harvesters always receive a fair and reasonable price for their product. In 2008 women in Tanzania (who normally earned less than $80 per year) earned $12 to $30 per day.
- An industry based on local baobab fruit is sustainable because the major product (unlike extractive products like coal, petroleum, and minerals) is a renewable resource.
- Unlike many Western industries, baobab fruit harvesting is ecologically friendly because it uses the fruit of the tree rather than the tree itself.

All of these features make the new African baobab fruit industry a highly successful effort at sustainable economic development. It avoids harmful consequences such as environmental degradation, increased incidence of disease, human rights abuses, and exploitation of the people it intends to help. But, most important, it is a home-grown development project, using local resources and giving the target population a real stake in creating and maintaining profitable employment. Because the major product of the development project (fruit from baobab trees) has played both economic and spiritual roles in the traditional culture, local harvesters protect their sacred baobab trees as well as earning a good livelihood from them. From an anthropological perspective, this project is culturally sensitive because local people are using their own resources, labor, and work procedures to earn a reasonable income. And, as a bonus, it is enabling the African harvesters/enterpreneurs to provide a highly nutritious food product to the rest of the world.

Cultural Survival of Indigenous Peoples

In recent years cultural anthropologists have become increasingly concerned with a particular type of cultural change—namely, the rapid disappearance of indigenous populations of the world. An **indigenous population** is a group of people who (1) are the original inhabitants of a region; (2) identify with a specific, small-scale cultural heritage; and (3) have no significant role in the government (Bodley 2008: 4). Classic examples of indigenous peoples are the hundreds of small-scale cultures in Asia, Africa, and the Americas that came under the influence of colonial powers during the past several centuries.

Many anthropologists are concerned about the survival of these indigenous peoples not because they are the subject of anthropological research, but because their disappearance is a basic human rights issue. A growing number of cultural anthropologists feel strongly that indigenous populations over the past several centuries have been negatively affected by the onslaught of civilization. Cultural patterns—and in some cases the people themselves—have been eradicated as a direct result of civilization's pursuit of "progress" and economic development.

The industrial revolution in nineteenth-century Europe was "revolutionary" to the extent that it led to explosions in both population and consumerism, which in turn had drastically negative effects on indigenous peoples. The technological efficiency of the industrial revolution resulted in a quantum leap in population growth. At the same time that populations were expanding in the industrializing world, there was a corresponding growth in consumerism. If economies were to grow and prosper, production had to be kept high, which could be accomplished only if people purchased and consumed the products of industry. In order to meet the needs of a growing population with ever-increasing desires to consume, people needed to control and exploit natural resources wherever they might be found.

A number of anthropologists, historians, and journalists have documented specific examples of the demise of indigenous populations over the past 150 years. In fact, one anthropologist, John Bodley (2007, 2008), has devoted much of his career to reminding us how the spread of civilization and industrialization has resulted in the creation of millions of "victims of progress" throughout the non-Western world. These tragic consequences—all in the name of civilization, economic development, and progress—have included everything from the annihilation of the entire population of Tasmania in the nineteenth century to the introduction of measles and influenza to the indigenous peoples of the Amazon when the government built roads through the Brazilian frontier.

The twenty-first century has presented additional challenges to the cultural survival of indigenous peoples. To illustrate, the Tikuna community in western Brazil (close to the border with Colombia and Peru) has become an important link in drug trafficking. Some young indigenous Tikuna men, working as drug "mules," use their knowledge of the rivers and dense rain forest to carry cocaine into Brazil's substantial drug market. Unfortunately, not only are a growing number of Tikuna men working in the illicit drug trade, but many have become addicted to both cocaine and alcohol. While facing unemployment, disease, poor health care, substance abuse, and the destruction of their natural environment, contemporary Tikunas are struggling to keep some vestiges of their traditional culture (Barrionuevo 2008).

But we need not go to the far corners of the earth to find tragic examples of the exploitation of indigenous peoples. The litany of atrocities committed against Native Americans in the name of progress and manifest destiny dates back to the earliest European settlements in the United States. The massacre of the Pequot in Connecticut in 1637 and the massacre of the Sioux at Wounded Knee in 1890 are just two examples from U.S. history. More recent examples of the demise, or potential demise, of indigenous cultures in the United States are far less violent but devastating nevertheless. To illustrate, a small tribe of 125 Native Americans currently are threatened with having their last remaining ancestral land flooded by a proposed expansion of the Shasta Dam in northern California. The Winnemem Wintu Indian tribe is no stranger to having their lands swallowed up in the name of water conservation. When the Shasta Dam was constructed in the 1930s, the tribe lost its ancestral lands along the McCloud River to the reservoir. Some 183 corpses were exhumed from their traditional graveyard and reburied, while tribal members watched their homes being destroyed. The plan now is to elevate the height of the dam by 18 feet, thereby inundating most of the remaining twenty sacred tribal sites. If even one site is destroyed, the symbolic circle of connection between it and the remaining nineteen sites will be broken, which would make the practice of Winnemem religion difficult at best and deprive the tribe of one of its major mechanisms for maintaining its tribal identity. One enterprising Winnemem, an ardent opponent of the proposed dam expansion, was making and selling T-shirts with the inscription "Homeland Security: Fighting Terrorism Since 1492" (D. Murphy 2004).

Not only do cultural anthropologists document the demise of indigenous peoples, but many also use their specialized knowledge to help these endangered cultures survive the homogenizing effects of globalization. In one of the most urgent forms of applied anthropology, a number of cultural anthropologists in recent years have contributed to the efforts of Cultural Survival, Inc., a nonprofit organization based in Cambridge, Massachusetts, that supports projects on five continents designed to help indigenous peoples survive the changes brought about by contact with industrial societies. In partnership with indigenous peoples, Cultural Survival advocates for native communities whose rights, cultures, and dignity are threatened by (1) strengthening their languages and cultures, (2) educating their communities about their rights, and (3) fighting marginalization, discrimination, and exploitation.

Founded in 1972 by Harvard anthropologist David Maybury-Lewis, Cultural Survival works to guarantee the land and resource rights of tribal peoples while supporting economic development projects run by the peoples themselves. As part of their work with Cultural Survival, cultural anthropologists have conducted research on vital cultural issues, served as cultural brokers between the indigenous peoples and government officials, and published literature informing the public about the urgency of these survival issues. To help support its work, Cultural Survival has maintained, for more than three decades, the premier databank for anthropological and social scientific information on the indigenous peoples of the world. This vast collection of literature is available free of charge from the Cultural Survival website (www.culturalsurvival.org). *Cultural Survival Quarterly*, the organization's major publication, is an award-winning periodical specializing in articles written by anthropologists and non-anthropologists, with a number of pieces written by indigenous peoples themselves. A periodic newsletter, *Cultural Survival Voices,* is circulated to more than 350 indigenous organizations worldwide, providing them with the practical information they need to protect their cultures and native territories.

At any given time Cultural Survival is conducting ongoing projects around the world. One such project entails working with Panama's largest indigenous group, the Ngobe, whose homeland is being threatened by a hydroelectric dam being built on the Changuinola River (E. Lutz 2007, 2008). Numbering about 170,000 people, the Ngobe, who occupy a remote area in western Panama, have traditionally supported themselves by subsistence agriculture and fishing. In the last several years, however, a U.S. construction company, in partnership with the Panamanian government, has started building a major hydroelectric dam on the river that runs through the Ngobe homeland. It has been estimated that the new dam will swallow up the homes and lands of more than a thousand people. Other Ngobe, who will not lose their land, will become even more isolated by losing their transportation routes. Moreover the dam will disrupt the migration of several fish species that make up a significant portion of the Ngobe diet.

Even though the new hydroelectric dam will provide a much-needed supply of "clean" energy, the Ngobe case has become a human rights battleground largely because of the heavy-handed way the U.S.-based AES Corporation and the government of Panama have treated the Ngobe people. Many of the Ngobe, under enormous pressure to sell their lands to the government, put their thumbprints on sales contracts that they could not read and did not understand. In other cases, people's homes were destroyed and their lands confiscated in the absence of even bogus contracts. When the local people staged a peaceful protest against the dam project in

This Ngobe woman plays the maracas as part of a protest against the hydroelectric and mining projects, which indigenous people say threaten their way of life. This was just one of many protests surrounding the Columbus Day celebrations in Panama City on October 12, 2009.

January 2008, government police in riot gear attacked the protesters with clubs; by the end of the day they had arrested fifty-four people, including thirteen children and two infants. After this incident the construction site was cordoned off to any outsiders who sought to meet with the Ngobe.

Organizations like Cultural Survival—and its local Panamanian partner, the Alliance for Conservation and Development (ACD)—intensified their efforts to block the dam project until these blatant human rights injustices were resolved. The ACD pressed the government to legally justify its cordoning off of Ngobe property. It also conducted workshops for indigenous peoples on their legal rights as Panamanian citizens and, more practically, on how to file legal complaints with their government. Cultural Survival has sponsored former Peace Corps volunteers to return to Ngobe communities to document human rights violations.

In addition to these in-country efforts, Cultural Survival worked on a larger legal project to stop the dam and protect Ngobe human rights. With the help of a group of U.S. law students, Cultural Survival submitted a petition to the Inter-American Commission on Human Rights, an intergovernmental group that had the authority to ask the Panamanian government to stop the dam project. The dam was completed over the protests of the Ngobe people, environmentalists, and human rights advocates in Panama, however, and in spite of precautionary measures taken by the Inter-American Commission on Human Rights. In early June 2011, the construction company began filling the reservoir, which flooded the homes of the Ngobe who had refused to negotiate a settlement with the company. Recently the Ngobe people and the various opponents of the dam had cause to celebrate when Panama's National Public Service Authority (ASEP) decided to prevent AES Corporation from building a second dam on the Changuinola River.

Climate Change and Applied Anthropology

The third, and final, global challenge of the twenty-first century that we will consider in this chapter is climate change. As recently as the start of this millennium, there was an ongoing debate among scientists, politicians, and pundits about whether or not climate change was real, and if it was, whether it was caused by civilization or was simply part of a natural cyclical pattern of climatic variations. That debate has largely been resolved. With the exception of some hard-line deniers, most responsible voices in the world accept climate change caused by global warming as a fact. Three questions remain: (1) How serious a problem is it? (2) What are the consequences of climate change likely to be? (3) What can be done to avoid the damaging, perhaps cataclysmic, effects on our natural environment?

The Intergovernmental Panel on Climate Change (IPCC), the premier organization for the assessment of climate change, is a scientific body made up of the world's leading experts who voluntarily contribute their work. The IPCC reviews and evaluates the most recent scientific data to provide the world with a clear view on the current state of climate change and its potential consequences. The differing viewpoints that exist within the scientific community are reflected in the IPCC reports. Moreover, the IPCC is candid about which of its findings are in dispute and which are not. Among those findings on which virtually all of the contributing scientists agree are the following (Emanuel 2009: 183–84):

- The amount of carbon dioxide in the atmosphere has increased approximately 35 percent since the start of the industrial period.
- The earth's average surface temperature has increased by 1.2 degrees Fahrenheit during the past century, with much of the increase occurring after 1975.
- 2010 and 2005 were the warmest years (in terms of average temperature) since temperatures have been instrumentally recorded (the past hundred years).
- As a direct result of the melting of polar ice caps, sea levels have risen 2.7 inches over the past forty years.
- The annual mean amount of arctic sea ice has decreased by 15 to 20 percent since satellite measurements began in 1978.

This is what the world's climate scientists agree on. Even more alarming are the findings on which *most* scientists agree, but on which there is *some* disagreement.

- The dramatic increase in average temperature over the past three decades is due primarily to rising levels of greenhouse gases.
- Unless levels of greenhouse gases are reduced, global average temperatures will increase between 2.5 and 9.0 degrees over the next century.
- As a result of the continued melting of the arctic ice caps, sea levels will rise between 6 and 16 inches over the next century.
- The incidence, intensity, and duration of floods and droughts will increase in the future.

As a professional group, cultural anthropologists have known for years that climate change is a reality and not merely the opinion of paranoid physical scientists. Unlike economists, political scientists, politicians, and policy makers, cultural anthropologists study and live with those populations that are the first to experience the negative consequences of climate change. Cultural anthropologists are able to document the very real consequences of global warming on people, including those who live in small-scale, nonindustrialized societies in marginal areas of the world, living as pastoralists, hunters, fishermen, and subsistence farmers. Since these people live so close to the earth, they have acquired a wealth of knowledge about their immediate environment and, as a result, are sensitive to minute changes in animal behavior, water temperatures, amounts of rainfall, planting cycles, climate, and soil conditions. In fact, it is because people in small-scale societies know so much about their ecology that they have been able to make the cultural changes needed to successfully adapt to their changing environments over the past millennia. Even today Inuit hunters know when to move their hunting grounds farther north so that their snowmobiles don't fall through the ice. Anthropologists are able to show how people have altered their lifestyles to accommodate the changing environment. Research results from anthropological studies are absolutely necessary for policy makers who have to address the very real problems resulting from global warming. And it is important to recognize that people living in marginal ecological niches have long been making adjustments to a changing environment without the help of USAID, the World Bank, or Oxfam.

The Republic of Kiribati, located in the central Pacific, provides an excellent example of how vulnerable some small-scale societies are to climate change. Although some consider Kiribati (population 98,000) an idyllic paradise, it is one of the poorest nations in the world (Beck and Blair 2008). Kiribati may become the first nation to fall victim to global warming. It comprises thirty-three coral atolls that are less than 1,000 feet across and barely above sea level. In 1999 two small, uninhabited Kiribati islets disappeared underwater due to rising sea levels. Rising ocean tides are causing two

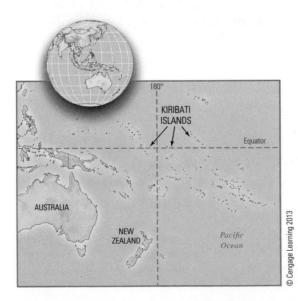

additional problems. First, the people are rapidly becoming unable to grow their basic tuber crop because the pits in which the crops grow are being inundated with sea water. And second, continual flooding by high tides is making the freshwater supply too brackish to drink. Today the people of Kiribati are among about a million people worldwide living on coral islands who are losing their livelihoods and cultures as their land is being consumed by the rising sea levels. There is very little that the government of Kiribati (with its meager resources) can do, other than to explore the possibility of moving their people permanently to large landmasses like Australia or New Zealand.

People from low-lying Pacific Island nations are not the only ones vulnerable to climate change. In the extreme opposite environment, the million people presently living in the Bolivian city of El Alto (a neighboring city to La Paz, which is the highest capital city in the world) are threatened by too little water rather than too much water. Each year the people of El Alto can see their once-majestic glaciers, a source of water and electrical power, shrinking. A World Bank report concluded that El Alto's glacier (called Illimani), and many other lower-altitude glaciers throughout the Andes, could totally disappear in the next several decades, thereby eliminating their water supply. As of 2010 the demands for water in El Alto have already exceeded the supply, and the problem is getting more acute because some of the water is being sold off to the wealthier residents of La Paz. With a lack of drinking water as well as water for irrigation and power generation, the people of El Alto could become the first urban casualty of climate change (Hicks, Fabricant, and Revilla 2010; Rosenthal 2009).

As we can see from the cases of low-level Kiribati and high-altitude El Alto, millions of people are already being negatively affected by climate change. If climate change continues on its present course, most scientists agree that many more millions will suffer, some so severely that their societies will cease to exist. One of the cruelest ironies, of course, is that most of these vulnerable populations are trying to adapt to problems not of their own making. Climate change has been caused primarily by the industrialized world's (Europe, Japan, Russia, the United States, India, and China) burning of fossil fuels, which produces the globe-warming gases. While scientists and politicians have been debating the causes of global warming and their effects on human existence in the future, cultural anthropologists have

This housing area (foreground) in El Alto, Bolivia, overlooks the capital city of La Paz. Both cities have been experiencing water shortages in recent years, due largely to retreating glaciers.

been documenting the very real changes occurring *on the ground* among the most vulnerable peoples and cultures, as well as bringing their research findings and recommendations to the attention of policy makers. Irrespective of what decisions are made at world climate conferences, anthropological data on the communities that are most immediately affected will be vital for policy makers who work to avoid the more deleterious effects of climate change, or at least ameliorate them after they have occurred.

The challenges facing these vulnerable peoples of the world should serve as a wake-up call to those in the developed world who will be facing these same difficulties down the road. Island states like Kiribati may be underwater in a few decades, but so could much of Florida and all of Manhattan just decades after that. Ethnographic accounts of the human costs of climate change will, no doubt, serve as a dramatic incentive for leaders in the industrialized world to reassess some of their basic assumptions about climate change, their role in causing it, and their responsibility in fixing it. And, it will expose the industrialized world to cultures that have radically different worldviews. To illustrate, many people in the industrialized world place a high value on consuming unlimited amounts of energy, allowing markets to solve all problems, and thinking that a system of "cap and trade" will really control the amount of greenhouse gases escaping into the atmosphere. By way of contrast, the people in Kiribati and El Alto have a worldview that values respect for the earth and a solemn responsibility to protect the natural environment for future generations. This alternative way of looking at the world is poignantly related by Casey Beck and Austin Blair (2008):

> On my first night (in Kiribati) a group of middle aged women threw a botaki (party) for me. Every guest at the botaki is expected to give a speech. When it was my turn, I told the women that I was there to learn about Kiribati culture in the face of climate change. I explained climate change to them, and their immediate reaction shocked me. If burning gas is contributing to climate change, one woman said matter-of-factly, then we should use our generators less. The others nodded in agreement. . . . Kiribati uses the fourth-smallest amount of oil of any country in the world and both produces and uses the sixth lowest amount of electricity. Yet, when these women learned that their actions, however insignificant, might contribute to climate change and affect others around the world, their first reaction was to reduce their own consumption.

Conclusions

If the many cultures of the world are not becoming a single homogeneous megaculture, then what is the most sensible foreign policy strategy for interacting with other peoples of the world? Rather than deliberately trying to eradicate cultural differences, a more workable approach is some type of **multiculturalism**—that is, an official policy that recognizes the worth and integrity of different cultures at home and abroad. Such an approach, which has been operating effectively in Switzerland and Canada for generations, requires the basic anthropological understanding that culturally different people are not inherently inferior and consequently should not be ignored, excluded, or marginalized. Rather it is possible to live together in peaceful coexistence, provided we understand the logic of culturally different peoples and are willing to negotiate with them in good faith and without exploitation.

At the very least, multiculturalism requires an awareness that people from other cultures, who do not share our cultural assumptions, probably do not sympathize with some of our behaviors, ideas, and values. For example, living in a culture that highly prizes individualism, most middle-class North Americans see themselves as strong, competitive, assertive, and independent achievers. People with a more collective value orientation, in contrast, view North Americans in far less flattering terms as self-absorbed, greedy materialists with hardly a shred of altruism. Many Americans are proud that they are sufficiently motivated by the value they place on individualism to achieve power, fame, and financial security by working seventy hours per week to be able to afford payments on a $75,000 luxury vehicle such as a Cadillac Escalade SUV. Many Swedes, however, look at the values and behavior of a thirty-something lawyer from Chicago, for example, as being selfish and dismissive of others. Working seventy hours per week translates, for them, into less time spent with one's family and fewer of the social activities that lead to a more balanced life and a healthier society. Moreover, working so hard to be able to afford a luxury like a Cadillac Escalade SUV is considered antisocial because driving this cousin of the military assault vehicle increases the cost of gasoline for everyone, destroys the environment quicker than a more conventional automobile, and essentially makes the statement that my vehicle, while keeping me and my children safe in the event of an accident, could kill you and your children. So, here are two radically different perceptions of the same behavior—one by Americans and one by Swedes. We are not arguing here that Americans need to give up their individualism or the high value some of them place on seventy-hour workweeks. Nor are we suggesting that Americans should agree with the typically Swedish interpretation. What is important, however, is that we learn to recognize the perceptions of other people, try to understand the reasons behind those perceptions, and acknowledge their right to have their perceptions. And when we do these things, we will be well on our way to adopting a multicultural strategy for interacting with culturally different peoples, both at home and abroad.

The reason that most anthropologists since the nineteenth century have insisted on looking at the rationality of another culture within its proper cultural context is that it will enable us to better understand that culture. And when we reach this greater understanding, we will be in a position to interact with people more rationally, humanely, and collaboratively. The rationale behind a multicultural approach to dealing with the rest of the world is that it can lead to win–win situations, whereby global solutions are likely to be more sustainable.

Multiculturalism remains the best hope for enabling all people to have the security, prosperity, and freedom they desire and deserve. And yet multiculturalism should not be seen as a totally selfless and altruistic philosophy. Rather it should be considered a win–win opportunity. Kishore Mahbubani poignantly captures the value of multiculturalism in this parable:

> There was a farmer who grew award-winning corn. Each year he entered his corn in a state fair, where it won a blue ribbon. One year, a newspaper reporter interviewed him and learned something interesting about how he grew it. The reporter discovered that the farmer shared his seed corn with his neighbors. "How can you afford to share your best seed corn with your neighbors when they are entering corn in competition with yours each year?" the reporter asked. "Why sir," said the farmer, "didn't you know? The wind picks up pollen from the ripening corn and swirls it from field to field. If my neighbors grow inferior corn, cross-pollination will steadily degrade the quality of my corn. If I am to grow good corn, I must help my neighbors grow good corn." (2005: 203–4)

Here is the point of this simple tale: The only way we can be safe and prosperous is if we enable our neighbors to be safe and prosperous as well.

Out in the Real World: A Cultural Anthropologist Revitalizes the Small Town of Star, North Carolina

Anthropologists often work in rural communities studying social changes brought on by economic development and cultural forces of change. Globalization has created dramatic economic and social shifts not only around the world but also in rural areas and small towns in the United States. The central region of North Carolina has been profoundly affected by globalization due to the relocation of manufacturing jobs (primarily in textiles and furniture) to other countries, especially during the 1990s and early 2000s.

For years rural areas in North Carolina, and indeed throughout the country, have experienced the loss of farms, corporate downsizing, a shift to service-sector employment, and the substitution of mega chain stores for small, main-street businesses. Moreover, factory closings have led to the loss of not only vibrant small-town main streets but also community identity, community leadership, and, in many cases, social cohesion. In 2006 Central Park (North Carolina), a rural, sustainable-development, not-for-profit organization directed by anthropologist Nancy Gottovi, took over a former sock factory in the small town of Star, North Carolina (population 803). In 2003 the sock company had relocated its manufacturing operations to Central America, thereby eliminating more than a thousand local jobs. Because many small businesses had been supported by the town's largest employer, the closing of the factory led to the closing of most small businesses, abandoned buildings, and a shuttered-up downtown.

Gottovi was interested in how the former factory building could be used to create a new "economic engine" for the town while at the same time providing opportunities for the community's leaders to craft a new identity that was not based solely on textile manufacturing. As an anthropologist, Gottovi wondered whether a community-based approach to development could meet the needs of individuals, workers, and businesses as well as the greater needs of the whole community. For example, during its days of operation, the large factory, with its multiple shifts of diverse workers, had provided a common "public" space for members of the community to come together. Conversations "around the water cooler" informed a wide cross section of community members about births, deaths, and other individual and family life events. When the factory was closed, there were few such opportunities for adults to maintain social networks, other than in churches, which are often segregated socially and by ethnicity.

Traditional economic development professionals tend to focus on what is commonly called the "big buffalo hunt": recruiting large manufacturing industries to rural areas to provide as many jobs as possible in as short a time as possible. However, this has proven to be a risky strategy for small communities that do not have the economic diversity and size to absorb the ebb and flow of plant closings. Increased globalization means that industries are more footloose than ever; they are likely to move their operations according to the "bottom line" at a faraway corporate headquarters. The loss of several hundred jobs overnight can be devastating to a small town, as the residents of Star discovered in 2003.

Another critical issue for Gottovi was how to stop the "hollowing out" of rural small towns such as Star through the loss of its most talented young people who leave in search of better economic and social opportunities. Gottovi's group focused on ways to build links between high school and post-secondary education, particularly in sustainable energy, creative arts, and local food production, as a relatively inexpensive way of capturing and retaining creativity and innovation in the community.

In 2006 Gottovi and her colleagues opened STARworks Center for Creative Enterprise in the abandoned factory building. STARworks provides training in glassblowing, ceramics, and sustainable energy, which includes biodiesel production from waste vegetable oil collected from restaurants, geothermal heating and cooling of homes, and a small-scale, organic, community-supported agriculture program. Not only has STARworks been successful in providing a place for young rural people to engage in innovative, creative work in the small town, but it also provides social opportunities for area residents—particularly youth—to combat the rampant boredom that often drives talented young people to urban areas. Creative types have traditionally felt isolated in small towns, yet STARworks has been able to attract people from all over the United States and the world to come to Star to work in its programs and businesses.

Gottovi's STARworks is one example of making a transition from an export-based manufacturing economy to one that is more "consumption" based. Cultural facilities and programs such as STARworks bolster the local economy. By bringing in new artists and other creative entrepreneurs, such centers spur new local spending, including revitalization of main streets and low-income housing for artists' spaces, and attract tourism. They also provide indirect opportunities and skills, including grant-writing and other capital investment abilities, new ideas, and new local leadership. Anthropologists have often studied the interaction between the local and the global in order to avoid disassociating economic issues from local meaning. The STARworks case study is an example of how a local culture, with the help of anthropological insights, is redefining itself in response to external forces of globalization.

QUESTIONS FOR FURTHER THOUGHT

1. What is meant by "Think globally, but act locally"?

2. What should STARworks do to continue to attract the young "creative class" to relocate and work in Star, North Carolina?

3. After five years of operation, STARworks has "incubated" businesses that focus on clay processing for potters, furnace construction for glassblowers, biodiesel fuel production, geothermal heating and cooling, and organic vegetable growing. What other business enterprises should STARworks include in its economic development project in the abandoned sock factory?

SUMMARY

1. The basic trends of the post–World War II era that concern anthropologists are world immigration patterns; the rise of religious fundamentalism; rapid urbanization in Africa, Asia, and Latin America; the spread of world health pandemics such as AIDS; environmental degradation; and the widening gap between the rich and the poor throughout the world.

2. A major concern of anthropology in the last half century has been sustainable economic development for the poor and marginalized peoples of the world. Because anthropologists study the alleged beneficiaries of economic development projects in a face-to-face way, they are in the best position to ascertain whether the projects are actually helping the local populations.

3. Development anthropologists look at the gap between the haves and the have-nots in terms of either *modernization theory* (the poor must strive to attain the cultural characteristics of the nonpoor) or *world systems theory* (the exploitation of the poor by the rich is the main cause of the widening income gap).

4. Many of the anticipated benefits of economic development (rising incomes and GNIs) have turned out to be illusory or downright detrimental in terms of health, environmental degradation, dietary quality, family breakdown, and social pathology.

5. Cultural anthropologists, through such organizations as Cultural Survival, work to help indigenous populations survive the onslaught of civilization and "economic progress."

6. Anthropologists work on the ground with the first people who are affected by environmental changes due to global warming, and they work with policy makers to help find social solutions.

7. With the world and all of its 5,000-plus cultural groups becoming increasingly interconnected, all nations must become more multicultural—that is, more adept at understanding and dealing with people from different cultural traditions. If the world is to successfully meet the challenges of this century, people can no longer afford to have an "us versus them" mentality, because resolving our problems depends on cross-cultural understanding. And, no academic discipline is better equipped to provide cross-cultural understanding than anthropology.

KEY TERMS

indigenous populations 316	modernization theory 310	multiculturalism 325 world systems theory 310

Appendix

Graduate Programs in Applied Anthropology Registered with COPAA—Consortium of Practicing and Applied Anthropology (http://www.copaa.info/programs_in_aa/list.htm#sc27)

University of Alaska—Anchorage

American University

University of Arizona

California State University—East Bay

California State University—Long Beach

University of Florida—Gainesville

The George Washington University

University of Georgia

Georgia State University

Indiana University—Purdue University at Indianapolis

University of Kansas

University of Kentucky

University of Maryland

University of Memphis

Mississippi State University

University of North Texas

Northern Arizona University

Northern Illinois University

Oregon State University

San Jose State University

University of South Florida

University of Texas at San Antonio

Wayne State University

Glossary

acculturation A specific form of cultural diffusion in which a subordinate culture adopts many of the cultural traits of a more powerful culture.

achieved status The status an individual attains during the course of her or his lifetime.

adaptive nature of culture The implication that culture is the major way human populations adapt or relate to their specific habitat in order to survive and reproduce.

affinal relatives Kinship ties formed through marriage (that is, in-laws).

ambilineal descent A form of descent in which a person affiliates with a kin group through either the male or the female line.

ambilocal residence A residence pattern in which a married couple may choose to live with either the relatives of the wife or the relatives of the husband.

American historicism Headed by Franz Boas, a school of anthropology prominent in the first part of the twentieth century that insisted on the collection of ethnographic data (through direct fieldwork) prior to making cross-cultural generalizations.

anthropological linguistics The scientific study of human communication within its sociocultural context.

applied anthropology The application of anthropological knowledge, theory, and methods to the solution of specific societal problems.

arbitrary nature of language The meanings attached to words in any language are not based on a logical or rational system but rather are arbitrary.

archaeology The subfield of anthropology that focuses on the study of prehistoric and historic cultures through the excavation of material remains.

arranged marriage A marriage in which the selection of the spouse is outside the control of the bride and groom.

artifact A type of material remain (found by archaeologists) that has been made or modified by humans and that can be removed from the site, such as tools and arrowheads.

ascribed status The status a person has by virtue of birth.

attitudinal data Information collected in a fieldwork situation that describes what a person thinks, believes, or feels.

authority The power or right to give commands, take action, and make binding decisions.

avunculocal residence A residence pattern in which a married couple lives with or near the husband's mother's brother.

band societies The basic social units in many hunting-and-gathering societies; characterized by being based on kinship and having no permanent political structure.

behavioral data Information collected in a fieldwork situation that describes what a person does.

bilateral descent A type of kinship system in which individuals emphasize both their mother's kin and their father's kin relatively equally.

binary oppositions A mode of thinking found in all cultures, according to Claude Lévi-Strauss, based on opposites, such as old–young, hot–cold, and left–right.

bound morpheme A morpheme that can convey meaning only when combined with another morpheme.

bride service Work or service performed for the bride's family by the groom for a specified period of time either before or after the marriage.

bridewealth Goods transferred from the groom's lineage to the bride's lineage to legitimize marriage.

cargo cults Revitalization movements in Melanesia intended to bring new life and purpose to a society.

carrying capacity The maximum number of people a given society can support, given the available resources.

caste A group in a rigid system of social stratification in which membership is determined by birth and social mobility is nonexistent.

chiefdom An intermediate form of political organization in which integration is achieved through the office of chiefs.

class A ranked group within a stratified society characterized by achieved status and considerable social mobility.

closed system of communication Communication in which the user cannot create new sounds or words by combining two or more existing sounds or words.

code switching The practice of adapting one's language depending on the social situation.

collecting data The stage of fieldwork that involves selecting data-gathering techniques and gathering information pertinent to the hypothesis being studied.

communal cults A type of religious organization in which groups of ordinary people conduct religious ceremonies for the well-being of the total community.

consanguineal relatives One's biological or blood relatives.

contagious magic A form of magic based on the premise that things, once in contact with a person (such as a lock of hair), continue to influence that person after separation.

corporate lineages Kinship groups whose members engage in daily activities together.

council of elders A formal control mechanism composed of a group of elders who settle disputes among individuals in a society.

crime Harm to a person or property that is considered an offense by society.

cross cousins Children of one's mother's brother or father's sister.

cult In the early anthropological literature, a nonjudgmental term that refers to a religious group that has its own set of beliefs, practices, and rituals. In popular discourse, a pejorative term referring to an antisocial group of religious extremists whose goal is mass suicide.

cultural anthropology The scientific study of cultural similarities and differences wherever and in whatever form they may be found.

cultural diffusion The spreading of a cultural trait (that is, a material object, idea, or behavior pattern) from one society to another.

cultural ecology An approach to anthropology that assumes that people who reside in similar environments are likely to develop similar technologies, social structures, and political institutions.

cultural linguistics The study of the relationship between language and culture.

cultural materialism A contemporary orientation in anthropology holding that cultural systems are most influenced by such material things as natural resources and technology.

cultural relativism The idea that cultural traits are best understood when viewed within the cultural context of which they are a part.

cultural resource management A form of applied archaeology that involves identifying, evaluating, and sometimes excavating sites before roads, dams, and buildings are constructed.

cultural universals Those general cultural traits that are found in all societies of the world.

culture shock A psychological disorientation a person experiences when attempting to operate in a radically different cultural environment.

Dalit The politically correct term for those formerly called Untouchables in India.

dance Intentional, rhythmic, nonverbal body movements that are culturally patterned and have aesthetic value.

descent A person's kinship connections traced back through a number of generations.

descriptive linguistics The branch of anthropological linguistics that studies how languages are structured.

deviance The violation of a social norm.

diachronic analysis The analysis of data through time, rather than at a single point in time.

diffusion The spreading of a cultural trait (that is, a material object, idea, or behavior pattern) from one society to another.

displacement The ability to talk about things that are remote in time and space.

divorce The legal and formal dissolution of a marriage.

document analysis Examination of data such as personal diaries, newspapers, colonial records, and so on.

double workload The situation in which employed married women, particularly those who have children, are both employed for wages and primarily responsible for housework and child care.

dowry Goods or money transferred from the bride's family to the groom or the groom's family in order to legalize or legitimize a marriage.

ecclesiastical cults Highly complex religious organizations in which full-time clergy are employed.

ecofacts Physical remains—found by archaeologists—that were used by humans but not made or reworked by them (for example, seeds and bones).

enculturation The process by which human infants learn their culture.

endogamy A rule requiring marriage within a specified social or kinship group.

ethnic group A group of people who share many of the same cultural features.

ethnocentrism The practice of viewing the customs of other societies in terms of one's own while often believing that one's own culture is superior to all others.

ethnographic fieldwork Research carried out by cultural anthropologists among living peoples in other societies and among subcultures of our own society.

ethnographic mapping A data-gathering tool that locates where the people being studied live, where they keep their livestock, where public buildings are located, and so on, in order to determine how that culture interacts with its environment.

ethnography A strategy of anthropological research, and an anthropological description of a particular contemporary culture by means of direct fieldwork.

ethnolinguistics The branch of anthropological linguistics that studies the relationship between language and culture.

ethnology The comparative study of cultural differences and similarities.

ethnomusicology The study of the relationship between music and other aspects of culture.

ethnoscience A theoretical school popular in the 1950s and 1960s that tries to understand a culture from the point of view of the people being studied.

event analysis Photographic documentation of events such as weddings, funerals, and festivals in the culture under investigation.

evolutionism The nineteenth-century school of cultural anthropology, represented by Tylor and Morgan, that attempted to explain variations in world cultures by the single deductive theory that they all pass through a series of evolutionary stages.

exogamy A rule requiring marriage outside of one's own social or kinship group.

extended family The family that includes in one household relatives in addition to a nuclear family.

features Archaeological remains that have been made or modified by people and cannot easily be carried away from the site, such as house foundations, fireplaces, and postholes.

female infanticide The killing of female infants.

femininity The social definition of femaleness, which varies from culture to culture.

feminist anthropology A theoretical approach that seeks to describe and explain cultural life from the perspective of both women and men.

feminization of poverty The trend of women making up the world's poor; refers to the high proportion of female-headed families that live below the poverty line, which may result from the high proportion of women working in occupations associated with low prestige and income.

fictive kinship Relationships among individuals who recognize kinship obligations even though the relationships are not based on either consanguineal or affinal ties.

fieldnotes The daily descriptive notes recorded by an anthropologist during or after observing a specific phenomenon or activity.

fieldwork The practice in which an anthropologist is immersed in the daily life of a culture in order to collect data and test cultural hypotheses.

free morpheme A morpheme that can convey meaning while standing alone without being attached to other morphemes.

French structuralism A theoretical orientation holding that cultures are the product of unconscious processes of the human mind.

functionalism A theory of social stratification that holds that social inequality exists because it contributes to the overall well-being of a society.

gender The roles, behaviors, and attributes a society considers appropriate for members of the two sexes.

gender ideology A system of thoughts and values that legitimizes sex roles, statuses, and customary behavior.

gender roles Expected ways of behaving based on a society's definition of masculinity and femininity.

gender stratification The hierarchical ranking of members of a society according to gender.

grammar The systematic rules by which sounds are combined in a language to enable users to send and receive meaningful utterances.

graphic arts Forms of art that include painting and drawing on various surfaces.

headless societies Societies that have no political leaders, such as presidents, kings, or chiefs.

historical linguistics The branch of anthropological linguistics that studies how languages emerge and change over time.

holism A perspective in anthropology that attempts to study a culture by looking at all parts of the system and how those parts are interrelated.

horticulture Small-scale crop cultivation characterized by the use of simple technology and the absence of irrigation.

human sexuality The sexual practices of humans, which vary from culture to culture.

human variation An area of investigation in physical (biological) anthropology that examines genetically inherited traits (sex, skin color, body proportions, head shape, and facial features) of contemporary human populations throughout the world.

hunting and gathering A form of subsistence that depends on a combination of hunting, fishing, and gathering wild foods found in the natural environment.

imitative magic A form of magic based on the idea that the procedure performed resembles the desired result; for example, sticking a doll-like image with pins will harm the person the doll represents.

incest taboo The prohibition of sexual intimacy between people defined as close relatives.

indigenous population People who are the original inhabitants of a region, identify with a specific cultural heritage, and play no significant role in government.

individualistic cults The least complex type of religious organization in which each person is his or her own religious specialist.

industrialization A process that results in the economic change from home production of goods to large-scale mechanized factory production.

innovation A recombination of already existing items within a culture.

intensive agriculture A form of commodity production that requires intensive working of the land with plows and draft animals and the use of techniques of soil and water control.

intermediaries Mediators of disputes among individuals or families within a society.

interpreting data The stage of fieldwork, often the most difficult, in which the anthropologist searches for meaning in the data collected while in the field.

interpretive anthropology A contemporary theoretical orientation holding that the critical aspects of cultural systems are subjective factors such as values, ideas, and worldviews.

invention A new combination of existing cultural features.

kinship system Those relationships found in all societies that are based on blood or marriage.

law Cultural rules that regulate human behavior and maintain order.

Leopard-Skin Chief An intermediary between a murderer's family and the family of the victim; found among the Nuer of the Sudan.

levirate The practice of a man marrying the widow of a deceased brother.

liberation theology A form of Catholicism found throughout South and Central America in which priests and nuns are actively involved in programs that promote social justice for the poor.

linked changes Changes in one part of a culture brought about by changes in other parts of the culture.

magic A system of supernatural beliefs that involves the manipulation of supernatural forces for the purpose of intervening in a wide range of human activities and natural events.

mahdist movements Revitalization movements in the Muslim world.

male gender bias A preference found in some societies for sons rather than daughters.

masculinity The social definition of maleness, which varies from society to society.

matriarchy The rule or domination of women over men.

matrilineal descent A form of descent in which people trace their primary kin connections through their mothers.

matrilocal residence A residence pattern in which a married couple lives with or near the relatives of the wife.

millenarian movements Social movements by repressed groups of people who are looking forward to better times in the future.

modernization theory The idea that differences in economic development may be explained by inherent sociocultural differences between the rich and the poor.

monochronic culture A culture in which people view time in a linear fashion, place great importance on being punctual and keeping on schedule, and prefer to work on one task at a time.

monogamy The marital practice of having only one spouse at a time.

moots Informal hearings of disputes for the purpose of resolving conflicts; usually found in small-scale societies.

morphemes The smallest linguistic forms (usually words) that convey meaning.

morphology The study of the rules that govern how morphemes are formed into words.

multiculturalism A public policy philosophy that recognizes the legitimacy and equality of all cultures represented in a society.

multilineal descent Descent traced through both the mother's and father's lines; includes both ambilineal and bilateral descent.

multilinear evolution The mid-twentieth-century anthropological theory of Julian Steward, who suggested that specific cultures can evolve independently of all others even if they follow the same evolutionary process.

nation A group of people who share a common identity, history, and culture.

nativistic movement A religious force for social change found among Native Americans.

negative sanctions A mechanism of social control that enforces a society's norms through punishments.

neoevolutionism A twentieth-century school of cultural anthropology, represented by White and Steward, that attempted to refine the earlier evolutionary theories of Tylor and Morgan.

neolithic revolution A stage in human cultural evolution (beginning around ten thousand years ago) characterized by the transition from hunting and gathering to the domestication of plants and animals.

neolocal residence A residence pattern in which a married couple establishes its own place of residence apart from the relatives of either spouse.

nomadism The movement pattern of pastoralists that involves the periodic migration of human populations in search of food or pasture for livestock.

nonverbal communication The various means by which humans send and receive messages without using words (for example, gestures, facial expressions, and touching).

nuclear family The most basic family unit, composed of wife, husband, and children.

nutritional deprivation A form of child abuse involving withholding food; can retard learning, physical development, and social adjustment.

oath A declaration to a god to attest to the truth of what a person says.

occupational segregation The separation of different occupations in a society along gender lines.

open system of communication Communication in which the user can create new sounds or words by combining two or more existing sounds or words.

ordeal A painful and possibly life-threatening test inflicted on someone suspected of wrongdoing to determine guilt or innocence.

organic analogy The early functionalist idea that cultural systems are integrated into a whole cultural unit in much the same way that the various parts of a biological organism (such as a respiratory system or a circulatory system) function to maintain the health of the organism.

paleoanthropology The study of human evolution through fossil remains.

paleopathology The study of disease in prehistoric populations.

pan-tribal mechanisms Mechanisms such as clans, age grades, and secret societies found in tribal societies that cut across kinship lines and integrate all the local segments of the tribe into a larger whole.

parallel cousins Children of one's mother's sister or father's brother.

participant-observation A fieldwork method in which the cultural anthropologist lives with the people under study and observes their everyday activities.

participatory action research A mode of research whereby the anthropologist and the community work together to understand the conditions that produce the community's problems to find solutions to those problems.

pastoralism A food-getting strategy based on animal husbandry; found in regions of the world that are generally unsuited for agriculture.

patrilineal descent A form of descent in which people trace their primary kin relationships through their fathers.

patrilocal residence A residence pattern in which a married couple lives with or near the relatives of the husband's father.

phonemes The smallest units of sound in a language that distinguish meaning.

phonology The study of a language's sound system.

photography The use of a still or video camera to document the ecology, material culture, and even social interactions of people during ethnographic fieldwork.

physical anthropology (biological anthropology) The subfield of anthropology that studies both human biological evolution and contemporary physical variations among peoples of the world.

plastic arts Artistic expression that involves molding certain forms, such as sculpture.

political integration The process that brings disparate people under the control of a single political system.

polyandry The marital practice of a woman having two or more husbands at the same time.

polychronic culture A culture in which people typically perform a number of tasks at the same time and place a higher value on nurturing and maintaining social relationships than on punctuality for its own sake.

polygyny The marital practice of a man having two or more wives at the same time.

positive sanctions A mechanism of social control that enforces a society's norms through rewards.

positivism A philosophical system based on observable scientific facts and their relationship to one another.

postmodernism A school of anthropology that advocates the switch from cultural generalization and laws to description, interpretation, and the search for meaning.

preferential cousin marriage A marriage between either parallel or cross cousins.

primatology The study of nonhuman primates in their natural environments for the purpose of gaining insights into the human evolutionary process.

problem-oriented research A type of anthropological research designed to solve a particular societal problem rather than to test a theoretical position.

proxemic analysis The study of how people in different cultures use space.

psychic unity A concept popular among some nineteenth-century anthropologists who assumed that all people, when operating under similar circumstances, will think and behave in similar ways.

psychological anthropology The subdiscipline of anthropology that looks at the relationships among cultures and such psychological phenomena as personality, cognition, and emotions.

public opinion What the general public thinks about some issue; when public opinion is brought to bear on an individual, it can influence his or her behavior.

purdah The Hindu or Muslim system of sex segregation, which keeps women in seclusion and/or requires them to wear clothing that conceals them completely.

qualitative data People's words, actions, records, and accounts obtained from participant-observation, interviews, group interviews, and relevant documents.

quantitative data Data that are counted and interpreted through statistical analyses.

race A subgroup of the human population whose members share a greater number of genes and physical traits with one another than they do with members of other subgroups.

rebellion An attempt within a society to disrupt the status quo and displace the people in power.

religion A set of beliefs in supernatural forces that functions to provide meaning,

peace of mind, and a sense of control over unexplainable phenomena.

research design The overall strategy for conducting research.

revitalization movements Religious movements designed to bring about a new way of life within a society.

revolution An attempt to forcibly overthrow the entire government or social order.

rites of passage Ceremonies that celebrate the transition of a person from one social status to another.

rites of solidarity Ceremonies performed for the sake of enhancing social integration among groups of people.

sanctions Any means used to enforce compliance with the rules and norms of a society.

Sapir–Whorf hypothesis The notion that a person's language shapes her or his perceptions and view of the world.

separatist Christian churches Small-scale churches that break away from the dominant church to gain greater political, economic, social, and religious autonomy.

serial monogamy The practice of having a succession of marriage partners, but only one at a time.

sex The biological or genetic differences between males and females.

sexual asymmetry The universal tendency of women to be in a subordinate position in their social relationships with men.

sexual dimorphism The difference in form between men and women.

shaman A part-time religious specialist who is thought to have supernatural powers by virtue of birth, training, or inspiration.

shamanistic cults A type of religious organization in which part-time specialists called shamans intervene with the deities on behalf of their clients.

shifting cultivation (swidden cultivation, slash-and-burn method) A form of plant cultivation in which seeds are planted in fertile soil prepared by cutting and burning the natural growth; relatively short periods of cultivation are followed by longer fallow periods.

small-scale society A society that has a relatively small population, has minimal technology, is usually preliterate, has little division of labor, and is not highly stratified.

social control Mechanisms found in all societies that encourage people not to violate the social norms.

social mobility The ability of people to change their social position within a society.

social norms Expected forms of behavior.

socialization The process of teaching young people the norms in a society.

sociolinguistics The branch of anthropological linguistics that studies how language and culture are related and how language is used in different social contexts.

song duel A means of settling disputes over wife stealing among the Inuit involving a public contest of derisive songs and lyrics.

sorcery The performance of certain magical rites for the purpose of harming other people.

sororate The practice of a woman marrying the husband of her deceased sister.

specialized political roles Specific tasks expected of a person or group, such as law enforcement, tax collection, dispute settlement, recruitment of labor, and protection from outside invasions.

state A particular type of political structure that is hierarchical, bureaucratic, centralized, and has a monopoly on the legitimate use of force to implement its policies.

state system of government A bureaucratic, hierarchical form of government composed of various echelons of political specialists.

structural functionalism A school of cultural anthropology, associated most closely with Radcliffe-Brown, that examines how parts of a culture function for the well-being of the society.

structured interview An ethnographic data-gathering technique in which large numbers of respondents are asked a set of specific questions.

subculture A subdivision of a wider culture that shares some features with the larger society and also differs in some important respects.

supernatural belief systems A set of beliefs in forces that transcend the natural, observable world.

symbol Something, either verbal or nonverbal, that stands for something else.

synchronic analysis The analysis of data at a single point in time, rather than through time.

syntax The linguistic rules, found in all languages, that determine how phrases and sentences are constructed.

theory A general statement about how two or more facts are related.

transformational The quality of an artistic process that converts an image into a work of art.

transhumance The movement pattern of pastoralists in which some of the men move livestock seasonally.

tribal societies Small-scale societies composed of autonomous political units with common linguistic and cultural features.

unilineal descent Descent traced through a single line (such as matrilineal or patrilineal) rather than through both sides (bilateral descent).

universal male dominance The notion that men are more powerful and influential than women in all societies.

unstructured interview An ethnographic data-gathering technique—most often used in the early stages of fieldwork—in which interviewees are asked to respond to broad, open-ended questions.

varnas Caste groups in Hindu India that are associated with certain occupations.

vision quest A ritual found in some Plains Indian cultures wherein, through visions, people establish special relationships with spirits who provide them with knowledge, power, and protection.

witchcraft The use of inborn, involuntary, and often unconscious powers to cause harm to other people.

world systems theory The idea that differences in economic development may be explained by the exploitation of the poor by the rich nations of the world.

References

Abraham, Ebenezer Rajkumar, Sethumadhavan Ramachandran, and Velraj Ramalingam. 2007. "Biogas: Can It Be an Important Source of Energy?" *Environmental Science and Pollution Research* 14(1): 67–71.

Agosin, Marjorie. 1987. *Scraps of Life: Chilean Arpilleras*. Toronto: William Wallace Press.

American Anthropological Association. http://www.aaanet.org.

American Medical Association. 2002. http://www.ama-assn.org/ama/pub/category/4867.html.

____. 2008. http://www.ama-assn.org/ama/pub/category/12912.html.

Andreatta, Susan L. 1998. "Transformation of the Agro-food Sector: Lessons from the Caribbean." *Human Organization* 57(4):414–29.

Andreatta, Susan, Barry Nash, and Gretchen Bath Martin. 2011. "*Carteret Catch*™: Raising Awareness of Local Seafood through Community and Business Partnerships." *Human Organization* 70(3): 279–88.

Andreatta, Susan L., and Anne Parlier. 2010. "The Political Ecology of Small-Scale Commercial Fishermen in Carteret County, North Carolina." *Human Organization* 69(2): 180–91.

Baba, Marietta L.2009. "Disciplinary-Professional Relations in an Era of Anthropological Engagement."*Human Organization* 68(4):380–92.

Balsam, John, and Dave Ryan. 2006. *Anaerobic Digestion of Animal Waste: Factors to Consider* (a publication of the National Sustainable Agriculture InformationServices). Washington, DC: National Center for Appropriate Technology.

Bamberger, Joan. 1974. "The Myth of Matriarchy: Why Men Rule in Primitive Society." In *Women, Culture, and Society*. Michelle Zimbalist Rosaldo and Louise Lamphere, eds., pp. 263–80. Stanford, CA: Stanford University Press.

Barfield, Thomas. 1993. *The Nomadic Alternative*. Englewood Cliffs, NJ: Prentice Hall.

Barlett, Peggy F. 1989. "Industrial Agriculture." In *Economic Anthropology*. Stuart Plattner, ed., pp. 253–91. Stanford, CA: Stanford University Press.

Barnes, Sandra T. 1990. "Women, Property, and Power." In *Beyond the Second Sex: New Directions in the Anthropology of Gender*. Peggy Reeves Sanday and Ruth G. Goodenough, eds., pp. 253–80. Philadelphia: University of Pennsylvania Press.

Barrionuevo, Alexei. 2008. "A Tribe in Brazil Struggles at the Intersection of Drugs and Cultures." *New York Times* (December 6).

Barua, D. C. 2006. "Five Cents a Day: Innovative Programs for Reaching the Destitute with Microcredit, No-Interest Loans, and Other Instruments: The Experience of Grameen Bank." Global Microcredit Summit, Nova Scotia, Canada. http://www.microcreditsummit.org/papers/Workshops/7_Barua.pdf (accessed January 20, 2008).

Basso, Keith H. 1970. "'To Give Up on Words': Silence in Western Apache Culture." *Southwestern Journal of Anthropology* 26(3): 213–30.

Beattie, John. 1960. *Bunyoro: An African Kingdom.* New York: Holt, Rinehart& Winston.

Beck, Casey, and Austin Blair. 2008. "Inundation." *Cultural Survival Quarterly* 32(2).

Behar, Ruth. 1993. *Translated Woman: Crossing the Border with Esperanza's Story.* Boston: Beacon Press.

Belson, Ken. 2004. "No, You Can't Walk and Talk at the Same Time." *New York Times* (August 29): 4.

Benedict, Ruth. 1946. *The Chrysanthemum and the Sword.* Boston: Houghton Mifflin.

Bensman, Joseph, and Arthur Vidich. 1987. *American Society: The Welfare State and Beyond,* rev. ed. South Hadley, MA: Bergin & Garvey.

Binford, Lewis. 1980. "Willow Smoke and Dogs' Tails: Hunter-Gatherer Settlement Systems and Archaeological Site Formation." *American Antiquity* 45(1): 4–20.

Birket-Smith, K. 1959. *The Eskimos,* 2nd ed. London: Methuen.

Bodley, John. 2007. *Anthropology and Contemporary Human Progress.* Lanham, MD: AltaMira Press.

___. 2008. *Victims of Progress,* 5th ed. Lanham, MD: AltaMira Press.

Boroditsky, Lera. 2009. "How Does Our Language Shape the Way We Think?" In *What's Next:Dispatches on the Futures of Science.* Max Brockman, ed., pp. 116–29. New York: Vintage Books.

Brettell, Caroline B., and Carolyn Sargent. 2005. *Gender in Cross-Cultural Perspective,* 4th ed. Upper Saddle River, NJ: Prentice Hall.

Brewer, Jeffrey D. 1988. "Traditional Land Use and Government Policy in Bima, East Sumbawa." In *The Real and Imagined Role of Culture in Development: Case Studies from Indonesia.* Michael R. Dove, ed., pp. 119–35. Honolulu: University of Hawaii Press.

Callender, Charles, and Lee Kochems. 1983. "North American Berdache." *Current Anthropology* 24: 443–56.

Canedy, Dana. 2002. "Lifting Veil for Photo ID Goes Too Far, Driver Says." *New York Times* (June 27): A-l, 6.

Carpenter, Edmund. 1973. *Eskimo Realities.* New York: Holt, Rinehart & Winston.

Cash, Richard. 2010. *Advancing Differentiation: Thinking and Learning for the 21st Century.* Minneapolis, MN: Free Spirit Publishing.

Chagnon, Napoleon A. 1992. *Yanomamo: The Last Days of Eden,* 5th ed. San Diego: Harcourt Brace Jovanovich.

Chambers, Robert. 1994. "The Origins and Practices of Participatory Rural Appraisal." *World Development* 2(7): 953–69.

Charle, Suzanne. 1999. "A Far Island of Cultural Survival." *New York Times* (July 25, section 2): 1, 28.

Chavez, Leo. 1999. *Shadowed Lives: Undocumented Immigrants in American Society.* Harcourt Brace College Publishers.

Chomsky, Noam. 1972. *Language and Mind.* New York: Harcourt Brace Jovanovich.

Chura, Hillary. 2006. "A Year Abroad (or 3) as a Career Move." *New York Times* (February 25): B-5.

Cohen, Eugene N., and Edwin Eames. 1982. *Cultural Anthropology.* Boston: Little, Brown.

Cohen, M. N., and G. J. Armelagos, eds. 1984. *Paleopathology at the Origins of Agriculture.* New York: Academic Press.

Confessore, Nicholas. 2006. "Spoonfuls of Culture Help Medicine Go Down." *New York Times* (June 4): 37.

Consortium of Practicing and Applied Anthropology (COPAA). 2010. "Programs in Applied Anthropology." http://www.copaa.info/ programs_in_aa/list.htm.

Coote, Jeremy, and Anthony Shelton, eds. 1992. *Anthropology, Art, and Aesthetics*. Oxford: Clarendon Press.

Coutsoukis, Photius. 2010. "Nobel Prizes by Country, Cumulative Prizes 1901–2009." http://www.photius. com/rankings/nobel_prizes_by_ country_cummulative_1901_2009. html.

Cox, Hillary. 2008. "The Tree of Life." *Cultural Survival Quarterly* 32(4).

Daly, Emma. 2005. "DNA Test Gives Students Ethnic Shocks." *New York Times* (April 3): A-18.

D'Antoni, Tom, and Alex Heard. 1998. "Subway Spirits." *New York Times Magazine* (October 25): 23.

Davis, Kingsley, and Wilbert Moore. 1988. "Wives and Work: A Theory of the Sex-Role Revolution and Its Consequences." In *Feminism, Children, and the New Families*. Sanford Dornbusch and Myra Strober, eds., pp. 67–86. New York: Guilford Press.

Dembo, Richard, Patrick Hughes, Lisa Jackson, and Thomas Mieczkowski. 1993. "Crack Cocaine Dealing by Adolescents in Two Public Housing Projects: A Pilot Study." *Human Organization* 52(1): 89–96.

DeVita, Philip R., ed. 1992. *The Naked Anthropologist: Tales from Around the World*. Belmont, CA: Wadsworth.

———. 2000. *Stumbling Toward Truth: Anthropologists at Work*. Prospect Heights, IL: Waveland Press.

Diamond, Jared. 1987. "The Worst Mistake in the History of the Human Race." *Discover* (May): 64–66.

———. 2001. "Death of Languages." *Natural History* (April): 30.

Digby-Clarke, Neil. 2007. "Marginalised Ju/'hoansi San at Nhoma Overcome Recent Setbacks." *Namibia Economist*. http://www.economist .com (accessed January 4, 2008).

Dreifus, Claudia. 2001. "How Language Came to Be, and Change: A Conversation with John McWhorter." *New York Times News Brief* (October 30).

Durkheim, Emile. 2001. *The Elementary Forms of Religious Life* (Carol Cosman, trans.). Oxford: Oxford University Press (orig. 1912).

Emanuel, Kerry. 2009. "Phaeton's Reins: The Human Hand in Climate Change." In *World in Motion: The Globalization and the Environment Reader*. Gary M. Kroll and Richard H. Robbins, eds., pp. 168–85. Lanham, MD: AltaMira Press.

Ervin, Alexander M. 2005. *Applied Anthropology: Tools and Perspectives for Contemporary Practice*. Boston: Allyn & Bacon.

Evans-Pritchard, E. E. 1940. *The Nuer*. Oxford: Oxford University Press.

Faris, James C. 1972. *Nuba Personal Art*. Toronto: University of Toronto Press.

Fattah, Hassan M. 2007. "A Familiar Set Helps to Create a New Cultural Market." *New York Times* (August 2): A-4.

Fentiman, Alicia. 2009. "The Anthropology of Oil: The Impact of the Oil Industry on a Fishing Community in the Niger Delta." In *World in Motion: The Globalization and the Environment Reader*. Gary M. Kroll and Richard Robbins, eds., pp. 32–44. Lanham, MD: AltaMira Press.

Finke, Roger, and Rodney Stark. 2005. *The Churching of America, 1976–2005: Winners and Losers in Our Religious Economy*. New Brunswick, NJ: Rutgers University Press.

Finnström, Sverker. 2008. *Living with Bad Surroundings: War, History, and Everyday Moments in Northern Uganda*. Durham, NC: Duke University Press.

Fish, Jefferson M. 1995. "Mixed Blood." *Psychology Today* 28(6) (November-December): 55–58, 60, 61, 76, 80.

Food and Agriculture Organization (FAO). 2005. *The State of Food Insecurity in the World*. Rome: FAO.

Fortes, M., and E. E. Evans-Pritchard. 1940. *African Political Systems*. London: Oxford University Press.

French, Howard W. 2007. "The Ship of State Shall Not Rock 'n' Roll." *New York Times* (October 25): A-4.

Friedl, Ernestine. 1978. "Society and Sex Roles." *Human Nature* 1(4): 68–75.

Friedl, John, and John E. Pfeiffer. 1977. *Anthropology: The Study of People*. New York: Harper & Row.

Friedman, Thomas L. 1999. *The Lexus and the Olive Tree*. New York: Farrar, Straus and Giroux.

Fuller, Thomas. 2007. "In Thai Cultural Battle, Name-Calling Is Encouraged." *New York Times* (August 29): A-4.

Gan, Lin, and Juan Yu. 2008. "Bioenergy Transition in Rural China: Policy Options and Co-benefits." *Energy Policy* 36(2): 531–40.

Gardner, R. Allen, and Beatrice T. Gardner. 1969. "Teaching Sign Language to a Chimpanzee." *Science* (August 15): 664–72.

Geertz, Clifford. 1973. *The Interpretation of Cultures*. New York: Basic Books.

____. 1983. *Local Knowledge: Further Essays in Interpretive Anthropology*. New York: Basic Books.

Gibbs, James L. 1963. "The Kpelle Moot." *Africa* 33(1).

Gilbert, Dennis. 2008. *American Class Structure in an Age of Growing Inequality*, 7th ed. Belmont, CA: Wadsworth.

Glossow, Michael. 1978. "The Concept of Carrying Capacity in the Study of Cultural Process." In *Advances in Archaeological Theory*. Michael Schiffler, ed., pp. 32–48. New York: Academic Press.

Gmelch, George. 1994a. "Lessons from the Field." In *Conformity and Conflict*, 8th ed. James P. Spradley and David McCurdy, eds., pp. 45–55. New York: HarperCollins.

____. 1994b. "Ritual and Magic in American Baseball." In *Conformity and Conflict*, 8th ed. James P. Spradley and David McCurdy, eds., pp. 351–61. New York: HarperCollins.

Goldschmidt, Walter. 1979. "Introduction: On the Interdependence Between Utility and Theory." In *The Uses of Anthropology*. Walter Goldschmidt, ed. Washington, DC: American Anthropological Association.

Goodall, Jane. 2005. *Harvest for Hope: A Guide to Mindful Eating*. New York: Warner Books.

Goodenough, Ward H. 1956. "Componential Analysis and the Study of Meaning." *Language* 32: 195–216.

Gorer, Geoffrey, and John Rickman. 1949. *The People of Great Russia*. London: Cresset.

Gross, Daniel, and Barbara A. Underwood. 1971. "Technological Change and Caloric Costs: Sisal Agriculture." *American Anthropologist* 73(3): 725–40.

Gwatirisa, Pauline, and Lenore Manderson. 2009. "Food Insecurity and HIV/AIDS in Low-Income Households in Urban Zimbabwe." *Human Organization* 68(1): 103–12.

Hadley, Craig, Amber Wutich, and Christopher McCarty. 2009. "Experience-Based Measure of Food and Water Security: Biocultural Approaches to Grounded Measures of Insecurity." *Human Organization* 68(4): 451–60.

Hanna, Judith Lynne. 1979. *To Dance Is Human: A Theory of Nonverbal Communication*. Austin: University of Texas Press.

____. 2005. "Dance Speaks Out on Societal Issues." *Anthropology News* 46(4): 11–12.

Harner, Michael J. 1973. "The Sound of Rushing Water." In *Hallucinogens and Shamanism*. Michael J. Harner, ed., pp. 15–27. New York: Oxford University Press.

Harris, Marvin. 1968. *The Rise of Anthropological Theory*. New York: Thomas Y. Crowell.

___. 1979. *Cultural Materialism: The Struggle for a Science of Culture*. New York: Random House.

___. 1999. *Theories of Culture in Postmodern Times*. Walnut Creek, CA: AltaMira Press.

Harris, Marvin, and Orna Johnson. 2003. *Cultural Anthropology*, 6th ed. Boston: Allyn & Bacon.

Heise, Lori, Mary Ellsberg, and Megan Gottemoeller. 1999. "Ending Violence Against Women." *Population Reports*, Series L, No. 11.http://info.k4health.org/pr/l11edsum.shtml (accessed July 14, 2010).

Herskovits, Melville. 1924. "A Preliminary Consideration of the Cultural Areas in Africa." *American Anthropologist* 26: 50–63.

___. 1972.*Cultural Relativism: Perspectives in Cultural Pluralism*. New York: Vintage Books.

Hewlett, Barry S., and Bonnie L. Hewlett. 2008. "Ebola, Culture and Politics: The Anthropology of an Emerging Disease." In *Case Studies on Contemporary Social Issues*. John Young, ed. Belmont, CA: Cengage.

Hicks, Kathryn, Nicole Fabricant, and Carlos Revilla. 2010. "The New Water Wars: Collective Action After Decentralization in El Alto, Bolivia." *Anthropology News* 51(1): 14–15.

Hoebel, E. Adamson. 1972. *Anthropology: The Study of Man*, 4th ed. New York: McGraw-Hill.

Holloway, Kris. 2007. *Monique and the Mango Rains*. Long Grove, IL: Waveland Press.

Hughes, Charles C., and John M. Hunter. 1972. "The Role of Technological Development in Promoting Disease in Africa." In *The Careless Technology: Ecology and International Development*. M. T. Farvar and John P. Milton, eds., pp. 69–101. Garden City, NY: Natural History Press.

Ishii, Keiko, Jose Alberto Reyes, and Shinobu Kitayama. 2003. "Spontaneous Attention to Word Content Versus Emotional Tone: Differences Among Three Cultures." *Psychological Science* 14(1): 39–46.

Jenkins, Henry. 2001. "Culture Goes Global." *Technology Review* 104(6): 89.

Jian, Li. 2009. "Socioeconomic Barriers to Biogas Development in Rural Southwest China: An Ethnographic Case Study." *Human Organization* 68(4): 415–30.

Kaplan, David, and Robert Manners. 1986. *Culture Theory*. Englewood Cliffs, NJ: Prentice Hall.

Katzner, Kenneth. 1975. *The Languages of the World*. New York: Funk & Wagnalls.

Khanna, Sunil K. 2010. *Fetal/Fatal Knowledge: New Reproductive Technologies and Family-Building Strategies in India*. Belmont, CA: Wadsworth.

Kluckhohn, Clyde. 1949. *Mirror for Man: Anthropology and Modern Life*. New York: Wittlesey House (McGraw-Hill).

Krajick, Kevin. 1998. "Green Farming by the Incas?" *Science* 281: 323–29.

Krause, Elizabeth. 2004. *A Crisis of Births: Population Politics and Family-Making in Italy*. Belmont, CA: Wadsworth.

Kroeber, Alfred L., and Clyde Kluckhohn. 1952. "Culture: A Critical Review of Concepts and Definitions." *Papers of the Peabody Museum of American Archaeology and Ethnology* 47(1).

Kulish, Nicholas. 2008. "Gay Muslims Pack a Dance Floor of Their Own." *New York Times* (January 1): A-4.

Kumar, Hari. 2005. "India's Harried Elite Now Turns, and Twists, to Yoga Lite." *New York Times* (February 1): A-4.

Kurtz, Donald V. 2001. *Political Anthropology: Power and Paradigms*. Boulder, CO: Westview Press.

Lacey, Marc. 2005. "Victims of Uganda Atrocities Follow a Path of Forgiveness." *New York Times* (April 18): 1.

____. 2006. "The Case of the Stolen Statues: Solving a Kenyan Mystery." *New York Times* (April 16): 4.

La Fontaine, Jean. 1963. "Witchcraft in Bagisu." In *Witchcraft and Sorcery in East Africa*. John Middleton and E. H. Winter, eds., pp. 187–220. New York: Praeger.

Lakshmi, Rama. 2004. "Factory Orders Dropping? Astrologer Is Go-to Guru for Struggling Corporate Executives." *The Washington Post* (July 4): A–1 7.

Lamont-Brown, Raymond. 1999. "Japan's New Spirituality." *Contemporary Review* (August): 70–73.

Lamphere, Louise. 1974. "Strategies, Cooperation, and Conflict Among Women in Domestic Groups." In *Women, Culture, and Society*. Michelle Zimbalist Rosaldo and Louise Lamphere, eds., pp. 97–112. Stanford, CA: Stanford University Press.

Larson, Reed W., Bradford Brown, and Jeylan T. Mortimer, eds. 2003. *Adolescents' Preparation for the Future: Perils and Promise*. Hoboken, NJ: Wiley-Blackwell.

Lave, Jean, and Etienne Wenger. 1991. *Situated Learning: Legitimate Peripheral Participation*. Cambridge: Cambridge University Press.

Lee, Dorothy. 1993. "Religious Perspectives in Anthropology." In *Magic, Witchcraft, and Religion: An Anthropological Study of the Supernatural*, 3rd ed. Arthur C. Lehmann and James E. Myers, eds., pp. 10–17. Mountain View, CA: Mayfield.

Lee, Richard B. 1968. "What Hunters Do for a Living, or How to Make Out on Scarce Resources." In *Man the Hunter*. Richard B. Lee and IrvenDeVore, eds., pp. 30–48. Chicago: Aldine-Atherton.

____. 2003. *The Dobe Ju/'hoansi*, 3rd ed. Belmont, CA: Wadsworth.

____. 2007. "The Ju/'hoansi at the Crossroads: Continuity and Change in the Time of AIDS." In *Globalization and Change in 15 Cultures: Born in One World, Living in Another*. George Spindler and Janice Stockard, eds., pp. 144–71. Belmont, CA: Wadsworth.

Lehmann, Arthur C., and James E. Myers, eds. 1993. *Magic, Witchcraft, and Religion*, 3rd ed. Palo Alto, CA: Mayfield.

Lewellen, Ted. 2003. *Political Anthropology: An Introduction*, 3rd ed. New York: Praeger.

Lewin, Ellen, ed. 2006. *Feminist Anthropology: A Reader*. Malden, MA: Blackwell Publishing.

Linton, Ralph. 1936. *The Study of Man*. New York: Appleton-Century-Crofts.

Little, Peter D. 1992. *The Elusive Granary: Herder, Farmer, and State in Northern Kenya*. Cambridge, UK: Cambridge University Press.

Little, Peter D., Abdillahi A. Aboud, and Clement Lenachuru. 2009. "Can Formal Education Reduce Risks for Drought-Prone Pastoralists? A Case Study from Baringo District, Kenya." *Human Organization* 68(2):154–65.

Loewe, Michael, and Edward L. Shaughnessy. 1999. *The Cambridge History of Ancient China*. Cambridge: Cambridge University Press.

Lomax, Alan, et al. 1968. *Folk Song Style and Culture*. Washington, DC: American Association for the Advancement of Science.

Luo, Michael. 2006. "Preaching the Word and Quoting the Voice: An Evangelist Thrives in Manhattan by

Embracing the City and Identifying with Its Culture." *New York Times* (February 26): 28.

Lutz, Ellen L. 2007. "Dam Nation." *Cultural Survival Quarterly* 31(4).

____. 2008. "Panama Dam Construction Steps Up the Pace." *Cultural Survival Quarterly* 32(1).

Lyson, Thomas. 2004. *Civic Agriculture: Reconnecting Farm, Food, and Community*. Medford, MA: Tufts University Press.

MacFarquhar, Emily. 1994. "The War Against Women." *U.S. News & World Report* (March 28): 42–48.

Mahbubani, Kishore. 2005. *Beyond the Age of Innocence: Rebuilding Trust Between America and the World*. New York: Public Affairs.

Malinowski, Bronislaw. 1922. *Argonauts of the Western Pacific*. New York: Dutton.

Mandelbaum, David G. 1970. *Society in India*, Vol. 1. Berkeley: University of California Press.

Marksbury, Richard A., ed. 1993. *The Business of Marriage: Transformations in Oceanic Matrimony*. Pittsburgh: University of Pittsburgh Press.

Marshall, Lorna. 1965. "The !Kung Bushmen of the Kalahari Desert." In *Peoples of Africa*. James Gibbs, ed., pp. 243–78. New York: Holt, Rinehart & Winston.

Martin, Jodie. 2008. "Feminization of Poverty: Women Constitute the Majority of the World's Poor." http://poverty.suite101.com/article.cfm/feminization_of_poverty#ixzz0qfvaEh4s (accessed June 12, 2010).

Mascia-Lees, Frances, and Nancy Johnson Black. 2000. *Gender and Anthropology*. Prospect Heights, IL: Waveland Press.

McCullough, Michael E., and Brian L. B. Willoughby. 2009. "Religion, Self-Regulation, and Self-Control: Associations, Explanations, and Implications." *Psychological Bulletin* 139(1): 69–93.

McGee, R. Jon. 1990. *Life, Ritual, and Religion Among the Lacandon Maya*. Belmont, CA: Wadsworth.

Mead, Margaret. 1928. *Coming of Age in Samoa*. New York: Morrow.

____. 1935. *Sex and Temperament in Three Primitive Societies*. New York: Morrow.

Mehrabian, Albert. 1981. *Silent Messages*, 2nd ed. Belmont, CA: Wadsworth.

Mehta, Suketu. 2004. "Bollywood Confidential." *New York Times Magazine* (November 14): 60ff.

Mendonsa, Eugene. 1985. "Characteristics of Sisala Diviners." In *Magic, Witchcraft, and Religion: An Anthropological Study of the Supernatural*. Arthur C. Lehmann and James E. Myers, eds., pp. 214–24. Palo Alto, CA: Mayfield.

Merton, Robert K. 1957. *Social Theory and Social Structure*. Glencoe, IL: Free Press.

Middleton, John, and Greet Kershaw. 1965. *The Kihuyu and Kamba of Kenya*. London: International African Institute.

Middleton, John, and David Tait, eds. 1958. *Tribes Without Rulers: Studies in African Segmentary Systems*. London: Routledge & Kegan Paul.

Miller, Barbara D. 1993. "Female Infanticide and Child Neglect in Rural North India." In *Gender in Cross-Cultural Perspective*. Caroline Brettell and Carolyn Sargent, eds., pp. 423–35. Englewood Cliffs, NJ: Prentice Hall.

Miller, Lisa. 1999. "The Age of Divine Disunity." *Wall Street Journal* (February 10): B-1.

Mills, George. 1957. "Art: An Introduction to Qualitative Anthropology." *Journal of Aesthetics and Art Criticism* 16(1): 1–17.

Mohn, Tanya. 2006. "How to Become a World Citizen, Before Going to College." *New York Times* (September 3): 6.

Montagu, Ashley. 1972. *Touching: The Human Significance of the Shin*. New York: Harper & Row.

Morgan, Lewis H. 1871. *Systems of Consanguinity and Affinity of the Human Family*. Washington, DC: Smithsonian Institution.

___. 1963. *Ancient Society*. New York: World (orig. 1877).

Murdock, George. 1945. "The Common Denominator of Cultures." In *The Science of Man in the World Crisis*. Ralph Linton, ed., p. 124. New York: Columbia University Press.

Murphy, Dean E. 2004. "At War Against Dams, Tribe Turns to Old Ways." *New York Times* (September 14): A-13.

Nanda, Serena. 1990. *Neither Man nor Woman: The Hijras of India*. Belmont, CA: Wadsworth.

___. 1992. "Arranging a Marriage in India." In *The Naked Anthropologist*. Philip DeVita, ed., pp. 137–43. Belmont, CA: Wadsworth.

National Association of Practicing Anthropologists (NAPA). 2010. "American Breakfast and the Mother-in-Law: How an Anthropologist Created Go-Gurt." http://www.practicinganthropology.org/ learn/?storyid=4.

Nettl, Bruno. 1980. "Ethnomusicology: Definitions, Directions, and Problems." In *Music of Many Cultures*. Elizabeth May, ed., pp. 1–9. Berkeley: University of California Press.

Nettl, Bruno, and Philip V. Bohlman, eds. 1991. *Comparative Musicology and Anthropology of Music*. Chicago: University of Chicago Press.

Newman, Katherine S. 1999. *No Shame in My Game: The Working Poor in the Inner City*. New York: Knopf.

Newport, Frank. 2004. "A Look at Americans and Religion Today." *The Gallup Organization* (March 23). www .gallup.com/poll/content/default .aspx?ci511089&pg52.

Oberg, Kalervo. 1960. "Culture Shock: Adjustments to New Cultural Environments." *Practical Anthropology* (July/August): 177–82.

Omidian, Patricia. 2010. *When Bamboo Bloom: An Anthropologist in Taliban's Afghanistan*. Long Gove, IL: Waveland Press.

Ortner, Sherry. 1974. "Is Female to Male as Nature Is to Culture?" In *Women, Culture, and Society*. Michelle Zimbalist Rosaldo and Louise Lamphere, eds., pp. 67–88. Stanford, CA: Stanford University Press.

Pew Forum on Religion & Public Life. 2010. "U.S. Religious Landscape Survey." http://religions.pewforum.org.

Pirog, Rich.2003. "Checking the Food Odometer: Comparing Food Miles for Local Versus Conventional Produce Sales to Iowa Institutions." Ames: Leopold Center for Sustainable Agriculture, Iowa State University. http://www.leopold .iastate.edu/pubs/staff/files/food_ travel072103.pdf.

Price, Sally. 2001. *Primitive Art in Civilized Places*. Chicago: University of Chicago Press.

Price, T. Douglas, and James A. Brown. 1985. *Prehistoric Hunter-Gatherers: The Emergence of Cultural Complexity*. Orlando, FL: Academic Press.

Prior, Ian. 1971. "The Price of Civilization." *Nutrition Today* 6(4): 2–11.

Pristin, Terry. 2002. "Behind the Legal and Private Worlds of the Veil." *New York Times* (August 11): L-4.

Rai, Saritha. 2004. "Short on Priests, U.S. Catholics Outsource Prayers to Indian Clergy." *New York Times* (June 13): 13.

Rasmussen, Knud. 1927. *Across Arctic America*. New York: G. P. Putnam's Sons.

Riding, Alan. 2004. "Babel, A New Capital for a Wider Continent." *New York Times* (May 2): 3.

Roesch, Roberta. 1984. "Violent Families." *Parents* 59(9)(September): 74–76, 150–52.

Rosaldo, Michelle Zimbalist. 1974. "Women, Culture, and Society: A Theoretical Overview." In *Women, Culture, and Society*. Michelle Zimbalist Rosaldo and Louise Lamphere, eds., pp. 17–42. Stanford, CA: Stanford University Press.

Rose, Susan A. 1994. "Relation Between Physical Growth and Information Processing in Infants Born in India." *Child Development* (June): 889–902.

Rosenthal, Elisabeth. 2006. "Genital Cutting Raises by 50% Likelihood Mothers or Their Newborns Will Die, Study Finds." *New York Times* (June 2): A-l0.

____. 2009. "In Bolivia, Water and Ice Tell a Story of a Changing Climate." *New York Times* (December 14): 1–7.

Rylko-Bauer, Barbara, Merrill Singer, and John Van Willigen. 2006. "Reclaiming Applied Anthropology: Its Past, Present, and Future." *American Anthropologist* 108(1): 178–90.

Rylko-Bauer, Barbara, Linda Whiteford, and Paul Farmer. 2009. *Global Health in Times of Violence*. Santa Fe, NM: SAR Press.

Ryu, Charles. 1992. "Koreans and Church." In *Asian Americans*. Joann Faungjean Lee, ed., pp. 162–64. New York: New Press.

Sahlins, Marshall. 1968. "Notes on the Original Affluent Society." In *Man the Hunter*. R. B. Lee and I. DeVore, eds., pp. 85–89. Chicago: Aldine.

Sanday, Peggy R. 2004. *Women at the Center: Life in a Modern Matriarchy*. Ithaca, NY: Cornell University Press.

Santos, Fernanda. 2009. "Musician Changes Tone of Impoverished Village." *New York Times* (October 13): A-10.

Sapir, Edward. 1929. "The Status of Linguistics as a Science." *Language* 5: 207–14.

Scaglion, Richard. 1987. "Customary Law Development in Papua New Guinea." In *Anthropological Praxis*. Robert Wulff and Shirley Fiske, eds., pp. 98–107. Boulder, CO: Westview Press.

Scudder, Thayer. 1999. "The Emerging Global Crisis and Development Anthropology: Can We Have an Impact?" *Human Organization* 58(4): 351–64.

Selzer, Richard. 1979. *Confessions of a Knife*. New York: Simon & Schuster.

Sen, Amartya. 1981. *Poverty and Famines: An Essay on Entitlement and Deprivation*. Oxford: Clarendon Press.

____. 2001. "The Many Faces of Gender Inequality." *New Republic* (September 17): 35–40.

Service, Elman R. 1975. *Origins of the State and Civilization*. New York: Norton.

____. 1978. *Profiles in Ethnology*, 3rd ed. New York: Harper & Row.

Sheflen, Albert E. 1972. *Body Language and the Social Order*. Englewood Cliffs, NJ: Prentice Hall.

Shiva, Vandana. 2000. *Stolen Harvest: The Hijacking of the Global Food Supply*. Cambridge, MA: South End Press.

Shweder, Richard A. 2007. "A True Culture War?" *New York Times* (October 27): op. ed. contribution.

Sieber, Roy. 1962. "Masks as Agents of Social Control." *African Studies Bulletin* 5(11): 8–13.

Slobin, Mark, and Jeff T. Titon. 1984. "The Music Culture as a World of Music." In *Worlds of Music: An Introduction to the Music of the World's Peoples*. Jeff T. Titon et al., eds., pp. 1–11. London: Collier Macmillan Publishers.

Smith, Bruce. 1998. *The Emergence of Agriculture*. New York: Scientific American Library.

Smith, Jeffrey M. 2003. *Seeds of Deception: Exposing Industry and Government Lies About the Safety of the Genetically Engineered Foods You're Eating.* Fairfield, LA: Yes! Books.

Society for Applied Anthropology. http://www.sfaa.net/.

Stavans, Ilan. 2003. *Spanglish: The Making of a New American Language.* New York: Rayo (HarperCollins).

Steinmetz, David. 2004. "World Christianity Under New Management." *Charlotte Observer* (July 12): 11-A.

Steward, Julian. 1963. *Theory of Culture Change: The Methodology of Multilinear Evolution.* Urbana: University of Illinois Press.

Stockard, Janice E. 2002. *Marriage in Culture.* Fort Worth, TX: Harcourt College Publishers.

Sturtevant, William. 1964. "Studies in Ethnoscience." *American Anthropologist* 66(3) (Part 2): 99–131.

Substance Abuse and Mental Health Administration. 2010. "National Survey on Drug Use and Health." http://alcoholism.about.com/cs/coke/l/blnida02.htm (accessed January 9, 2011).

Sundkler, Bengt. 1961. *Bantu Prophets of South Africa,* 2nd ed. London: Oxford University Press.

Sutton, Mark Q., and Anderson, E. N. 2009. *Introduction to Cultural Ecology,* 2nd ed. Lanham, MD: AltaMira Press.

Tannen, Deborah. 1990. *You Just Don't Understand: Women and Men in Conversation.* New York: Morrow.

Tierney, John. 2003. "Letter from the Middle East." *New York Times* (October 22): A-4.

___. 2008. "Hitting It Off, Thanks to Algorithms of Love." *New York Times* (February 9).

Trilling, Bernie, and Charles Fadel. 2009. *21st Century Skills: Learning for Life in Our Times.* Hoboken, NJ: Jossey-Bass.

Tylor, Edward B. 1958. *Origins of Culture.* New York: Harper & Row (orig. 1871).

Udvardy, Monica, and Linda Giles. 2008. "Groundbreaking Repatriation of Two Kenya Memorial Statues." *Anthropology News* 49(l) (January): 30.

UNFPA (United Nations Fund for Population Activities). 2005. "State of the World Population." http://www.unfpa.org/swp/2005/presskit/factsheets/ facts-vaw.htm.

UNICEF. "State of the World's Children—2009 Report." www.unicef.org .sowc09.

Urdang, Stephanie. 2001. "Women and AIDS: Gender Inequality Is Fatal." *Women's International Network News* 27(4) (Autumn): 24.

U.S. Department of Labor. 2010. "Employment Status of the Civilian Population by Sex and Age." http://www.bls.gov/news.release/empsit .t01.htm (accessed July 14, 2010).

Vallely, Paul. 2010. "The Big Question: What's the History of Polygamy, and How Serious a Problem Is It in Africa?" *The Independent* (January 6). http://www.independent.co.uk/news/world/africa/the-big-question-whats-the-history-of-polygamy-and-how-serious-a-problem-is-it-in-africa-1858858.html.

Van Esterik, Penny. 1989. *Beyond the Breast-Bottle Controversy.* New Brunswick, NJ: Rutgers University Press.

Van Gennep, Arnold. 1960. *The Rites of Passage.* Chicago: University of Chicago Press (orig. 1908).

Van Willigen, John. 2002. *Applied Anthropology: An Introduction,* 3rd ed. Westport, CT: Bergin & Garvey.

Wallace, Anthony F. C. 1966. *Religion: An Anthropological View*. New York: Random House.

Waring, Marilyn. 1989. *If Women Counted: A New Feminist Economics*. New York: HarperCollins.

___. 2004. *Counting for Nothing: What Men Value and What Women Are Worth*. Toronto: University of Toronto Press.

Weber, Max, 1958. *The Protestant Ethic and the Spirit of Capitalism*. New York: Charles Scribner's Sons (orig. 1904).

Weiner, Annette. 1976. *Women of Value, Men of Renown*. Austin: University of Texas Press.

Wcise, Elizabeth. 2010. "Sign Language No. 4 Most Studied Foreign Language." *USA Today*. http://www.usatoday.com/news/education/2010–12–08–1Alanguages08_ST_N.htm (accessed December 17, 2010).

White, Leslie. 1959. *The Evolution of Culture*. New York: McGraw-Hill.

Whyte, M. K. 1978. *The Status of Women in Preindustrial Societies*. Princeton, NJ: Princeton University Press.

Wines, Michael. 2007. "In a Land of Homemade Names, Tiffany Doesn't Cut It." *New York Times* (October 1): A-4.

Witherspoon, Gary. 1977. *Language and Art in the Navajo Universe*. Ann Arbor: University of Michigan Press.

Wolf, Eric. 1964. *Anthropology*. Englewood Cliffs, NJ: Prentice Hall.

World Bank. 2011. "Literacy Rate, Youth Female (% of Females Ages 15–24). http://data.worldbank.org/indicator/SE.ADT.1524.LT.FE.ZS(accessed March 18,2011).

World Health Organization.2009. "What Do We Mean by 'Sex' and 'Gender'?" http://www.who.int/gender/whatis-gender/en/index.html (accessed July 14, 2010).

Wright, Melissa W. 2006. *Disposable Women and Other Myths and Global Capitalism*. New York: Routledge.

Yardley, Jim. 2005. "Fearing Future, China Starts to Give Girls Their Due." *New York Times* (January 31): A-3.

Yellen, John. 1990. "The Transformation of the Kalahari !Kung." *Scientific American* (April): 96–104.

Yellin, Emily. 2004. *Our Mother's War: American Women at Home and at the Front during World War II*. New York: Free Press.

Index

Page numbers followed by *t* or *f* indicate a table or figure.

American Sign Language (ASL), 118, 133–134
Amish community subculture, 37
ancestor-god sacrificial rituals, 255
Ancient Society (Morgan), 84
Andreatta, Susan, 72–74, 163
androgynous (gender identity), 199
animal husbandry, 144, 153, 157–158
anthropological linguistics, 3–4, 5t, 11–12
Anthropological Society of Washington, 60
anthropological theories, 81–96
    American historicism, 86, 96t
    cultural materialism, 93, 96t
    diffusionism, 85–86, 96t
    ethnoscience, 91, 96t
    evolutionism, 84–85, 96t
    feminist anthropology, 91–92, 96t
    French structuralism, 90–91, 96t
    functionalism, 86–87, 96t, 178
    neoevolutionism, 88–90, 96t
    postmodernism, 93–95, 96t
    psychological anthropology, 87–88, 96t
    questions asked by, 83–84
    structural functionalism, 87, 96t
    theory (defined), 83
anthropologists
    defined, 3
    field of study, 3–4
    National Research Council recruitment, 64
    new product development, 27–28
anthropology
    branches of, 5t
    defined, 3–4
    non-academic careers in, 24t
    special features of, 65–67
    theories of, 81–96
anthropology, contributions of, 21–26
    appreciation of other perspectives, 23
    balance contradictions, 23–24
    broad perspective development, 23
    cognitive complexity development, 25–26
    enhancement of global understanding, 21–222

global teamwork emphasis, 24–25
influences on culture, 33
perceptual acuity development, 26
applied anthropologists, 68, 75
    career choices for, 74–79, 76t
    cultural relativism and, 67
    international agency consultations, 62
    policy development activities, 64
    specialized roles of, 67–68, 70–71, 75
    studies abroad, 77–79
    work for hiring agencies, 65
    Zimbabwe HIV/AIDS studies, 58–59
applied anthropology, 5t, 57–79
    career choices in, 74–79, 76t
    climate change and, 320–325
    continuum of, 63t
    defined, 61
    non-applied vs., 60–64
    participation-observation method, 62
    public/private research funding, 60
    recent history of, 64–65
    theoretical continuum of, 63t
applied anthropology, examples of
    development anthropology, 71–72
    ecological anthropology, 72–74
    medical anthropology, 70–71
    urban anthropology studies, 68–70
applied archaeology, 5t
applied linguistics, 5t
applied physical anthropology, 5t
Arapesh culture (New Guinea), 88, 198
archaeology
    agricultural discoveries, 152, 159
    artifacts, features, ecofacts, 9
    branches of, 5t
    cultural development research, 307
    cultural resource management, 5t, 11
    described, 4, 8–9
    importance of culture to, 33
    Krajick's Peruvian research, 141
    relevance of, 10–11
    role of archaeologists, 3, 9–10
Argentina, pastoral practices, 159
arranged marriages, 181–183
art, 283–303
    as aspect of culture, 34, 45f

per capital gross national income data, 309t

world systems theory, 310–311

education/education systems

anthropological research in, 61, 69, 306

as component of culture, 45f

cultural transmission and, 43

dance education in Cuba, 297

development anthropology projects, 15

gender inequalities, 196, 204, 206–207, 210, 216–218

gender stratification and, 206–207

influence in pastoral cultures, 138–139

limited access in Zaire, 54

marriage and, 179, 182, 185

modern vs. traditional nations, 310

role in technology adoption, 72

role of music in, 290–291, 295

educational anthropology, 5, 17, 61

Egypt

agricultural development, 89, 159

art in, 292

diffusionism in, 85

ecclesiastical cults in, 272

government systems, 228

mating practices, 180

neolithic communities, 153

Eisenstein, Sergei, 299

The Elementary Forms of Religious Life (Durkheim), 253

emasculation rite (Hijra of India), 200

emic view (perspective of local people), 65–66, 87, 91, 94

emotional function, of religion, 263–266

employment

benefit of bilingualism, 133

food/water security and, 109

gender inequity and, 206, 207

gender stratification, 207

in Inuit villages, 149

kinship group pressures, 190

urban anthropology focus, 14

enculturation, 37, 50t

endogamy rules of marriage, 180–181

environmental anthropology, 5t, 16, 72–74

carrying capacity, of environments, 142

human adaptation studies, 140–141

epidemics, global, 168–169

Ervin, Alexander, 62–63

ethics of cultural anthropology, 106–107

ethnic group (defined), 51

ethnocentrism

cultural relativism and, 19

defined, 18

examples of, 18–19

personal avoidance of, 39

ethnographic mapping, fieldwork method, 103

ethnographic methods, of cultural anthropology, 96–106

data-gathering techniques, 101–104

field research, stages of, 99–101

fieldwork, 96–98

gains and pains of fieldwork, 105–106

preparations for fieldwork, 98–99

ethnography, 12–14

adolescent drug dealer study, 68

defined, 97

descriptive ethnography, 63t

ethnographic interviewing, 62

research methods, 98

ethnolinguistics (cultural linguistics), 5t, 12, 122

ethnology, 12–14, 33

ethnomedical perspective, of epidemics, 168

ethnomedicine, 14

ethnomusicology, 295–296

ethnoscience theory, 91, 96t

Europe

climate change contribution, 323

fishing rights, 150

19th century industrial revolution, 317

reproductive health issues, 207

world systems theory and, 311

evaluator (applied anthropologist role), 68

evangelical churches, 253, 256

Evans-Pritchard, E. E., 233

multilinear evolution theory (Steward), 89–90

multilingualism, 127

Mundugumor culture (New Guinea), 88, 198–199

Murdock, George, 255

music, 294–296
  Balinese contributions, 290
  Chinese government choices, 292
  continuity/changes in, 300–301
  educational role, 290–291
  egalitarian vs. stratified societies, 296t
  ethnomusicology, 295–296
  Javanese/Sri Lankan contributions, 294
  urban revitalization in Brazil, 284

Nairobi (Kenya) housing unit design, 32

Nanda, Serena, 182, 200

Nandi culture (of Kenya), 178

nation-states, 232–233

National Association of Practicing Anthropologists (NAPA), 27, 65

National Environmental Policy Act (1969), 65

National Historic Preservation Act (1966), 65

National Institutes of Health (NIH), 60

National Museums of Kenya, 303

National Public Service Authority (ASEP) (Panama), 320

National Research Council, 64

Native Americans
  atrocities against, 318
  bridewealth marriage custom, 186
  communal forms of religion, 266
  educational experiences of, 115
  exploitation of, 318
  gender alternatives, 199–200
  linguistic language styles, 125
  nativistic movements, 276
  Navajo art contributions, 286, 288
  patrilineal descent practice, 173
  self-governance studies, 61
  subordinate role of women, 205
  Taos Pueblo art contributions, 293

vision quest ritual, 266–267

nativistic movements (Native Americans), 276

Navajo culture, 186
  art contributions, 286, 288
  bridewealth compensation, 186
  gender roles in, 203
  Kluckhorn's studies, 40–41
  language, 123
  matrilineal descent system, 174

negative sanctions (of social control), 235–237

neoevolutionism, 88–90, 96t

neolithic revolution, 152–154

neolocal residence, 177

Nestlé baby formula controversy, 70–71

Netsilik Eskimos, dance contributions, 298

Nettl, Bruno, 296

New Guinea
  Customary Law Project, 245–246
  Highland culture, 173–174
  Kapauku Papua culture, 173–174, 186–187
  sex/temperament study, 198–199

New Guinea Highland culture, 173–174

New Zealand, pastoral practices, 158

Ngobe culture (western Panama), 319–320

nomadic movement patterns, 157

non-applied anthropology, 60–64

nonverbal communication, 129–131
  active listening and, 26
  American Sign Language, 118, 133–134
  emphasis in Asian cultures, 125–126, 130
  hand gestures, 129, 130
  importance of, 129
  posture (body stance), 131
  shared symbols as, 35–36
  touching, 131

norms of society, 234–235

North America
  indigenous peoples, 317
  languages of, 115
  pastoral practices, 158
  social controls, 236

Stavans, Ilan, 127

Steward, Julian, 89–90
    See also cultural ecology; multilinear
       evolution theory

Sting (musical artist), 301

Stockard, Janice, 187

structural functionalism, 87, 96*t*

structured/unstructured interviews,
    102–103

Sturtevant, William, 91, 96*t*
    See also ethnoscience

subculture (defined), 37

subsistence agriculture. *See* horticulture

subsistence strategy, for obtaining food,
    139, 157

Sudan
    applied anthropological studies, 78
    Nuer people, 122–123
    racial/ethnic differences, 51

Suitablematch.com (matchmaking ser-
    vice), 182

Sundkler, Bengt, 262

supernatural beliefs, 43, 251–280
    art and, 291, 298, 303
    described, 238–239
    humanistic studies of, 4
    intervention of intermediaries, 241
    oaths and ordeals, 242–243
    rituals for appeasement of forces, 255
    shamanistic cults, 265–269,
       271–273, 277
    sorcery, 43, 168–169, 238–239, 256,
       258–259
    supernatural (defined), 256
    terrorism-religious beliefs link, 252
    witchcraft, 43, 239, 259–260, 264
    See also religion; religious
       organizations

Sweden, filmmaking contributions, 299

swidden cultivation technique,
    143*f*, 155

symbols
    communication through, 113
    defined, examples, 35
    emotions evoked by, 289
    of humans, complexity of, 11
    interpretive anthropology study of, 94

kinship diagram usage, 171*f*, 172*f*

religious symbols, 262

social integration contributions,
    289–290

Trobriand Island culture, 92

synchronic analysis, of language, 121

syntax (language component), 120, 121

*Systems of Consanguinity and Affinity of
    the Human Family* (Morgan), 84

Tagliapietra, Lino, 301

Taliban terrorist group (Afghanistan), 83

Tannen, Deborah, 12

Tchambuli culture (New Guinea), 88,
    198–199

technology
    agricultural, 43
    cultural interconnectedness of, 45*f*
    global connectedness through, 21
    minimal, in some cultures, 33
    See also Internet

text messages (texting), 34, 132

Thailand
    applied anthropological fieldwork, 64
    naming conventions, 114
    Nestlé baby formula controversy,
       70–71

theoretical anthropology, 63*t*, 64

theories of anthropology. *See* anthropo-
    logical theories

Tikuna community (Brazil), drug traffick-
    ing, 317–318

Titon, Jeff, 294–295

touching (nonverbal communication), 131

transgender (gender identity), 199

transhumance movement patterns, 157

*Translated Woman: Crossing the Border
    with Esperanza's Story* (Behar), 95

Transportation Security Administration
    (TSA), 22

tribal societies, 63, 225–226, 227, 232,
    236–237

Trobriand Islanders, study of Malin-
    owski, 92

Truth and Reconciliation Commission, 245

tuberculosis epidemic, 168

Tutu, Desmond, 245

Wolf, Eric, 4

Women for Women International (NGO), 218

World Bank
anthropology research support, 60
El Alto glacier report, 323
female illiteracy data, 206
female poverty data, 208
gross national income report, 309*t*
male vs. female loan data, 209

World Health Organization (WHO), 60, 70–71

world systems theory, of economic development, 310–311

Wounded Knee massacre (1890), 318

Wutich, Ambert, 108

Yanomamo horticultural society, 154

Yemen
female illiteracy, 206–207
high birth rate, 207

YouTube videos, 112

Zimbabwe, HIV/AIDS rates, 58

Zimbalist Rosaldo, Michelle, 92
See also feminist anthropology

Zuckerberg, Mark, 112

Zuni culture (New Mexico), 175